Mental Health, Spirituality and Wellbeing

A Handbook for Health and Social Care Professionals, Service Users and Carers

Edited by
**Sarajane Aris, Hilary Garraway
and Hannah Gilbert**

Spirituality, Mental Health & Wellbeing

Published by:
Pavilion Publishing and Media Ltd
Blue Sky Offices, 25 Cecil Pashley Way
Shoreham by Sea, West Sussex
BN43 5FF

Tel: 01273 434 943
Email: info@pavpub.com
Web: www.pavpub.com

Published 2021

A catalogue record for this book is available from the British Library.

ISBN: 978-1-914010-62-0

Pavilion Publishing and Media is a leading publisher of books, training materials and digital content in mental health, social care and allied fields. Pavilion and its imprints offer must-have knowledge and innovative learning solutions underpinned by sound research and professional values.

Editors: Sarajane Aris, Hilary Garraway and Hannah Gilbert
Production editor: Mike Benge, Pavilion Publishing and Media Ltd
Cover design: Emma Dawe, Pavilion Publishing and Media Ltd
Page layout and typesetting: Phil Morash, Pavilion Publishing and Media Ltd
Printing: CMP Digital Print Solutions

To the memory of Professor Peter Gilbert who edited the first version of this Handbook. To all those who have lost their lives as a result of the global pandemic, and to all the unsung heroes and those who have tirelessly helped and cared for people across the world suffering from Covid-19.

Contents

Contributors

Sarajane Aris is a Consultant Clinical Psychologist, Associate Fellow of the British Psychological Society and Fellow of the Royal Society of Arts. She mentors both women leaders across the world in the not-for-profit sector and clinical psychologists across the career span. She is a committee member for both the British Psychological Society's Leadership and Management (L&M) Faculty for the Division of Clinical Psychology, and the Political Psychology Section. She setup and led the first Senior Clinical Psychologists pilot mentoring scheme (2015) and, via the steering group she set up, as the L&M Lead, has actively supported the development of the recent successful Clinical Psychologists as Leaders Mentoring pilot scheme (2018-2020).

She was Head of Adult Psychology Services for Derbyshire Healthcare Foundation Trust for 10 years and Director of Policy for the British Psychological Society's Division of Clinical psychology (2012/13). She has worked within the NHS for over 40 years. She was the national lead for Spirituality for the British Psychological Society (2002-2010), and the psychology representative on the National Mental Health and Spirituality Forum during this time. She was responsible for setting up Derbyshire Mental Healthcare Foundation Trusts Spirituality Strategy and Steering Group (2009-11)). She has facilitated and run a variety of training courses and workshops, in areas such as mindfulness, leadership, wellbeing, and death and dying over the years.

Sarajane has also worked for the Healthcare Commission, now Quality Care Commission as an associate. She founded the Transpersonal Network for Clinical and Counselling Psychologists and therapists in the UK (1997-2011), has been involved in organisational change, coaching and development work for a variety of organizations such as Avon and Wiltshire Mental Health Partnership NHS Trust, the Cancer Help Centre, now the Penny Brohn Centre, Bristol, amongst others. Sarajane has contributed various chapters to books and articles on leadership, consciousness and spirituality in mental health, amongst others. She is co-author of the second edition of *Counselling and Helping* with Professor Richard Velleman (2010) and *Beyond Resilience from Mastery to Mystery* with Professor Stephen Murgatroyd (2017).

Her life is informed by the principles of love, compassion, wisdom and truth, and a wish to serve and collaborate with whomever she connects with.

Dr Hilary Garraway, BSc. MSc. DClinPsychol CPsychol is a Consultant Clinical Psychologist and BABCP accredited CBT therapist, supervisor and trainer. She works full time as an adult psychology lead in Barnet, Enfield and Haringey Mental Health Trust, and before that she worked in Early Intervention in Psychosis teams. Hilary has been a therapist for over 30 years and has worked in the NHS for about 20 years as well as a range of settings including residential child care, youth and community work and the voluntary sector. Hilary has trained in person-centred art therapy, ecotherapy, spiritual direction and creative writing. Hilary also trained as an adult education teacher and is an honorary lecturer at University College London, University of Hertfordshire and King's College London.

Hilary has developed a CBT approach which is described in her book *Holistic CBT* along with a group manual based on this approach called *Free to be Me*. Hilary has been a trustee for various charities and is currently a trustee for two charities which develop whole person health care and is the former chair of the National Spirituality and Mental Health Forum and former British Psychological Society spirituality lead. Hilary has a special interest in psychospiritual development and integrating spirituality into therapy, and describes her spirituality as Celtic and Contemplative within the Christian tradition. Together with her husband, she has set up a charity in Grenada and they are in the process of establishing a therapeutic retreat house there.

They have two adult children and a labradoodle dog.

Dr Hannah Gilbert has a BA (Hons) in Anthropology from Durham University, and a PhD in Sociology from the University of York. Her doctoral thesis explored experiences of spirit amongst the spirit mediumship community in Britain. She recently retrained as a psychotherapist and is now a lecturer in Integrative Psychotherapy and Counselling at the University of Roehampton. She also works for the Compassionate Mind Foundation and runs compassionate mind training workshops.

Dr. Haben Ghezai, **Dr. Nancy Nsiah**, **Dr. Prabhleen Sandhu** and **Dr. Yvette Arthur** are a group of clinical psychologists from ethnic minority backgrounds. They have over 10 years' combined experience working in mental health across the lifespan. They recently formed a collective organisation called 'Intercultural Psychology Consultants' (IPC), offering specialist consultation, workshops, teaching and therapy to organisations and individuals around topics relating to race, culture and religion, as it pertains to mental health and wellbeing. They have a keen interest in working with marginalised groups and communities and are passionate about decolonising the non-Western mind and working with individuals in ways that support cultural and religious forms of healing. They advocate for individuals to have access to culturally sensitive psychological therapies as well as raise awareness of the importance of cultural sensitivity and diversity being embedded in the culture of the workplace.

Haben is a Senior Clinical Psychologist working within the NHS in a forensic inpatient and as the Interim Adult Team Manager within a leading human rights organisation working with survivors of torture. Nancy works within a specialist, tertiary care paediatric hospital as a Clinical Psychologist supporting children with long-term health conditions. Prabhleen is a Clinical Psychologist working in paediatric healthcare and child and adolescent mental health services. Yvette is a Highly Specialist Clinical Psychologist working within an NHS Early Intervention Service for people experiencing psychosis for the first time.

Ben Bano has been a social worker for 45 years. He worked as Director of Older People's Services and Social Care. On retirement, he took a particular interest in spirituality and its application to Mental health as well as dementia. He has contributed to various books including *Spirituality and End of Life Care*. He also produced a video titled 'It's still ME Lord' for Caritas Social Action Network. He is Director of 'Welcome Me as I Am', which promotes mental health and dementia awareness in Faith Communities (www.welcomemeasiam.org). He is also currently Chair of the National Spirituality and Mental Health Forum.

Dr Sara Betteridge is a Counselling Psychologist and Family Therapist who has specialised in faith-based approaches (with a particular focus in Islam) and the Open Dialogue systemic way of working. Her work as a Muslim mental health chaplain/spiritual care advisor in a mental health NHS Trust alongside her doctoral thesis which focused on ways of incorporating faith into different psychotherapeutic models; have contributed to her extensive experience in this field. She continues to work as an Individual and Family Therapist, Group facilitator, Supervisor, and Trainer in both Open Dialogue and in working with faith in therapy and mental health services.

Dr Adam Boughey is a Lecturer in Adult Nursing and a Post Doctoral Researcher in the Department of Nursing, School of Health and Social Care, Staffordshire University, Stoke-on-Trent, Staffordshire, UK.

As a medical student, **Ross Bryson**, who had grown up in Africa (and now in multicultural Birmingham), became convinced that a Western worldview and the bio-medical model of human functioning did not adequately explain his observations of life. His medical career has included specialist training in General Practice, time working in community child health and drug addiction in the UK and developing primary healthcare in Africa. He supports the Royal College of GPs' view that GPs are specialists in whole person medicine. For over 30 years he has been a GP partner in an urban setting in Birmingham. In this context, he expanded the concept of a primary healthcare team to include a counsellor, family therapists and Chaplains for Wellbeing, while also setting up a voluntary sector organisation to address social and spiritual needs. His personal spirituality has been shaped by seeking to understand Jesus in his historical Jewish context, which in turn has shaped his practice of whole-person medical care in the NHS today.

Liz Bryson has a background in education. She and her GP husband Ross, worked for a short time in health and community development in the West Africa. They are both passionately interested in the concepts and practice of whole person care. For the last eight years, Liz has worked as part of the Chaplaincy team at Birmingham Women's and Children's Hospital. She specialises in spiritual play and staff support offering pastoral, spiritual and religious care to patients, families and staff. Her journey in understanding the needs of the human spirit has been shaped by raising four adult children; caring long-term for a disabled child; experiencing and processing loss through the death of an adult daughter; mentoring individuals and couples; and working with Ross in developing Chaplaincy in General Practice, jointly writing the Association of Chaplains in General Practice Handbook and establishing its accreditation process.

Alexis Carey is a Health Psychologist in Training, who is currently completing a Health Psychology Professional Doctorate at the Staffordshire Centre for Psychological Research & Centre for Health Psychology, Staffordshire University, Stoke-on-Trent, UK.

Isabel Clarke is a Consultant Clinical Psychologist who trained in mid life with the intention of effecting change in mental health services. Her interest in spirituality and work with people diagnosed as experiencing psychosis combined in the edited book *Psychosis and Spirituality*, and *Madness, Mystery and the Survival of God*. These publications led to conferences, an internet presence and contributing to the foundation of the Spiritual Crisis Network (SCN) in the UK in 2005. She has been active in SCN ever since, as she sees it as providing a vital alternative way of making sense of exceptional/unusual experiences. She has continued to work within the NHS, where she has developed a radical, trans-diagnostic, mindfulness-based model within acute (hospital and community) and Increasing Access to Psychological Therapies (IAPT) services, as described in the 2018 book *Third Wave CBT Integration for Individuals and Teams: Comprehend, Cope and Connect*. She also authored *Meeting Mental Breakdown mindfully: how to help the Comprehend, Cope and Connect Way*. For more information, see her website: www.isabelclarke.org

Sally Coleman was born and brought up in the Far East, in Singapore and Malaysia, and then mostly lived in several different places in the UK, apart from a jaunt to Houston Texas for four years. She is a daughter, a mother and a grandmother who identifies as queer; a loaded word that, in her opinion, needs redeeming as something to be proud of. It also refuses in some senses to impose particular boundaries/ expectations!

Sally currently lives and works in Sheffield, a city that enables her to live at an equal distance between most of her five children!

She is passionate about reading and enjoys hill-walking, which inevitably includes her bringing along her camera which is not popular with walking companions who'd rather go for a fast stomp! She usually tries to keep fit by swimming, which she finds helps with her mental health, and she expresses herself through the mediums of poetry and abstract painting. If someone were to ask her if she was spiritual or religious, she would say spiritual, and yet she works for the institutional church. She is a Methodist Minister.

Dr Peter Fenwick was a senior lecturer at King's College, London, where he worked as a consultant at the Institute of Psychiatry. He was the Consultant Neuropsychologist at both the Maudsley and John Radcliffe hospitals, and also provided services for Broadmoor Hospital. He worked with the Mental Health Group at the University of Southampton, and held a visiting professorship at the Riken Neurosciences Institute in Japan.

Peter is the president of the Horizon Research Foundation, an organisation that supports research into end-of-life experiences. Before this he was the President of the British branch of the International Association for Near-Death Studies. Peter has been part of the editorial board for a number of journals, including the Journal of Neurology, Neurosurgery, and Psychiatry, the Journal of Consciousness Studies and the Journal of Epilepsy and Behaviour. He is the co-author of *The Art of Dying*.

Mike Gartland is an Anglican priest and UKCP analytical psychotherapist with a research background in Theravada Buddhist psychology and medieval Christian mysticism. He has led the development of the Pastoral and Spiritual Care service in South West Yorkshire NHS Partnership Foundation Trust and teaches extensively in the field of comparative mysticism. He has wide experience in leading contemplative retreats and spiritual development workshops.

Prof Paul Gilbert, FBPsS, PhD, OBE, is a Professor of Clinical Psychology at the University of Derby and was for many years a Consultant Clinical Psychologist at the Derbyshire Health Care Foundation Trust. He has researched evolutionary approaches to psychopathology for over 35 years with a special focus on shame and the treatment of shame-based difficulties, for which compassion-focused therapy (CFT) was developed. Paul has written extensively, and taught and lectured all over the world. He has written and edited 22 books, including the best-selling *Overcoming Depression* and *The Compassionate Mind*, and established the Compassionate Mind Foundation in 2006. He was awarded an OBE for services to mental healthcare in March 2011. His latest books are *Living Like Crazy* and the forthcoming edited *Compassion Focused Therapy: Clinical Practice and Application*.

Dr Lucy Grimwade is a Consultant Child and Adolescent Psychiatrist working in community mental health services in Durham, TEWV Mental Health Trust. She is secretary to the Spirituality Special Interest Group of the Royal College of Psychiatrists, and has published in the area of spirituality, mental health and young people. She completed her higher speciality training project on the topic of spirituality assessment in a psychiatry context. She is beginning to work across TEWV trust to raise awareness of the need in this area. Before starting medicine she studied anthropology with an emphasis on Islamic Society. Lucy's personal spirituality is Christian and she and her husband and three teenage kids attend Hillsong Church, Newcastle. Her relationship with Father-God is the source of inspiration, strength and comfort in every detail of her life. She experiences God as an all-powerful-unconditionally-loving attachment figure, who has power to re-create and heal.

Professor Peter Hawkins Ph.D. has been coaching senior executives and their leadership teams for over 40 years across many sectors and in many different countries. He has been the leading global pioneer and thought leader in Systemic Team Coaching having carried out extensive research, written a number of the bestselling books and provided trainings to people from over 100 different countries. He previously played a similar role in Coaching Supervision.

He is Emeritus Professor of Leadership at Henley Business School, joint founder and Co-Dean, with Professor David Clutterbuck, of the Global Team Coaching Institute, Chairman of Renewal Associates, UK. He is currently researching and developing the greater role coaching can play in addressing the climate and ecological crisis.

He is also the author of over hundred publications including many best-selling and internationally translated books including: *Leadership Team Coaching* (Kogan Page, 2011; 4th ed, 2021) (translated into Chinese, Japanese and Spanish, Hungarian); *Leadership Team Coaching in Practice* (Kogan Page, 2014; 3rd ed, 2022); (translated in Chinese); *Systemic Coaching: Delivering Value Beyond the Individual* with Eve Turner (Routledge 2020); *Creating a Coaching Culture* (McGraw Hill, 2012) (translated into Dutch); *Coaching, Mentoring and Organizational Consultancy: Supervision, Skills and Development* (with Nick Smith), McGraw-Hill/Open University Press, 2nd ed, 2013); Hawkins P and Ryde J (2020) *Integrative Psychotherapy in Theory and Practice: A relational, systemic and ecological approach*. London: Jessica Kingsley.

He is passionate about how we transform human consciousness for humans to be fit to live on this planet we share and is a committed gardener and grandfather.

Prof Jamie Hacker Hughes is a clinical psychologist, psychotherapist, clinical neuropsychologist, supervisor, researcher and academic. After a short service commission in the army and five years in sales and marketing, Jamie studied psychology, psychopathology and clinical psychology at UCL, Cambridge and Surrey universities. Jamie initially worked in the NHS, first in intellectual disabilities and then in adult psychological health, specialising in psychological trauma, then returning to the MoD as a military psychologist and running a military research team at King's College, London, before becoming defence consultant advisor and head of clinical psychology at the MoD. In this capacity, he visited Bosnia, Kosovo, Iraq, Afghanistan and Northern Ireland to support and supervise colleagues. In 2014, he established a military veterans and families research unit, the Veterans and Families Institute, at Anglia Ruskin University, and he also holds visiting and honorary professorial appointments at Hertfordshire, Northumbria and Lomonosov Moscow State universities. He is a registered psychologist specialising in psychotherapy, an EMDR consultant and a registered applied psychology supervisor.

Jamie is committed to inclusivity, social justice and ending psychological stigma (he has had a diagnosis of bipolar two for the past 20 years, first made when he was a newly qualified clinical psychologist) and, as well as his specialist field of anxiety, stress and trauma, he is particularly interested in the dialogue between faith and psychological health and is also currently involved with a number of organisations working with refugees, asylum seekers and migrants. He founded the first Society Presidential Task Force, on refugees, asylum seekers and migrants. Jamie became the 91st President of the British Psychological Society in April in 2015 and initiated a three-year review and transformation of the Society's structure. He has also been a director of EMDR UK and Ireland, the United Kingdom Psychological Trauma Society (UKPTS) and the Child and Family Practice. He is also honorary president of the Cardiff Samaritans and patron or trustee of a number of charities.

Jo Hemmingfield is Director of Hemmingfield Consultancy. She sits on the Division of Clinical Psychology's Executive Committee as lead for Experts by Experience. Jo also has a role as a Coproduction Consultant at Sheffield Health and Social Care NHS Foundation Trust. She offers consultancy on strategic development, ensuring lived experience is at the heart of organisations. Jo has written numerous articles, organised and spoken at many events and conferences on how to work collaboratively, particularly with service users, as well as on power, distress, language and culture. Jo is relieved to have (reasonably successfully) raised her two children to adulthood. In her spare time she enjoys making pottery and likes to visit beaches.

Paul Jenkins is the Chief Executive of the Tavistock and Portman NHS Foundation Trust and was appointed in December 2013. He was previously the Chief Executive of Rethink Mental Illness, the leading national mental health membership charity. He was awarded an OBE in 2002 for his role in setting up NHS Direct. Outside of his role at the Tavistock and Portman, Paul is Chair of the NHS Confederation's Mental Health Network and of the Cavendish Square Group of the London Mental Health Trusts. He is also a Trustee of the Joseph Rowntree Foundation.

Paul has worked in the health and care sectors since 1985, combining roles in central government, the voluntary sector and the NHS. He led the establishment of NHS Direct, the nurse-led telephone and online information service that was established in 1998.

At the Tavistock and Portman NHS Foundation Trust, Paul has supported a number of significant developments including the development and dissemination of Thrive, a new population health model for children and young people's mental health services. He has overseen the expansion of the Trust's work on training and education including a significant increase in student numbers and the launch of the Trust's Digital Academy, opening the Trust's courses to wider audiences in the UK and internationally.

Recently, Paul has led the Trust through the testing times of the Covid-19 pandemic, which has seen massive changes to how the Trust operates, moving rapidly from face-to-face services to socially distanced, digital and online services.

Dr David Lukoff, PhD, is a licensed psychologist and co-author of the DSM-IV and DSM-5 diagnostic category 'Religious or Spiritual Problem', which increased awareness of the need to address spiritual issues in clinical practice. He has published over 80 articles on spirituality and mental health, and is an active workshop presenter internationally on spiritual competency, grief, death, recovery, and spiritual crises. He is a Professor Emeritus of Psychology at the Institute of Transpersonal Psychology in Palo Alto, CA, and previously served on the faculties of Harvard and UCLA. He founded the Spiritual Competency Academy which offers accredited training programs on mindfulness, forgiveness and spiritual assessment.

Dr Erica Mapule McInnis is a Chartered Clinical Psychologist (UK) and Founder, Director, and Principal Clinical Psychologist for Nubia Wellness and Healing www.nubiawellnessandhealing.co.uk. Her maternal grandfather was a businessman, and several maternal aunts were schoolteachers. This ancestral lineage inspired her to develop the first online African Psychology Emotional Wellness School in the UK (2020). She was awarded a Churchill Fellowship (2016) with post-fellowship funding to develop 'Know Thy Self - Adinkra Cards', an African-centred therapy engagement tool with diverse wellness applications. This inspired further African Psychology Wellness Tools such as a *Post Pandemic Planning Workbook* and an *African-Centred Wellness Journal*. These put the best of traditional African culture and wellness into practice in accessible, contemporary formats. In response to the disproportionate impact of the Coronavirus pandemic in communities of African ancestry, she received a Covid-19 Action fund grant from the Winston Churchill Memorial Trust (WCMT) to develop an online Masterclass in African Psychology Series. She has publications in several peer-reviewed journals and book chapters, over 28 years of NHS experience and is an occasional lecturer for University Clinical Psychology training programmes.

Speaking engagements on African Psychology include Kensington Royal Palace (London, 2019), The High Commission for Trinidad and Tobago (Belgravia, London, 2019), a Mental Health Foundation (MHF) Podcast (aired July 2020), a feature in an award-winning documentary 'Black Girls Don't Cry' (BBC Radio 4, 2019), and a Mentally Yours podcast 'An African-Centred Approach to Mental Health' (aired 9 November 2020). Dr McInnis is a professional member of the Association of Black Psychologists (ABPsi) and is Black British of Jamaican parentage.

Chrissie McGinn & Richard Hewitt of Wisborough Transformation aim to celebrate the best in everyone. They facilitate Conscious Caring groups in healthcare, leadership development in organisations, and individual personal development. They regularly lead retreats, teach meditation, run workshops and have a counselling practice. They are Spiritual Companions and trained as Interfaith Ministers. They have run leadership and personal development programmes in the UK and abroad, mainly in Australia, for more than 30 years. They taught management in health and social care at what is now the University of Chichester. Richard was a Management Development Advisor in the distributive industry, having worked for Marks & Spencer previously. He was a Director of the West Sussex Enterprise Centre and CPD Advisor to the Sussex Chartered Institute of Personnel & Development. Chrissie worked in several capacities for Birmingham Social Services, including Home Help Organiser, Industrial Relations Officer, and Trainer. She was also partner of a medical locum agency. She taught psychology and learning & development at what is now Brighton University.

Prof Wilfred McSherry is a Professor in Nursing at the Department of Nursing, School of Health and Social Care, Staffordshire University/University Hospitals of North Midlands NHS Trust, England. He is also a part-time Professor VID Specialized University College Bergen/Oslo, Norway.

Abigail Methley gained her BSc and MRes in Psychology from Bangor University. She completed her NIHR funded PhD at the University of Manchester, investigating access to health care services for people with multiple sclerosis, before completing her Doctorate in Clinical Psychology in 2017. Since qualifying, she has worked with people with a range of neurological and mental health conditions, including in an older adults' mental health and memory assessment service. She is a Senior Clinical Psychologist within an NHS neuropsychology service in addition to independent practice. She is a clinical supervisor and publishes regularly in the scientific and practice-based literature.

Ivor Moody has been Vice Dean and Canon Pastor of Chelmsford Cathedral since 2010. He is also Chair of the Mid-Essex Inter Faith Forum and Chair of Essex Mind and Spirit, a community voluntary organisation that seeks to promote positive relationships between faith and spirituality and mental health issues, and to challenge the stigma which often surrounds mental health. He is also Chaplain to Essex County Council, and in 2017 had his first book published, called *Songs for the Soul*. Ivor has spent all his professional life in the Diocese of Chelmsford. After completing a theology degree at Kings College London and training for the ministry at The College of the Resurrection Mirfield he served curacies at St. Margaret's,

Leytonstone and St. Margaret's, Leigh on Sea, before becoming vicar of St. John the Baptist, Tilbury Docks. He then took up a post as University Chaplain at the Chelmsford Campus of the Anglia Ruskin University, before taking up his current post with Chelmsford Cathedral.

Rebecca Nye is a children's spirituality researcher and consultant whose work addresses school, church and hospital contexts. Taking a psychological perspective, she conducted a landmark study of children's spirituality with David Hay, *The Spirit of the Child* (Jessica Kingsley, 2006, revised edition). She is now committed to interdisciplinary approaches to children's spirituality, evident in her leading role in the 'Godly Play' movement which draws on psychological, theological and pedagogical theories. Rebecca has been an Associate Lecturer in Child Psychology and Childhood Studies at the Open University since 2009, and a post-graduate supervisor for the Cambridge Theological Federation since 1999. She is currently part of an NIHR research project about the spiritual needs of children facing end-of-life.

Reverend Robin Pfaff has over 20 years' experience of working in healthcare chaplaincy, managing multi-faith chaplaincy teams both in a District General Hospital in East London, as well as in Community and Mental Health in the South West of England. He is an ordained minister of the Swiss Reformed Church. To deepen his understanding and interest he has trained as a Jungian Art Psychotherapist.

Dr Adam J Powell is a research associate in Religion and Medical Humanities at Durham University. His research blends the cognitive and social sciences to explore how and when religion constructs and conserves identity and wellbeing. His work has been translated into eight languages and featured in outlets such as Forbes, Slate, and BBC Science Focus.

Nirmala Ragbir-Day is a health economist by profession and is currently Spiritual Care Trainer at the South West Yorkshire Partnership NHS Foundation Trust, UK. She is a member of the Pastoral and Spiritual Care team and her main role is delivering spiritual training and development to staff, service users and carers in the Trust. Her talks, workshops, seminars and retreats revolve around spirituality in healthcare, mindfulness and self-compassion.

Dr Steve Taylor, PhD is the author of 13 books on psychology and spirituality, and is a senior lecturer in psychology at Leeds Beckett University. He is past chair of the Transpersonal Psychology Section of the British Psychological Society.

His books include *The Clear Light*, *The Leap*, *Spiritual Science* and his new book *Extraordinary Awakenings*. His books have been published in 20 languages, and his articles and essays have been published in many academic journals, magazines and newspapers, including *The Psychologist*, *Philosophy Now*, *The Journal of Humanistic Psychology* and *The Journal of Transpersonal Psychology*. He regularly appears in the media in the UK and writes blog articles for *Scientific American* and for *Psychology Today*. Steve lives in Manchester, England, with his wife and three young children. His website is www.stevenmtaylor.com.

Jeremy Timm lives in East Yorkshire with his husband Mike, and an aged border terrier. Mike and Jeremy have been together for over twenty years, and in 2009 contracted a Civil Partnership, which was later commuted to marriage when the opportunity arose. He trained as a priest in the Church of England but was not ordained until he completed his time at college in Durham. This led to Jeremy working as a Lay reader in the Church. Following years with no official role he took up the position of Reader again, working with 6 churches until his Permission to Officiate was rescinded when he married Mike. For over a decade he was a trustee of Changing Attitude, a campaigning group, working for a change in the position and official teaching of The Church of England regarding the place of LGBTIQ folk in its life and ministry. He is currently a member of a dispersed contemplative community, Contemplative Fire, which is an Acknowledged Community by the Church of England.

Dr Cassandra Vieten is Executive Director of the John W Brick Foundation, Director of Research at the Arthur C Clarke Center for Human Imagination at the University of California, San Diego, and a Senior Fellow at the Institute of Noetic Sciences, where she served as President from 2013-2019. Her research has focused on spirituality and health, transformative experiences and practices, the development of mindfulness-based interventions for emotional wellbeing, and development of media technologies to inspire awe. She received her Ph.D. in clinical psychology at the California Institute of Integral Studies, and completed her research training in behavioural genetics at UC San Francisco. She has authored three books, including *Spiritual and Religious Competencies in Clinical Practice: Guidelines for Psychologists and Mental Health Professionals*, has published numerous articles in scientific journals, and is an internationally recognised keynote speaker and workshop leader.

Prof Fraser Watts is Visiting Professor in Psychology of Religion at the University of Lincoln, and Executive Secretary of the International Society of Science and Religion. He was formerly Reader in Theology and Science in the University of

Cambridge, and President of the British Psychological Society. His books include *Psychology for Christian Ministry* (Routledge, 2002, with S Savage & R Nye), *Psychology, Religion and Spirituality: Concepts and Applications* (CUP, 2017), *Living Deeply: A Psychological and Spiritual Journey* (Lutterworth, 2018), and *A Plea for Embodied Spirituality: The Role of the Body in Religion* (SCM, 2021).

Prof Michael West, CBE is Senior Visiting Fellow at The King's Fund, London, and Professor of Organisational Psychology at Lancaster University, Visiting Professor at University College, Dublin, and Emeritus Professor at Aston University, where he was formerly Executive Dean of Aston Business School. He graduated from the University of Wales in 1973 and was awarded a PhD in 1977 for research on the psychology of meditation. He has authored, edited and co-edited 20 books, and has published more than 200 articles in scientific and practitioner publications on teamwork, innovation, leadership and culture, particularly in healthcare. He is a Fellow of the British Psychological Society, the American Psychological Association (APA), the APA Society for Industrial/Organisational Psychology, the Academy of Social Sciences, the International Association of Applied Psychologists and the British Academy of Management. He is an Honorary Fellow of the Royal College of Physicians and Surgeons of Glasgow.

He led the English Department of Health Policy Research Programme into cultures of quality and safety. He also led the NHS National Staff Survey development and initial implementation. He assisted in developing the national framework on improvement and leadership development in England (Developing People, Improving Care - 2016) and in Northern Ireland in developing the Collective Leadership Strategy for Health and Social Care (2017). He is supporting Health Education and Improvement Wales to develop the national health and care compassionate leadership strategy in Wales. He co-chaired, with Dame Denise Coia, the two-year inquiry on behalf of the UK General Medical Council into the mental health and wellbeing of doctors Caring for Doctors, Caring for Patients (2019). He led the review for The King's Fund (commissioned by the RCN Foundation) into the mental health and wellbeing of nurses and midwives across the UK, The Courage of Compassion: Supporting Nurses and Midwives to Deliver High Quality Care (2020). His latest book (2021) is *Compassionate Leadership: Sustaining wisdom, humanity and presence in health and social care* (London: Swirling Leaf Press). He was appointed a CBE in the Queen's Birthday Honours List 2020 for services to compassion and innovation in healthcare.

Prof William West is a Visiting Professor in Counselling and Spirituality at the University of Chester where he supervises a number of PhD and doctorate students who share his interests in spirituality, faith, diversity and culture. William is a

Fellow of the British Association for Counselling and Psychotherapy. His most recent book, co-edited with Greg Nolan, was *Extending Horizons in Helping and Caring Therapies*.

Reverend Canon Professor James Woodward, Ph.D. was born in Durham in 1961. He was educated at Spennymoor Grammar School and then at King's College London, where he read Theology. After a year working at St Christopher's Hospice in London, he spent two years training for Ministry in the Anglican Church at Westcott House, Cambridge. Ordained in 1985, he has worked as a Curate, a Bishop's Chaplain, a Hospital Chaplain and from 1996 in Parochial Ministry in the Diocese of Birmingham. From 1998 to 2009 he was the Master of the Foundation of Lady Katherine Leveson, Temple Balsall, Vicar of St Mary's Church and the Director of the Leveson Centre for the Study of Ageing, Spirituality and Social Policy. In this post he pioneered work in both Church and society to encourage better thinking and practice in the support and care of older people. From 2009 to 2015 he was a Canon of Windsor. He was appointed Principal of Sarum College in September 2015 and Professor of Theology at Winchester University in 2017. He has written widely in the area of Pastoral Theology. He has taught in a number of universities including the Open University and in Warwick Business and Medical Schools and the University of Birmingham. He has written and edited 15 books.

Rev. Prof. Stephen G. Wright, FRCN MBE, works as a spiritual director and trustee for the Sacred Space Foundation (see www.sacredspace.org.uk). Before this he had a long and distinguished nursing career in practice and academia and the National Health Service, the Royal College of Nursing and as a consultant to WHO. He published many works on the research, theory and practice of nursing and was awarded an MBE by the Queen for his services to nursing, and the profession's most distinguished accolade: a Fellowship of the Royal College of Nursing. His personal and professional life took an about turn some 30 years ago through a series of life-changing spiritual experiences. Consequently, he developed an interest in spiritual matters and the connection with wellbeing, and co-founded the Foundation, to support those in spiritual crisis. He was made an Honorary Fellow of the University of Cumbria in 2013 for his work connecting spirituality and health. Three books explore the nature of healing relationships: *Therapeutic Touch, Sacred Space – right relationship and spirituality in health care* and *Reflections on spirituality and health. Coming Home* (2nd ed, 2017) is a personal and scholarly account of spiritual awakening and support.

He currently works with individuals seeking personal and spiritual guidance, and with organisations developing the practice of healing, spiritual care, conflict resolution, staff support, compassion and leadership. He is an ordained interfaith minister, bringing a rich experience of spiritual practice from many faiths to his work, as well as being a member of the Iona Community. With the support of the Diocese of Carlisle, he established the Kentigern School for contemplatives in 2018. His other recently published works include teachings in circle dance and poetry, and titles including *Burnout* (2012), *Contemplation* (2017), *Kentigern: a life and a Lakeland pilgrimage* (2019) and *A Grasmere Pilgrimage* (2020). His latest book, *Heartfullness – a 12 step guide to awakening*, is nearly complete.

Foreword

By Jamie Hacker Hughes

'*Something deep within us*' – after Peter Gilbert

I have to confess something right from the start: I am a clinical psychologist with a long-held faith and religious beliefs, held long before my journey into psychology, mental health (or psychological health, as I would rather call it) and clinical psychology. The path that I have taken has, I strongly believe, been shaped and formed by the Divine. I believe that the journey that I have made and the work that I carry out are those of service: to my patients (or clients), to my community and, often, to organisations and causes further afield. I pray for my patients (the term I prefer is 'patients', although I am equally happy with 'clients' or 'service users' as alternatives) not only between our sessions and often long after our work together is finished. I also pray (silently, of course) during sessions, and I know, because I have often been told, that my patients pray for me, and I am very much aware of their prayers. I do not in any way 'wear my faith on my sleeve' in my professional work, but if and when asked whether I have one, I answer openly and honestly.

I come with an agenda, therefore, and with a long-held view that spirituality, however we may choose to define it, is an integral part of work in wellbeing and psychological health.

Defining spirituality is very much an individual and cultural matter. The editors of this handbook have understandably chosen not to get caught up with definitions and discussions about terminology. As they rightly state in the introductory chapter, this was addressed extensively in the first edition of this handbook, and many of the authors in the chapters that follow seek to tackle this question from their varying perspectives.

What I would say, however, and what several authors of the chapters in this handbook say too, is that spirituality is something that is very much distinct from religious belief (everyone is spiritual, but not everyone is religious, in the words of one of the authors), although often the two can be very much intertwined. Rather, spirituality, as I and many others see it, refers to the sense of the other, the numinous, the Divine. I don't think that I can do better than to quote the words of Peter Gilbert, the progenitor of the first edition of this handbook and the pioneer, within the UK at least, of the work to embed awareness and understanding of spirituality into work in the fields of mental health and wellbeing. Spirituality, Peter wrote, is all about "something deep within me" and, of course, deep within all of us, whether we are aware of it or not.

And so to this handbook, newly edited by Sarajane Aris, Hilary Garraway and Hannah Gilbert, which was conceived nearly 10 years after Peter's original in 2011, *Spirituality and Mental Health*. The title and contents now embrace the term 'wellbeing', which has come to the fore, and which speaks to the current emphasis within the health agenda. What the editors have also set out to do, as they explain in their introductory chapter, is to "capture a decade of development while retaining the core resources offered by the original text."

It was therefore a hugely exciting prospect to be asked to write a short foreword to this new edition, and to be able to read all of its nearly 30 chapters in their pre-publication versions. Needless to say, I accepted the invitation eagerly and with alacrity.

More so because the time for a new and revised edition of this handbook, addressing as it does these three interlinked topics, has definitely come. This time, now, is what the Ancient Greeks would have called a 'Kairos' moment, not just an opportune moment but a critical moment; the right moment.

Why? Because, as many of its contributors allude to, this handbook is not a mere anniversary project. Whilst marking, commemorating and celebrating anniversaries is tremendously important too, this book has been assembled and its chapters written at a time of global crisis: the Covid-19 pandemic, global poverty, the Black Lives Matter movement and the growing awareness of prejudice, discrimination and its effects, the climate crisis, and other phenomena affecting our daily lives, the health, mortality and wellbeing of our sisters, brothers and loved ones, not only here at home but right across the length and breadth of our fragile and vulnerable planet. All of these things threaten the sustainability of our environment, the survival of our species and of many, many others. A Kairos moment indeed. Never has this handbook been needed more, I would argue, than now.

And so this carefully curated book sets out to do 'what it says on the tin'. Not only to "retain … the core resources offered by the original text", but also to "capture a decade of development" since the publication of Peter Gilbert's original.

Some of those original resources and projects are still alive and well. Here we can read, for example, about developments in initiatives to integrate spirituality into mental health services. These are evidenced in developments of spiritual wellbeing groups within local mental health services and, nationally, the formation of an APPG (All Party Parliamentary Group) on Faith and Society at

Westminster. Also, some of these concepts now form part of national policies and NHS policies (Spiritual Care Matters, NHS Scotland, 2009; No Health without Mental Health, 2011).

Our spiritual needs, the way we become aware of them, and the way in which we can access spiritual resources, whether internal or external, differs hugely, not only from one cultural or faith tradition to another (there is a very helpful chapter here on 'Spiritness' in African spirituality which speaks to this), but also as we travel along life's path, from our birth, through milestones, hardships and crises, to our eventual deaths.

Thus, the spirituality of children and young people, addressed very helpfully in one of the chapters here, is very different to that of adults. And, similarly, the needs of older adults regarding the spiritual dimension of their psychological health and wellbeing are understandably different to those of younger adults. These are all topics that are addressed in this book, together with philosophical approaches to help us to understand these issues. And, of course, all our journeys, spiritual or otherwise, end with one certainty – death. Here, too, an understanding of the spiritual issues and their impact on our physical and psychological health and wellbeing, can help all who are involved in life's final chapter, whether as professionals, carers and/or relatives.

Another facet of this handbook is a very practical one. A chapter on assessing spirituality is an example, as is a chapter on integrating spirituality within therapy. There is a chapter on spiritual care in general practice, another on spiritually informed care in mental health services. Other chapters focus on the interface between spirituality and mental health, on race and religion and on Christian perspectives on mental health. There is input, too, on Eastern religions, as well as on the relationship between faith and mental health written from a service user's experience, an expert by experience indeed. One chapter argues that all psychological health professionals should be trained in spiritual competences. Another chapter, as well as describing a small research study in the area, gives very practical advice and information for those wishing to carry out research in the areas of spirituality, mental health and wellbeing. The important areas of burnout and compassionate leadership are also addressed.

But the handbook looks at other areas too. As well as looking at the current context and debating the language of spirituality and moving on from that to consider areas of application and practice, the book examines in detail the concepts of the whole person, diversity and inclusion, sexual identify, compassion, connectedness, love and leadership.

The editors want us, in addition to considering our current context, understanding, practice and research, to consider the future. The inclusion of a chapter on eco spirituality is an example.

How are we, as professionals, users, academics or any other interested party or general reader, to embrace these ideas and concepts and assimilate some of the ideas and challenges presented here into our professional, working, personal daily lives? How can insights gained into the spirituality of ourselves and those we work with and care for have positive effects on our mental (or psychological) health and wellbeing?

This re-envisioned handbook is not, I would suggest, a book to be read from cover to cover and then placed on a bookshelf, never to be opened again. Rather, it is a resource to be accessed and dipped into again and again. Moreover, from the very outset the handbook, its editors and contributors, ask us to engage with the material, to reflect on its content and how these interact with and inform our personal lives and professional work. We are asked regularly throughout its pages, to consider the mental health, wellbeing and spiritual aspects of our lives and work, not only to enhance our understanding but to resource us more fully in our current and future lives and work.

So, as the editors once again remind us in their introductory chapter: "we are living in extraordinary times", a Kairos moment. Sometimes books arrive at precisely the right moment and I believe this is a perfect example of such a book. And I also believe, by the way, that this is no accident.

I commend it to you. Use it to resource your understanding of and engagement with these areas, and then keep using it, engaging with it, and enjoying it.

Professor Jamie Hacker Hughes, July 2021

Introduction: Where are we now?

Chapter 1:

Introduction: the current context

By Sarajane Aris, Hilary Garraway & Hannah Gilbert

'It is the spiritual dimension of our consciousness and being that truly connects us, and takes us beyond our quarrels and conflicts. We are ever evolving, eternally interconnected beings.' Sarajane Aris

In the beginning...

Never before has there been a more crucial time to attend to, address, and work with, spiritual dimensions and realms of our being and consciousness.

Spirituality and Mental Health was originally published in 2011 by Pavilion Publishing, edited by Professor Peter Gilbert, Emeritus Professor of Social Work and Spirituality at Stafford University, one of the many distinguished positions he held. Peter was project lead for spirituality for the National Institute for Mental Health England (NIMHE) from its inception, set up after the devastating consequences of 9/11 by the Director of NIMHE and Mental Health Services, Anthony Sheehan. Sadly, shortly after editing the first edition of this handbook, Peter tragically passed away from the effects of motor neurone disease. The book aimed to "bring a spiritual dimension to mental health services." It was and remains a well-received and widely used handbook across mental health, public sector and related services, and also by a range of people including experts by experience, professionals and non professionals, leaders of services, academics, researchers and educators.

Ten years on, the book is in need of substantial revision, so that its users can be kept up to date with developments, research and opportunities that have arisen in this field since Peter's untimely death. The book aims to be inclusive of a range of perspectives, and offers an opportunity to hear from both well-known authorities in the field and not-so-well known contributors.

Pavilion approached Sarajane Aris, who had contributed a chapter on psychological approaches to spirituality for the original handbook, to act as editor of a new edition. The task would be to capture a decade of development while retaining the core resources offered by the original text. As Sarajane had retired from mental health services in 2011, she wanted to engage younger editors who were involved on the ground as current practitioners, to create a strong editorial team. Both Hannah Gilbert and Hilary Garraway agreed to come on board and work as an editorial team, contributing their experience and network of contacts for the new book. What an exiting, rich, unfolding process and journey it has been together, to safeguard Peter Gilbert's legacy, build the content afresh, taking into account the current climate and issues across the world, and gather evidence of the continued importance of the work he championed and, in many ways, pioneered.

'We are living in exceptional times'

There are many converging issues that provide a backdrop to this present edition of the handbook. We are writing it within the context of many changes and challenges, but also potential opportunities; the suffering and trauma the whole world is experiencing and living through with the devastating impact that Covid 19 is having on physical, mental and spiritual health. We are being faced with untimely deaths of significant numbers of people across the world.

We are witnessing the huge impact of Covid 19 on people who have underlying health issues, and who are from ethnic minorities – the stark differences between people are laid bare. Social, ethnic, age and gender inequalities in society are revealed as problematic, both in socio-economic terms but also psychologically: vulnerabilities are different for different groups as highlighted by Public Health England Covid Report (2020), and the British Psychological Society's position papers (February & June, 2020).

These issues are not solely about Covid 19. 'Black Lives Matter' and the need to revisit issues of inequality, injustice and equity, are presenting very real, urgent challenges and issues to address, but also potential opportunities for all age groups.

We are only just beginning to see the traumatic impact of the Covid 19 pandemic on children's lives, particularly with regard to their wellbeing, schooling and development (Waite *et al*, 2021) as well as impact of Covid 19 on older people, their mental health and wellbeing, with the need to self-isolate preventing human contact. This social contact is so crucial in our human development at all ages, as Bowlby and Harlow demonstrated in their studies on the impact of lack of attachment on monkeys and young children in the 1960s (Bowlby, 1969; Harlow *et al*, 1965). Families are losing loved ones without being able to properly say goodbye or be with them, or comfort them in times of illness and tragedy. This will inevitably cause psychological distress for those unable to say goodbye or grieve their loss naturally (Eisma *et al*, 2021). Visiting restrictions for families with relatives and loved ones in care have made the display of compassion difficult: email and Zoom are no substitute for hugs, touch and the nuances of in-person and engaged conversations. We are all living with the incessant trauma.

Various studies have been set up to look at these impacts, such as the Covid 19 Longitudinal Research Hub, by organisations such as UCL Social Research Institute[1], and various government bodies[2].

Relief is potentially at hand with the swift development of vaccines, but at the same time the virus is mutating. The landscape is ever-shifting, the map and route not constant or clear, and so being redrawn, calling us continually to stretch ourselves, to think outside the box and to reconsider our assumptions – both a potential opportunity or a potential threat, depending on our perspective.

We are also seeing the devastation of people's livelihoods, with a deep recession and what is described as a 'K' shape recovery just emerging: that is to say a portion of the population and businesses recover quickly and fully, while others suffer a great deal. Some sectors are recovering and others are not. No generation or country across the world is unaffected, either by the virus or by its impact on the global economy and the recession/depression that may follow. At the time of writing this, we are not near the end of this pandemic and its effects, more 'at the end of the beginning'. The 'fallout' from this and the ensuing mental health problems, some of which may be a natural response to an unnatural situation, are just emerging. Never has there been a more important time to address and develop our mental health, spirituality and wellbeing.

The paucity of effective political leadership across the world, with many potentially explosive global situations and conflicts rising around the world, all add to the sense of uncertainty and complexity, pushing us to look within and consider alternative ways of being. Many leaders urgently need to learn about wise and compassionate leadership. This is a time when a focus on spirituality, mental health and wellbeing are so necessary in all sectors of society.

And yet there are even larger challenges. All of the above needs to be seen within the context of climate change and ecological crises, in which people and much of

---

1   CLOSER (Covid 19 Longitudinal Research Hub): UCL Social Research Institute. closer@ucl.ac.uk

2   Covid 19 Impact Inquiry: https/www.ukri.org

the natural world are potentially at risk. Both in the long term and the short-to-medium term, dramatic challenges face us due to global warming, extreme weather events and population growth. The lives of many people across the world are being turned upside down, with extreme heat or constant flooding or drought forcing them to leave their homes and countries. There are therefore widespread anxieties and uncertainty about our future and its existence.

But it is not all 'doom and gloom'. At the same time as we see challenges and disruption everywhere, we are also witnessing great acts of kindness and compassion. Innovative developments are pushing through the crisis, demonstrating creative new ways of delivering services, from restaurants to sport. We are seeing spontaneous helping, community engagement and the gifts of time and energy making a difference to the lives of others, many who offer anonymous gifts of support. The great gift of the 99-year-old veteran Sir Tom Moore walking his garden to raise money for health service workers is but one example of many.

Wellbeing is now emerging as a major priority across the world. Ways to develop wellbeing are in the spotlight – with a greater emphasis on developing and sustaining wellbeing. New and innovative developments are emerging in health, education, and universities across the world. Wellbeing policies are being developed by governments, universities and mental health services. As a consequence, wellbeing services are expanding; for example Wellbeing Hubs are developing locally and regionally, and NHS resources are being directed to develop a variety of wellbeing services. As editors, we therefore felt it important that the new handbook included wellbeing both in its title and in the content.

Given this context, as we reflect on our current times, just pause to reflect for yourself on the following questions, and see what arises.

Reflective questions

- What sense are you making of what we are living through and what will be left for generations to come?

- What are you being called to attend to? In ourselves, others, our community, our country, in the world, and beyond?

- Are you/we being called to consider ourselves more broadly and deeply than our everyday existence?

- Are you/we being called to look at our interconnectivity and connectedness in a different way?

- What is it that enables and sustains your wellbeing? What nourishes you?

It is the contention of the editors of this handbook that we are being called, amongst many other things, to look at what is really meaningful to us: what matter's most and what is the meaning of 'self' and 'life' – truly spiritual questions that support our wellbeing. Peter Gilbert referred to this in his first chapter of the original handbook, saying:

"…spirituality relates to a person's inner spirit, and therefore to their experiences of being human, their meaning and purpose in life: their human quest; what makes them tick; what keeps us well when life throws its challenges at us. Spirituality may also be related to a belief in a personal God, a cosmic life force, and / or an organised religious grouping. A Sikh, Christian, Muslim, Jew, Hindu etc. may feel as close to God while walking in the hills as worshipping in their gurdwara, church, mosque, synagogue or temple." (Gilbert, 2011)

Whatever spirituality may be for you, the reader, hold it in your heart and mind as you read this handbook.

Given what we are living through, and likely to be living through for some time, the editors felt that there is even more reason for this new and revised handbook to be made available for a range of individuals, professionals, managers, CEOs and leaders working within mental health and other sectors. It is, we hope, a resource and tool-box to use to strengthen and develop spirituality, mental health and wellbeing, in order to respond to the threats, challenges and changes each of us are experiencing and may continue to experience for a number of years.

No-one has any idea how the future will unfold – what the dangers and the opportunities are, as the Chinese symbol for crisis depicts (see Figure 1.1). We need to hold both ends of the spectrum or continuum, the opportunities or challenges, as we move forwards in an uncertain world, in which no-one has a clear map. We are perhaps being called to question what we think we know as our reality, and consider our world and our fellow human beings differently, in order to attend to another dimension of consciousness, the true nature of our being. We are perhaps being called to be in the moment, rather than know exactly where we are headed. Palmer (2004) describes how: "…farmers on the Great Plains, at the first sign of a blizzard, would run a rope from the back door to the barn", to prevent people from getting lost in the storm. Spirituality perhaps offers something like that rope to hold on to when the way ahead is unclear.

CRISIS

Danger   Opportunity

Figure 1.1: Chinese symbol for crisis

This handbook is perhaps timely in moving us all to think about and reflect on a new landscape and the need to connect with deeper resources to nourish and sustain our wellbeing on our journey through life.

The handbook

We have tried to bring together a broad range and rich tapestry of perspectives and themes related to spirituality, mental health and wellbeing, for experts by experience, carers, a range of public sector workers, organisations, leaders, and services relevant to the present and moving towards our future. Given that this is the second handbook, we have assumed the reader has a basic understanding of mental health, spirituality and wellbeing, in order to avoid going over the basics and focusing instead on new developments. We are therefore not devoting space to definitions of 'mental health' 'spirituality' or 'wellbeing' in this introductory chapter as these are often defined throughout the chapters. We have aimed to be inclusive, to draw together contributions from a range of perspectives, both well known and less well known contributors, and to explore mental health, wellbeing, and spirituality across the life cycle.

We have divided the book into four sections, the themes of which will be returned to in our final chapter:

Section One covers an introduction from the authors to set the current context of the handbook, an update on some key Mental Health Trust Spirituality projects 10 years on from the time at which Peter Gilbert led their developments to integrate spirituality within mental health services. It includes a chapter introducing African psychology and spirituality, and a chapter on finding meaning and purpose in a 'covid' impacted world. This is in order to set a tone and include a breadth of perspectives from the beginning of the handbook.

Section Two is split into three parts:

1. Mental health spirituality and wellbeing across the life cycle, looking at childhood, older adults, and death and dying.

2. Therapeutic practice. This includes chapters on spirituality, mental health and wellbeing assessments, spiritual crises, integrating spirituality into therapeutic interventions, an expert by experience's views of the intersection of faith and mental health, a perspective on spirituality and psychotherapy, a perspective on research and spirituality in mental health, and a chapter on spiritual competencies.

3. Themes and Journeys. This part of the section includes chapters on psychological and Christian perspectives on mental health, voices, visions and the spiritual journey, and also spirituality and LGBTQ.

Section Three covers the landscape of spirituality, leadership, services and training including burnout, and spiritual care in general practice from a range of perspectives. It includes a chapter on the challenges for the formal healthcare system in embracing spirituality. The thread running through each chapter is about the power of love and compassion to transform. Compassionate leadership, while always important, has never been more necessary than it is now with what are we witnessing amongst our politicians and leaders, some of those who lead us here in the UK, and across the world.

Section Four looks to the new landscape of the future. This covers reflections on race, religion and wellbeing, eco-spirituality in the context of climate change, the call of the new spiritualties, and ending the handbook with a chapter taking us 'Beyond Separation'. We will return to these themes in the final chapter of the book.

Conclusion: the current and future unfolding landscape for *Spirituality, Mental Health and Wellbeing*

As we said at the beginning of this chapter, there has never been a more crucial time to attend to, address, and work with, the spiritual dimensions and realms of our being and consciousness. For some individuals, spirituality is the heart of who we are, for others it is a little explored area. Could spirituality eventually be seen and become the heart of and foundation for our mental health and wellbeing, and the services that support these? Could spirituality become seen and recognised more widely as both an inherent and essential part of our community and world wellbeing, which will take us beyond our ordinary ways of coping?

We hope this handbook goes some small way to enabling all our readers to do just that.

Below are some final reflections for you to begin the journey. You may want to make a note of these at the beginning of the handbook and see what arises for you as you go through the chapters.

- Again – what are you being called to attend to?
- What would you like the journey onwards for your own and humanity's spirituality, mental health and wellbeing to look like?
- What can you be doing to enable this to happen in a real way, both personally and professionally?

An ending quote for reflection: "Only love and compassion can bring true and lasting transformation." – **Rasheed Ogunlaru**

References and links

Bowlby, J. (1969), *Attachment and loss, Vol.1:* New York: Basic Books.

British Psychological Society (BPS) Position Paper by BPS Racial and Social Inequalities Group (2020), *Taking the conversation forwards.*

British Psychological Society and Division of Clinical Psychology Briefing Paper (2020), *Psychological impact of the response to the coronavirus / Covid-19 on older people.*

Eisma, M.C., *et al.* (2021) Acute grief after deaths due to COVID-19, natural causes and unnatural causes: An empirical comparison. *J Affect Dis.*

Gilbert P (2011) *Spirituality and Mental Health.* Pavilion Publishing

Harlow H.F., Dodsworth R.O., & Harlow M.K. (1965) Total social isolation in monkeys. *Proceedings of the National Academy of Sciences of the United States of America.*

Jones, C. (2021) Three Charts Show A K-Shaped Recovery. Forbes.com

Palmer, P. (2004) *A Hidden Wholeness.* US: Jossey-Bass

Public Health England Covid Report (2020) Beyond the Data. *Understanding the impact of Covid 19 on BAME groups.*

Waite,P., *et al.* (2021) *Co-Space Study.* Oxford University

The Health Foundation (2021) *The wider impacts of Covid 19 on the health monitoring tool.* www.gov.uk.

Chapter 2:
Integrating spirituality into mental health services

By Ivor Moody, Robin Pfaff & Ben Bano

Introduction

Background to the National Spirituality and Mental Health Forum

As the second millennium approached, an interest was developing in a more holistic approach to mental health, with a focus on mind, body and the spirit. Within this context the National Spirituality and Mental Health Forum (NSMHF) was created by a consultative group exploring the relationship between different religions and mental health. This was initiated by the former Health Education Authority (HEA) during the 1990s and became a multi-faith charity with trustees representing all nine major faiths recognised by the Department of Health, supported by MIND and Rethink, together with representative humanists and atheists. More recently, within the context of the 'parity of esteem' agenda, the Forum has been particularly concerned about the contribution of spirituality to working with people affected by the Covid-19 pandemic. As a result, a number of online seminars have addressed this theme.

Background to the National Mental Health Spirituality Project

Professor Peter Gilbert was a key figure within the NSMHF, eventually taking over chairing from the then NSMHF Chair and National Director Paddy Cooney, when he was employed by the National Institute of Mental Health England (NIMHE) to lead the Spirituality and Mental Health Project. At that time he was also the National Director for Social Care. Peter Gilbert recognised the importance of spirituality within mental health and social care services.

Following the 9/11 terrorist attacks in the US, their immediate aftermath and the burgeoning Islamophobia, in collaboration with Anthony Sheehan, chief executive of NIMHE (National Institute for mental health in England), they established spirituality as a major project within the NIMHE Programme. (NIMHE had been established by the government as the vehicle for delivering modern mental health services.) Peter, on behalf of NSMHF, obtained support and patronage from various sources, including with the then Archbishop of Canterbury, Rowan Williams. NSMHF was successful in obtaining a major grant from the Department of Health to develop a National Spirituality Project in the NHS for three years. This three-year spirituality project developed and co-ordinated various other spirituality projects and pilot sites across the country, conducted various training programmes, national events and networking opportunities to raise awareness of the importance of spirituality in mental health services. Peter Gilbert spearheaded this project and, along with colleagues, established links with spiritual care staff and others working in the area of spirituality across the country.

The National Spirituality Project aimed to establish a spirituality link person in every one of the 68 mental health trusts of that time. Ideally, a trust is best served by having three key people in post: a spirituality lead at board level, a spirituality lead in service delivery and a professional spirituality lead such as a chaplain. As well as establishing local networks, the project created a regional structure to facilitate communication between the NSMHF, mental health trusts and third sector organisations as well as faith communities. The National Spirituality Project led by Peter Gilbert bore rich fruits and led to an increased awareness of the importance of spirituality within mental health care, a focus on Chaplaincy across mental health trusts in England and Wales, whilst also linking and including psychologically related spirituality projects, such as described in Isabel Clarke's chapter, 'Voices, Visions and the Spiritual Journey'. In particular, the spirituality project established the recognition of the common bonds of spirituality as 'something deep inside me' as compared to specific faith beliefs.

Despite the tragic terminal illness and death of Peter Gilbert from Motor Neurone Disease in 2013, the work that Peter and others achieved through the National Spirituality Project sowed many seeds. The fruit of this is seen in chaplaincy and spirituality projects throughout mental health trusts across the country. The remainder of this chapter showcases the development and continuation of this work with two such projects, the first from Somerset and the second from Essex. Another example can be found in Chapter 19 by Nirmala Ragbir-Day & Mike Gartland. This describes the work carried out in South West Yorkshire Partnership Trust and the development of 'Spirit in Mind'.

Spirituality and mental health: a perspective from community and mental health chaplaincy in Somerset

Conversations about spirituality and mental health might automatically lead to thoughts about healthcare chaplaincy. Chaplains often have to explain their role to people both in the NHS and beyond. As the words 'chaplain' and 'chapel' sound very similar, many still make an assumption that a chaplain's primary role is a religious one, and a Christian one in particular. Many are surprised to learn that healthcare chaplains are employed by the NHS[3]. This fact has profound consequences for their work. Healthcare chaplains not only have to be accountable to their own faith/belief traditions and their relevant authorising bodies, but also endorse NHS values and principles. Some of these may stand in uncompromising conflict with a faith tradition's doctrine, for example if we consider the NHS's equal opportunities policies or LBGT rights.

Some healthcare chaplaincies have tried to address some of these challenges by renaming their department to include the term 'spiritual care'. A new difficulty may arise if spiritual care is only associated with chaplaincy. In my view, spiritual care concerns the entire organisation and all its staff, so that a culture is created in which kindness and thoughtfulness can flourish.

If we are truly committed to providing person-centred care, we need to know how to sensitively explore a person's core values, and how their hopes, fears, dreams, beliefs and values impact on their identity and wellbeing. These are deeply personal conversations. My experience is that members of staff are sometimes unsure if they are permitted to explore these.

Providing spiritual care is often done through very simple acts of thoughtfulness and kindness, for example by remembering a person's preferred name or that they take one spoonful of sugar in their coffee. By remembering and acknowledging the individual in small but very important gestures, we can help people know that they are not just a number in a long caseload.

Chaplains know that the majority of spiritual care is provided by other members of staff in their routine work of providing person-centred care. When chaplains are embedded in an organisation, it often means that a space is created for the spiritual, religious and cultural dimensions to be voiced and heard.

---

3   The standards and a register for healthcare chaplains has been developed by the UK Board of Healthcare chaplains.

In my experience, most patients access chaplaincy in very informal ways. Last year only 7% of referrals originated from a patient "wanting to discuss a significant matter". The majority of referrals (59%) stated that the patient welcomed engagement with a chaplain or chaplaincy volunteer, and 34% came into contact with chaplaincy by attending one of our groups or events. Providing easily accessible, inclusive and welcoming opportunities for people to meet chaplains to start a conversation seems to be of value.

Chaplains are completely dependent on the wider multi-disciplinary team to be involved. Other healthcare professionals need to know and understand the principles of chaplaincy, so that they can support patients' access when required. We now have a chaplaincy champion on most wards and in many teams. This healthcare professional acts as a bridge between their workplace and the chaplaincy department. The chaplaincy champion can help colleagues discern the spiritual needs of patients and explain when and how to make a referral. By creating a network, the chaplains can easily update the various wards and teams about important changes, for example that we are now able to use 'Attend Anywhere', the NHS's video consultation software. To support patients in their understanding of what chaplains can offer, we have supplemented our information leaflet with a short film on their role. It maps out who can be referred, how and what to expect once a referral has been made. The film explains that chaplains are NHS employees working within the multi-disciplinary team who will contribute to writing into the patient's notes to ensure that their spiritual needs are recognised and being met.

We have since learnt that making short films provides easily accessible learning experiences and fosters engagement with chaplaincy. In addition to other short teaching films, we are now regularly creating films to mark important events, like Mental Health Awareness Week, Holocaust Memorial Day or Chinese New Year. The resources can be easily found on the chaplaincy website, so that other healthcare professionals can make them available to patients when the time is right for them.

For the last year, during the covid pandemic, we have also been offering a weekly, virtual gathering which is open to everybody. The first 15 minutes is a formal space for people to pause and reflect on a theme that has been developed by the core members of the group. The format followed usually involves lighting a candle, then an action that links all participants, a focus on breathing, listening to a poem and a piece of music, and an invitation to make/bring an object linked to the theme. This gathering is followed by a virtual coffee break, where attendees can talk about the experience of having participated.

In recent years, the chaplains have reduced the number of traditional religious services held on inpatient units. These have been replaced by Spiritual Wellbeing Groups in which a theme is creatively explored. If a participant expresses having a personal religious faith, the chaplain will follow this up to ensure that the patient's religious needs continue to be met while in hospital. In my experience, it is enormously helpful if chaplains have creative skills to augment verbal communication. Many patients are able to express themselves through art and music, which requires the chaplain to be able to understand and value these forms of communication. For example, when celebrating harvest, the chaplain might work together with the occupational therapist to make bread with patients.

Without the help of staff on the wards or based in the community, our small chaplaincy department struggles to be effective. Finding ways to ensure good collaboration, mutual high regard and open dialogue is essential for spiritual care to thrive. This will benefit our patients and carers, but also ensures a high degree of wellbeing and satisfaction within our various workplaces.

Essex Mind and Spirit: understanding the journey

It takes courage to strike out on your own; independently to travel a different way. Essex Mind and Spirit (EMS) struck out on its own in 2012, though with ongoing links to the NSMHF. Formerly, the work of fostering a positive relationship between faith and spirituality and mental health issues fell under the auspices of the charity InterAct, based at Moulsham Mill in Chelmsford. Financial insecurities meant that this work faced the axe, but it proved the catalyst for the establishment of an independent community voluntary organisation dedicated to ensuring that the conversation started between faith groups and those working with and enduring mental health issues would continue.

My journey to the role of Chair of EMS began when I became Chaplain to Anglia Ruskin University (Chelmsford Campus). It was the first time as a priest in the Church of England that I had to grapple with mental health issues in a sustained way. For many, the journey to university can mean loneliness, isolation, debt, homesickness, academic rigour and much else besides. Chaplaincy was able to draw alongside those experiencing marginalisation and disempowerment and explore how faith and spirituality could contribute positively to the pastoral care of those with difficult mental health journeys.

EMS operates through the formation of 'cluster groups' situated around Essex and coordinated by volunteers who themselves are either mental health professionals and/or members of faith communities. They seek to cluster together individuals and agencies living and working in local communities to explore different aspects of mental health care and provision. In short, to encourage thought and networking about what is often regarded as a neglected 'Cinderella' subject. One of the organisers of the Colchester group says:

"We seek to inform and discuss topical issues from a mental and spiritual point of view. We arrange meetings with speakers who have experience and knowledge of various subjects. Wherever possible we like to involve local people. I have learnt a lot about mental health conditions through being part of the cluster group and listening to experts."

Another from a cluster group based in Epping says:

"The group is focused on holistic care, especially the value religious and spiritual care can provide responding to mental health challenges. The cluster holds regular networking events, hosted at local hospital sites. The cluster has always had a strong mix of NHS professionals including GPs, a Trust Governor, NHS chaplaincy and nursing and counselling professionals. The cluster was linked to training and recruiting local people to form the bulk of a chaplaincy services to patients in the West. The model developed has been so successful it has been rolled out across all the Trust sites."

The above quote is from someone who is a mental health nurse, Christian minister and is also head of Chaplaincy and Spiritual Care for the Essex Partnership University Foundation Trust (EPUT) and a Trust governor. His various roles therefore enable the cluster group to have a voice at all levels of the county's NHS mental health provision.

A key tenet of EMS is that we welcome people of all faiths and no faith. Mental ill health is no respecter of culture and creed. This is reflected in the membership of our steering group, which meets quarterly to support the work of the cluster groups and oversee the direction of travel for EMS. It confronts societal stigma around mental health issues, and a cultural reticence to talk about mental health problems, a phenomenon which crosses all sections of society. One of the cluster groups is based in Basildon, supported by Basildon Council, and is organised and chaired by Sidra Naeem from the Muslim community. The group is called 'Women Together' and seeks to provide fellowship, support and encouragement for women, many of them refugees, and from various minority communities. She writes:

"This group aims to integrate vulnerable women from different backgrounds into the community. This is achieved by organising coffee mornings, craft activities, keep fit classes, talent competitions and the delivery of lectures on topics related to inter faith, educational matters and mental health. The group also liaises with outside agencies and Essex Police to invite outside speakers and specialists on mental health to attend and deliver talks at Women Together."

Choosing to accompany someone on their journey can have remarkable results. One respondent from the Basildon cluster group has said:

"Before I started attending Women Together I was unemployed. My marriage had ended due to domestic violence, and consequently I was suffering from depression and lacked confidence. Through one of the speakers who delivered a talk, I managed to get myself a job! This in turn gave me back my confidence and I felt I could offload my problems to the ladies in a safe environment. Women Together signposted me to Wickford Mind, where I also received counselling. I am now an altogether better person."

Another cluster group is based in Mid-Essex, at Chelmsford Cathedral. Its convenor is a Pastoral Assistant whose role is to work with clergy and volunteers at the cathedral in the care and nurture of the congregation and the community. As well as providing another networking forum for local charities, societies, faith leaders, service users and volunteers, the Mid-Essex cluster group also acts as a training hub. Pastoral Assistants and those in preparation for this role come and learn about the relationships between faith and spirituality and mental health as part of their ongoing training and formation for their work in their own parishes and communities. The Mid-Essex convenor reflects:

"In Mid-Essex we have recently organised talks focusing on the support available locally for carers, victims of trafficking and drug abuse. They have formed a much-appreciated part of our contribution to pastoral care training."

Every three years, EMS has organised a county-wide conference held at Chelmsford Cathedral. In 2014 there was a conference on 'Spirituality and Mental Health in a Multi Faith Context', and it proved to be a turning point for EMS and its work. One of the recommendations made by the conference delegates was for EMS to undertake a 'mapping project' across Essex to find examples of constructive interaction between faith communities and the voluntary and statutory services in the provision of care for those experiencing mental ill health. Several such projects were identified and the results reported at a conference. One of the conference delegates suggested making contact with the All Party Parliamentary Group on Faith and Society. This group, under the Chairmanship of the Rt. Hon. Stephen

Timms MP, had started a national programme of 'Faith Covenants' designed to foster and encourage conversations between the faiths sector and voluntary and statutory organisations and district, borough and county councils. The purpose of these Covenants is to encourage these providers of care to recognise that many faith-based organisations, some of them very small and working 'at the coalface' amidst scattered communities, are delivering a huge variety of community care to a very high standard and deserve recognition as valued partners in the delivery of social care. These faith covenants encourage those faith groups to realise that what they do as care providers is part of a bigger picture, and to give them greater access to networking and funding opportunities.

So, what had started as a project by one small, community voluntary organisation resulted in the establishment of the Essex Faith Covenant (EFC) with the Essex County Council in 2017 (to which the author is also Chaplain). It was the first covenant to be county wide in its scope and operation, and to date it has 33 signatories from faith groups, inter faith forums and other organisations across Essex.

This major development in the work and direction of EMS has helped to further cement relationships with other caring agencies and organisations in Essex. This has been especially relevant with the onset of the COVID-19 pandemic in helping others focus on the resulting rise of mental ill health and distress. The author, along with other members of the EFC and the Mid-Essex Inter Faith Forum, were invited onto a 'Faith and Communities Tactical Coordination Group' (F&CTCG) convened by Essex County Council to tackle the impact of the pandemic from a faiths and cultures perspective. One of its major focuses was advice on funerals and the management of loss and bereavement across Essex's many and diverse communities.

The most recent county conference organised by EMS in 2017 was on 'Dementia and Faith and Spirituality', and it established an ongoing friendship with The Alzheimers Society. EMS has hosted Dementia Friends sessions both virtually and through the local cluster groups and through representation on the Pan Essex Dementia Action Alliance. Most recently it encouraged the membership of The Alzheimers Society on the F&CTCG to represent the alarming statistic that 22% of dementia deaths are COVID related.

EMS works alongside other caring agencies across Essex in a multi-agency, multi-faith, multi-disciplinary approach dedicated to the understanding and management of mental health issues. At the time of writing it remains unclear what the landscape will look like post-COVID-19. No one can be certain. But if there is one word which summarises all that has been described so far, it is 'friendship'.

A journeying alongside those who suffer and are sad. A non-condemnatory, non-judgemental listening to all those who have stories to tell, and a partnership with others, gently and without proselytizing, who share the same intention to make a difference to others' lives. This is something that has always defined EMS, and it will continue to do so whatever the future holds.

Websites for further information

www.spiritualitymentalhealth.org.uk

www.healthcarechaplains.org

www.somersetft.nhs.uk/chaplaincy-and-spiritual

youtube.com/playlist?list=PLLHpeKyhww3oLR1Vsp1PYfzKFH3VBhMan

www.essexmindandspirit.co.uk

www.essexfuture.org.uk/action/unite-behind-a-sense-of-identity/essex-faith-covenant

www.interfaith.org.uk/involved/contact/mid-essex-inter-faith-group

www.southwestyorkshire.nhs.uk/spirit-in-mind/home

Chapter 3:

African Psychology & Spiritness in Twin Pandemics

By Dr Erica Mapule McInnis

Summary

In this chapter, we use the language of disease, prescription and vaccine to propose the paradigm of African Psychology to create a spirit of wellness, particularly for people of African ancestry. This is in the age of twin pandemics: of the microbial disease of COVID-19 and the structural 'disease' (and legacy) of the global system of White supremacy. We introduce the paradigm of African Psychology, explore African concepts of self, provide clinical case study material, and suggest means for inclusion of African Psychology in practitioner's clinical and managerial supervision. We argue spiritual health to be a precursor for mental health and provide African-centred outcomes.

The language of disease and pandemic

In the year 2020, the global mental health of people of African ancestry experienced trauma and psychic terrorism from the occurrence and media circulation of the death of George Floyd. This is not to say circulation should not happen, but this knowing provoked re-traumatisation from vicarious trauma and unresolved historical trauma[4]. This is proposed as global 'psychic terrorism', as it both is and results in the systematic use of terror to immobilise and/or destabilise a person's fundamental sense of security and safety by assaulting his or her consciousness

---

4   According to SAMHSA (2014) 'Individual trauma results from an event, series of events, or set of circumstances that are experienced by an individual as physically or emotionally harmful or life-threatening and that have lasting adverse effects on the individual's functioning and mental, physical, social, emotional, or spiritual wellbeing'. Vicarious trauma is the negative psychological symptoms people can gain from witnessing or being told of traumatic events.

and identity (Nobles, 2015). The event that provoked these occurrences was a police officer in the US kneeling on George Floyd's neck, preventing him from breathing for over eight minutes (BBC World News, 2020). The term 'global system of White supremacy' is used to describe a world structured due to historical events which results in worse experiences for people of highest skin pigmentation (darkest complexion), although the impact may differ due to coping, resilience, and other factors (Eddo-Lodge, 2017; Fuller, 2016; McIntosh, 2003). The language of disease is used because a disease is contagious, caused by something, causes harm, and has symptoms (negative effects) (Cambridge University Dictionary, 2021).

It is reasonable to suggest that the events leading to the death of George Floyd were either in part or full examples of the effects of a global system of White supremacy, and furthermore triggered the tribal/ancestral self (Akbar, 1998) in many of African ancestry both on the continent of Africa and in the diaspora. Moreover, it may have caused many to wonder, dependent upon their stage of racial identity, whether 'this is what happens to people like us', 'this could happen to me', 'will I be next?', 'this happens to us too often regardless of my good conduct or right to a fair process for any misdemeanour'. The legacy and ongoing 'mental and spiritual disease'[5] of a global system of White supremacy for people of African ancestry, provokes such fears (Fuller, 1971/2016; Woodson, 1933/2012).

This triggered the tribal/ancestral self which has memories from experiences of ancestors. Furthermore, it impacted at a spirit[6] level; as extinguishing the important breath (the Ba[7]) was symbolic of attempts to stop the existence of people of African ancestry (literally take away their breath), a regular occurrence (given a history of lynching), and fearfully repeatable (will this continue) (Akbar, 1998; Grills *et al*, 2016). Furthermore, this event was for many another indicator of lack of belonging in countries their ancestors built (Andrews, 2017). Yet there is scope for recovery of this 'trampled and battered' spirit. Black Lives Matters (BLM) campaigns were re-launched as the latest in a series of movements to both highlight and decrease maltreatment of people of African ancestry (Day, 2015; Johnson, 2020). Nevertheless, a spirit weakened by racial battle fatigue left many with few

---

5   The global system of White supremacy is referred to as a 'mental disease' due to its persistent thinking/ conceptualising of people of high skin pigmentation as inferior rather than in need of appropriate support or a product of unhelpful and debilitating environments. The global system of White supremacy is referred to as a 'spiritual disease' as it removes the humanity (spirit) of people of high skin pigmentation seeing them as less than human so deserving of interactions and interventions which does not meet their needs or is degrading.

6   There are many definitions of spirit. Ani (1994) refers to it as a greater cause, creative force, energy, and meaningful level of existence. Grills (2002), a passion or sense of purpose. Nobles (2006), the 'essence' of a person; humanity; relationship with a creator, ancestor, or self. He goes on to propose the use of the term 'spiritness' as we are spirit beings having a physical existence.

7   The 'Ba' (breath) in ancient Nile Valley civilisations (eg ancient Egyptian) was the essence of the self, the spirit of the person and an allegory for the universality of life (Akbar, 1998).

physical, mental, social or economic resources to fight the co-existing pandemic of COVID-19 which disproportionately devastated communities of African heritage in the diaspora (Adams, 2020; Jaspal & Lopes, in press; The Health Foundation, 2020). Given a disease which is spread across a whole country or world is termed a 'pandemic' (Oxford English Dictionary, 2021), the language of twin pandemics is used to describe global majority people[8] simultaneously struck by both a system of White supremacy and COVID-19. This is not to say other communities did not experience twin pandemics, but for those of African ancestry, the institutionalised global system of White supremacy pre-existed (Kambon, 1998).

An ongoing aim of the disease of the global system of White supremacy is to de-spirit. At its height, this was necessary to convince those enslaved that escape was futile as they simply could not provide for themselves in the elements without a slave master. Another necessary feature of effective enslavement was suppression or denial of their culture of origin, promoting the adoption of the culture of their oppressors. Denial of culture often happened from removing original names of those enslaved and allocating the name of slave owners, in the knowledge that names often held key cultural information about who you were or could be (Nubia, 2017). Suppression of African culture was reinforced by allocating dignity and prosperity to those rejecting the culture of their ancestors, even though many practised their culture of origin in secret. For example, to avoid punishment, the religion of Santería in Cuba developed with hidden elements of the West African religion of Yoruba (Pérez y Mena, 2000). For many, a result of a partially hidden self was inter-generational de-spiriting (Nobles, 2006).

From an African-centred perspective, nothing is new, as descendants often have similar experiences to their ancestors unless they change the journey (Baruti, 2015). This begs the question, how did our ancestors' cope, survive and thrive with the resources they had? For those of us in the diaspora, these are ancestors who survived the horrors and indignity of race-based chattel enslavement, the middle passage when trafficked, plantation life, colonisation and more (Ani, 1994; 1997). It is of note that these ancestors were enslaved, not slaves. They descended from those who developed advanced civilisations in the Nile Valley and other parts of Africa (Browder, 1992; Walker, 2013). The task of recovery is to reclaim the knowing spirit of those ancestors, to nurture and propel us in the here and now.

---

8   Kambon (1998) asserts an African worldview, in which people of high skin pigmentation are a global majority rather than minority based on population.

A prescription: African Psychology

African Psychology provides a strengths-based approach to wellness, enlivenment of the spirit, preservation of healthy African character, and life-enhancing African cultural rituals. This approach was championed by the Association of Black Psychologists (ABPsi) when they broke away from the American Psychological Association (APA) in 1968, knowing they needed alternative methods to both understand and promote the betterment of people of African ancestry. This was necessary to reduce further damage from Western psychology, as was prolific at the time. This led them to use theories, practices and intuition they knew worked in their communities which kept the spirit, body and mind alive and well. They also travelled and researched both on the continent of African and in the diaspora, and documented many practices (Cokley & Garba 2018; Grills *et al*, 2018). A full explanation of Black Psychology/African Psychology is beyond the scope of this chapter but can be summarised as using the best of African thinking, culture and practices in constant exchange with the contemporary world for improvement in spiritual, emotional, mental and physical functioning (Karenga, 2010). As thinking evolved and the paradigm developed, the term 'Black Psychology' evolved to 'African Centred Psychology' and on to 'African Psychology' with many terms in between. This shift is important and emphasises a culture of reference, rather than a colour (Black). Indeed, the future trajectory is to fully embrace the term 'Sakhu Djaer' (Skh Djr), as a further refinement and a deeper extension of African Psychology's African essence (Nobles *et al*, 2016). This further shift steps away from the Greek (European) derived word of 'psychology'; to use indigenous language, knowledge and healing practices which proudly orientate us to Africa. Indeed, Nobles *et al* (2016) argues the ancient Egyptian derived term 'Sakhu Djaer' better explains the alchemy of what happens in the healing encounter which is to provide the means to illuminate the human spirit of wellness. This is because, in practice, interventions raise the spirit of the person, so the person is motivated, accessible, purposeful and is ready to accept messages and ideas for wellness from a range of cultural and psychological perspectives.

Spirit is important and critical in African Psychology. It is the essence of the person, fundamental, as we are 'spirit beings' having a human existence, and therefore our spiritness[9] is fundamental and always present despite appearing invisible to the naked eye (Nobles, 2006). Simply put, it is all that you are and what gets you through difficult moments. Of note, spiritness or spirituality can differ from religiosity, as religiosity is often a prescribed form of being spiritual often adopted by a community (Jackson-Lowman, 2014). Spirit is important, as enslavement had

---

9   Nobles (2006) (a champion of naming phenomenon for ourselves to advance a cause), proposes the use of the term 'spiritness' rather spirituality, as the latter indicates a derivative of, rather than existence in, its own right. Spiritness emphasises we are 'spirit beings' having a physical existence.

the fundamental task of keeping the body strong (for strenuous work on cotton, sugarcane and other plantations) but the mind and spirit weak and docile in order to respond well to instruction. Thus, the importance of the spirit was well known. To date, I propose we have not sufficiently recovered.

The task for us is to reclaim the spiritness of global ancestors who resisted and fought against enslavement, colonisation and its effects. These are ancestors such as Queen Nzinga of present-day Angola who resisted Portuguese colonisers for over 40 years; Ethiopians whose country was occupied but never colonised; Frederick Douglass who not only survived US enslavement but fought for the freedom of others; my maternal ancestor, Paul Bogle, who protested for better living conditions in Jamaica; and Harriett Tubman who went back and freed others from US enslavement. This is our call to action, to Revisit, Re-educate, Reclaim and Resurrect the 'Spirit of Wellness' so that emotional wellness forms a defence shield against acts of micro or macro aggression. The best way to fight the disease of an alien and oppressive culture is to embrace your own (Ani, 1997). African Psychology is suggested as a prescription amongst others.

Tenets of African Psychology

Key features in African Psychology include di-unital thinking (where two opposing ideas can exist at the same time), spiritual rather than materialistic orientation, and using the best of African culture prior to enslavement and colonisation which kept health to the point a valuable human cargo existed to be exploited (Karenga, 2010; Myers, 1993). African Psychology is a dynamic manifestation of unifying African principles, values and traditions. Furthermore, a system of thought and action which examines processes that allow for the illumination and liberation of the Spirit. It recognises:

1. Spirit permeates everything

2. Everything in the universe is interconnected

3. The collective (group connection) is the most salient element of existence

4. communal (in addition to individual) self-knowledge is the key to mental health (Nobles, 2006).

This is why the race-based transatlantic chattel slave trade was so damaging to inter-generational mental health, as at a spirit level it disconnected and severed ties between individuals, families and tribes. Alongside elements of African indigenous culture as the root of African Psychology, the branches of African Psychology look at experiences from the perspective of people of high skin pigmentation. Accordingly, for those rich in eumelanin (Afrika, 2009), the prescription of African Psychology needs to address disproportionately negative (or less favourable) outcomes and treatment in settings such as health, housing, education, the workplace and the criminal justice system (The Health Foundation, 2020). Such regular challenges can be major contributors to de-spirited functioning and health problems, thus, interventions need to be aware of influences upon individual's presentation and inclusive of healing cultural practices (Parham & Parham, 2002).

One outcome and model of healthy African-centred mental health is the ability to demonstrate the 5 dimensions of African character (Karenga, 2012; Parham *et al*, 1999, pg 97) which are:

1. Divinity (e.g. 'I have a relationship with God, the Universe or Creator', 'I have in me the positive qualities of God, the Universe or Creator')
2. Teachability (e.g. 'I can learn')
3. Perfectibility (e.g. 'I can become better')
4. Free Will (e.g. 'I can make choices and choose options which aid transcending limitations of my environments')
5. Moral Character (e.g. 'I treat myself and others in a good and responsible way').

An African-centred method to gain such spiritness and mental health can be by practicing or aspiring to the 7 Principles of Ma'at, derived from ancient Kemetic (Egyptian) text (Parham *et al*, 1999, pg 97) such as:

1. Truth (e.g. to become honest with yourself and others)
2. Justice (e.g. to act with fairness and justice)
3. Righteousness (e.g. doing the right thing and to live with optimal rather than sub-optimal values)
4. Harmony (e.g. functioning consistent with your internal environment, such as listening to what your body is telling you)
5. Order (e.g. developing a logical sequence which helps achieve a purpose or following an ethical order rather than adapting to unhelpful and impoverished environments)
6. Balance (e.g. balancing your day or week to include both productive and rest activities)
7. Reciprocity (e.g. doing for others as well as yourself).

African concepts of Self

There are many dimensions to African concepts of Self which go beyond the scope of this chapter (Grills & Ajei 2002; Obasi, 2002; Nobles, 2006; Somé 1998). Overarching themes are similar, regardless of the region in Africa. According to the African Concept of Self by Akbar (1998):

> *"The tribal self is the level of consciousness that is shared by everyone who is part of a particular 'tribal' experience. The 'tribe' identifies the collective historical and shared experiences that have shaped us in the particular form that we are."*

An example of a tribal experience is the legacy of enslavement and colonisation and how those whose ancestors endured so much are presently treated today. However, if enslavement and colonisation merely interrupted the trajectory of people of African ancestry, rather than defines it, what are these concepts of self? The Akan Model (Grills & Ajei, 2002; Nobles, 2006) is an African Concept of Self (what comprises the person) which includes Ancestors (Nananom), Community (Oman), Father (Ntoro), Personality/Character Spirit (Sunsum), Mother (Mogya), Siblings (Nuanom), Spirits (Abosom), Destiny (Nkrabea), and a Shadow (opposite which remains in the spirit world). From this concept of self, it is reasoned that events which negatively impact your destiny, adversely affect your community, interrupt the continuation of your maternal or paternal lineage, and affect your role for others. Thus it damages your spirit (essence) resulting in mental health problems. Why is it necessary to know an African model of self? Self-knowledge of a multi-dimensional self is fundamental as it leads to self-understanding which leads to self-mastery. Furthermore, this awareness of 'self' means the person acts to the benefit of themselves and furthers his or her wellbeing rather than to purely 'dance to the tune of others' (Akbar, 2017; 2003).

To summarise, African psychology believes wellness resides within the person and the conditions need to be created for that wellness to be excavated, unearthed and exposed (Nobles *et al*, 2016). To illuminate the "spirit of wellness" which already lies within, several conditions are necessary to assist this process. According to Hilliard (1999), people of African ancestry should participate in SBA. SBA is an ancient Egyptian[10] prescription which first appears in Kemetic texts during the Old Kingdom and again in the 11th Dynasty of the Middle Kingdom (Hilliard, 1999). This is an example of what is known as a West African concept of Sankofa (returning to the past to reclaim one's essence in order to go forward) which

---

10 Research suggests that early and later ancient Egyptians dynasties were Black (high in skin pigmentation) as demonstrated by analysis of eumelanin content of mummies (highly preserved remains), complexion in reliefs in tombs, and knowledge of the trajectory of their ancestors from deeper into Africa, from areas such as those now known as Ethiopia and Sudan (Diop, 1974; Walker, 2013).

includes reaching as far back as ancient Egypt and further. SBA is 'teaching, learning, wisdom and study or collectively deep thought' (Hilliard, 1999). To access this process, McInnis (2020a; 2020b) developed tools such as 'Know Thy Self – Adinkra Cards'[11] to increase accessibility to traditional symbolic African wisdom. In addition to access, it illuminates concepts relevant to traditional communities of African ancestry. This can be used in therapy as an engagement tool, in meditation to suggest a focus for the mind, and group work to build rapport. In short, deep thought (SBA) can mean rejecting what one is told preferring to analyse for oneself, which leads to adopting what assists one's cause, purpose and mission.

Spiritual vaccine (reaching the vibe in life and clinical work)

How do we create a spiritual vaccine? In short, the energetic spirited vibration of wellness needs to be created and maintained to inoculate against further attack. The energy associated with unresolved emotions such as hurt, betrayal, sadness and anger can become trapped in the body and cause mental (thinking), physical (disease), and spiritual (e.g. lack of purpose) pain. This needs to be processed through activities (rituals) involving spontaneity which attract the spirit (of ancestors and the essence of the person). These acts transmute the energy of pain to wellness, processing for release from the body. To elaborate, people of African ancestry traditionally maintained wellness and processed such pain through various acts which are listed in Box 3.1.

Box 3.1: Activities to promote wellbeing

- Increasing self-knowledge
- Singing
- Dancing
- Writing (including in contemporary times writing lyrics to music)
- Creating
- Connecting with like minded others
- Engaging with nature
- Listening to music
- Movement
- Chanting
- Drama

11 www.nubiawellnessandhealing.co.uk

- Connecting with ancestors
- Connecting with elders
- Creating and playing music
- Laughing
- Meditating
- Connecting with Jegnas (mentors)

(Ani 1997; Somé 1998).

These activities can all raise the energetic vibration of the person to a level where healing can be accessed. Think of how one feels after one listens to a piece of music which moves the soul (Harrell, 2018). One needs to incorporate these into daily life. The outcome is the opportunity for improved health in various domains such as spirit illumination (pursuing a purpose), enhanced emotions (feeling good), improved cognitive skills (enhanced thinking from reaching a vibration of creativity) and better physical status (optimising physical strength and resistance to infections) through life health-promoting behaviours. When the spirit is strong, all else follows.

Application of Black Psychology

Case studies

In clinical work as a clinical psychologist with a client who had a significant history of trauma, at the start of a talking therapy session the client often felt she could not describe her feelings. We introduced a brief meditation (which can shift the rhythmic vibration of the spirit (Anpu, 2017)) which she reported helped calm her to the extent she could access her thoughts. Later, we introduced a meditation near the end of the session as she reported feeling emotionally aroused from disclosing traumatic events and needed to calm herself before leaving the therapy room. She found meditations which focused on nature and breathing most useful.

Another client struggled with the death of several relatives in her family. She was offered and agreed to engage in a libation[12] (which she knew of) during which we poured water into a bowl and she recalled the gifts in terms of lessons learnt and goodness associated with the people who died. This contributed to changing the conversation from one of loss, to one of thanks and remembrance of benefits. This led to conversation in which happy memories and their ability to guide from the

---

12 Libation can be feeding (invoking) Ancestral energy (spirit) in the form of those who have transitioned.

spiritual realm was shared. In sessions, to explain phenomena difficult to explain with the constraints of the English language, we often conversed in Ebonics[13] (Nobles, 1996) and patois (a language widely spoken in Jamaica where our families both paused on the trip out of Africa). Laughter was often heard from our therapy room even when discussing the most distressing of experiences. Indeed, from my personal experience of Jamaican culture, laughter can be a medicine and way of coping with distressing times. To 'see the funny side of it' eases the pain and can lead to 'looking on the bright side' and for gains and benefits.

This case illustrates the importance of bringing the gifts gained from ancestors into the therapy room. Many cultural practices such as 'nine nights' have a similar function, where for several nights before burial or cremation of a dead body, the 'village' (sometimes in a contemporary setting) gathers to tell stories, sing, dance, play music, drink and be merry, thinking about the departed and receiving the vibration of the others in the community who join with them. The restrictions on numbers attending funeral services and social gatherings during the COVID-19 pandemic meant a generation did not know or experience this cultural practice for some time. For cultural practices to be passed on, they need to be regularly practised alongside documentation for the next generation.

In therapy sessions with another client, we used 'Know Thy Self – Adinkra Cards', which gave a hook for him to bring into the session his feelings about Spiritness/ Spirituality, God and 'Mother Nature'. This led to discussions about how he felt when he succumbed to family pressure to attend church with family. He felt:

1. His 'personal business' was shared with an entire church, possibly by well-meaning relatives.
2. Offence at being prayed for as he felt this created a single narrative around him as a misfortunate person in need.
3. Uncomfortable about certain church rituals he was expected to take part in for 'his own good'.
4. Angst, as some family members did not know his leaning towards African Spirituality and how he saw things differently from them.

A user-friendly informal tool such as 'Know Thy Self – Adinkra Cards' created the healing space for this person to think and express the stress he was feeling. Without this African-centred technique, he may not have brought into such a formal setting beliefs core to him. From my experience as a therapist, I find many individuals of

---

13 Ebonics is technically a Black vernacular language in its own right, rather than as a deficit of standard English (Nobles, 1996).

African ancestry are taught not to speak of family issues to others outside their immediate family or select others. This is often due to fear their presentation of deep-seated spiritual experiences will be misunderstood or abused, and in some cases lead to the application of inappropriate anti-psychotic medication or detention under the Mental Health Act (Department of Health, 2008). I felt the client was able to 'test the waters' with how I responded to his general conversation about cards. These cards had wisdom important to the lives of people of African ancestry which revealed information as he felt moved. The task of an African-centered psychologist (Sakhu Djaer) is to create such opportunities for healing spaces in their interventions. For the client, the task is to create healing encounters in their homes and life using such personal tools or means to raise vibrations.

Conclusions

This chapter was written during the second lockdown of the COVID-19 pandemic in the UK, which undoubtedly influenced terminology. This chapter proposed the prescription and vaccine of Black/African Psychology to recognise the spiritness of people of African ancestry. The use of techniques which activate the human spirit and illuminate the soul generates both mental health and mental wealth (cognitive, emotional, and spiritual deposits in the bank for later withdrawal). This is not new for those versed in these approaches but can be for the next generation. Therefore, we need to write it, live it, and teach it. Living through at least twin pandemics[14] (COVID-19 and the global system of White supremacy) negatively impacted the mental health and spirit of many while uncovering opportunities. Mental and spirit health are intertwined, with spiritness (such as a sense of purpose or relationship with a divine being) often a precursor for good mental health. It is of note that embracing the earlier African Psychology (derived from Ancient North African texts) does not exclude the later Eurocentric psychology (derived from the ancient Greek and Roman texts) it influenced (James, 1957/2013). Rather, it provides a challenge and correction by providing a deeper and richer context to understand and help those of African heritage. This chapter merely provides an introduction to a much deeper area of Spiritness in African Psychology and is intended as a primer.

In concluding this chapter, we are reminded that one function of the global system of White supremacy (which is so far-reaching, even European characteristics are often preferred in Africa and the Caribbean) is to take away our joy. Furthermore, it is to empower themselves as oppressors, by creating fear in us. This chapter aimed to bring a prescription of connecting with: like-minded others, joy, movement, and

---

14 It is acknowledged that for people of African ancestry, the global system of White supremacy exists alongside systems which prefer individuals of a certain gender, sexuality and orientation, class, ability and more (McInnis, 2020a).

self-development. This can be in various contexts such as life in general through the inclusion of wellness enhancing strategies, in clinical therapy settings and supervision. Spiritness (closely related to spirituality) is proposed to seek and maintain optimal functioning. If we orientate ourselves to heal and find what there is to laugh about and put our energy into new skills, self-improvement and improving others; the global system of white supremacy will stall, as it will have no feedback to draw strength from. We render it little power to make us act. In short, we de-spirit the power of the oppressor when we transmute their oppressive spirit to become the best version of ourselves. This does not mean we never protest. With a di-unital spirit, we do both. Ashe Ashe Ashe (So Be It in Yoruba)

Dedication

For my late mother, Minnette Elsada McInnis nee Ramus, who visioned great things for me and provided in every way without fail. Thank you. For my late father Jeremiah Eric McInnis, who was with me throughout, with proverbs of wisdom and your company. Zola-up (the Bantu word for love).

Acknowledgements

I wish to sincerely thank Dr Lawford Goddard and Baba Dr. Wade Ifágbemì Sàngódáre Nobles for significant assistance with re-drafting, and Dr Edwin Nichols for inspiration and comments on drafts.

References

Adams B (2020) Understanding racial battle fatigue. https://attheu.utah.edu/facultystaff/understanding-racial-battle-fatigue/ (accessed July 2021).

Afrika L (2009) Melanin. What makes black people black! Seaburn: NY

Akbar N (1998) Know Thy Self. Mind productions: Tallahassee, FL

Akbar N (2003) Akbar papers in African psychology. Mind productions: Tallahassee, FL.

Akbar N (2017) New Visions for Black Men. Mind productions: Tallahassee, FL

Ani M (1994), Yurugu: An Afrikan-centered Critique of European Cultural Thought and Behavior., Africa World Press, Trenton.

Ani M (1997) Let the circle be unbroken. Implications of African spirituality in the diaspora. Nkonimfo Publications: USA

Andrews K (2017) The west's wealth is based on slavery. Reparations should be paid. Guardian Newspaper https://www.theguardian.com/commentisfree/2017/aug/28/slavery-reparations-west-wealth-equality-world-race (accessed July 2021).

Anpu UR (2017) Meditations for African Americans. Igniting the inner light. Gye Nyame: USA

Archibong U & Darr A (2010) The Involvement of Black and Minority Ethnic Staff in NHS Disciplinary Proceedings. A report of research carried out by the Centre for Inclusion and Diversity, University of Bradford on behalf of NHS Employers and NHS Institute for Innovation and Improvement.

Armah AK (1978) The healers. An historical novel. Heinemann: Oxford

Baruti MKB (2015) Clarity. Remembrance, Reality & Vision. CreateSpace Independent Publishing Platform: USA

Browder AT (1992) Nile Valley Contributions to Civilization: Exploding the Myths: vol 1. Institute of Karmic Guidance: Maryland

BBC world news (2020) George Floyd: What happened in the final moments of his life. https://www.bbc.co.uk/news/world-us-canada-52861726 (accessed July 2021).

BBC News (2020). George Floyd death: The mental health impact. https://www.bbc.co.uk/news/av/uk-england-london-53009872 (accessed online 17 December 2020).

BPS (British Psychological Society) (2020) GUIDANCE The impact of Covid-19 on the wellbeing of psychologists. www.bps.org.uk/sites/www.bps.org.uk/files/Policy/Policy%20-%20Files/Impact%20of%20Covid-19%20on%20the%20Wellbeing%20of%20Psychologists.pdf (accessed July 2021).

Cambridge University Dictionary (2021) Cambridge University English Dictionary. Cambridge University Press: Cambridge, UK.

Cokley K & Garba R (2018) Speaking truth to power: how Black/ African psychology changed the discipline of psychology. *The Journal of Black Psychology* **44**(8) 695-721.

Day E (2015). #BlackLivesMatter: the birth of a new civil rights movement. Guardian Newspaper https://www.theguardian.com/world/2015/jul/19/blacklivesmatter-birth-civil-rights-movement (accessed July 2021).

Department of Health (2008) Code of Practice: Mental Health Act 1983. London: The Stationery Office.

Diop CA (1974) The African Origin of Civilization. Chicago, Illinois: Lawrence Hill Books.

Eddo-Lodge R (2017) Why I'm No Longer Talking to White People about Race. London: Bloomsbury Publishing.

Evans E (2020) Mourning in America: What grief can teach us about the protests of George Floyd's death. *Deseret News*. Jun 7, 2020. Available at: https://www.deseret.com/indepth/2020/6/7/21279520/george-floyd-funeral-al-sharpton-protests-riots-looting-mourning-grief-process (accessed July 2021).

Feagin JR (2014) Racist America: Roots, current realities, and future reparations. Routledge.

Fleming I & Steen L (2013) Supervision and clinical psychology: Theory, practice and perspectives, 2nd edition. Supervision and Clinical Psychology: Theory, Practice and Perspectives, 2nd Edition.

Fuller Jr, N (1972/ 2016) The United Independent Compensatory Code/System/Concept: A Compensatory Counter-Racist Code. Revised/ Expanded Edition. Neeley Fuller Jr: USA.

Gentleman A (2019) The Windrush Betrayal: Exposing the Hostile Environment. Guardian Faber: London

Grills C (2002) African-centered psychology. Basic principles. In: TA (Ed) Parham Counselling Persons of African Descent: Raising the Bar of Practitioner Competence. Sage Publishing Inc.

Grills C & Ajei M (2002) African-centered Conceptualizations of Self and Consciousness: The Akan Model. In: TA (Ed) Parham Counselling Persons of African Descent: Raising the Bar of Practitioner Competence. Sage Publishing Inc.

Grills CN, Aird EG & Rowe D (2016) Breathe, Baby, Breathe: Clearing the Way for the Emotional Emancipation of Black People. *Cultural Studies ↔ Critical Methodologies* **16** (3) 333–343.

Grills C, Nobles WW & Hill C (2018) African, Black, Neither or Both? Models and strategies developed and implemented by The Association of Black Psychologists. *The Journal of Black Psychology* **44** (8) 791-826.

Harrell SP (2018) Soulfulness as an Orientation to Contemplative Practice: Culture, Liberation, and Mindful Awareness. *The Journal of Contemplative Inquiry* **5** (1)

Harrell SP (2014) Compassionate confrontation and empathetic exploration: the integration of race-related narratives in clinical supervision. In: CA Falender, EP Shafranske & CJ Falicov (Eds) Multiculturalism and diversity in clinical supervision: a competency-based approach. American Psychological Association: USA.

Harrell SP (2000) A multidimensional conceptualization of racism-related stress: implications for the wellbeing of people of color. *American journal of Orthopsychiatry* **70** (1) 42-57.

Hawkins P & Shohet R (2012) Supervision in the Helping Professions, 4th edition. Maidenhead: Open University Press.

Hilliard AG (1995) The Maroon Within Us. Selected Essays on African American Community Socialization. Black Classic Press: Baltimore USA.

Jackson-Lowman H (Ed.) (2014) Afrikan American Women: Living at the Crossroads of Race, Gender, Class, and Culture. San Diego, CA: Cognella Academic Publishing

James GGM (1954/2013) Stolen Legacy. Start Publishing LLC: USA

Jaspal R & Lopes B (in press) Discrimination and mental health outcomes in British Black and South Asian people during the COVID-19 outbreak in the UK. Mental Health, Religion and Culture.

Johnson D (2020) *The George Floyd uprising has brought us hope. Now we must turn protest to policy* [online]. Available at: www.theguardian.com/commentisfree/2020/jun/30/black-lives-matter-protests-voting-policy-change (accessed July 2021).

Jones B & Nichols E (2013) Cultural Competence in America's Schools: Leadership, Engagement and Understanding. Information Age Publishing: Charlotte, NC.

Kambon KKK & Bowen-Reid TL (2010) Theories of African American Personality: Classification, Basic Constructs and Empirical Predictions/assessment. *The Journal of Pan-African Studies* **3** 83.

Kambon KKK (1998) African/Black Psychology in the American context: An African-Centered Approach. Nubian Nation Publications: Tallahassee, FL.

Karenga M (2010) Introduction to Black Studies. 4th ed. University of Sankore Press: Los Angeles

Karenga M (2012) Maat, The Moral Ideal in Ancient Egypt. A study in classical African ethics. Routledge: New York.

Kübler-Ross E & Kessler D (2005) On grief and grieving: finding the meaning of grief through the five stages of loss. New York, Scribner.

Obasi E M (2002) Reconceptualizing the notion of self from the African deep structure. In: TA (Ed) Parham Counselling Persons of African Descent: Raising the Bar of Practitioner Competence. Sage Publishing Inc

Obholzer A & Roberts VV (Eds) (2009). The unconscious at work: Individual and Organizational Stress in the Human Services. Routledge: UK.

McInnis EM (2020a) An African Psychology Perspective on White Supremacy within UK Clinical Psychology. *The Journal of Critical Psychology, Counselling and Psychotherapy* **20** (3) pp. 5-15.

McInnis EM (2020b) 'I am not your minority - Know Thy African Self'. In: Y. Ade-Serrano and O. Nkansa-Dwamena (Eds), Applied Psychology and Allied Professions Working with Ethnic Minorities. British Psychological Society: Leicester.

McIntosh P (2003) White privilege: Unpacking the invisible knapsack. In: S. Plous (Ed.), Understanding prejudice and discrimination (pp. 191-196). New York: McGraw-Hill.

Matthews J (2020) UK citizenship: Families plunged into to debt just for wanting to be British. A new report says the cost should be cut, ceremonies held in "iconic" venues and children born in the UK made citizens by right [online]. Available at: https://news.sky.com/story/uk-citizenship-families-plunged-into-to-debt-just-for-wanting-to-be-british-12156590?fbclid=IwAR1PPQ0mznpT0zUhkxjyCCQtKB5X_H1ePhSRpfcD3pokehnQjCcgWsxNaK4 (accessed July 2021).

Myers LJ (1993) Understanding an Afrocentric world view: introduction to an optimal psychology, Kendall Hunt, Iowa.

Myers LJ, Anderson M, Lodge T, Speight S & Queener JE (2018) Optimal theory's contributions to understanding and surmounting global challenges to humanity. *The Journal of Black Psychology* **44** (8) 747-771.

Nobles VL (1996) Ebonics: The Retention of African Tongues. In: Shujaa MJ & KJ Shujaa (eds.) *Encyclopedia of African Cultural Heritage in North America*. Thousand Oaks, CA: Sage.

Nobles W, Baloyi L & Sodi T (2016) Pan African Humanness and Sakhu Djaer as Praxis for Indigenous Knowledge Systems. *Alternation Journal* (18) 36-59.

Nobles W (2006) Seeking the Sakhu: Foundational Writings for an African Psychology. Third World Press, Chicago.

Nobles W (2015) Cultural resistance to psychic terrorism. In: M Shujaa & K Shujaa (Eds.) The SAGE encyclopaedia of African cultural heritage in North America (pp. 322-324). SAGE Publications, Inc.

Nubia O (2017) The power of names. Centre of Pan African Thought [online]. Available at: www.panafricanthought.com/video/the-power-of-names/ (accessed July 2021).

Oxford English Dictionary (2021) Oxford English Dictionary. Oxford University Press: Oxford.

Parham TA, Ajamu A & White JL (2016) The psychology of Blacks: centering our perspectives in the African consciousness (4th Edition). Routledge: New York.

Pérez y Mena, Andrés I (February 2000) Understanding Religiosity in Cuba. *Journal of Hispanic / Latino Theology* **7** (3) 6–34.

Pieterse AL (2018) Attending to racial trauma in clinical supervision: enhancing client and supervisee outcomes. *The clinical supervisor* **37** (1) 204-220.

SAMHSA (2014) Substance Abuse and Mental Health Services Administration (SAMHSA)'s Concept of Trauma and Guidance for a Trauma-Informed Approach. HHS Publication: Rockville, MD.

Scaife J (Ed.) (2001) Supervision in the mental health professions: A practitioner's guide. Brunner-Routledge.

Somé MP (1998) The healing wisdom of Africa: Finding life purpose through nature, ritual, and community. New York: Jeremy P. Tarcher/Putnam.

The Health Foundation (2020) Emerging findings on the impact of COVID-19 on black and minority ethnic people [online]. Available at: www.health.org.uk/news-and-comment/charts-and-infographics/emerging-findings-on-the-impact-of-covid-19-on-black-and-min (accessed July 2021).

Van Vandiver BJ, Cross WE, Worrell FC & Fhagen-Smith PE (2002) Validating the Cross Racial Identity Scale. *Journal of Counseling Psychology* **49** 71-85. 10.1037/0022-0167.49.1.71.

Walker R (2013) When we ruled 2nd Ed. Reklaw Education Ltd: London

WHO (World Health Organisation) (2021) Coronavirus [online]. Available at: www.who.int/health-topics/coronavirus#tab=tab_1 (accessed July 2021).

Willis WB (1998) Adinkra Dictionary: A Visual Primer on the Language of Adinkra. Pyramid Complex: USA.

Woodson CG (1933/2012) The Mis-Education of the Negro. EWorld Inc: New York.

Chapter 4:
Finding meaning and purpose in a Covid world

By Ben Bano

As I wrote this chapter, the second wave of the Covid-19 pandemic was raging around us. A third, indefinite lockdown had begun. Deaths from Covid-19 were exceeding 1,000 per day. Nearly 100,000 families had been left bereaved. Our world has probably been changed forever. Many of us have experienced unexpected bereavements, the loss of employment, income, and much of what sustains our mental health in everyday life. In addition to losing loved ones, there is the impact of the loss of contact with our family and friends – indeed, it seems that Covid can only be kept at bay through diminishing the social relationships which matter most to us. The virus strikes harshly at those who are already disadvantaged in our society. When this book is published, let us hope that the virus is well under control, although the longer-term effects are likely to be with us in coming years.

In the face of these and the many other challenges that face our world today, how might we help ourselves, and others, to find a sense of meaning and purpose in what is nothing less than an existential crisis both for individuals and our wider society? How might we address the question that many of us, and those who are close to us, might ask from time to time – 'What does my life mean to me?' 'Is life still worth living?' These are just some of the questions to which we need answers in order to sustain our mental health and wellbeing and that of the people we seek to help, as well as addressing these key existential issues.

In this chapter we will look at the contribution of spirituality in its broadest sense to answer these questions, which relate not just to the Covid-19 crisis but to many other challenging situations in our daily lives. We will explore what lessons we might learn from our responses to the traumas of earlier years, for example in the wake of the second world war. We will discuss the implications for those of us who act in the role of the 'wounded healer', and how we might understand the spiritual and existential concerns of those we accompany in this difficult journey.

We continue by reflecting on how we might help people to move forward and face an uncertain future with a degree of confidence and resilience. We will explore how our discernment of spiritual issues needs to be based on an approach grounded in compassion and love. We then conclude by highlighting some positive examples of how people have been able to find meaning and purpose at a challenging time.

The contribution of spirituality: 'something deep inside me'

Our late and esteemed friend Peter Gilbert, who died tragically in 2013, was at the forefront of reminding us about the need to find and understand that which is 'deep inside us'. In a Covid-dominated world, such a discovery might sustain and fortify us. In addition to official advice, Government guidelines and other sources of advice often omit the fortifying influence of spirituality on our mental health and wellbeing at a challenging time.

Here are some examples of how spirituality might be interpreted. Which of these speak to you? Do you have another perspective, from your own life experience?

- Spirituality can refer to the essence of human beings as unique individuals – what makes me, me, and you, you.
- The drive power, energy and/resourcefulness in a person.
- What is deepest within us – what gives us direction, motivation and enables us to survive difficult times.
- Spirituality is about what we do with the fire inside us and how we channel desire.
- Spirituality is a human quest for meaning, purpose, identity, self-transcending knowledge, meaningful relationships and a sense of the holy; it asks profound questions around suffering and what happens after death.
- It may or may not be associated with organised religion, or a personal belief in a transcendent deity.
- Spirituality offers a worldview that suggests there is more to life than what people experience on a sensory and physical level.
- While spirituality addresses issues of suffering and death, it is also a force for the restoration of hope and optimism.
- A sense of the spiritual in ourselves acts as a protective factor for our mental health and wellbeing.

Peter Gilbert (2006) described spirituality as 'something deep inside me', relating to the 'eternal questions':

■ Where do we come from?

■ Who do you think you are?

■ What are we doing here?

■ What meaning is there in mental and physical distress?

■ Is there such a thing as a 'good death'?

■ Is death a closed door or a gateway to another life?

Equally, he felt it important to describe the importance of the **soul**. He reminded us of the maxim of the Greek philosopher Plato: 'You will not cure the body without the mind, nor the mind without the soul, because the part cannot be well unless the whole be well'. This is helpful support for those who believe in a holistic approach to understanding mental health. Cook & Powell (2006) describe this approach: 'As we meet on the path of life there is one medicine constantly at our disposal that even comes free – this is the power to choose…'

We could suggest that the soul represents our inner beliefs and value base, while the spirit represents this value base in action in our everyday lives. The soul is a common concept across many faith groups. As Bano (2014) comments, Peter Gilbert reminded us that, for example, in Jewish thought the soul is God-given but passive, while the spirit is an active force. If the soul provides us with our value base, the spirit puts this into action. Spirituality needs to be understood in the context of the 'whole person', taking its place alongside the cognitive, physical and emotional aspects of our lives. And, following Plato's maxim, it forms a vital part of our identity and our personhood. My own experience of providing pastoral support to people with advancing dementia has convinced me that a focus on the spiritual unlocks memories and insights for someone whose cognitive functioning is gradually fading.

A sense of meaning and purpose – the contribution of Victor Frankl

Victor Frankl, a psychiatrist who himself experienced the horrors of life in Auschwitz, worked with patients who had been prisoners in concentration camps. In providing our therapeutic support, can we learn anything from psychological insights gained from Frankl's work during and after the second world war?

World War II gave psychological scars to the millions of people affected, not just caused by the traumatic experiences of wartime, but equally by the horrors of the Holocaust. It was also in this context that Victor Frankl developed the theory and practice of logotherapy. In the midst of despair and hopelessness, he had noticed that those victims who had been able to find a sense of meaning and purpose, even in the most horrific conditions, were most likely to emerge from their experience as survivors. To use Nietzche's phrase, 'He who has a Why to live for can bear almost any How'. Frankl observed that the prisoners who had given up hope for the future and given up on life were often the first to die. They lost their lives in the absence of something to live for. He realised how, even in the dire environment of a concentration camp, there could still be a purpose to life.

Frankl's development of logotherapy was best described in his book *Man's Search for Meaning*, published directly after the war and in many editions later. He had an innate optimism about human nature – in the darkness of war and the Holocaust, he believed that humans are still capable of doing good and of behaving ethically. Equally, he believed in freedom of will at a time when a deterministic view of human nature influenced by Nazi ideology had led the famous philosopher Heidegger to join the National Socialists in 1933.

He wrote: 'For one to survive even the worst conditions is the knowledge that there is a meaning to one's life'. When we cannot change the situation in which we find ourselves, however challenging this may be, we can at least change ourselves.

Dealing with adversity – the approach of Frankl

His advice appears challenging, to say the least: 'Homo patiens ranks before homo sapiens. Another imperative is contrasted with sapere aude and that is: patti aude, have the yearning to suffer! This courage, the courage to suffer: it all depends upon it. Pain needs to be accepted, saying yes to the destiny, take a stance towards it. This is the only way to approach and reach the truth, not through escape.'

Frankl was not afraid to use the term 'suffering' to describe a reality similar to that which many people in the pandemic will have experienced. This implies a degree of self awareness, not always obvious when confronted with the challenges of getting through the day.

Finding a sense of purpose: *Maria lost her husband unexpectedly during the peak of the Covid pandemic. At first, she was feeling lost, bewildered and confused* *and she felt aimless as she tried to fill her days as best she could. She did not feel that she needed bereavement counselling but later she felt she was drifting in her life, unable to find any way forward within her feelings of grief and loss. Her experience of seeking and receiving help enabled her to realise that life is worth living after all. Her counsellor suggested that she put together a number of photos and memorabilia to remind her of her husband.*

Maria's experience shows that, in spite of her suffering through the loss of her husband, she was still able to find a sense of purpose with the right help.

Helping someone to find meaning and purpose – the journey of hope

How might we set about the task of helping someone to find a sense of meaning and purpose? We may be in a professional or pastoral position, and at the time of writing our ability to be physically present with the person concerned may be limited or even non existent, so calling for a new and unfamiliar way of working. We need also to beware of the risk of 'medicalising' the experience of our clients, or diagnosing depression, when someone is experiencing distressing but normal feelings.

Perhaps the first task is to understand to what extent those we work with are in touch with, or might have considered these 'deeper' questions. While there is still much to do to ensure that spirituality has a place in the assessment and intervention process, we must not make assumptions about the readiness of someone to discuss these difficult issues, not least with colleagues who are perhaps sceptical, or feel that these conversations cross professional boundaries.

Are you a member of a multi-disciplinary team working in mental health services? Do you feel confident in raising the issue of spirituality in ward rounds or review meetings? If not, you may want to raise the issue informally with colleagues, or organise a discussion on the topic.

Perhaps the first step is to place ourselves in the position of the person we are helping.

Emmanuel Levinas, another philosopher who followed in the footsteps of Frankl, focused on the need to rethink the nature of suffering so that it could become a springboard in the process for change and growth. He saw the quality of the therapeutic relationship of the worker as key to this process of development.

For example, for a social worker and their client there is an opportunity for the development of a profound therapeutic relationship, in which the worker shows their empathy and understanding by entering into the suffering of the client. The term 'suffering' is not comfortable, but to move forward we sometimes can't shy away from understanding these difficult emotions.

Working with meaning and purpose – a process of discernment

Our first task in developing this relationship is to understand what the person might be going through, in as sensitive a way as possible. At the time of writing, this is a particularly challenging process due to social distancing rules. Peter Gilbert used the phrase 'sitting beside you'. If this is not possible physically, then we can do it in a metaphorical sense. Some of the following questions may form part of an extended interview. Allow enough time to engage in authentic listening – it may also be that several sessions may be needed to work with what are often sensitive and sometimes complex issues.

An assessment framework – some questions you might find helpful to raise:

■ Are there any things which might give you meaning and purpose in your life? What might they be? What are the important images which might reflect them?

■ Do you have any favourite photos or pictures which mean a lot to you? Can you tell me about them?

■ Are there aspects of your current situation which come into conflict with this meaning?

■ Do you have any sources of strength and hope?

■ How have you coped with crises in the past?

■ Do you have a sense of being called and of obligation in your life? Tell me about them?

■ Do you have any favourite activities? Do you have any achievements you can share with me?

■ Are you a member of a Faith Community? Is this a help or a hindrance? If yes, in what ways does your belief help you? If not, then what might be the negative aspect of your faith belief? This type of exploration will not always be easy and could result in some difficult and painful memories – so time might be needed to enable these and related issues to be worked through. We need to remember also the potential downside of a focus on spirituality, for example the image of a God who is prepared to let a person commit suicide, as well as blaming a God for misfortunes which have been endured.

'My faith helps to give me a sense of meaning and purpose but as I grew up I was often made to feel unworthy in the eyes of God. It was a thoughtful pastor who helped me to see that in God's eyes none of us are unworthy – we are all precious in the eye of God'. – Member of a faith community

And as we grow older...

Finding meaning and purpose as we grow older becomes increasingly important. There may be situations in the assessment process when verbal questions are inappropriate and when we may have to understand someone's meaning and purpose in other ways, for example through pictures and symbols. This can also help in working with people with a learning disability.

Alice suffers from advancing dementia and has been confined to her bedroom in her care home for more than six months during the Covid pandemic. She finds virtual communication difficult and sometimes confusing.

She has also not been able to see her family. Her key worker has worked with her family to devise a life story book which contains photos of significant events in her life, such as her marriage and past holidays. Through sharing her memories using the life story book her key worker has helped Alice to find again a sense of meaning and purpose in difficult circumstances. Her family has been encouraged to write regular letters to Alice with photos which can stimulate her memory. Her key worker knows the importance of her faith for Alice and ensures that she can experience familiar hymns and prayers. She is encouraged to remember and say her prayers in the way that she has done in the past.

Do you work with people who may not be able to express themselves verbally? In what ways could you help them to find a sense of meaning and purpose?

Carl Jung, who became increasingly preoccupied with the health of the soul, wrote in relation to older age: 'We cannot live in the afternoon of life according to the programme of life's morning – for what was great in life's morning – money making, social existence, family and posterity will be little at evening – whoever carries into the afternoon the law of the morning will pay for it with damage to his soul.' (Jung, 1933)

Moving forward – the contribution of positivity

The ways in which we might move forward are very individual – each of us has our own way of finding sources of strength and hope. The spread of an uncontrollable virus can give rise to a feeling of fear and hopelessness, but positive emotions such as love and gratitude can help to provide a sense of balance in helping us to find meaning and purpose. Our human need for connection can still be maintained even while retaining a physical distance. The search for meaning and purpose can also lead to the discovery of new or previously hidden aspects of ourselves. Here are some examples:

Helping others: *'I have come to realise that in this Covid crisis I need not be a helpless bystander. We all depend on each other to rescue humanity from this crisis – that's why I knew I had to play my part during the Covid crisis and I have become a volunteer with the local foodbank.*

Helping others is perhaps one of the deepest human instincts; its foundations are to be found in all major faith beliefs.

Giving back: *'Mum was admitted to her residential home a year ago. She has been on her own for much of the last few months in her room for most of the day. But she is not passive – she radiates a sense of optimism – one the carers rang to tell me how much it meant to her when Mum said a prayer for her and her colleagues.'*

Reciprocity is important in finding meaning and purpose – giving, even in our darkest times, we may still feel that we have something to give back to others. We all have gifts we can share, but we might need someone to help us to discover these.

Developing a structure and routine to my life: *'During the lockdown I found the isolation of living for long periods on my own very difficult. And then I was helped by my counsellor to try to find some meaning in my situation.*

After I saw a programme on religious life, based on a well-developed routine, I realised that I needed to structure my life into a daily rhythm if I was to survive lockdown. I now make sure that I develop a routine – which includes practising mindfulness and meditation. I have come to realise that silence and tranquillity are important gifts. I have come to realise that these experiences can sometimes compensate for my lack of social contact with others. And I am even exploring whether to take up my old hobby of painting.'

The ancient hermits of the desert had much to teach us – they learnt the value of meditation and contemplation, as a key to maintaining their mental equilibrium. There is much we can learn from the rhythm of monastic life, in which the day is divided into periods of reflection, work, as well as leisure.

Spending time together: *'During lockdown we as a family spent much more time together than we otherwise would have done. And yet up to now we had all been functioning in our own bubbles, doing our own thing. We could not 'escape' the family by seeing friends. One evening we turned off the TV and I reflected with my wife on the meaning and purpose of our family life – and we realised that we needed regular times during day when we could come together as a family – perhaps sitting together for a meal rather than eating and watching the TV.*

All too easily our lives as a family are played out as individuals – sometimes we need to find strength from having regular times together.

Looking after myself: *'During this difficult period I have been the main carer for my mother who had a serious stroke a year ago. I went through a period of mixed emotions feeling resentful as well as feeling guilty that I should feel like this. But I have been helped to see that my caring is not just a chore – it's an act of love and compassion. In giving myself to the care of Mum, I experience a sense of purpose and fulfilment. I have also learnt to practise giving thanks for the things which we have to keep us going both physically and mentally.'*

Many people who are carers feel a sense of both frustration and guilt. The realisation that we need to look after ourselves is important, for example through the practice of self-compassion.

I have learnt to appreciate the natural world: *'During the period of lockdown I could only leave my flat for an hour each day for a walk in our local park. Gradually my walk became more than just exercise – I began to appreciate the beauty of nature through paying attention to the trees and the wildlife around me.'*

As the integrity and health of our planet is increasingly under threat, the ability to appreciate the world around us provides a welcome relief from negative and difficult feelings.

A reflective exercise: have you been able to find and develop a sense of meaning and purpose in difficult times? If so, what have you found most helpful in moving forward?

Conclusion

In this chapter we have looked at how 'something deep inside me' is present in all of us and that the understanding of our behaviour needs an approach which encompasses body mind and soul. At a time of crisis and ongoing stress, the task of helping someone to identify the meaning and purpose in their lives is more important than ever. And it pays dividends in helping someone to move forward with a renewed sense of hope and optimism.

Some key messages:

- In a time of turmoil and upheaval, the discovery of 'something deep inside me' can be provide a vital force in sustaining our wellbeing and mental health.

- At times when we feel we are suffering, if we're not able to change our situation we can at least think about how we can change ourselves.

- For those involved in working with people with existential dilemmas, the task has to be approached with empathy and sensitivity.

- Hope and optimism are key aspects of the journey to develop meaning and purpose in adverse situations.

References

Bano B (2006) *In my end is my beginning* in Bano, B and Hawes, A (eds) *Crossing the River.* Pavilion Publishing and Media (2014)

Cook C and Powell A (2006) *Spirituality and Psychiatry.* Social Perspectives Network.

Frankl V (2006) *Man's Search for Meaning'.* Beacon Press (first published in 1946)

Gilbert P (2010) *Something so deep inside me.* Presentation to the Mental Health Social Care Strategic Network.

Jung CG (1933) *Modern Man in Search of a Soul* Kegan Paul, London.

Mental Health, Spirituality and Wellbeing

Across the Life Cycle

Chapter 5:

Children and young people's mental health and spirituality

By Lucy Grimwade and Rebecca Nye

> When Ryan was seven years old he came home from school to find his mum dead. She had committed suicide. Now eight, he has never spoken about her or her death at school, something all too apparent to his teachers and classmates who sense he is increasingly weighed down carrying this unspeakable pain. One day, as part of their RE lesson on parables, the teacher tells a story to the children. The children sit in a circle to focus on the objects used to tell the story quietly. It is a reflective storytelling style so the story is not overshadowed by the storyteller's persona nor the distraction of audience participation. The story describes the 'kingdom of heaven' as being like when a person searches and searches for a great pearl, and on finding it, he gives up everything for it. As the story ends the teacher invites the children to comment on the character's behaviour. Most say he must have been crazy to give up so much for apparently so little. There's a lot of laughter and ridiculing of this silly man. Then the teacher asks, 'Is there anything you'd give up everything for?' Again most are negative, but Ryan speaks up. 'Yes, my Mum is that pearl. I'd give up everything to have her back.' All seem aware of the breakthrough Ryan's comment represents, as well as its poignancy, and there's a prolonged moment of stillness and respect. Finally, the boy nearest to Ryan reaches out to pat Ryan's arm.

> *Mia is 12, has been losing weight and looks permanently tired and anxious. The school nurse is aware that her dad has chronic alcoholism and that things must be hard at home. As they chat, Mia says she can cope, so long as she 'does prayers and stuff' every night to ensure that her dad doesn't have a 'bad day'. She worries that sometimes she just falls asleep before she's done enough, 'Cos if I manage about an hour or more, my Dad can be quite good the next day'. Mia also mentions it's easier to stay awake on an empty stomach, suggesting she is deliberately restricting her food intake. She justifies this saying that it 'makes prayers better too doesn't it, like fasting and stuff that my friends do at Ramadan. I know what they mean, it really is like you are closer to God that way.'*

These two cases demonstrate in different ways that spirituality can be a potent reality in childhood. It is certainly not something that is 'adults only', nor something that occurs only to children with obvious religious backgrounds. The crucial primary response we can make is to assume spirituality *does* feature in children's lives, and that to ignore that reality can negatively impact children's wellbeing in itself.

These cameos also highlight that spirituality is not simply a panacea or 'short cut' to wellbeing. Sometimes, as in Ryan's story, spirituality is part of the coping, recovery or adjustment process in a positive way. For others, like Mia perhaps, spirituality can seem to contribute to the stressors and disorder in a young person's life. The experience of spiritual distress as a child will be explored towards the end this chapter too.

The taboo of engaging in a child's spirituality

Treading sensitively through this can feel like walking through a minefield. When spirituality, often out of the blue, is expressed to us in some way, we may be unsure about where to start. But the general taboo around intruding into the 'private' territory of religious belief and cultural practices can feel even stronger when our clients are children: we worry that we may be insensitive to the child's family, community or culture, or over-influence a child with our own beliefs. We may tend to steer away from this area with the child, but follow it up indirectly with adult family members instead. It is important to be aware of our instinctive avoidance of this area, and any inclination to ignore the feelers children put out about spiritual things – experiences, thoughts, behaviours or motives. Ultimately this avoidance sends children messages that this topic is banned, perhaps even irrelevant or wrong.

This chapter will provide a brief guide to research findings which establish common features of natural childhood spirituality and to explore some of the ways these contribute to their wellbeing. It will equip you to notice children's spirituality, talk to them about it, and help them reflect on it.

> **Exercise**
>
> When you were a child, what seemed 'sacred' to you?
>
> Could you talk to anyone about this sense of the sacred?
>
> Can you think of a time when a child you've worked with tried to share something spiritual? How did you feel and what did you do? What do you wish you had done or said?

Children's natural spirituality

Psychiatrist Robert Coles (1992) published *The Spiritual Life of Children*, a landmark account of conversations with a wide range of children from many faiths and cultures. It raises immediate questions.

- Can children have spiritual lives? If so, from what age?
- What kind of children? Do they need to be religious?
- In what sense are they 'spiritual'? Is it about what they say, what they believe or having certain experiences?
- Are children aware of this? Does it 'count' if they are not?
- Do they seek it, or does it just happen to them?

These questions highlight some of the assumptions many people make about children and the quality of their experience. There's a tendency to assume that any spirituality is either drummed into them by indoctrination or they are simply very unusual.

However, a detailed series of case studies of 40 'ordinary' school children in the UK, most of whom had no family faith background, yielded a rich variety of spiritual experiences, spiritual views and self-taught spiritual practices drawing on not only some religious knowledge, but also ideas from science, stories and films, and significant relationships (Hay & Nye, 1998). In fact, children's spirituality can have a particularly authentic quality to it because it arises out of everyday moments and isn't necessarily yoked to a particular kind of language or faith, as Louise's example below illustrates. Their spirituality is not only connected to deliberately 'spiritual' places, actions or statements, such as at church or temple, weddings and funerals, or restricted to religious statements of belief or traditional spiritual narratives. They are as likely to find any aspect of their environment spiritually stimulating, provoking awe (which can be a kind of fear) or wonder, or prompting an intuitive (but powerfully intense) awareness of transcendence.

For Louise (10) at playtime on a sunny day, the blue of the sky was 'holy', and the greenness of grass was a kind of meta-physical mystery ('Where does green even come from?').

Recalling her experience of gazing through her brother's telescope she remembered very powerful feelings: 'It all has a meaning, but you can't think of the meaning… all of the… um… growing, flying and just imagining things. And it all just fits into 'one' and it's just like a big explosion in your mind.'

Nevertheless, children (and those who care for them) can worry that they will be labelled as weird and face rejection should they talk about their experiences.

'Because they might think I'm stupid or something… it's embarrassing' (Nadeem, 10, explaining why he'd never mentioned his spiritual ideas and feelings with his family or friends)

'It's one of those things you can't explain… it really doesn't make sense to other people.' (Anya, 11)

'Perhaps they [family] do it too [pray] themselves, but they'd tease me if they knew I did.' (Seema, 10)

'And sometimes I think about which God's real… and after the universe… what is the universe? Is it going on for ever… [it] gets annoying trying to think about it… you think your brain is gonna get all scrambled like.' (Tim, 10)

'Sometimes I feel very lonely when I am alone with God because I can't see God and I can't hear God, I just think about God, and I feel really, really lonely.' (Beth, 10) (quotes from Hay & Nye, 1998)

So paradoxically, although spirituality is often about sensing a deep sense of connectedness (to God, to Self, to others or to nature), there's an inherent loneliness in this realm of experience for children – 'no one else thinks or feels like this'.

In answer to the sorts of questions posed above, numerous recent studies have systematically documented that:

■ Children *can* and *do* experience spirituality in words and feelings, affecting thoughts and behaviours.

■ This is ubiquitous among *all* kinds of children.

■ This is largely spontaneous and natural.

In other words, childhood spirituality is 'normal', and possibly more prevalent than in adulthood. Large scale studies in Finland found that 60% of 11-year-old children and 80% of seven-year-old children reported having experienced a sense of divine presence at least once in their lives to date (Tamminen, 1991). It is common for adults to report that the most vivid spiritual events of their lives occurred in childhood, though expressing this or finding anyone to take this seriously was very hard (Robinson, 1983).

Whilst studies of very young children are harder to undertake, from a psychological perspective younger children may have heightened perception and capacity for spiritual experience (e.g. for feelings of awe, wonder, sense of mystery or value, a search for meaning and pattern, or experiences of feeling totally overwhelmed (Kimes Myers, 1997)). The difference for the younger child is that they normally lack a recognisable language to frame this to themselves, let alone express it (Watts *et al*, 2002).

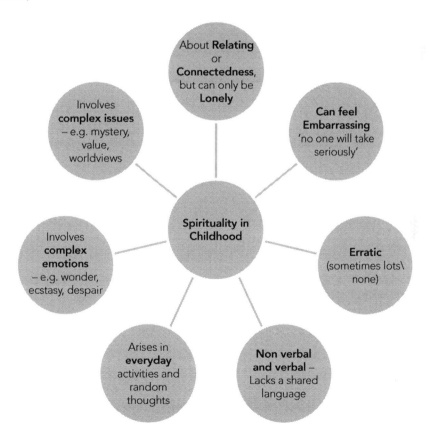

Figure 5.2: Summarises the key features associated with children's spirituality (Nye, 2009).

The functions of childhood spirituality

Finding meaning

Coles (1992) explained how spirituality helps children find meaning and answer the profound questions that life throws up:

'Children try to understand not only what is happening to them, but why; and in doing that, they call upon the religious life they have experienced, the spiritual values they have received, as well as other sources of potential explanation.' (Coles, 1992, p.100)

It can help them to make meaning, find resolution, or cope. This highlights the importance of supporting (not sidestepping) the child's instinct to process life events 'spiritually', in asking questions such as 'Who am I?', 'Is there any meaning to this?', 'What about good and evil?', 'Is anything permanent?' 'Does everything end?' Young people suffering mental illness or trauma often feel these questions more pressingly. 'Why is this happening to me?' 'Does anyone love me?' 'Am I bad?' 'Who can I trust?' 'Am I going to hell?'

Attachment and self-value

Often spirituality is about relating to 'something beyond', often called 'God'. The first of Erickson's (1959) developmental stages is 'trust vs mistrust' when the infant learns to what degree their primary care giver can meet their needs consistently. Bowlby and Ainsworth go on to explain the fundamental importance of the bond formed between the infant and the primary caregiver and how it affects future ways of relating to others. Kirkpatrick (1998) explains how God can be an attachment figure. Where God is experienced as unconditionally loving and accepting, available and powerful, God can even be 'the perfect attachment figure'.

Bella had a long history of depression after she had been neglected as a child. She told of a memory she clung to, of singing a Sunday School song to herself, 'Jesus loves me, this I know', and feeling a presence with her. She knew she would always be loved and would never be alone.

The problem of shame

Humankind and our children grapple with the problem of suffering, pain and our individual roles in causing it. We carry a burden of shame and guilt which can be unbearable. Children and young people can have this shame projected onto them from abuse done to them; their circumstances or illness can lead them to perpetrate abuse onto others; a feature of mental illness can be unfounded, unreasonable feelings of guilt; a harsh religion can sometimes accentuate rather than relieve this. And so we see a complex interplay between trauma, harmful behaviour, illness, emotions of guilt and shame, and spiritual/religious responses to these. A healthy supportive spirituality or religion can offer a way out, through forgiveness.

Developing one's values, finding direction

Adherence to a set of values (e.g. religious, political or environmental) provides a young person with a foundation from which they can make decisions in life. Without this they are pushed around by every whim of social media, friendship or lobby group (Cotton *et al*, 2006).

Communicating

In Ryan's example at the start of the chapter, the 'spiritual' story functioned as a way to say something about the proportions of his loss, his love and his needs, and what seemed the first chance for explicit peer support. Children can be offered this additional route to expressing complex emotional needs and reactions.

Exercise

Influential development psychologist Erik Erikson suggested that 'the most deadly of sins is the mutilation of a child's spirit'. Why do you think encouragement or hindrance of spirituality could affect a child so much?

Think of a recent encounter with or observation of a child. Can you identify any 'big issues' they may have been wrestling with. How was this evident – in words, play, behavior, silence?

What is mental illness in childhood and adolescence?

Young people's mental health difficulties can be understood on multiple levels: genetic, biological and neurodevelopmental; core beliefs and thinking styles; attachment; systemic (e.g. family dynamics); trauma and bullying; culture and social setting, to name a few. Considering the young person's spirituality completes the holistic understanding, making a bio-psycho-socio-spiritual formulation. We will now consider how to incorporate spirituality into our assessment and care of children with mental health difficulties.

Working with children's spirituality

A child's spirituality will not appear 'on demand', especially in a time-limited meeting. We therefore need to be listening out for signs of spirituality in all our encounters with young people.

We might assume that children can only process what they can verbalise. However, children frequently develop or intuit their own concept of 'God', developing an internal, non-verbal frame of reference that may be vibrant and sophisticated compared to their ability to articulate it. We therefore need to adjust our language to fit theirs as well as listen for the non-verbal.

Whilst so much about spirituality revolves around a sense of connectedness of the child to 'more than just me', there is the fear that no one shares these experiences – so they can be defensively guarded. It is imperative to validate the young person's beliefs and experiences. Permission to talk about this usually taboo topic, may be given simply by asking a single question early on in the therapeutic relationship (e.g. 'Do you have any faith or beliefs that are important to you?') The young person can then come back to this topic when they are comfortable. If no mention is made of spirituality, a young person may assume it is off limits.

Where further conversation is welcome, the clinician's role is to listen and validate the young person's experiences and beliefs, then to enable the young person to reflect on how their spirituality interacts with their wellbeing. If any concerns emerge, the clinician must tread carefully before making any challenge, and enable the young person to reflect and see how a belief or practice may be unhelpful.

Trust the child to be the expert in themselves and their spirituality. The clinician only has to be an expert in mental health and in communication. Knowledge of religion, while helpful, can lead to making assumptions about the beliefs of the young person.

Talking to adolescents about their spirituality

Adolescents are establishing their beliefs and are becoming more able to express them. The image of a flower can be used as an aide memoire for five areas of questioning that can build a picture of the young person's spirituality. This should be used entirely flexibly as some areas will be more pertinent than others. These areas were identified using a literature review of articles describing spiritual assessment of young people in a mental health context, further examined by an expert panel including service users and clinicians with expertise in both spirituality and mental health (Grimwade et al, unpublished).

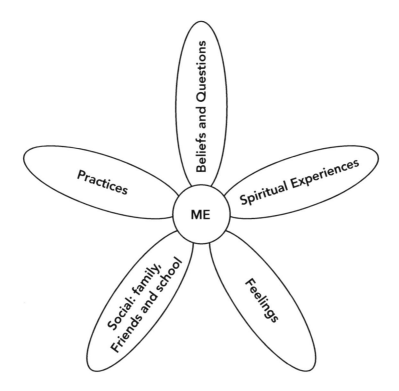

Beliefs and questions

- Could you tell me more about what you believe?

- What do you think about God(s)?

- What does God(s) think about you?

- Questions about the young person's image of God(s) will suggest the type of attachment they may have: if their God is distant, condemning or controlling; or compassionate, forgiving and accepting.

- If you could ask God anything, what would you ask? Fosarelli found this question uncovers the issues young people are grappling with (Sexson, 2004).

- What do you think happens after death? Beliefs about life after death can inform risk assessment or suggest routes to decrease risk.

- Do any of your beliefs conflict with the treatment your doctor recommends? e.g. Young people may require vegetarian formulations of medications.

Practices

What do you do to support your spirituality? For example, do you ever pray or meditate? How does this help you? Is there anything hard about it?

Social

What do your family think of your beliefs? Your friends? Teachers? Are you part of a faith community? How is it supportive? Are there any difficulties?

Experiences

Have you had any spiritual experiences? What did they mean to you?

Feelings

How does your spirituality make you feel? Do you think your spirituality helps you feel loved? Belonging? Accepted? Safe?

Bringing it together: a 'formulation'

	Spirituality's effect on wellbeing	Stress/ ill-health's effect on spirituality
Healthy, helpful or positive	How can we harness your spirituality to build your wellbeing?	Are there questions you are asking, or a spirituality you want to explore?
Unhealthy, unhelpful, or negative	What areas of your spirituality are causing difficulty or stress?	Has your ill-health got tangled with or distorted your spirituality?

The information from the 'flower' can be used to help the young person reflect on how their spirituality can be harnessed to build recovery and resilience. This can be worked into their care plan.

When the young person's spirituality is validated and a trusting relationship is built, a clinician may very tentatively reflect on any difficult aspects which may be contributing to mental health difficulties. Common types of negative spiritual issues among children include fixations about death, or obsessions about specific religious ideas (at least their own interpretation of those) such as sin, lack of perfection, the reality of evil (the devil, witches, ghosts, hell) or the sinister omniscience of God 'watching them'. Eaude (2009) makes the case that supporting agency may be an important factor in the relationship between child mental and physical health and spiritual wellbeing. In other words, that rather than protecting or distracting children from suffering, it can be important to enable children to face, for themselves, aspects of their life circumstances that take them deep beneath the surface issues of the immediate crisis.

Some seemingly negative aspects of their spirituality might actually be the illness influencing the spirituality: for example, the guilt and unworthiness of depression;

the perceptual disturbances of trauma and psychosis; or the repeated frustrated rituals of obsessive compulsive disorder.

Where young people are asking existential questions, or wanting to explore spirituality, they may want help. It is never appropriate for a professional to impose their own spiritual or anti-spiritual beliefs on the young person. Great care must be taken to give them choice, which requires both that they be informed and have freedom; all in a safe context. Chaplaincy or the young person's own faith leader can be called on to give expertise in this area.

Supporting young people's spirituality

Stories
Stories (from spiritual traditions, fairy-tales and myths) allow children to raise, or simply find recognition of, spiritual issues such as redemption, birth and death, chaos and order in the widest sense (Crompton, 1998). Often, relating to stories 'about others' can reduce the embarrassment factor. Stories, songs and music can also help to contain the complexity of spiritual feelings for children (e.g. delight, despair, adversity, courage) and responses, and act as sources of comfort, strength or illumination. The story may be more effective than anything a practitioner's carefully worded response could offer.

Bhagwan suggests that 'The greatest sacred stories are our own' (Bhagwan, 2009, p228), and encourages the practice of helping children to tell, write or make visual representations of their own life story, including those elements that transcend their immediate existence – the 'before me, beyond me' connections to the past and possible future.

Rituals
Rituals are important ways that people process life events at a spiritual level. They can help to address issues of loss, grief and hope (such as at a funeral), or more generally offer ways to connect with others in experiences of spiritual life, including responses of wonder, reverence, comfort, gratitude, protection and uncertainty (e.g. Shabbat, Puja or Holy Communion). Children *can* benefit from being part of these rituals, as they offer a predominately *non-verbal* and shared (not lonely) approach to this area of experience. The repetition of actions and signs also supports a more gradual kind of processing, rather than a 'now I get it' kind of understanding, which discussion tends to demand. Equally, it is worth paying attention to any rituals the child has created – possibly another clue to their wellbeing (or stress, as in Mia's case at the beginning of this chapter), and to the success of self-administered spiritual 'therapy'.

Creative arts

Creativity, including art, movement, or poetry can help express those 'hard to communicate' aspects of spirituality non-verbally (Broadbent, 2004). Silence and meditation can also have a role (Galanki, 2005; Goodman, 2005). Children should also be encouraged to create something tangible, which may become an important symbol of their situation – with a capacity to hold together the emotional complexity of that more effectively than words, and with more permanence than conversation.

Again, children may already have their own important symbols that support their spiritual processing. For example, a terminally ill child treasured a 'guardian angel' trinket. This seemed like a source of comfort and protection for the girl, but in fact she was frustrated that her family could not face talking to her about dying, and so privately this angel became the focus for her thoughts, questions and feelings about 'becoming an angel' herself – in fact her 'death' symbol.

Conclusion

This chapter has focused on how spirituality can affect children's wellbeing, and how adults with responsibilities for children's mental health can best respond to this. The first step is to recognise the universal but individual and powerful reality of spirituality to young people. Mental health clinicians, with help from chaplaincy and faith leaders, can help young people to reflect on how spirituality impacts the young person's mental health: harness the resource; challenge the stressors; facilitate growth and disentangle spirituality from illness.

References

Bhagwan, R (2009) Creating sacred experiences for children as pathways to healing, growth and transformation *International Journal of Children's Spirituality,* **14**: 3, 225 – 234.

Broadbent, J (2004) Embodying the abstract: Enhancing children's spirituality through creative dance. *International Journal of Children's Spirituality* **9**: 97–104.

Coles, R (1992) *The Spiritual Life of Children* T. & T. Clark Ltd.

Cotton S, Zebracki K, Rosenthal S L *et al* (2006) Religion/Spirituality and adolescent health outcomes: a review. *Journal of Adolescent Health* **38** 472-480.

Crompton, M (1998) Children, Spirituality, Religion and Social work. Aldershot, UK: Ashgate.

Eaude, T (2009) Happiness, emotional wellbeing and mental health - what has children's spirituality to offer? *International Journal of Children's Spirituality* **14**: 3, 185 – 196.

Erikson Erik H. (1959) Identity and the Life Cycle. New York: International Universities Press.

Galanki, E (2005) Solitude in the school: a neglected facet of children's development and education. *Childhood and Education* **86**, 573-80.

Goodman, T (2005) Working with children: Beginner's Mind. In: *Mindfulness and Psychotherapy* CK Germer, CD Siegel and PR Fulton (Eds). New York, Guildford Press.

Hay, D & Nye, R (1998) *The Spirit of the Child*. Harper Collins.

Kimes Myers, B (1997) *Young Children and Spirituality*. Routledge

Kirkpatrick, L. A. (1998) God as a substitute attachment figure: A longitudinal study of adult attachment style and religious change in college students. *Personality and Social Psychology Bulletin* **24**(9) 961–973.

Moreira-Almeida, A., Koenig, H.G. and Lucchetti, G. (2014) Clinical implications of spirituality to mental health: review of evidence and practical guidelines. *Brazilian Journal of Psychiatry* **36** (2) 176-182.

Nye, R (2009) *Children's Spirituality: What it is and Why it Matters* Church House Press.

Robinson, E (1983) The Original Vision: A study of the religious experience of childhood. New York: Seabury Press.

Tamminen, K (1991) *Religious development in childhood and youth: An empirical study*. Helsinki: Suomalainen Tiedeakatemia.

Watts, F, Nye, R & Savage, S (2002) *Psychology for Christian Ministry*. Routledge.

Sexson, S.B. (2004) Religious and spiritual assessment of the child and adolescent. *Child and Adolescent Psychiatric Clinics of North America* **13** (1) 35-47.

Chapter 6:
Spirituality in an older generation

By Abigail Methley & James Woodward

This chapter presents a brief overview of the need to consider spirituality in the older generation from a mental health and theological perspective. It presents context on the clinical interplay between mental health and spiritual needs observed within services, highlighted through clinical vignettes with accompanying questions for reflection to assist continuing professional development. From a theological perspective, the chapter explores the importance of listening to the stories of old age and opens up some of the research that explores the generativity of the spiritual in third and fourth age.

A perspective from a UK older people's mental health service: Dr Abigail Methley, Senior Clinical Psychologist

The proportion of older adults in the UK population (defined as age 65 years and above) has been steadily increasing. In statistics from 2016, there were 11.8 million UK residents aged 65 years and over, representing 18% of the total population. By 2066, predictions suggest the total number will be 20.4 million, comprising 26% of the total population, with the fastest growth in the over 85 age bracket. This positive change in life expectancy will also present challenges on a public health level, including the estimation that one million people in the UK will have dementia by 2025, increasing to two million people by 2050.

Within the cohort of older people, a subset will experience mental health needs in later life. An estimated 22% of men and 28% of women over the age of 65 in the UK experience depression, and an estimated 40% of older people seen within GP clinics have mental health needs.

Older adults experience many factors that may lead to poorer mental health. These include intergenerational trauma and poor childhood attachment, difficulties with emotion recognition, high levels of shame and self-criticism. They are at increased risk of completing suicide attempts due to both access to means and pharmacological factors, and frequently present with forms of self-harm which are missed by clinical services (such as deliberately withholding pain medication). Some may struggle with independence and many are at risk of domestic violence, neglect, and emotional and financial abuse (from a spouse or partner, inter-generationally, or, in the case of emotional and financial abuse, by paid carers).

Older people grew up with many stereotypes and stigma about mental health, beliefs about expressing emotions and relationships with gender, and the need to not tolerate difficult feelings but to find a pharmacological or biological 'fix'. All of these may make accessing professional support harder than for a younger person. In addition, society holds many offensive beliefs about older people which have been made clear during the Covid-19 pandemic. These include the beliefs that older adults are naturally dependent, incompetent, a burden on society, that depression is inevitable, that you cannot 'teach an old dog new tricks' and that economic resources are best diverted to younger (often working) age groups. Sadly, these beliefs are often shared by health care professionals, restricting access to supportive services and leading to systemic underfunding of services for older people. In combination, these barriers may mean that older people hold little hope for recovery or improvement in their mental health needs in later life.

The elements of mental distress people present with are impossible to disentangle from spiritual distress, and they often include a sense of unfairness ('why me?'), unworthiness, hopelessness, guilt and punishment, a sense of isolation and anger, feelings of vulnerability and abandonment (by other humans and by their God or a higher power), and confusion. Similarly, older people requiring support from mental health services may:

- struggle with self-acceptance and acceptance of physical, cognitive and emotional changes
- find it difficult to reflect on positive life events (often due to a paucity of these where childhoods were abusive or neglectful)
- experience isolation rather than solitude (often due to exclusion and stigma)
- struggle with the loss of roles and possessions, including finances
- experience rigid beliefs with strong self-judgement
- experience increased fear of death
- experience activation of painful prior attachment styles in later life
- experience a lack of connection with others and the natural world.

The Interpersonal Theory of Suicide described by Thomas Joiner (2005) explains how, in addition to having access to the means with which to end life by suicide, individuals must also experience two psychological states: perceived burdensomeness and a sense of low belonging and social alienation. As such, it is possible to see how spirituality may decrease this experience, by increasing a person's sense of purpose and worth, and providing a sense of community and connection, even where this does not link to a formal place of worship. In comparison, it is also easy to see how a lack of spiritual experience may predispose people to low mood and hopelessness.

Formulating these needs through a spiritual rather than biological lens of depression enables the accommodation of significant triggers for low mood in later life such as bereavement and role loss. It also enables the use of spirituality to enable people to see recovery from low mood not just as a remission from illness but as a journey into self-discovery and an increased awareness of the missing factors required for contentedness, such as connection and positive self-worth. The spiritual recovery process therefore involves not a cure but the development of a way of living a meaningful life in the context of limitations. This focuses on restoring self-esteem through a personal commitment to growth, discovery and transformation. Within mental health services there are many interventions which support this, including age-adapted cognitive behaviour therapy, acceptance and commitment therapy, compassion-focused therapies, mindfulness-based approaches and ecotherapy, all with a growing evidence base for older adults. These approaches can be supported jointly by mental health professionals, families, and community religious leaders who can provide both credibility and the specific information needed to challenge shame or guilt related to interpretations of religion or religious practices (for example, interpretation and examples of religious scripture).

There is still considerable stigma regarding dementia, and individual experiences of dementia are influenced by how dementia is framed within broader societies and communities. Societies which value people only on the basis of their cognitive, physical and occupational functioning, chronically devalue people with dementia and other disabilities. The biomedical focus within health care services and the media may prevent the development of psychosocial, spiritual and theological perspectives on dementia (for further information, see MacKinlay, 2017). More spiritually based approaches have the potential to support people with dementia by broadening our understanding and definitions of the value of human life, supporting people to find continuity and purpose even in the face of changes in functioning, changing the language around dementia from one of burden to one of value, and supporting ongoing relationships and communication.

Examples are provided below of amalgamated and anonymised clinical vignettes. With these, consider the following questions:

1. Who or what provides strength and hope?
2. How do they use spirituality?
3. How do they express spirituality and how would they describe it?
4. What type of spiritual support do they require?
5. What does suffering or distress mean to them?
6. What are their spiritual goals?
7. How does or could their faith help them cope and/or challenge their wellbeing?

Case 1: questioning spirituality after bereavement

Mrs A attended services after the traumatic death of her long-term spouse. She was suicidal and experiencing severe symptoms of depression. She had been raised in a Christian community but did not consider herself religious and had no religious practices. To try and manage her grief she was re-engaging with texts from many different religions in the hope that one would help her connect with her spouse, make meaning of her loss and help the loss feel less absolute. She would spend many hours a day reading religious texts and contacting leaders from various religious and spiritual communities. Doing so helped provide her with a framework to make sense of her grief, provided a sense of connection with others through understanding the universal experience of loss, and helped provide a sense of hope and a continuous relationship with her spouse.

Case 2: reconciling spirituality and abuse in religious settings

Mr B attended services for intervention for Post Traumatic Stress Disorder due to historical childhood sexual abuse within an organised religion setting. He had been raised within a strongly religious community which made disclosure of the abuse very difficult and prevented both protection from his abuser and recovery. As an older adult he was deeply against organised religion but reported that he held spiritual beliefs and was searching for meaning in his current life and past experiences.

Case 3: reconciling spirituality and dementia

Mr C was a devout Muslim and his faith had played a crucial role throughout his life, in his self-identity, community and religious practices. As dementia progressed in his later years, he began to struggle to read the Quran, at times forgot when he should be attending daily prayers, could no longer complete his annual pilgrimage to Mecca, and, due to changes in his language and cognitive abilities, felt that he was not always able to share the spiritual wisdom he wished to with his family and younger members of his community.

A theological perspective: Revd Canon Professor James Woodward

Listening to our story

Each of us is a biography, a story. Each of us is a singular narrative, which is constructed continually and unconsciously, by, through and in us – through our perceptions, our feelings, our thoughts, our actions, and not least through our discourse; our spoken narratives. Biologically, physiologically, we are not so different from each other. To be ourselves we must have ourselves – possess, and if need be re-possess, our life stories. We must 'recollect ourselves'; recollect the inner drama, the narrative of ourselves. Each person needs such a narrative. We best understand spirituality in older age by attending to the narratives of older people, by holding a space within which they can articulate their lives and be heard (Phelan & Rabinowitz, 2008).

'Reading' old age challenges us about what we are not learning and who we are learning from. The liminal edge of living is one of the places the energy and life remains persistent and possible. In anthropology, liminality (from the Latin word līmen, meaning "a threshold") is the quality of ambiguity or disorientation that occurs when participants stand at the threshold between their previous way of structuring their identity, time, or community, and a new way, which the rite establishes. We might regard old age as a liminal period of generativity and spiritual growth (McAdams, 2006).

It could be that one of the elements necessary for wellbeing in older age is our capacity to live with this very unresolvedness in ourselves and others. Being prepared to articulate our experiences, to interrogate ourselves into a deeper truth and wisdom, form part of our ability to embrace and live with ambiguity, paradox and uncertainty. Wellbeing will be shaped by the quality of our listening and the readiness not to evade or deny some of the complexities of the ever-unfinished work of living and loving. As we commit ourselves to a deeper understanding of the sheer variety of human life and choices, then there is the possibility of a more textured and enlightened understanding of living.

Spiritual flourishing?

We all listen to and tell the stories of our lives in fragments. It is never easy to see the whole, especially in an age where information moves so quickly in our distracted society. Modernity has blessed us with immediate access to information but distanced us from perspective that comes from a slower and more reflective pace of living.

We want to live well and flourish at all stages of our lives. There are at least four categories of flourishing, and they become more essential to maintain as we grow older. The first, and the one we are most familiar with, is physical fitness – the bodily strength, resilience and agility that are stimulated by appropriate exercise. Intellectual flourishing, the second category, comes from keeping our minds and intellects engaged and active. The third, our social flourishing, requires the formation and maintaining significant friends and relationships that journey with us in good times and in bad. No less important (but sometimes difficult to define) is spiritual flourishing.

The organising question here is this: how might we age well? For some, spiritual flourishing can only occur in communities of persons, most particularly a religious community. Therefore, we must recognise our responsibility for one another, and we must be open to let others be responsible for us! Others have not been enabled to flourish within organised religion and have sought flourishing from a variety of sources. Some of the discourse around spirituality has become deeply individualised – a form of heroic quest in which each individual travels alone in his or her own inner spiritual world. But, understood as embodied, spiritual flourishing would necessarily have to develop within the context of a spiritually flourishing community – that is, within a community characterised by deep and meaningful relationships with one another and with God (Moberg, 2001).

In short, and in the context of ageing, an embodied sense of spiritual flourishing requires all of us to acknowledge our dependence and need for the scaffolding of our lives by communities of other persons in order to thrive and flourish.

These four categories are important at all stages of life and how we have managed them will have implications for how we flourish in old age. In each of these categories we have more or less control and the ability to change. How we have responded will be important; it may be the case that ageing well may depend on how we embrace and negotiate the stages of our living, especially those aspects of life over which we have little control. Spiritual flourishing may also be related to the balance and interconnections that we nurture between the physical, the social, the intellectual and the spiritual. Finding the space to reflect on our story, we might learn about ourselves – where we have been, where we are now, and, it is to be hoped, where we are going. This adventure of embracing our flourishing with friends and family may help us discover our strengths and weaknesses and come to terms with the lives we have led. Perhaps we might see part of our spiritual flourishing as our preparedness to go deeper into our experience of human contradictions and ambiguities. What possibilities lie in discovering and naming patterns in our living, and so articulating the nature of our longings, desires and restlessness?

In listening to parents and grandparents, I have become aware of the desire to leave a cherished legacy. A person needs to believe that his or her life has mattered and that it has had a purpose or an impact on the world. One of the reasons why we need to open up to the possibilities of reimagining age is to paint a richer and more textured picture of how we can so live together to cherish older people and the shape of their narratives. We flourish when we empower one another to adapt to old age.

When old and young alike (or, even better, together) reflect on their lives, here are some of the areas of life that might be important. The chapters of a reflective life might look something like this:

- the major branching points in my life

- my family or home community

- my career or major life work

- the role of money in my life

- my health and physical living

- the loves and hates over my lifetime

- my sexual identity and sexual experiences

- my experiences with death and ideas about dying

- the history of my aspirations and life goals and the meaning of my life.

(Coleman, 2011)

Finding meaning and sustaining purpose: belief and ageing

In Erikson's well-known account of the life cycle, he demonstrates his commitment to and sympathy for religion. He describes religious faith as the mature adult virtue, which grows out of trust. Peter Coleman and his work at Southampton University have engaged in some fundamental questions relating to the widespread existence of spiritual experience and to its consequences for the person's life.

It is significant that the developmental theorists in central Europe and America who challenged the negative picture of ageing which was afflicting Western society in the 20th century – psychologists such as Carl Jung, Erik Erikson, David Gutmann – took their inspiration from observations in earlier and more traditional societies (Gutmann, 1987).

As they realised, religion was, in the past, the central part of the cultural support of ageing. In these former societies, the role of older people was to engage more fully, more deeply, with religious practice, to become often the very voice-piece of the deity. So the failure of Western post-enlightenment culture to adapt to the rising tide of older people in its populations could also be understood as a failure of religion. Some authorities have even attributed the problem to Christianity. Christianity, of all the great religions, gives apparently little significance to ageing. The evidence from the US still provides a consistent picture of the increasing importance of religion with age. Religious beliefs, behaviour, and experiences that reflect spirituality all increase with age, third age and usually beyond 55. The only exception is diminished attendance at religious services among the very old. This is understandable due to reduced health and mobility, but this is often compensated by increased rates of other forms of religious and spiritual activity. Moberg (2001) emphasises that this pattern of results has been consistently found over the last 50 years as successive generations have aged and died, despite the predictions that it would diminish as secularisation sweeps through society. Therefore, it cannot be considered only as a cohort or period effect. Also, other US evidence suggests that the processes involved in ageing affect people's interest in religion. Most hospitalised patients, for example, say that religion has become more important to them (Koenig, 1994).

At this point it may be helpful to draw upon the research work of Carstensen and Hartel (2006) and Thornstam (2005). The research work of Carstensen and her team reached a number of perhaps surprising conclusions about older people. This work is part of a movement away from decline models of ageing to a lifespan developmental model, which considers how particular processes and strategies facilitate adaptive ageing. Research offers a stark contrast between a picture that clearly demonstrates decreased biological, physiological and cognitive capacity alongside evidence that suggests that people are generally satisfied in old age and experience high levels of emotional wellbeing. Carstensen offers a view of ageing as series of adaptations, which shed significant light on resilience and wellbeing across adulthood.

There is some acknowledgement of the reality that many older adults are faced with a number of unavoidable or inescapable negative events and experiences. The loss of loved ones, adapting to different work circumstances, tensions and difficulties in relationships, can all work to contribute to significant levels of physiological distress which are bound to affect physical and mental health. Social isolation greatly exacerbates the disruption, and will compromise wellbeing.

We should note these challenges to older people's flourishing alongside the significant contribution by Carstensen to gerontology, of the argument that we should be freeing ourselves from the presumption of decline. Within the context of understanding the whole person, theology can play its part in exploring new ideas and concepts that have the possibility to illuminate age and ageing in modern society by placing greater priority on the spiritual and meaningful dimensions of life.

Tornstam

The research work of Tornstam originated in Sweden in the field of gerontological sociology. The model of Gerotranscendence (Tornstam 2005) suggests that human longevity includes the potential for a transcendent movement away from the materialistic and rational point of view common in the first half of life. He suggests that successful completion of such a shift is accompanied by an increase in life satisfaction. This sits with and complements the work of Carstensen, which suggests that older people become more open to the transcendent and the spiritual. This has the capacity to help us all to age well.

The theory of gerotranscendence grew from the decades Tornstam spent in making careful observations of people living in old age, as follows:

1. In older age, coming to terms with yourself occurs and there is a deepening of a process of discovery that reveals previously hidden aspects of self, both good and bad.

2. There is, in the second half of life, a decrease in self-centeredness. With this increasing awareness that the individual is not at the centre of the universe, there is a change from egoism to altruism.

3. There is rediscovery of childhood and the pleasure of recalling episodes from one's childhood.

This developmental theory of positive ageing also offers some distinctive and radical changes in the area of relationships in older age. Here is summary of these core findings:

1. The character and importance of social contacts change in late life. Older people become more selective and less interested in superficial relationships. There is an increased need for solitude.

2. A distinction between one's self and one's role becomes increasingly obvious.

3. Attitudes to wealth change. There is less acquisitiveness and a greater awareness that possessions can ensnare and confine a person.

4. There is a new-found joy in transcending nonsensical social norms. This developmental trend is behind the popular declaration, 'When I get old I will wear purple'.

5. A deeper appreciation develops for the large grey areas separating right and wrong. This is accompanied by an increasing reluctance to give advice to others.

Finally, there are what Thornstam names as cosmic dimensions of Gerotranscendence. These might be summarised as follows:

1. Time and space long thought to be fixed and unchanging are now seen as possessing blurred boundaries. Past and present sometimes merge, and the immediate presence of long-absent relatives can be sensed.

2. There is often a renewed interest in genealogy and one's relationship with past generations.

3. The fear of death recedes. The curiosity about what comes next may develop.

4. There is a renewed interest in nature and connections with the vast living world that surrounds us all.

The combined work of Carstensen and Hartel and Thornstam challenges us to reconsider the spiritual prospects of older age and to see within our life span the possibilities of creativity and power. We will remain ignorant of the depth and breadth of this potential and power as long as we insist on simply comparing youth to age (Woodward, 2008).

Summary

The proportion of older adults in the population is increasing, and within this cohort is a substantial group of people with mental health needs and cognitive changes, including dementia. Older adults experience many life events and factors predisposing them to poor mental health and barriers to receiving quality mental health care, including effective interventions to address the complex interplay between mental health and spiritual needs. Framing discussions through a more spiritual lens provides a chance to improve our understanding of the narratives and life stories that are key to a person's coherent and positive sense of self and identity. An altered focus from decline to flourishing enables an improved understanding of how we may age well with meaning and purpose, drawing on the strengths of older age and the power of connected communities.

References

Carstensen, L. L., & Hartel, C. R. (Eds.) (2006) *When I'm 64*. Washington, DC : National Academies Press.

Coleman, P.G. (2011) *Belief and Ageing, Spiritual pathways in Later Life*. Bristol: The Policy Press.

Gutmann, D (1987) *Reclaimed Powers: Towards a new psychology of men and women in later life*. New York: Basic Books.

Harding MM, Kwong J, Roberts D, Hagler D & Reinisch C (2019) *Lewis's Medical-Surgical Nursing E-Book: Assessment and Management of Clinical Problems*, 11th Edition. St Louis: Mosby.

Joiner T. (2005) *Why people die by suicide*. Cambridge, MA, US: Harvard University Press.

Koenig, H K (1994) *Aging and God: Spiritual pathways to mental health in midlife and later years*. Binghamton, NY: The Haworth Press.

MacKinlay E. (2017) *The Spiritual Dimension of Ageing*. London, UK: Jessica Kingsley Publishers.

McAdams, D. (2006) *The Redemptive Self, Stories Americans Live By*. New York: Oxford University Press.

Moberg, D O (2001) *Aging and Spirituality: Spiritual Dimensions of Aging Theory, Research, Practice and Policy*. Binghamton, NY: The Haworth Press.

Phelan J. & Rabinowitz P. (2008) *A Companion to Narrative Theory*. Blackwell.

Tornstam, L. (2005) *Gerotranscendence, A Developmental Theory of Positive Aging*. New York: Springer Publishing Company.

Woodward J (2008) *Valuing Age*. London: SPCK.

Chapter 7:

The need for spirituality in the dying process

By Peter Fenwick

Chapter summary

Death is a universal experience. And yet death, our own death at least, is something we don't like to talk about, or even think about. It seems to be traditional in our Western culture to act as though it is never going to happen – or at least not to us. We have an existential fear of dying; we are quite happy to talk about someone else's death, but will do anything to avoid thinking or talking about our own. This is called Freud's paradox.

Many people would say they are frightened of death, but when questioned more closely what most of us fear is not death itself – is there much point in fearing the inevitable? – but the process of dying; the anticipation of annihilation. And this is an area about which many doctors are either ignorant, or they find difficult to talk about.

The only way to discover what dying is really like is to talk to those people who have witnessed death, watched what actually happens just before and at the time of death, and seen how those who are dying react to what is happening to them. And when we have done this, we can only come to one realistic conclusion. Death is nothing to be afraid of.

What do the dying need?

Until quite recently, medical treatment of the dying has been focused almost entirely on the patient's physical needs – pain control and easing the end of life. And yet for many patients these are not paramount. A study by YouGov for Dignity in Dying (2008) suggested that the greatest fear for 32% of Britons is to die alone. As death has become more and more medicalised, many more people die in the clinical environment of a hospital, where often the relatives as well as the patient may be unprepared for the death, and fewer and fewer people are able to die in their own homes, surrounded by their family.

If someone is to die in peace, they need to understand the mental and spiritual experiences they may have, which often accompany the process of dying. A firm spiritual faith is a comfort to some, but many may also need help and advice with practical and personal matters, or difficulties in their life situation which need resolution.

A tranquil death is most likely if the patient can actually talk about any anxieties or problems they have, with their family if possible, otherwise with a member of the hospice or nursing staff. Unfortunately, economic factors and sheer pressure of work mean that it is hard for the nursing staff to spend as much time with their patients as they would like. A report by Dr Robin Youngson (2008) suggests that when the need to satisfy budgets is primary, a lack of compassion can negatively affect the welfare of patients. Nurses and doctors, he says, cannot spend as much time as they should with patients because targets are driven by the need to satisfy budgets rather than by care and quality. Families, too, may suffer from this. More than half of the complaints received relate to end-of-life care and demonstrate the lack of empathetic understanding from medical staff which led to relatives being unprepared to face the death of their loved one, or being given no time to arrange for other family members to be present at the time of death (Mayor, 2007).

Few physicians discuss what dying might be like, or the patient's spiritual needs as they approach death. When we discovered this through our own research, we produced a pamphlet (Brayne & Fenwick, 2018) primarily for carers, which describes the dying process and suggests how carers can help the dying understand and come to terms with what is happening to them.

The phenomena of the dying process

What do the dying describe? When I began my own research into this area, I found that we got two very different pictures of the process of dying. The view of the medical profession was that it is simply a switching off, an end to everything, while the nurses and carers who actually spent time with their patients gave a totally different picture, as did the people who described being with their own family members as they are dying at home.

The descriptions of all these people give us a much clearer picture of what it is like to die. They describe visits to the dying person from dead relatives who say they will come to help them on their journey. They hear the dying person talk of transiting in and out of another reality – somewhere they really want to go and are reluctant to return from. And the experiences they describe all have one thing in common: they are nothing to be afraid of. Quite the reverse in fact. It's almost as though the whole process is designed to be reassuring – not only for the dying themselves but to those who are with them.

Deathbed visions

One of the most common phenomena reported around the time of death is the occurrence of visions, occasionally of unknown or spiritual presences, but usually of dead relatives. These visions are clearly so real to the dying person that they often interact with them, and expect others to see them too. This is what one nurse told us they had witnessed when caring for a dying patient.

"I was attending a patient with a fellow nurse – again around 4 in the morning. The patient asked us to stand one on each side of him because he wanted to thank us for looking after him. He then looked over my shoulder towards the window and said, 'Hang on I will be with you in a minute, I just want to thank these nurses for looking after me'. The patient repeated himself a couple of times then died!"

These visitors seem to come with a definite purpose, to help the person through the dying process. They draw closer as death draws nearer, often sitting on the person's bed, and promise to return and go with them on their journey when the time comes. This account, given by a woman describing the last days of her 90-year-old mother who was dying of pneumonia, shows very clearly the parallel worlds the dying seem able to inhabit. During all this time, her heart and oxygen levels were being monitored and were steady.

"She occasionally mentioned that she was aware that people were watching over her, and that they were in the gardens surrounding the hospital. She couldn't describe them, but she knew that they were there to help her, 'If her head fell forward". She said to my son that she also saw "Dad" in the hospital room (as she used to call my father), and wasn't bothered by this.'

It is interesting that these experiences seem to depend on neither expectation nor religious faith – they seem to bewilder and amaze believers and non-believers alike. By far the most common reaction is to feel the visitor as a comforting presence, there to help with the dying process and escort them over the borders of death. The apparitions are nearly always seen as welcoming, and the dying person responds with interest or joy.

I was impressed by the head of a hospice in Canada who I once talked with at a conference. Often her patients lived in isolated places and might be some way away from home and relatives. But, she told me, "No one ever dies alone in my Hospice". She described how she would wait until the dying person had a deathbed vision and then told them that the next time they were 'visited' they should take their visitor's hand and leave with them.

Travelling to a new reality

The dying often talk about transiting between their real world and an alternative reality towards which they want to go. The following account was sent to me by someone who described what she witnessed the day before her mother died:

"Suddenly she looked up at the window and seemed to stare intently up at it... She suddenly turned to me and said, 'Please Pauline, don't ever be afraid of dying. I have seen a beautiful light and I was going towards it... It was so peaceful I really had to fight to come back." The next day when it was time for me to go home I said, "Bye mum, see you tomorrow". She looked straight at me and said, "I'm not worried about tomorrow and you mustn't be, promise me." Sadly she died the next morning... but I knew she had seen something that day which gave her comfort and peace when she knew she had only hours to live.'

Our end-of-life experience research early in 2020 suggested that experiences like this were not uncommon, and that the dying process appears to involve an instinctive need for spiritual connection and meaning. But we also found that although almost all the carers we interviewed, from palliative care teams, nursing homes and hospices, were aware of and interested in the phenomena they had observed, very few understood their significance and even fewer had been properly trained in this area. Perhaps this is not surprising, because the doctors we talked to were quite confident that we would find nothing like this ever happened to *their* patients. The prevailing culture of the institutions was such that these experiences were something of a taboo topic and were not generally acknowledged or discussed. Carers received little training in how to respond if their patients had such experiences and wanted to talk about them. However, in the last ten years many academic papers describing what happens when people die have been published and the medical profession is now much less resistant to accepting that these phenomena do occur and need to be acknowledged and understood.

Terminal lucidity

Terminal lucidity – what the Victorians called 'Lightening up before death' – is a sudden and unexpected alerting in patients, usually about 24 hours before they die. Patients who have had dementia for a number of years and been unable to recognise family members or remember their names may suddenly sit up in bed, recognise those around them, greet them by name, say goodbye, and then lie back and are frequently dead within two hours. This sudden improvement may not only be in their mental state – patients who have had a stroke and been unable to use their limbs for several years may suddenly find they are able to do so. The literature shows that serious mental conditions such as being deaf or mute since childhood, having schizophrenia or brain damage may also be reversed at this time. The mechanism for this extraordinary reverse in pathology is unclear, but a study at the National Institute of Health has been funded to investigate them further. It is important for the relatives to understand that this sudden improvement is not an indication that the patient is recovering, but that they are entering the final stage before death itself.

Talking to the dying

The realisation that you are in fact going to die starts when you are told so by your doctor. The patient may then have many internal questions, but apart from, "How long have I got, doctor?" only a few are discussed with the medical team. What most people would really like to know is what will it be like? Do I really have to go through this?

What to say, and how to say it

Death isn't easy to talk about at the best of times, and for someone who is having to come to terms with the end of their own life it can be harder still. Hard, too, for those who are caring for them. But if someone has had one of the experiences described above, they may want to talk about it, and it will probably make it easier for you to talk to them about what is happening. Watch their body language and look them in the eye. Be ready to listen to them, encourage them to describe who or what they have seen. By all means, ask them questions about their experience, show that you are curious about what happened and that you are interested in it. But whatever you do, don't question its validity, or dismiss or belittle it, even if it is entirely alien to your own belief system. If you are able to mention other, similar experiences you have heard about, this would help them to feel that what happened is a normal – and very positive – part of the dying process.

Perhaps it is not surprising that these experiences have not been taken seriously by the medical profession. Visions are usually attributed to medication, the pathological process of dying, or to expectation based on religious belief. But their nature and clarity, and the fact that many of those who experience them have no particular religious belief and certainly no expectation of a visit, makes none of these explanations tenable. Whether these phenomena are 'true' in a literal sense is unimportant. The fear of death is one of the most fundamental and universal human fears, and what these experiences seem to do is to extinguish this fear, and help to reassure the dying that death need not be the fearful process they may have imagined, but can be something that is positive, even joyful. And seeing the effect the experiences have on the dying person may also have a profound and lasting impact on family members who witness them or are told about them.

Reconciliation

One of the most impenetrable barriers to a 'good death' is unfinished business, and one of the most essential facilitators is reconciliation. If we are to die in peace we need to forgive others, seek their forgiveness, and forgive ourselves for any wrongs or misunderstandings. If you are caring for the dying, the most valuable thing you can do for them is to make sure they have the opportunity, however late in the day, to try to mend broken or troubled relationships. This is not only so that the dying person can let go in peace, but so that the people left behind can have a peaceful and guilt-free parting. How important this is can be seen from the following account by Les Wilson of something that happened to him 40 years ago, when he was just 21 years old:

"My father and I had never got on and thus I left home 6 months after leaving school at the age of 16 years. I managed to find work and get myself stabilised in the south of England where I worked in the transport industry. I never visited home in the following five years, nor did I think about the family I had left behind in Yorkshire.

However, one morning at 7.30am as I was on my way to work I found a sudden urge to visit my home in Yorkshire. I just felt a sudden need to do this.

When I arrived at my parents front door my Mum came rushing out in tears and threw her arms around me saying 'Thank God you're here... we hadn't a clue where to get in touch, but your dad is dying of cancer and you're the only one left to see him'.
I went upstairs and made my peace with my dad who said that now he had seen all his family he was ready to go, and, next morning, when my elder brother called to see him, he was dead in his bed.

I could not explain this phenomenon and it has troubled me ever since."

The fear of sudden death

Covid-19 has brought death to the forefront of all our minds. Many people who have previously regarded themselves as too young or too fit to consider imminent death suddenly realise it is a possibility, and that such a death would be likely to take place rapidly in an intensive care unit, probably when they were unconscious. Without time to prepare for death, would they too have the experiences that we have been talking about? A consultant in a Canadian hospice told me that he used a description of the near death experience as a model of the dying process and found that this was a great comfort to the dying. We know that many people who have had near-death experiences such as a sudden accident or heart attack describe, when they recover consciousness, visiting the same area of love and light the dying so often describe, even though the people they meet are not there to help them on their 'journey', but to send them back because it is not their time. All the information we have suggests that, however you die, the process of death remains the same.

What happens to consciousness as we die?

Dr. Monika Renz, a Swiss palliative care theologian who has studied a large number of dying patients in hospices, has taken our knowledge of the dying process a step further in her recent and most comprehensive and interesting research; what happens to consciousness as we die.

She showed that there seem to be three stages in the death process which mark the alterations that consciousness undergoes. These she calls pre-transition, transition and post-transition. In the pre-transitional state, the person realises that dying is inevitable, they may fear losing control, and realise that they will have to give up everything they are attached to. It is in this state that the dying person may suffer from the anxiety and struggle, which is called terminal restlessness. Inability to accept this will hold them in the pre-transitional state and lead to further suffering. It is worth asking them if anything particular is worrying them, or if they would like you to contact a friend or relative for them. It is important to take any final requests they may make seriously – they may make all the difference between a restless and a peaceful death.

But once they have acknowledged and accepted the inevitable, they will pass into the next, transitional, stage, and may have vivid dreams or simply lie quietly and stare. Finally, they may pass into the final, peaceful state of post-transition, becoming serene, in a state beyond anxiety pain or powerlessness. Although they may be unable to speak, they can still hear and can communicate by gestures or single words. Such transformative experiences are comparable to a spiritual awakening; the patient shows an expansion of consciousness with love and light, rather than its cessation.

What can protect us from the fear of death?

The progress from pre to post-transition is not essentially linear, the patient may pass back and forth from level to level during the days preceding death. But Dr. Renz has noted that there seem to be various protective factors which make it easier to reach this final peaceful state. The people who seemed to suffer least during the dying process, to pass most easily to the post- transitional state, were the ones who were meditators, or who prayed regularly, or had had a previous near-death experience. But perhaps the most unexpected protective factor was one which is open to us all. Curiosity. So, this is the message for us all; death is nothing to be afraid of, as with birth it is one of the two greatest transitions we will ever make, to another state of consciousness. Once you have mended your relationships and can be at peace with yourself, you need do nothing more to ensure a peaceful death except this one thing. Be curious.

References

Brayne, S. & Fenwick P. (2018) *Nearing the End of Life: A Guide for Relatives and Friends of the Dying.* Brown Dog Books.

Campaign for Dignity in Dying (2008) Survey finds that being alone is Britain's biggest fear about death, https://www.dignityindying.org.uk/news/survey-finds-alone-britains-biggest-fear-death/

Mayor, S. (2007). Care of dying patients and safety dominate report on NHS complaints. *The BMJ*, 2007, **334**: 279

Youngson, R. (2008) Compassion in healthcare: The missing dimension of healthcare reform? *Futures Debate*, The NHS Confederation, https://www.researchgate.net/publication/281256034_Compassion_in_healthcare-The_missing_dimension_of_healthcare_reform#fullTextFileContent

Mental Health, Spirituality and Wellbeing

Therapeutic Practice

Chapter 8:
Assessing spirituality

By Hilary Garraway

Chapter summary

This chapter begins by considering our own spirituality as a useful therapeutic resource and then goes on to discuss the importance of spirituality and why it is sometimes not included in an assessment. It then covers some basic tools to use in the assessment of spirituality within mental health settings. We will also consider the possibility of spirituality as a source of difficulty as well as spirituality being a source of support and wellbeing.

Spirituality as foundational to therapy

When someone comes to therapy, they are putting their trust in the therapist to understand and to help bring about constructive change. As therapists we therefore have a duty of care to listen to the whole person in order to truly understand them, rather than simply listen to the particular aspects of their life that we choose to focus on. Many people come to therapy with a deep spiritual journey and with a range of spiritual experiences that have shaped their world view. Some come with spiritual questions or a crisis of faith, and some come when faith is all they have got left to hold on to. These aspects of spirituality could hold the key to their anxiety or be the source of strength they need in order to move on. If we do not explore these areas, we could be missing vital pieces of the therapeutic jigsaw.

However, before we start thinking about assessments, we need to remember that therapy is primarily a relationship. Foundationally, it is about who we are and how we say things rather than what we say: it is more about presence than practice. The tools of therapy begin with ourselves and what we bring as a person in who we are. So, understanding and assessing our own spirituality and potential biases is a first step – how do we make sense of our world and how do we find meaning and purpose? What spiritual resources do we draw on to feel grounded? How can we hope for our clients to be grounded if we do not feel that ourselves?

As therapists, we need to be centred, showing warmth and compassion, so that the client feels that the therapy room is a safe place and that there is a glimmer of hope for their situation. This does not come from simply knowing therapeutic techniques or the latest research, but comes from our own spirituality as therapists – what centres and grounds us? Where do we draw our own sense of peace and wellbeing from? How do we make sense of the chaos and suffering we see in the world? These are key questions to ask ourselves in order to be effective in helping our clients from a holistic point of view. A spiritual practice can be foundational for being in the present moment with each client, being fully present to their world and their needs. Effective therapy begins with 'being' before 'doing' – it begins with our own stillness and centred peace so that our therapy comes from a place of genuine compassion, deep listening and authentic availability.

Dilemmas in exploring spirituality

Spiritualty is often neglected within therapy for a number of reasons. If spirituality is not significant within our own lives or is a subject with which we feel uncomfortable, then it may not be something we will readily wish to explore with our clients. Research suggests that clients are more likely to be religious or spiritual than their psychologists (e.g. Neeleman & Lewis, 1994), and psychologists may therefore be less likely to see spirituality as a relevant area to explore. There are sometimes concerns about starting to explore this area and then not knowing what to do with the information acquired, and not having a framework with which to work with it. Therapists may not feel confident to ask questions in this area if they have not had previous training in how to explore spirituality within therapy.

There can be concerns about spirituality being a very personal or emotive area, so therapists may decide that it is best left unexplored. Yet therapists may ask about the intimacies of a marriage or the details of a traumatic event along with other personal or emotive areas. There may be concerns about saying the wrong thing, causing offense or coming across as ignorant in this area. Alternatively, if they have their own faith or spiritual worldview, a therapist may have a fear of imposing this on others or being seen to proselytize. Therapists routinely ask about relationships, and in particular assess family dynamics. For some clients, the most important relationship is with a divine or spiritual being, and yet this is a relationship which can be left unexplored. As a result, this can also mean that important relationships within a faith community, crucial to wellbeing, are also left unexplored.

Therapists may not ask about a client's faith because they feel it is not appropriate for the client to consider what aspects of their faith are helpful or not. As therapists, we may have no difficulty asking about family life and exploring the different aspects within families, yet sometimes we do not feel able to do this with aspects of a person's faith. As with families, there are various helpful and unhelpful aspects within spirituality and faith communities and this is why it is useful to explore both in an assessment. It is important that the therapist remains impartial about whether a person's faith or image of God is helpful or not. It is the therapist's role to explore these issues, to ask the questions and to allow the client space to reflect on what is helpful. Spirituality is often a key way in which clients cope with difficulties (Koenig *et al*, 2001) and so it is important to assess and include these coping strategies. For example, Pargament *et al* (1998) found some religious coping styles contributed to wellbeing, while others hindered it.

There is a danger that spirituality is seen as synonymous with religion. If someone does not tick the box of being part of a religion, then spiritualty may not be considered relevant. However, if we see spirituality as being about meaning and purpose, about values and worldviews, of what energises, what gives a sense of belonging and interconnection, then we all have a spirituality. It is at the heart of our identity. Sometimes therapists say that they will be led by the client, so if the client brings the subject up then the therapist will explore it. Yet research suggests that clients avoid talking about their faith or spirituality for fear of it being dismissed, challenged or pathologised (Dein, 2004). This can lead to some clients feeling trapped in a double taboo – not feeling able to talk about their faith in secular mental health services, while at the same time not feeling able to talk about their mental health in their faith community where they may be perceived as not trusting God enough, or possibly that their difficulty is due to demonic influences or jinn.

One useful starting point in considering these areas is to begin with spiritual competencies. An example of such a list of competencies is on p182 and described in more detail in Chapter 14.

Reflective exercise

You may find it helpful to pause at this point in order to reflect on the dilemmas outlined above. Are any of these relevant to you or influence your therapeutic practice? You may also find it helpful to reflect on how you are progressing in terms of spiritual competencies, noting any areas that you could develop further.

Introducing the topic of spirituality and faith

There are various approaches and tools that can be used to assess spirituality. Crucially, it is important to ensure that it is not a tick box exercise but a genuine conversation in which the therapist is curious to understand the person's unique spirituality. Ideally, it is best not to ask what religion a person is because sometimes people will say they are Christian just because they are British, for example, or Muslim if they come from a Muslim country. This does not necessarily relate to their own belief system or spirituality, but more about how they identify with a state religion. In terms of useful therapeutic material, we need to understand about a client's personal belief system, what is it about being part of that faith which helps them or makes their life more difficult and how their faith and mental health inter-relate. Unless this question is followed up with further questions, then naming a faith does not really give much information. Also, there is an increasing number of people who would describe themselves as 'spiritual but not religious', who would answer that they do not have a religion whilst having a meaningful spiritual life. Even using the terms 'worldview' or 'beliefs' in a question rather than 'religion' can lead to different responses due to a growing cultural shift in people having less affiliation to formal religions.

However, if a person has, for example, completed an assessment checklist that asks about religion, it can be helpful to follow this up by asking how religion is part of their lives and what that means to them. It can be useful to keep in mind the difference between intrinsic religion and extrinsic religion (Allport & Ross, 1967). Intrinsic religion is that which is integrated into a person's life and holds some meaning for the person, such as a Muslim who feels strengthened by praying five times a day and who believes that different things come into his life because Allah has sent them. Extrinsic religion, meanwhile, is compartmentalised and the focus is more about secondary benefits their faith brings them, such as socialising with people after Friday prayers, even if the rest of the week their religion doesn't affect their life in anyway.

If a person does say that they have a religion, it is important not to assume what that means. It needs exploring. Each religion has different subgroups within it, such as the Sufi and Sunni groups within Islam, or, within Christianity, Catholic worship has different emphases than worship at a Pentecostal church. There is also an overlap between culture and religion. For example, a Muslim from Bangladesh may have different practices than a Muslim from Sudan due to cultural traditions being integrated within the faith. As clinicians, we cannot be expected to know about all the different faith groups. Instead, it is important to draw from the client's understanding of their own faith; to ask about their own experiences and the personal significance of their particular faith.

It is often more helpful to ask open-ended questions that naturally follow on from talking about a client's difficulties, rather than ask a direct question about religion. Below are some examples of this:

- What do you rely on when you feel hopeless?
- Is there anything in your life that gives you strength in these difficult times?
- Does anything in your life give you any sense of meaning or purpose?
- What keeps you going and gets you out of bed each day?
- Do you feel part of a community that supports you?

As we have already noted, some clients feel cautious talking about their spiritual beliefs or faith, so more explicit questions such as the following can be useful:

- Would you describe yourself as religious or spiritual?
- Has a faith or spirituality ever been part of your life?
- Are there spiritual beliefs which you hold on to that help you?
- Has your mental health impacted on any spiritual practices that you do?
- Have you had any spiritual experiences that have been significant in your life?

Spirituality assessment tools

There are a range of tools that can be used to guide the conversation, though even with questionnaires and useful acronyms they are best used as frameworks to create open-ended questions rather than used in a rigid way.

A useful acronym that is easy to remember is **HOPE** (adapted from Anandarajah & Hight, 2001):

- **H**ope, meaning, comfort, strength, peace, love and connection – what gives these to your client? What keeps them going?
- **O**rganised religion – are they part of one? How involved are they?
- **P**ersonal spirituality and practices – what do they believe and do?
- **E**ffects on mental health care and end of life issues – has their mental health changed their beliefs and practice? Does their spirituality help with suicidal thoughts? Do they believe anything happens to a person after they die?

Another model that can shape the assessment is the **5 Rs** (Govier, 2000):

■ **Reason** and **reflection** – the ability to reflect on mental health and general life experiences, and how their spirituality impacts this.

■ **Religion** – involvement in a faith community, having a spiritual practice.

■ **Relationships** – with others, God or a divine being and with self.

■ **Restoration** – how their spirituality contributes or limits their recovery.

A final acronym is **FICA** (Puchalski & Romer, 2000):

■ **F**aith and belief – do you consider yourself spiritual or religious? Is spirituality important to you? What gives your life meaning?

■ **I**mportance – what importance does your spirituality have in your life? Has your spirituality influenced how you take care of yourself and your health? Does your spirituality influence you in your healthcare decision making?

■ **C**ommunity – are you part of a spiritual community? Is this of support to you and how? Is there a group of people you really love or who are important to you?

■ **A**ddressing spirituality – How would you like me to address these issues in your healthcare or therapy? How can this be incorporated into your therapy or care plan?

Cognitive Behaviour Therapy (CBT) separates out thoughts, feeling and emotions. You may find it helpful to use the common CBT cycle (see Figure 8.1: CBT cycle of spirituality) to ask about these different aspects in terms of spirituality. For example, spiritual practices could include prayer, walking in nature, meditation and yoga; spiritual experiences could include a sense of peace when someone prays or having a sudden insight; spiritual beliefs could be that this insight has come from God, that you are being guided by God and that your life has significance.

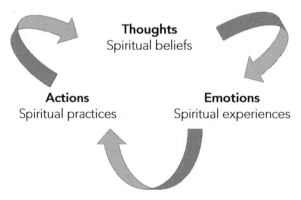

Figure 8.1: CBT cycle of spirituality

The box below lists some questionnaires that can be used to assess spirituality. As with any questionnaires, it can make the assessment more formal and less fluid. However, you may find them useful as resources and potential areas to explore.

Spirituality questionnaires

- Spiritual wellbeing scale (Paloutzian & Ellison, 1982).
- Multidimensional measurement of religiousness and spirituality (Idler *et al*, 2003).
- Spiritual History Scale (Hays *et al*, 2000)
- Religious Coping Questionnaire – RCOPE (Pargament *et al*, 2000).
- Meaning in Life questionnaire (Frazier *et al*, 2006).

Systemic therapy uses genograms to explore different issues within a family tree. A spiritual genogram, such as the example in Figure 8.2, can be a useful way to map out a family's spirituality (e.g. McCullough, 2004). These can be particularly helpful to map out family member's religious affiliations when someone has converted from one religion to another, or when there are different faiths held within a family. The following questions can be useful to reflect on with the client:

- How important was/is religion or spirituality in the family?
- Who do they feel is the most/least spiritual?
- How was spirituality expressed in your family?
- What influence did/does spirituality have on family beliefs, values, underlying messages and behaviours?
- How does the family celebrate festivals or mark life events such as a births, deaths and marriages?
- Was spirituality/religion a source of strength or source of conflict in the family?
- How has this changed over generations?
- How has your family's spirituality influenced you personally?

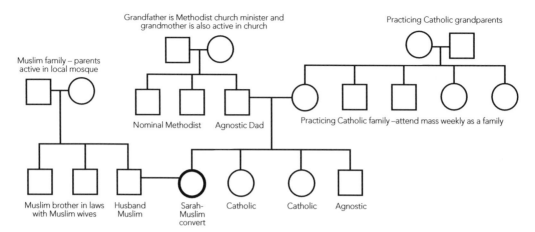

Figure 8.2: Spiritual genogram

If someone has a belief in God or a divine being, you could explore this in terms of:

■ how they were taught about this as a child

■ what have they experienced of this as they have grown up

■ how has that view changed as they became an adult.

If there is a sense that someone's faith or spiritualty has changed over time, a client may find it helpful to draw a timeline of key events that have shaped this journey. This helps to show how spirituality is not a static concept but is often a changing dynamic, involving an ongoing search for the sacred and of spiritual development.

Assessing difficulties within spirituality

We often find that spirituality is a source of strength; it helps to give people meaning and a framework to understand the world in order to cope with difficulties. This is supported by research such as that done by Koenig (2001). However, as with most aspects of life, there can be difficulties within spirituality. These can interact with mental health difficulties or undermine the therapy process. For example, if someone has an image of God in which they feel unable to be forgiven or that they are being constantly judged and condemned, that may impact on a person's capacity to use therapy or to benefit from it. They may feel unworthy of progressing in therapy or that there is no hope for them.

A person's psychological difficulties can interact with their spirituality. For example, a religious person with OCD (Obsessive Compulsive Disorder) may use set prayers or prayer beads as part of their compulsive behaviour. Part of the assessment process may therefore be about understanding when prayer is helpful and when is it part of the OCD behaviour and how these can be distinguished from each other. As well as psychological difficulties impacting on spirituality, the reverse can also occur with unhelpful spiritual beliefs maintaining psychological difficulties. For example, religious beliefs about judgement in an afterlife have been found to be underlying health anxieties in some clients (Wells & Hackman, 1993).

Some difficulties experienced by individuals are specific to certain religions, such as the shared historical trauma of the Holocaust for Jewish people. Clients may also experience prejudice or abuse for belonging to a certain faith tradition. A Muslim, for example, may experience Islamophobia or a Jew targeted by anti-Semitic abuse. Even in what may be seen by some as a 'Christian country', people from this faith tradition can be bullied or ostracised for their beliefs.

With issues specific to a certain faith tradition, therapists can sometimes feel daunted that they do not know enough about a particular faith and so may avoid the topic altogether. However, therapeutic listening and gentle questions can allow a client the space and permission to explore these issues, which encourages the client to reflect on these difficulties and to come to their own conclusions.

Another difficulty can arise when clients are given conflicting advice from both their faith community and their mental health services, causing increased stress and confusion. They may not feel able to talk about these difficulties in therapy, unless the area of spirituality has already been explored within the assessment. There is a danger that these conflicting understandings from their faith group and mental health services are compartmentalised instead of explored and integrated. These spiritual beliefs about mental health can sometimes be stigmatising for the individual, even though they may come with good intentions. For example, in a mosque a person may be told that their mental health difficulties are due to jinn, or the evil eye, and that they need to do certain rituals and to stop taking medication. In a church, they may be told that they need deliverance from evil spirits or that they need to pray with more faith. Some religious communities, such as some orthodox Jewish communities, may advise a person against seeking help from mental health professionals and instead encourage the person to gain support within their own community. Some faith traditions may encourage the person to receive the difficulties as a test from God to be endured rather than to seek help. For example, in the Buddhist tradition, suffering is seen as part of life due to attachments and so the individual may feel guilty if they seek help through therapy.

Generally, being part of a faith community has been shown to be good for wellbeing and health (e.g. Koenig, 2001). Often such a community is able to provide caring support and reduces isolation. Faith traditions usually warn against suicide, self-harm and the use of drugs and alcohol, and encourage a balanced, healthy lifestyle. They also tend to encourage people to be altruistic and encourage healthy values such as forgiveness, gratefulness and compassion. Therefore, clients may use these spiritual teachings to encourage themselves to have healthy therapeutic goals alongside input from their therapy. However, being part of a faith group can occasionally cause difficulties. As with any group of people where there are positions of leadership, there are risks of abusive power, controlling practices and various forms of abuse. Within faith groups there can be the addition of spiritual abuse. This can include 'coercion and control, manipulation and pressuring individuals, control through the misuse of religious texts and scripture, and providing a 'divine' rationale for behaviour (Oakley *et al*, 2018). However, with safeguarding practices becoming more commonplace in faith traditions, there is less risk of this occurring. Nevertheless, it is still worth considering where relevant within the assessment.

Within the diagnostic framework DSM-5 (Diagnostic and Statistical Manual of Mental Disorders (American Psychiatric Association, 2013)), religious or spiritual difficulties are listed as other issues that 'may need some clinical attention'. Examples given are 'distressing experiences that involve loss or questioning of faith, problems associated with conversion to a new faith or questioning of other spiritual values'. A person may be coming to therapy with a diagnosis of depression but underlying this may be spiritual doubts or questions that they do not feel able to voice within their family or faith community. These may be the main issues that are maintaining their depression, and yet if the question is never asked about spirituality, they may never find the courage or words to voice it, leading to the potential for misdiagnosis.

Conclusion

Assessment is often an ongoing process in therapy. If spirituality is explored with a person in the initial assessment, it can be integrated within the formulation and explored further as part of the ongoing therapeutic process. By introducing the topic early on, it allows the client to voice spiritual issues later within therapy. Although some therapists may feel deskilled in this area, and may not have received any specific training in exploring a client's spirituality, they can use their existing therapeutic skills to explore this area. They can ask questions, be curious, show compassion and actively listen. In this way they can allow space for clients to explore their spirituality as an important dimension of their life, and often the source of their deepest strength.

References

Allport & Ross (1967) Personal and religious orientation and prejudice. *Journal of Personal Social Psychology* **5** 432-443.

American Psychiatric Association (2013) Diagnostic and statistical manual of mental disorders (5th ed.). Arlington, VA.

Anandarajah, G.M. & Hight, E.M. (2001) Spirituality and medical practice: Using the HOPE as a practical tool for spiritual assessment. *American Family Physician* **63** (1) 81-88.

Dein (2004) Working with patients with religious beliefs. *Advances in Psychiatric Treatment.* **10** 287-94.

Frazier, Oishi and Kaler (2006) The Meaning in Life Questionnaire: Assessing the presence of and search for meaning in life. *Journal of Counseling Psychology.* **53** 80-93.

Govier, I (2000) Spiritual care in nursing: A systematic approach. *Nursing Standard.* **14**, **17**, 32-36.

Hays, Meador, Branch & George (2000) The Spiritual History Scale in Four Dimensions (SHS-4) Validity and Reliability *The Gerontologist.*

Idler *et al* (2003) Measuring Multiple Dimensions of Religion and Spirituality for Health Research. *Research on Aging* 25 no.4.

Koenig, McCullough & Larson (2001) *Handbook of Religion and Health.* Oxford University Press.

McCullough (2004) Genograms and African American Families: Employing Family Strengths of Spirituality, Religion, and Extended Family Network. *Michigan Family Review* **09** (1) pp30-36.

Neeleman & Lewis (1994) Religious identity and comfort beliefs in three groups of psychiatric patients and a group of medical controls. *International Journal of Social Psychiatry* **40** 124-34.

Oakley LR, Kinmond KS & Humphreys J (2018) Spiritual abuse in Christian faith settings: Definition, policy and practice guidance. *Journal of Adult Protection* **20**(3/4), 144-154.

Paloutzian RF & Ellison CW (1982) Loneliness, spiritual wellbeing and the quality of life. *Loneliness: A Sourcebook of Current Theory, Research, and Therapy* 224-237.

Pargament KI, Koenig HG & Perez LM (2000) The many methods of religious coping: Development and initial validation of the RCOPE. *Journal of Clinical Psychology* **56** 510-543.

Pargament KI, Smith BW, Koenig HG & Perez L (1998) Patterns of positive and negative religious coping with major life stressors. *Journal for the Scientific Study of Religion* **37** 71-725.

Puchalski C & Romer AL (2000) Taking a spiritual history allows clinicians to understand patients more fully. *Journal of Palliative Medicine* **3** (1) 129-137.

Wells A & Hackman A (1993) Imagery and core beliefs in health anxiety: Content and origins. *Behavioural and Cognitive Psychotherapy* **21** 265-273.

Chapter 9:
Spiritual crises

By David Lukoff

Spiritual crises are quite common during different stages of the lifespan. In addition, they can be associated with a wide range of spontaneous experiences such as conversion to a new faith, near-death experiences (NDE) and mystical experiences, and also be related to spiritual practices such as yoga and meditation. As more people engage in spiritual practices and leave their religions of family origin to experiment with other religious beliefs and practices, mental health practitioners are likely to see more people in the midst of spiritual crises. Collaboration with religious professionals and spiritual leaders can help clients utilise their faith-based communities and their spiritual practices as resources in their recovery from, and positive integration of, spiritual crises.

Spiritual crises are quite common, and may be the norm rather than the exception for people during different stages of the life span. For example, in one survey, 75% of adults reported experiencing a spiritual struggle at some time in their life (Pargament & Exline, in press). Spiritual struggles have also been reported by people from all demographic groups, diverse religious traditions, and even among atheists (e.g. Sedlar *et al*, 2018). For example, among older adults with depression, 50% reported spiritual struggles (Murphy *et al*, 2016). Yet spiritual crises are potential sources of growth and can be a turning point for personal exploration, discovery and transformation (Desai & Pargament, 2015).

Polls have shown dramatic increases in the number of people who are engaging in spiritual practices, as well as who are using psychedelic substances which can induce such experiences (Yockey *et al*, 2019). Polls have also shown dramatic increases in the number of people who are having spiritual experiences. When the Gallup Poll asked respondents whether they agreed with the statement: "I have had a profound religious experience or awakening that changed the direction of my life" (with slight variations over the years), complete agreement with this statement as applying to themselves increased from 20% in 1962 to 34% in 1978 to 41% in 2002 (Gallup, 2001). The Religious Experience Research Unit at Oxford University in England (Hay, 2006) reported in 1987 that 48% of British citizens claimed they had had a powerful spiritual experience. A follow-up survey (2000) found 60% reporting such experiences. Gallup polls have also found increases in reports of experiences such as NDEs, contact with the dead, extrasensory perception, visions and out-of-body experiences (Gallup & Lindsay, 1999). Other polls have found beliefs in telepathy (54%), clairvoyance (25%), and contact with the dead are quite common (Wahbeh *et al*, 2019).

People in the midst of such experiences have difficulty obtaining support from either the healthcare system or religious organisations: "Both Western religion and science lack the cognitive models and language to describe such states in a nuanced way... with a viable cultural language" (Douglas-Klotz, 2001, p71). Many forms of organised Christianity have eliminated elements of experiential spirituality. Consequentially, "If a member of a typical congregation were to have a profound religious experience, its minister would very likely send him or her to a psychiatrist for medical treatment" (Grof & Grof, 1986). Or they may find themselves considered blasphemous, heretical, or even possessed (Bentall, 2007). In addition, many people undergoing a spiritual crisis have no reference with which to frame their experience. Thus, they may not be able to lucidly communicate what has happened, may fear that others will consider them insane, feel unable to broach this topic with other people in their lives, including clergy, because of guilt, shame, or fear of stigmatising responses. Experiences such as mystical experiences, NDEs, and paranormal experiences appear to challenge our understanding of the world, and have been ignored or pathologised by mainstream psychology. However, they often include spiritual content that people having the experience believe is important. Many who have had NDEs and paranormal experiences report that their lives have been radically altered on a deep, spiritual level. Many also report having developed a heightened reverence for nature and human life, a positive attitude, altruistic value changes, personality transformation, and spiritual development. But they can also be distressing and lead to contact with mental health professionals (Ring & Rosing, 1990).

Spiritual crises and mental healthcare

In 1994, the fourth edition of the *Diagnostic and Statistical Manual of Mental Disorders* (1) included a new V-code (retained in DSM-5), entitled "Religious or Spiritual Problem".

This category can be used when the focus of clinical attention is a religious or spiritual problem. Examples include distressing experiences that involve loss or questioning of faith, problems associated with conversion to a new faith, or questioning of other spiritual values which may not necessarily be related to an organised church or religious institution (p685).

The acceptance of religious and spiritual problems as a new diagnostic category in the DSM is a reflection of increasing sensitivity to spiritual crises in mainstream clinical practice. In the UK, the Spirituality Special Interest group of the Royal College of Psychiatrists and the Transpersonal Section of the British Psychological Society have become leading authorities by providing extensive resources for mental health professionals on spiritual crises.

In this chapter, the terms 'spiritual' and 'religious' are distinguished even though they are overlapping constructs. 'Religion' here refers to an organised belief system, guided by shared values, practices and understandings of the divine, and involvement in a religious community. 'Spirituality' is defined more broadly as an individual's internal sense of connection to something beyond oneself, which could be perceived as a higher power or God, and/or a more general sense of the sacred, consciousness, or interconnectedness to all of nature and life (Mahoney & Shafranske, 2013).

Types religious problems

Particularly for persons whose meaning systems have been strongly shaped by a theistic religious tradition, religious struggles can be related to supernatural beings, such as tension or with disconnection from their God, or to demonic or evil beings. Others may struggle in relationships with congregants and/or leaders within their own tradition. For example, people may feel judged by their family or community because of differences in religious/spiritual beliefs, or they may struggle with injustice or malpractice at the institutional level. The typology below is based on systematic literature reviews and a content analysis of all published articles on religious/spiritual problems in the healthcare and scientific literature between 1987 and 1999 (Lukoff *et al*, 1999).

Loss or questioning of faith

Loss of faith is specifically mentioned in the DSM-IV/DSM-5 definition of religious problems. Loss of faith can involve questioning of a person's whole way of life, purpose for living, and sources of meaning. In addition, a person's social world can be affected, since religion is for many an important part of their social support network. Barra *et al* (1993) conducted a survey and also reviewed anthropological, historical and contemporary perspectives on loss and grief. They found that loss of a sense of religious connectedness frequently resulted in individuals experiencing feelings of anger and resentment, emptiness and despair, sadness and isolation. In addition, the transitions from one stage of spiritual development to another are often experienced as a crisis of faith (Fowler, 1995). A powerful example of the potential impact of loss of faith comes from research conducted by Pargament *et al* (2001) on elderly patients who felt alienated from God, felt they were being punished, or felt abandoned by their church community. Such people were at greater risk of dying (a 19–28% increase) within the next two years, compared with those who had no such religious conflicts.

Changes in religious membership

Due to intermarriage, mobility and the breakdown of geographic limitations to church membership, about half of people in the US convert to new religions or change their denominational membership during their lifetime (Pew, 2008). When people move to a community which does not have a branch of their original religious group, the change may be experienced as forced separation from a previously valued religious community. Conflicts can also occur between the beliefs of a spouse from a different religious background or differences in which one was raised and a new social environment, for example peers at a new school. Nearly one-third of the college students seeking help from university counseling centers report experiencing distress from religious or spiritual problems (Johnson & Hayes, 2003). Wortmann *et al* (2012) also note that, "The college years are a time of many transitions that are often marked by significant losses...[which] may lead to grief, distress, and religious or spiritual concerns" (p303).

Intensification of belief

Another type of religious crisis can occur when a person converts to a new religious identity or intensifies their religious beliefs and adherence to religious practices, especially if their family or friends are not supportive. If the patient is newly religious, the therapist needs to help identify and work on conflicts between the patient's former and current lifestyles, beliefs and attitudes. Spero (1987) described the case of a 16-year-old adolescent from a reform Jewish family who underwent a sudden religious transformation to orthodoxy. The dramatic changes in her life, including long hours studying Jewish texts, avoidance of friends, and conflicts over food at meals, led her parents to schedule an appointment with a psychiatrist who determined that no mental disorder was present. The therapy then dealt with the impact of religious transformation on her identity and family relations. Similarly, conversion to a new religious identity can also disrupt peoples' lives.

New religious movements and cults

New Religious Movements (NRMs) need to be distinguished from socially destructive cults. All religions originally began as cults and were originally perceived as a threat to the status quo. 'New Religious Movement' is the term that sociologists use to refer to new religious groups that are not destructive, whereas 'cult' carries the implication that the group uses intimidation, coercion and indoctrination to systematically recruit, initiate and influence inductees.

But even the assumption that cult involvement is always dysfunctional has been disputed. Galanter (1983) studied members of the Unification Church and found that most members had a high level of distress before conversion. For the vast majority, such "radical religious departures" are part of adolescent or young adult identity exploration, and most ex-members (67%) looked back on their experience as something that made them wiser for the experience. Since over 90% of persons who join cults leave within two years, Post (1993) pointed out that, "if brainwashing goes on, it is extremely ineffective" (p373).

Terminal and life-threatening illness

Although listed here as a religious problem, both religious and spiritual functioning can be disrupted by serious illness. This is particularly true in the case of terminal illnesses that raise fears of physical pain, the unknown aspects of the dying process, and the uncertainty about life after death (Doka & Morgan, 1999). Anger at God, belief that their illness was a punishment for their sins, and discontinuation of religious practices have been reported by people with terminal and life-threatening medical illness as well as mental disorders (Hathaway, 2003). In the US, the Joint Commission on Accreditation of Healthcare Organizations has mandated that spiritual care be a component of hospice care (The Joint Commission, 2007). Many terminal patients return to their childhood religious beliefs and practices, while others search for new forms of spirituality.

Types of spiritual problems

Mystical experience

Mystical experiences represent a fundamental dimension of human existence and are reported across all cultures. Wulff (2000) defined mystical experiences as "Non-ordinary states of conscious awareness leaving strong impressions of having encountered a higher reality" (p397). Scientific investigation of this phenomenon dates back to William James, who maintained that such experiences led to the founding of the world's religions. As described earlier, surveys assessing the incidence of powerful spiritual experiences in the general population show that it has been rising over the past few decades. Most adults in the US and UK report having had such experiences.

Historically, psychological theory has described the mystical experience as symptomatic of ego regression, borderline psychosis, a psychotic episode, and temporal lobe dysfunction. Freud reduced the "oceanic experience" of mystics to "infantile helplessness" and a "regression to primary narcissism" (Lukoff, 1985). However, most clinicians do not currently view mystical experiences as pathological (Allman *et al*, 1992). In a survey, psychologists reported that 4.5% of their clients over the past 12 months brought such an experience into therapy (Lannert, 1991).

Near-death experience

The NDE is a subjective event experienced by persons who come close to death or who confront a potentially fatal situation. Since 1975, when Raymond Moody first focused public attention on the NDE in his book, *Life After Life*, the NDE has been the focus of considerable scientific research. NDEs can be accompanied by intense emotions, difficulties coping in daily life, confusion of inner and outer worlds, trouble sleeping, ego-inflation, a sense of the importance of symbolism and myth, meaningful coincidences, and seeing flashbacks or spirits. Despite generally positive outcomes, significant intrapsychic and interpersonal difficulties frequently arise in the wake of an NDE (Greyson, 2013).

Modern medical technology has resulted in more people experiencing an NDE. Gallup Polls estimated that about 5% of the adult US population have had an NDE, making it a clinically significant and pervasive phenomenon. NDEs are recognised as fairly common occurrences in modern ICUs, as is the need to differentiate between NDEs and ICU psychoses, which can occur as a side-effect of medical treatments (Greyson, 2013).

Paranormal experiences

Paranormal experiences span most of the world's religions and cultures. They include extrasensory occurrences such as:

■ clairvoyance

■ telepathy

■ poltergeist phenomena

■ precognition

■ synchronistic events

■ after-death communications.

Polls show that paranormal experiences are fairly widespread, and the percentage has been increasing. About 75% of Americans hold some form of belief in the paranormal, such as extrasensory perception, ghosts, telepathy, clairvoyance, astrology, communicating with the dead, witches, reincarnation or channeling (Gallup, 2002). Confusion and the fear that "I'm going crazy" are common reactions to spontaneous paranormal experiences. Some people report feeling isolated from others because they are afraid to talk about these experiences with their friends and family (Watt & Tierney, 2013).

Meditation and spiritual practice-related experiences

The National Center for Health Statistics in the US reported that the use of meditation increased more than threefold, from 4.1% in 2012 to 14.2% in 2017, and from 3.1% to 8.4% in children (Clarke *et al*, 2018, p1). Practitioners of yoga have also increased, from 9.5% to 14.3% between 2012 to 2017. Despite the preponderance of health benefits from meditation (Vieten *et al*, 2018), some Western meditation practitioners report anxiety, dissociation, depersonalization, agitation, and distressing muscular tension. Cebolla *et al*, (2017) surveyed 342 individuals who practiced meditation. They found that 25.4% of the participants reported experiencing unwanted effects of varying degrees of severity including anxiety, panic attacks, physical pain, depersonalisation, symptoms of depression, and dizziness. However, most of these unwanted effects did not last long and were not severe enough to require psychological intervention.

Kundalini awakening is a well-documented outcome from intensive yoga practice and can involve considerable distress (Hoffman, 2013). Qigong has also been associated with a cultural syndrome involving transient psychotic-like episodes recognised in Chinese medicine as "qigong psychosis" (Shan, 2000). People who use books, DVDs and online videos to practice on their own without the supervision of a knowledgeable teacher may be at a higher risk for such practice-related problems.

Possession

In possession states, a person enters an altered state of consciousness and feels taken over by a spirit, power, deity, or other person, who assumes control over his or her mind and body. Generally, the person has no recall of these experiences in the waking state. The deliberate induction of possession states has been part of valued religious rituals in many cultures and throughout human history, including in many ancient cultures such as Egypt and Greece, and also appears in early Christianity. Many contemporary forms of evangelical Christianity consider it desirable to be possessed by the Holy Spirit, with physical manifestations that include shaking and speaking in tongues.

The DSM-5 notes that possession can also be normative behaviour in many cultures, and not meet criteria for dissociative identity disorder. A report of possession experiences can lead to an inappropriate diagnosis of a dissociative or psychotic disorder, particularly among members of immigrant groups. More than half (57%) of Latinos in the US believe that people can be possessed by spirits (Ramos *et al*, 2017). Interaction with spirits of various kinds is also seen in some New Age spiritualities as well as references to the supernatural, superstition, magic and voices of dead people.

What helps people having spiritual crises?

'Religious and spiritual struggle' is a term used in research that overlaps with religious and spiritual problems. Religious/spiritual struggles, defined as expressions of conflict, question and doubt regarding matters of faith, deities and religious relationships, have been linked with depression, paranoid ideation, somatisation, anxiety, post-traumatic stress disorder (PTSD), suicidal ideation, social isolation, and lower life satisfaction, as well as immune system declines, slower rehabilitation from disease, and declines in emotional and physical health, and higher mortality (Exline, 2013).

Individuals in the midst of intense religious and spiritual experiences have been hospitalised and medicated when less restrictive interventions could have been used (Lukoff, 2007). Spiritual crises should be approached using the same clinical skills that are applied to other problems, including attitudes of openness and tolerance, respect for diversity, self-awareness, sensitivity and genuineness. The foundational skill in dealing with the spiritual crises of clients from different backgrounds and belief systems is being at ease and open to discussing and collaboratively exploring religious/spiritual topics regardless of how they align with the clinician's personal worldview. Clients who experience their therapist as having an open stance reported better outcomes and a stronger therapeutic alliance and are more likely to share religious/spiritual problems when they experience their practitioner as culturally humble (Vieten & Lukoff, 2021).

Conducting a spiritual assessment is a way to obtain information on a client's religious/spiritual background, beliefs, practices and experiences that can be helpful in determining the appropriate interventions that a client would benefit from. Since 1999, a spiritual assessment documented in each patient's chart is a requirement in over 26,000 healthcare organisations accredited by the Joint Commission in the US. The author developed – and for 30 years has taught mental health professionals – a spiritual assessment interview that covers clients' spiritual strengths, beliefs and practices, and also addresses spiritual problems (Vieten & Lukoff, 2021). More specific knowledge may be required that necessitates collaboration with clergy or other religious professionals to determine whether a client's symptoms are normative within a particular religious tradition or are signs of serious mental disorders.

In an online survey of 245 people who had self-assessed themselves as having had a spiritually transformative experience (STE) (defined as a discrete experience of an altered state of consciousness that brings about a profound transformation in the spiritual identity and life expression of the experiencer), participants rated how helpful 84 practices, habits and behaviours were to coping with and integrating their STE (Brook, 2019). Twelve practices were rated by all participants as essential (4.0 in a Likert scale of 1-4) including (a) practicing compassion, humility, forgiveness, honesty and gratitude; (b) practicing self-awareness and exploring the unconscious; and (c) supportive practices such as finding serene environments, reading spiritual literature, praying and sharing with another person. Another key finding was that psychiatric care and medication were usually not helpful by persons integrating STEs.

In working with clients who have paranormal or other distressing spiritual experiences, Hastings (1983) suggested that, "The focus of this counseling should be to assist the person toward balance, integration, and judgment relating to apparent or genuine parapsychological experience" (p143).

He described seven steps for working with someone who has had such experiences:

1. Ask the person to describe the experience or events.
2. Listen fully and carefully, without judging.
3. Reassure the person that the experience is not 'crazy' or 'insane'.
4. Identify or label the type of event.
5. Give information about what is known about this type of event.
6. Where possible, develop reality tests to discover if the event is genuine or if there are non-psychic alternative explanations.

Treatment for people having problematic possession episodes should include social integration of the experience within their community and collaboration with the leaders of that patient's religious community. This may require a posture of cultural humility in which the healthcare professional seeks to understand the nature of the possession in a curious and respectful manner (Griffith, 2010). Some clinical programs have been developed for people experiencing spiritual struggles which make use of interventions such as naming and normalising spiritual struggles, addressing struggle-related stigma and shame, finding support for spiritual struggles, reframing spiritual struggles in a more hopeful context, and making meaning out of spiritual struggles, e.g., spiritual struggles among older trauma survivors (Bowland *et al*, 2012), clients with both a major depressive disorder and a medical illness (Pearce & Koenig, 2016), and child survivors of slavery in Haiti (Wang *et al*, 2016). Studies on the effectiveness of these interventions have been generally positive.

Conclusion

With increased participation in spiritual practices such as meditation and yoga, the incidence of spiritual crises associated with these practices is likely to increase. Also, it can be expected that the incidence of spiritual crises seen in treatment is likely to increase as more people leave their religions of family origin and experiment with other religious forms. Collaboration with religious professionals and spiritual leaders can help clients utilise their faith-based communities and their spiritual practices as resources that provide social support to promote sustained recovery.

References

American Psychiatric Association (1994) *Diagnostic and statistical manual of mental disorders (4th ed.).* Washington, DC: Author.

Brook MG (2019) Struggles reported integrating intense spiritual experiences: Results from a survey using the Integration of Spiritually Transformative Experiences Inventory. *Psychology of Religion and Spirituality.*

Cardeña E, Lynn SJ & Krippner S (Eds) (2012). V*arieties of Anomalous Experience: Examining the scientific evidence.* American Psychological Association.

Pearce MJ & Koenig HG (2016) Spiritual struggles and religious cognitive behavioural therapy: A randomized clinical trial in those with depression and chronic illness. *Journal of Psychology and Theology* **44** (1) 3-15.

Pew Research Center (2008) *U.S. Religious Landscape Survey.* New York, NY: Pew Forum on Religion & Public Life.

Ramos AI, Woodberry RD & Ellison CG (2017) The contexts of conversion among US Latinos. *Sociology of Religion* **78** (2) pp. 19-145.

Sedlar AE, Stauner N, Pargament KI, Exline JJ, Grubbs JB & Bradley DF (2018) Spiritual struggles among atheists: Links to psychological distress and well-being. *Religions* **9** (8) 242.

Spero MH (1987) Identity and individuality in the nouveau-religious patient: Theoretical and clinical aspects. *Psychiatry* **50** 55-71.

Vieten C, Wahbeh H, Cahn BR, MacLean K, Estrada M, Mills P, Murphy M, Shapiro S, Radin D, Josipovic Z & Presti DE (2018) Future directions in meditation research: Recommendations for expanding the field of contemplative science. *PloS one* **13** (11) p.e0205740.

Wortmann JH, Park CL & Edmondson D (2012) Spiritual struggle and adjustment to loss in college students: Moderation by denomination. *International Journal for the Psychology of Religion* **22** (4) pp.303-320.

Chapter 10:

Therapy for the whole person: integrating spirituality within therapy

By Hilary Garraway and Sara Betteridge

Chapter summary

This chapter begins with some introductory thoughts and in particular encourages us to reflect on our own spirituality and how this might impact on the therapy we offer. We then explore two main approaches to working with the whole person – firstly incorporating spirituality within cognitive behaviour therapy (CBT), and in particular using Holistic CBT, and secondly offering a case study in which the psychologist and client share an Islamic faith.

Introduction

"An holistic approach to the patient, which takes account of their physical, cultural, social, mental and spiritual needs, would seem to have a particular significance within mental health services. Spirituality and an individual's religion or beliefs are increasingly acknowledged as playing an important role in the overall healing process. Most religions have developed symbols and analogies as a way of interpreting and coping with life events, and these are seen as tools that might be integrated into the medical healing process."
(Department of Health, 2009)

Despite this recommendation within an NHS publication and significant research to support it (e.g. Koenig, 2001), most mental health services still have some way to go in order to provide a holistic approach that acknowledges spirituality. If we are, as the above quote suggests, to have a bio-cultural-psycho-social-spiritual approach, then one of the most effective ways to do this is ensuring that the assessment covers all these areas. As we explored in Chapter 8 on assessing spirituality, this can produce a range of information which can then be integrated into the therapy. For example, if clients have spiritual practices which they find helpful then these can be encouraged to enhance their wellbeing. Likewise, a client may need the therapeutic space to explore difficult questions about their values or their life's direction, particularly if these lead to conflict with their family or faith group and they need a neutral space to voice these issues. Working with a holistic model can be particularly helpful when mental health services have, for example, diagnosed a person with psychosis but the client sees their unusual experiences as a spiritual crisis. By mental health services acknowledging that a client's experiences have a spiritual dimension alongside a biological and psychological dimension, this can move the either/or discussion to a both/and discussion. This can sometimes help the client to engage with psychological and medical input while still holding a spiritual understanding of their experiences.

As with any issue that is addressed within therapy, it is important to first reflect on our own biases or assumptions, which may cloud our perceptions and shape our responses. Hodge (2004) warned of religious counter transference in which our own spirituality has an effect on clients. He suggested that this may be particularly strong when therapists have left a particular religion leading to significant biases against a client from a similar faith background. As we consider exploring a client's spirituality within therapy, it may be helpful to reflect on the following questions in terms of your own spirituality.

- How would I describe my spirituality?

- Have I ever had any religious affiliation?

- Have I had experiences that I would describe as spiritual? If so, what are these and how would I describe them?

- What would I list as my five core values in life?

- In what ways has my spirituality helped me?

- Has there been anything unhelpful about my spiritual journey or experiences?

- Do I have any spiritual practices, and if so, what are these? Is there something I could do to deepen my spirituality?

- Does my spirituality influence how I understand and formulate issues with clients? If so, in what ways?

- In what ways does my spirituality affect how I relate to clients or how I practice as a therapist?

- In what ways does it shape my language at work?
- Are there any spiritual issues that a client may raise which I would find difficult to explore? Why?

Various schools of psychology have offered ways to approach the spiritual dimension of our being. Jung's analytic approach (Jung,1933) uses imagery and symbolism and encourages people to reach levels of personal growth and transcendence, recognising a spiritual purpose in life. Jung's work, alongside that of psychologists such as Abraham Maslow and William James, set the foundations for what is now known as transpersonal psychology. This field of psychology acknowledges the transpersonal aspect of life such as spiritual experiences and exploring higher levels of consciousness, and seeks to integrate ancient wisdom from faith traditions within psychology. This has offered approaches such as Psychosynthesis (Assagioli, 1965) and Integral psychology (Wilber, 1994) and various other transpersonal approaches which recognise a mind-body-spirit interconnection as well as a connection with the divine or something greater than ourselves. The transpersonal psychotherapist, John Rowan, described transpersonal approaches as those which:

'...*emphasize the spiritual centre in people; the direction of the person, the higher potentials of the person, the deeper perspective given by a sense of the divine... to do with the higher unconscious as distinct from the lower unconscious.*' (Rowan, 2005)

Developments in positive psychology have also opened up possibilities to integrate spirituality within therapy. For example, the concept of post-traumatic growth (Tedeschi & Calhoun, 1995) can be used to identify a client's spiritual resources, helping people to find meaning following traumatic events. Positive psychology has introduced a more strengths-based approach, such as encouraging people to identify character strengths and virtues such as forgiveness, spirituality and gratitude (e.g. Seligman, 2002).

A range of therapeutic groups have also been developed to explore spirituality with clients, particularly with severe and enduring mental health difficulties. For example, an open spiritual issues group in a day hospital that was psychodynamically based gave space for clients to explore their religious backgrounds and spiritual beliefs (Kehoe, 1998). Another example is a semi-structured group for community mental health clients which explored a different topic each week and looked at individual spiritual journeys, spiritual resources, spiritual strivings, spiritual struggles, forgiveness and hope (Phillips *et al*, 2002).

Practical considerations can help to acknowledge spirituality such as booking appointments which do not fall on key religious festivals for certain clients, using examples that are culturally and religiously relevant within therapy and being mindful of the language used, adapting it to the client's terminology where possible. If there are particular religious issues coming up in therapy you may wish to seek advice from chaplains or consider doing some joint work with a chaplain or with someone from the client's faith group. There are various online resources and faith-based mental health groups to which you can also signpost clients for more specific help (see the list of useful websites at the end of this chapter). It is also important to remember that the client is the expert of their own spirituality, rather than putting this expectation on yourself as the therapist. For example, if a client relies on their faith as a source of support, then this can be encouraged by asking them to find certain scriptural quotes or prayers to reinforce therapeutic goals or encouraging them to ask their faith community to support them with a particular goal in therapy.

Spirituality within CBT

Historically, CBT was built on behavioural therapy with added ideas from cognitive psychology, which tended to see human functioning as similar to a computer. CBT offered ways to change unhelpful thinking and behaviour in order to address a wide range of mental health difficulties. CBT has further developed to provide a range of approaches under the collective term of 'third wave' approaches (behavioural therapy and then cognitive approaches being the first two waves). These third wave approaches, also known as 'contextual CBT' are less about changing thoughts and more about changing our focus and relationship with these thoughts. These more recent approaches have offered more possibilities to integrate spirituality into CBT.

Perhaps the most significant addition to CBT has been the introduction of mindfulness, which is traditionally a spiritual practice. Mindfulness has its roots in Buddhism but is found in all faith traditions such as centering prayer and related practices within contemplative Christian traditions as well as various Sufi traditions within Islam. This process of non-judgmentally observing thoughts and emotions is a core feature of Mindfulness-based cognitive therapy (Teasdale *et al*, 2000) as well as being a key component of Acceptance and Commitment Therapy (Hayes *et al*, 1999). Mindfulness is explored more fully in Chapter 26 along with another third wave therapy, Compassion Focused Therapy (Gilbert, 2009), which is an evolutionary approach to therapy. Mindfulness is used to help people move into an observer position in order to become less enmeshed in unhelpful thinking and to be able to let thoughts and emotions pass. They are than able to respond in more healthy ways. Dialectical Behaviour Therapy (DBT) offers skills for distress tolerance and emotional regulation and includes mindfulness and prayer within these resources (Linehan, 1999). Along with the third wave approaches already mentioned, DBT encourages clients to be more mindful and respond from a 'wise mind' in order to slow their emotional responses down to respond in less impulsive ways. Acceptance and Commitment Therapy (ACT) offers a similar approach but also explicitly encourages clients to identify their values in order to encourage value-based behaviour so that, despite psychological difficulties, a person can do what is important to them, in line with their values. This can therefore offer the opportunity for clients to talk about values based on their spiritual beliefs and to explore how they can live according to these values. As well as including mindfulness, these approaches also include other aspects of spirituality such as compassion and non-judgmental acceptance.

Traditional CBT has been adapted for different faith traditions such as incorporating Biblical quotes for Christians (e.g. Propst *et al*, 1992; Williams *et al*, 2002) and incorporating verses from the Quran for Muslims (e.g. Azhar & Varma, 2000). There is also adapted CBT for Judaism (e.g. Paradis *et al*, 1996) and for Taoism (Zhang *et al*, 2002). The Center for Spirituality, Theology and Health at Duke University has produced religiously integrated CBT Manuals available online (see Resources at the end of the chapter). Although there is some evidence that these approaches help clients from particular faith backgrounds to engage with the therapy (e.g. Propst *et al*,1992), there is little evidence to suggest that clients need to be matched with therapists of the same religious background (e.g.Hawkins *et al*, 1999). However, what the research suggests is that religious clients prefer working with therapists who recognise the importance of their faith and integrate it into therapy regardless of the therapist's own spirituality (e.g. Post & Wade, 2009). Generic spirituality has been integrated within CBT through adding an existential focus such as spiritually augmented cognitive behaviour therapy (D'Souza & Rodrigo, 2004) which encourages clients to find some form of meaning in life. There is also a three domain model exploring behavioural, cognitive and existential domains, proposed by Rashid Skinner in Waller *et al* (2010).

Holistic CBT

Another way of integrating spirituality within CBT is Holistic CBT (Garraway, 2016; 2021) which adds the concept of the human spirit to the CBT formulation, and could be seen as a transpersonal approach to CBT. Clients are encouraged to reflect on this concept of spirit according to their own faith or spiritual beliefs so that the approach can be used with people of any faith including humanistic and atheist beliefs. In general, the spirit is seen as a source of inner strength, motivation and inherent wisdom which can be a catalyst for change. It is also seen as the potential and essence of the person and the source of a healthier version of self. By incorporating the spirit into the centre of standard CBT maintenance cycles, the unhealthy thoughts and behaviours are seen to be limiting the spirit and hiding the person's potential, whereas the healthy cycles are enabling the spirit to be released and helping the person to move closer to their full potential. These two cycles can be used as a basic Holistic CBT (HCBT) formulation as shown in Figure 10.1: Basic HCBT cycles. In this model, the thinking is divided into the content of the thoughts (automatic thoughts) and the thought processes such as rumination and mindfulness (labelled as 'how I think' in the Figure 10.1)

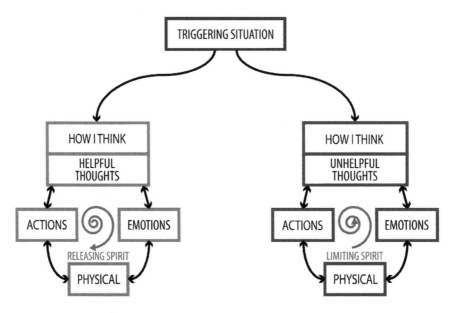

Figure 10.1: Basic HCBT cycles

HCBT also incorporates other factors in order to see the individual within their wider context so that external influences are added to the formulation, such as their physical and socio-economic environment, the different cultures with which they identify and their social networks. The model also includes spiritual influences which means that clients who believe in a spiritual world can incorporate this into the formulation. This may include a belief in a God who cares for them, or beliefs about jinn or evil spirits influencing them or angels protecting them. This leads to the full HCBT formulation showed in Figure 10.2: HCBT formulation

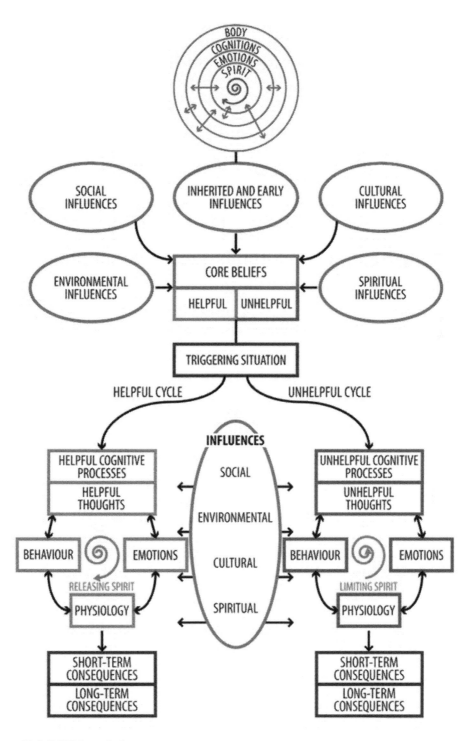

Figure 10.2: HCBT formulation

This HCBT model has been used to form a 16-week personal development course called 'Free to be Me', which systemically takes participants through the different aspects of the HCBT formulation and encourages them to explore their identity and the potential it holds. CBT tools are used to help participants to address unhelpful thinking styles and behaviours which limit this potential and, along with reflective writing, art exercises, considering the body more and ecotherapy, the programme encourages a more holistic approach to CBT. This approach sees spirituality as a key part of life and an important influence on our wellbeing. As a result, it offers a CBT formulation and framework to explore spiritual beliefs and practices. It encourages a reflective and creative approach to help people to identify factors which move them towards their ideal self and factors that move them away. The image of a tree is used throughout the course to represent the human spirit and participants draw a tree diagram which reflects their unique identity. This process helps them to identify resources, characteristics and people which strengthen their true identity, as well as factors such as talents and dreams that grow from their inner spirit.

Islamic case study

The following case study shows another way in which spirituality can be incorporated into therapy and describes a therapeutic intervention by a counselling psychologist working with a client called Sonia. (Her name has been changed to maintain anonymity.)

Sonia is a middle-aged British woman of Pakistani origin. She is married with three children aged 12, eight and six. Sonia presents with severe anxiety and panic attacks that occur on a daily basis – these tend to happen in places where she feels trapped such as the car or a supermarket. A few months prior to coming to therapy, Sonia's husband left the family home saying he could no longer live with her because of her controlling behaviour. Although Sonia knew that things were not good, she was shocked by his actions and it prompted her to seek professional help. It transpired that for most of their relationship she had controlled every detail of their lives, which was dictated by her levels of anxiety. This would include small details such as what they watched on TV, where they went or what they ate, to bigger issues such as allowing her mother and elder brother to have a say in their marriage and their lives.

During the assessment and initial therapy sessions it became clear that underlying her anxiety, Sonia was constantly trapped in a cycle of guilt and anger towards her mother. When her mother would ask her to do something for her, Sonia would obey in the hope of getting her mother's approval because she had been consistently told that to not obey would make her a bad daughter in the eyes of God. However, once Sonia had carried out the task and still experienced criticism from her mother, she would feel incredibly angry and resentful towards her and would withdraw until the next request.

Sonia's parents had a turbulent and violent marriage. She often witnessed her father verbally or physically abusing her mother. During her childhood they went from being financially stable to poor due to her father not being able to manage his business or finances. When the family had been financially stable, they had owned a restaurant, but during this time Sonia was often left alone in the flat above the restaurant at a young and vulnerable age. Sonia describes having a very difficult relationship with her mother who was highly critical of her. She would often put her down, calling her 'fat' and telling her that she wouldn't achieve much, as well as having a lot of emotional and practical control of her life such as controlling her bank account when she was a working adult.

Sonia was clear that her belief in God and her religious practice were key to how she had coped and was continuing to cope with the challenges in her life. She also identified her husband and children as protective factors because they were encouraging and supporting her to get help. However, some of her beliefs were maintaining her guilt and anxiety. In particular, she held a belief that 'saying no' to her mother was a sin in the eyes of God for which she would be punished.

There were a number of aspects to the therapeutic work with Sonia but for the purposes of this chapter we will focus on the ones which combined using her faith to help with the therapeutic process. This took two forms: one was around challenging the view that Sonia could not say no to her mother and the other was in building self-compassion.

It was clear that a major part of Sonia's anxiety presentation was related to her relationship with her mother (whether directly or indirectly). She remained stuck in this cycle because she feared that God would punish her if she did not do as her mother requested. Together, we explored this from an Islamic perspective; we took each of her mother's demands or behaviours and assessed whether they were reasonable or not, and what the impact of carrying them out would be on Sonia's life. For example, Sonia's husband was unhappy in the area they lived and had wanted to move out for many years, Sonia had always refused because her mother had not wanted to move out of the area. We explored this issue in depth, on the one hand Sonia's mother resided with her son (Sonia's brother) and was therefore being taken care of from an Islamic perspective. Also, in Islamic tradition, the wishes of a husband have an equal if not slightly higher importance than those of her mother, providing his wishes are not anti-Islamic or deliberately harmful to anyone. In this particular situation, his wishes needed to be considered because living there was making him very unhappy. Sonia also felt that this was part of the controlling nature of her mother, which continued to build significant amounts of resentment and anger inside her towards her mother. The conclusion Sonia arrived at was that God would not be angry or punish her for moving with her husband because although this would make her mother unhappy, she was being adequately cared for by Sonia's brother and she would still see Sonia and her family. The anger and resentment she was building up towards her mother was having a negative effect on her relationship with God and so reducing this anger could potentially help both her relationship with her mother and with God, as well as helping to repair her relationship with her husband.

Sonia agreed to move with her husband and children a few hours' drive away from her mother. Since doing so, her panic attacks in supermarkets or when walking around in the new town have dramatically reduced. She later reflected that she and her husband felt that this was because she wasn't subconsciously afraid that she was going to bump into her mother and subsequently be criticised by her.

Once Sonia had moved, this allowed us to really explore her relationship with her mother and the impact it had had on her. It was discovered that, not only had it left her with an extremely critical view of herself with low self-esteem, but that it had also left her with a distorted view of her relationship with God. We soon realised that, in order for Sonia to be able to start to build her own self-esteem and self-worth, she needed to understand and believe that God really did love her – imperfections and all. As we unpicked painful stories from her past which fuelled the self-hate, we explored how her mother's behaviour's really left Sonia feeling and we reframed what might have been happening with her mother in that situation. We explored what God might have thought about it as opposed to what her mother told her God was thinking. This slowly started to allow Sonia to see that she needed to be shown compassion in those moments and that she needed to separate her mother's criticism towards her from both her view of herself and God's view of her. For example, just because her mother criticised her for being fat it, a) didn't mean that she was fat and b) it didn't mean that God thought she was fat or bad.

Sonia began to see that, believing that God is not only with her but also loves her and wants her to love herself, allowed her to start the very difficult process of showing herself compassion and love. This took the form of finding Islamic lectures on the loving, kind and compassionate nature of God, finding scripture which also evidenced that and by using prayer to connect with God's love and bringing His loving presence into the therapy room.

This case study shows how the client's presenting problems of anxiety were based on key relationships in her life, including her relationship with God. By exploring her spiritual beliefs within the therapy, this led to more holistic approach and sustained change and illustrates how therapy can be provided for the whole person.

Useful websites

www.spiritualcompetency.com

www.mindandsoulfoundation.org

www.mentalhealth4muslims.com

www.spiritualcrisisnetwork.uk

www.spiritualitymentalhealth.org.uk

www.rcpsych.ac.uk/spirit

www.bbc.co.uk/religion/religions

www.llttfwg.com

www.jamiuk.org

www.spiritualityandhealth.duke.edu/index.php/13-religious-cbt-study

References

Assagioli R (1965) *Psychosynthesis: A collection of basic writings*. New York: The Viking Press.

Azhar & Varma (2000) Mental illness and its treatment in Malaysia. In: Al-Issa Al-Junun Mental illness in the Islamic world. Madison CT International Universities Press.

Department of Health (2009) *Religion or belief A practical guide for the NHS*.

D'Souza & Rodrigo (2004) Spiritually augmented cognitive behavioural therapy. *Australasian Psychiatry* **12**, 2.

Garraway (2016) 'Free to be Me': Introducing an holistic approach to Cognitive Behaviour Therapy *Clinical Psychology Forum*.

Garraway (2021) *Holistic CBT. A Strengths-based Approach Integrating Body, Mind and Spirit within the Wider Context* Pavilion Publishing and Media.

Garraway (2021): *Free to be Me*. A Course Manual to Offer Holistic CBT as a Group or Individual Therapy Pavilion Publishing and Media.

Gilbert (2009) *The compassionate Mind*. London: Constable.

Hawkins *et al* (1999) Secular vs. Christian inpatient CBT programs; Impact on depression and spiritual wellbeing *Journal of psychology and theology* **27** (4) 309-318.

Hayes *et al* (1999) *Acceptance and Commitment Therapy*. London Routledge.

Hodge (2004) Spirituality and people with mental illness; developing spiritual competency in assessment and intervention. **Families in Society 85** (1) 36-44.

Jung (1933) *Modern Man in Search of a Soul*. London: Kegan Paul Trench Trubner.

Kehoe (1998) Religious issues group therapy. *New Directions for Mental Health Services* **80** 40-55.

Koenig, McCullough & Larson (2001) *Handbook of Religion and Health*. Oxford University Press.

Linehan, Kanter, & Comtois (1999) Dialectical behavior therapy for borderline personality disorder: Efficacy, specificity, and cost effectiveness. In: DS Janowsky (Ed.) *Psychotherapy Indications and Outcomes* (p. 93–118).

Paradis CM, Friedman S, Lazar RM, Grubea J (1996) Cognitive behavioral treatment of anxiety disorders in Orthodox Jews. *Cognitive and Behavioral Practice* **3**, 271–288.

Phillips, Lakin and Pargament (2002) Development and Implementation of a Spiritual Issues Psychoeducational Group for those with Serious Mental Illness. *Community Mental Health Journal* **38** (6) 487-495.

Post B & Wade N (2009) Religion and Spirituality in Psychotherapy: A practice-friendly review of research. *Journal of Clinical Psychology* **65** 131-146.

Propst LR, Ostrom R, Watkins P, Dean T & Mashburn D (1992) Comparative efficacy of religious and nonreligious cognitive-behavioral therapy for the treatment of clinical depression in religious individuals. *Journal of Consulting & Clinical psychology* **60** 94-103.

Rowan J (2005) *The Transpersonal: Spirituality in psychotherapy and counselling*. Routledge.

Seligman M (2002) *Authentic Happiness: Using the new positive psychology to realize your potential for lasting fulfillment*. Random House Australia.

Teasdale JD, Segal ZV, Williams JMG, Ridgeway VA, Soulsby JM & Lau MA (2000) Prevention of relapse/recurrence in major depression by mindfulness-based cognitive therapy. *Journal of Consulting and Clinical Psychology* **68** 615–623.

Tedeschi R & Calhoun L (1995) *Trauma & transformation: Growing in the aftermath of suffering*. Sage Publications.

Waller, Trepka, Collerton & Hawkins (2010) Addressing spirituality in CBT. *The Cognitive Behaviour Therapist* **3** 95-106.

Wilber (1994) *Integral Psychology: Consciousness, spirit, psychology, therapy*. Shambhala Publications.

Williams, Richards and Whitton (2002) *I'm Not Supposed to Feel Like This: A Christian approach to depression and anxiety*. Hodder & Stoughton.

Zhang, Young, Lee, Li, Zhang, Xiao, Wei, Feng, Zho &, Chang (2002) Chinese Taoist cognitive psychotherapy in the treatment of generalized anxiety disorder in contemporary China. *Transcultural Psychiatry* **39** 115–129.

Chapter 11:

How faith brought me to a place of some wholeness: an expert by experience perspective

By Jo Hemmingfield

Summary

Faith can be a really important way we understand ourselves, and for some, like me, it is the most important way. These understandings, like those in mental health, can have power to help and heal or, when abused, to oppress and crush. The CHIME model (Leamy, 2011) focuses on Connection, Hope, Identity, Meaning and Empowerment. It is useful to think about how recovery, understood in this way, might connect with common ideas and themes for people from bible-based faith traditions. This will be related to ideas about anxiety and peace. Finally, we will think about the powerful impact of taking formal and informal roles in life and how that can support or undermine our mental health.

This chapter was written in the winter of 2020 and early 2021 during the coronavirus pandemic.

Life and life to the full

Many years ago I used mental health services. I did not appreciate this experience and found it dehumanising, degrading and disempowering. I was medicated, diagnosed and restricted. For the last 16 years I have been working with the Division of Clinical Psychology initially as a service user representative and subsequently as an expert by experience. For the last three years I have been working within the NHS in the same Trust that I was a patient, but in the role of a coproduction consultant. This path has helped me to understand what helps people lead freer, fuller lives, what boxes them in and oppresses them, how we can all be silenced, and some of the things that set us free. It is intriguing to consider concepts from psychology through the lens of faith and notice the commonalities and differences, testing out the usefulness of both.

My journey is one of mental ill health and of recovery – one of faith and life. You will have your own story of challenge and triumph, of joy and despair and hope and hopelessness. This is the story of how spirituality and mental health have woven themselves through my last decades, but also an account of what I have learned about myself, my understanding of faith, the mental health system and church. I've discovered that fullness of life is finding joy in the emptiest of places, knowing inner calmness that goes beyond understanding, and learning to love my fellow humans in all of our frailty, vulnerability, creativity, strength and courage. Humility has been thrust on me as part of my identity as someone who has struggled with my own mental health. Humility, however, comes with a beautiful gift – it is the antidote to arrogance.

Many of us during the pandemic and lockdown have had our worlds shaken. People who have never struggled with distress, have found that things have been taken away from them that has left them worried and in despair. The question of where our hope comes from has never been more relevant.

Pause for reflection

To what extent do you believe and trust in:

- The NHS? Yourself? Science? Your family? The Universe? Your discipline? Nature?
- To what extent do you believe and trust in a divine or supernatural force – someone or something beyond the physical world?
- How do you feel about belief systems different to your own? Do you dismiss some and remain curious about others? What makes the difference?
- What have been difficult and challenging experiences in your life?
- What helps you to live with this? Distraction? Forgetting? Learning and growth?

What is spirituality to me?

My faith is a Christian one, based on the promise of living life to the full. It is based on a belief that the essence of the bible is a message about how I should live my life. As such the aspiration is to love, to forgive, to be generous, avoiding accusations, not to judge others as well as myself. Beyond a way of life or what you might consider a values-based approach there is a connection and a friendship, with a love and a power beyond ourselves who is always working for good.

What is mental health?

However, as we think about spirituality through one particular lens, it is worth considering that mental health is not a single narrative. There are many different perspectives – some at odds with one another. As someone who has used services and worked with professional groups as well as in the NHS, I have had lots of opportunities to understand and witness different practice. Some practice holds the preference and pace of the person using services at the heart of everything. It is beyond patient centred and is person centred. The walk is light of touch and alongside. The relationship between practitioner and service user is temporary and based on a respectful connection between two humans who are both potentially vulnerable as well as potentially resilient. Some leaders in the NHS understand that their staff cannot be super human and celebrate that reality. Other settings are rule based and blaming. When things go wrong, as inevitably they sometimes do in systems of humans working with humans, then fellow workers are severely judged with little space for understanding or compassion.

Historically, the mental health system would ask people what is wrong with them. What are their 'symptoms' and what kind of 'mental illness' they have, in order to find a diagnosis that best fits their presentation. There is debate about the usefulness of this way of thinking. The scientific validity and reliability of diagnostic categories of mental health problems have been challenged (DCP Position Statement). Different practitioners diagnose the same patient with different 'mental illnesses', which leads to an alarming degree of subjectivity. The 'bible' of psychiatry, the *Diagnostic Statistical Manual of Mental Disorders V*, has been questioned and the industrialisation of pharmaceutical companies in the creation of new categories of psychiatric difficulties is questionable at best.

There has been a transformation in understanding that we can no longer divide people into those who use services and those who run services; the 'mentally normal' and the 'mentally troubled', the 'noble us' and the 'troubled them'. Now we can embrace an understanding where all of us face challenges and difficulties. Suffering and loss are experiences that are part of being human. Some of us have more privileges and resources available to us to support us when these challenges come. Be that as it may, experiencing loss is an inevitable part of all of our human experience, as is the challenge of healing, growing and starting again.

> **Pause for reflection**
>
> ■ What have been your experiences of organised faith systems or religions?
> ■ What have you liked and connected with?
> ■ What have you wondered and been curious about?
> ■ What have you disliked?
> ■ What have been your experiences of loss and suffering?
> ■ What has helped you cope with these?

What is the relevance of spirituality to mental health? CHIME Recovery factors

The Recovery Movement, with its emphasis on 'Nothing about us, without us' (Mental Health Strategy, 2011) and its message of hope has been a crucial shift in mental health care. Many senior clinicians today were trained at a time when people who were labelled as suffering from a psychiatric disorder had to expect that they would lead a limited life. Psychiatric patients could no longer expect to live a full and free life but would live with the fear of relapse just around the corner. Monitoring our every thought and mood for signs of something outside of whatever 'normal' is, we were considered 'other'.

CHIME, with its factors of Connection, Hope, Identity, Meaning and Empowerment, is a model of recovery that connects well with my spiritual journey. There are both strengths and limitations in understanding from a psychological or a spiritual standpoint and it is interesting to consider helpful overlaps as well as points of difference.

Connection – with ourselves, one another and with all life

Connection is with ourselves, one another, life around us and with all things – the planet and maybe even beyond. This can be being aware of the presence of energy and spirit in all life around us, in every breath we take, every beat of our hearts, every step and every decision. Within my faith tradition this spirit and the energy they bring is the Holy Ghost, or Holy Spirit. Many people report that sense of life, energy and spirit within as really heightened when experiencing what the mental health system would describe as crisis and what doctors used to call a spiritual crisis.

The sense of love and joining together can be within nourishing relationships in families, communities and even sometimes workplaces. It might be experienced fleetingly while dancing in a nightclub or at a festival, or joining with others in an online game.

With all life and all things, there is this potential for the joy of connecting with life. This can be from growing plants, to learning to understand our pets, the sensation of the wind and rain and the temperature of the world. The distinct sound of different leaves in the tops of different trees on a windy day. The experience of stillness and solitude in a public park, leaning against a discreet tree after a day of 'toxic hurry', where stillness and solitude don't feel a right. How taking oneself out of our own mental world then leads, almost mysteriously, to an awareness of physical self, and a divinity and connection that is beyond us.

Connection with our fellow human beings can be wonderful and complicated. Sometimes we bring one another joy, and sometimes we can cause each other pain. The ability to forgive when we are hurt or to forgive ourselves when we have been petty or cruel, is a way of letting go of bitterness. This does not mean that we have to trust those who have hurt us, unless we are sure they are truly sorry and have changed.

Hope: possibility of change and a different life

Hope has been really important to me. I am fortunate in that I have always had hope that things could get better. Noting progress, remembering how life, sometimes miraculously, has changed, and counting blessings helps to hold onto hope. From a spiritual perspective in the Christian tradition, we 'live by faith and not by sight' and know that there are plans to help us prosper and not to harm us, plans to give us a hope and a future.

The idea is that, although your circumstances can look grim, and objectively it can seem that there is no way out or no pathway to a good life, an all powerful God's intentions towards us are good, that all we need to do is ask and he will help. This is alongside the belief that he is all powerful and all loving, beyond my wildest imagination. But remembering all that and living it out is a whole different matter. However the journey can be a really liberating place to be.

Identity: who are we?

Being given a diagnosis, like that of bipolar disorder, can lead to many questions about your identity. Things that could have been taken for granted may no longer be. Enthusiasm and passions can be written off as mood swings. Thoughts and feelings are no longer to be trusted and are simply symptoms. If thoughts and feelings cannot be trusted, then what does it say about identity? What about anger? Is there any place to be angry?

Who we are is really important and this can be a challenge to mental health. Some therapeutic perspectives are underpinned by an evolutionary account of how we got here. The message that this brings is that we are all an accident of chance and unimportant. Are we to think that those of us who have been described as having a 'severe and enduring mental health condition' are simply broken, and as many of us have been told, to lower our aspirations? Any ambitions are considered 'delusions of grandeur'. The 'A disorder4everyone' (2021) movement is one important attempt to consider the usefulness of historical ways of defining mental health.

A spiritual understanding of identity is much more positive, as is being deeply connected to the divine. This deep connection is described as an adopted child, chosen, as a sister and friend. The Holy Spirit lives in me and I in him. There is nothing special about any one of us in this regard. This friendship and close connection is freely and equally available to anyone. We are all forgiven and a fresh slate is available to all of us at any time. The idea of grace is that we are able to receive all of these advantages without deserving it. It is not possible to earn this clean slate by doing good things, but it is only because of the generosity of God. Grace really helps to take the pressure off.

Meaning: purpose in every moment

When people recover from a mental health crisis, they can be left in a very empty place. The expectations that they had had about their lives are often taken away. Some people report having been specifically told to lower their aspirations and ambitions. It is true that striving at another person's pace can be counterproductive and ultimately dispiriting, which can be experienced as depression. Learning to choose our own goals and set our own pace is an important aspect of knowing oneself that can support future growth. "You're not recovering quickly enough" can never be a helpful message.

Seeing less purpose and meaning in life can be a difficult place to be. A bible-based faith tradition believes that all of us are created for a purpose. That purpose is to live in the way of love, forgiveness and grace, and to invite others to do the same. Other understandings conceptualise human existence as accidental. There are opportunities to value yourself, based on being created and chosen, rather than being an accident or a mistake that can support recovery.

It is easy to run into difficulties based on what we consider to be meaningful. If we only value people in 'important' professions – doctors, lawyers, teachers. If we only 'see' people whose relationship status is married, who have managed to produce beautiful, well-behaved and talented children. If we privilege white perspectives, the male narrative and graduates ahead of all others, and do that unquestioningly, then it is easy to feel discounted and unimportant.

If we only value celebrity status or academic titles, then it is easy for any of us to feel unimportant or irrelevant. If instead we value every interaction, we see each moment as a chance to nurture ourselves and others, and see that we have many opportunities every day to lift ourselves up and those around us, it is much easier to start to build a life of purpose. When we value every person and their views and perspectives as equal citizens and members of the wider community, then this is a different story.

Empowerment: structural oppression and personal liberation

The notion of empowerment in itself is an interesting one as it relates to mental health. We can all have oppressive experiences in life. Some groups, due to structural inequalities and associated stereotypes can often be perceived as 'less than'. The structures in the mental health system and faith groups can perpetuate this oppression and be complicit in creating pressures and stress that can disempower and aggravate mental health problems.

In the UK, it is easy for someone who is white, educated and (sort of) middle class, like me, to think that there are enough opportunities for any citizen to make a living and enjoy life. This is far from the truth, but unless you have experienced being a member of a disadvantaged group, these structural disadvantages can be invisible or seem negligible.

There has been the recent spotlight shone on brutal ill-treatment of citizens in the US by authorities tasked with keeping people safe, a notable case being George Floyd, who was murdered in full view of the world at the hands of police who had their knee on his neck despite his pleas that he could not breathe and for his mum. The shockwaves ricocheted across the world. The pandemic had created circumstances which we had fewer distractions and it was harder to turn away – the world responded with compassion.

Racism is everywhere and all our structures evolved within a racist society that systematically disadvantages those who are black and brown. As a white woman, this is not something that I have personally experienced, although I have experienced stigma due to having a history of a mental health problems. People of colour have had particularly oppressive experiences at the hands of the mental health system – prejudice and misunderstandings further deepening mistrust between BAME communities and an NHS that has the values and culture of middle-class white people.

Church leadership also is still primarily white and male. The role of women is rarely discussed. Churches that welcome people from the LGBT+ community are exceptions to the norm. The bible esteems all people as equal before God, but the church esteems some above others, and when people arrive whose faces do not fit, it is too easy for them to get lost in this lack of clarity.

Those in important roles in our lives can either encourage us to dream of fuller lives, or they can ask us who we think we are to dream? We all can take important roles in relation to others and there is always the challenge of how we use this power. When encountering the mental health system, we trust it, when we are at our most vulnerable, to treat us well. When we enter a church, we expect the culture and values to reflect those of love and acceptance found in the way Jesus lived. When we have the powerful roles of parents, older siblings, teachers, nurses, therapists, doctors, lawyers, academics – do we lift those up around us, support, nurture and encourage plans for a better life, or do we discourage, tell people their face doesn't fit and respond with micro-aggressions? We can choose to support one another or undermine one another's wellbeing. Do we silence one another, alluding to race or mental health as reasons people should lower their expectations in life? Are some of us receiving coaching, mentoring and supervision whilst others receive treatment? How do we ensure that all aspects of worship, teaching in faith groups, leadership and mental health care reflect all of us and our concerns throughout all our lives, not just some of us.

Pause for reflection

- In what ways can faith be liberating?
- In what ways can the mental health system be liberating?
- In what ways can faith and faith groups oppress?
- In what ways can the mental health system oppress?
- How can we support one another to live free and full lives by capitalising on the best of both?

Recovery, discovery or transformation

The CHIME recovery model has some interesting perspectives that map well onto key ideas in a Christian tradition. For some, the process can be understood more as discovery or even transformation rather than recovery. A new way of being is created through learning and growing. In addition to the CHIME model, it is useful to consider the relationship between anxiety and peace as seen through the lens of biblical teaching.

Anxiety and calm, fear and peace

There is a lot of anxiety and fear for the future right now in relation to the impact of Covid and lockdown on all of our mental health and the economy. There is a fear of a mental health surge and widespread reports of hopelessness. The bible says lots about anxiety, worry and fear. The message "do not be afraid because I am with you" mitigates against fear and anxiety. The bible promises a peace that surpasses all understanding, which sounds incredible. In practice, this calmness of spirit is attained by surrendering anything that we feel guilt for from the past and anything that causes us shame. Forgiveness and healing can then be received, which come with the gift of calmness. In addition, anything that we might worry, be anxious about or be afraid for in the future can (with wisdom about any action we might need to take) be surrendered. Once this is done, then maintaining peace is through noticing when this state changes, through what might be considered your conscience and taking this in prayer, where, in relationship with the Holy Spirit, it is possible to understand where these fluctuations come from. This leads to the process of forgiveness, healing and trusting. There is a liberation that allows us to live fully in the present moment.

From words in the bible to transformation in our lives

It is one thing knowing what the bible says but how does this become a reality if you are not really feeling it. Some churches advise people to collect verses that are meaningful to them and read them frequently or speak them over themselves. The words that are written in the bible are considered to be different from other words and "sharp as a surgeon's scalpel, cutting through everything, whether doubt or defence".

In conclusion

The faith walk, at its best, is one of invitation and choice. The ways in which faith is organised can make it a place of common purpose, family and community. Essentially, it seems that some of the aims of the faith life and the mental health system could be a shared goal – to support one another to live as full and free a life as possible within systems where we are alert to unhelpful 'othering', inequalities and discrimination. It could be that, by mental health practitioners understanding the aspects of faith that line up with potential aims of the mental health system, they could both align and work together for everyone's good.

References

adisorder4everyone (2021) *A Disorder for Everyone* [online]. Available at: http://www.adisorder4everyone.com (accessed July 2021).

British Psychological Society (2013) *Classification of behaviour and experience in relation to functional psychiatric diagnoses: Time for a paradigm shift*. DCP Position Statement [online]. Available at: www.bps.org.uk/sites/www.bps.org.uk/files/Member%20Networks/Divisions/DCP/Classification%20of%20behaviour%20and%20experience%20in%20relation%20to%20functional%20psychiatric%20diagnoses.pdf (accessed July 2021).

HM Government (2011) *No health without mental health: A cross-government mental health outcomes strategy for people of all ages* [online]. Available at: https://assets.publishing.service.gov.uk/government/uploads/system/uploads/attachment_data/file/213761/dh_124058.pdf (accessed July 2021).

Leamy M, Bird V, Le Boutillier C, Williams J & Slade M (2011) Conceptual framework for personal recovery in mental health: systematic review and narrative synthesis. *The British Journal of Psychiatry* **199** pp445-452.

Chapter 12:
Spirituality and psychotherapy

By William West

Summary

Spirituality and religion remain an important part of many people's lives in the UK in the 21st Century, having a significant impact on people's physical and mental health. To not consider a client's spirituality as part of their therapy is to miss out what could be either a great asset for the client's wellbeing or possibly a problematic one, or perhaps a mixture of both. In this chapter, besides providing some information on working with spirituality in therapy, I also invite the reader to consider their own relationship with spirituality and faith as a way of making sense of, and being more able to work with, their clients' spirituality.

Introduction

As I write this, we are in the thick of the Covid crisis, which raises existential questions for most, if not all, of us. These are likely to remain active even when the worse of the pandemic is over. For many of us, these issues have a spiritual and for some a distinctly religious element. In the UK, Covid infections and Covid deaths have occurred disproportionately among BAME communities and among working class people. Life as we know it has been, and continues to be, re-envisioned. These challenges inevitably inform our work with clients around faith and spirituality.

When we as therapists first meet a new client, it is important to notice their presence in the therapy room and the impact of their presence on us and what sense we make of that. Part of this will inevitably involve noticing their gender, ethnicity, class, age, sexuality, spiritual and religious beliefs and any possible disabilities. Of course, the therapist is present themselves and will be likewise be noticed by their would-be client. It is surprising how much information clients pick up about us even if not communicated explicitly.

Very few of us are indifferent to spirituality and religion – it has that kind of effect on us. Most, if not all, therapists should be at peace around faith. It is important that we as therapists do not fill all the psychological space that is available in the room. We need to leave the space as empty as possible, intentionally a safe space, in which the client can open up and explore the issues that matter to them.

There is much to absorb and reflect on in this first encounter with a new client; some aspects will be clearer than others, and a deeper truth will likely emerge over time. It will be interesting to note what they share as their reason(s) for seeking therapy and the way in which they express this. It is important for us, as therapists, to reflect on and explore the impact on us, on many levels, of this first encounter with a new client. For me, these encounters are embodied and spirited. By this I mean that I have a visceral engagement with clients. I experience them within my body, within my emotions and within my spirit. The challenge, which never ends, is to make sense of this impact on me and to see how this can be put to the client in the service of their process of therapy.

I remember once meeting a counsellor who was a committed and rather fundamentalist Christian. She told me how she had recently met a married man who she was convinced God wanted her to marry. I was struck, indeed worried, by her lack of doubt, her lack of questioning whether this was true. Her version of faith caused her to believe that it was God's will that she should carry it out, come what may. Meeting her was a one-off encounter at a conference, so I do not know what happened next. (All of the examples I share here have been changed to preserve anonymity, but do reflect real experiences.)

Religion in the UK today

A poll by YouGov carried out in December 2016 in the UK investigating people's religious and spiritual beliefs, found that its respondents replied: I believe in either God or a higher spiritual power 28%; I do not believe in either God or a higher power 38%; I believe in some kind of spiritual power only 20%; I am unsure of my belief regarding either of these 14% (from www.faithsurvey.co.uk/uk-christianity. html accessed September 2020).

In the UK census of 2011, 59.5% defined themselves as Christian, 4.4% as Muslim, 1.3% as Hindu and 25.7% as no religion (Ibid). Of course, identifying as a Christian, Muslim or Hindu does not mean you necessarily attend services. In England, Church of England attendance declined from 1,370,400 in 1980 to 660,000 in 2015; Catholic Church declined from 2,064,000 to 608,000. Most other Christian churches showed a decline apart from New Churches, Orthodox and Pentecostal (Ibid).

Clearly more people define themselves as religious then regularly attend services. Certainly, in the Church of England, congregations are getting, by and large, smaller and older.

What do we mean by religion or spirituality?

My preferred answer is: what do these words mean to you and those you work with? This does not usually seem to satisfy people when they ask me such questions! Common dictionary definitions talk of religion as the framework – buildings, clerics, books, beliefs under which people gather, whilst reserving spirituality for the individual's own beliefs and experiences (also usefully discussed in Harborne, 2008). Many agree, but some do not. I notice that even the words we use to talk about these issues are under challenge and often passionate dispute. These words – 'spirituality' and 'religion' – really matter to many people. I think the polarisation and controversies around religious beliefs in recent years, partially fuelled by social media, has increased this mattering.

It is also worth remembering that religions encompass a range of views among both religious leaders and their congregations. This includes varying interpretations of sacred texts. Although many people of faith remain conservative, there are a number who take a more liberal stand on issues such as gay marriage, LGBT+ issues in general, and sexual and racial equality. For example, the views, practices and theology of Quakers or Unitarians differ from those of the Church of England or the Catholic Church. Within Islam, Sufis occupy a very different place to Sunni or Shia Muslims. Or again, Orthodox Jews are different to United Reform Jews. Of course, there can, and often is, a range of views within any one congregation or faith group.

I once worked with a young Afro-Caribbean man who had just started university. His key issue was a developing realisation that he was gay. It was completely unacceptable to both his family and his Christian Church for him to be gay. Either he accepted his sexuality but received the disapproval and ostracism of his family and faith community, or he rejected it and lived a false life. Either way there would be a great loss involved for him.

A well-prepared therapist needs to have some background knowledge on the major faiths and ethnicities in Britain today. But when working with a client whose faith is important to them, it is crucial to hear their own positioning on faith issues, including any tensions that arise between their individual faith and that of the religion they belong to. It is also most useful to hear how the client makes use of their faith, including what practices such as prayer, contemplation, meditation and yoga they draw on, and how this might sustain them or create difficulties.

I once had a friend who was a fairly devout Buddhist whose partner became pregnant and for various reasons she chose to have an abortion. He was conflicted over this decision but accepted it nonetheless. He had then stopped seeing his Buddhist teacher because he thought he would not approve of the abortion. I challenged this by saying to him that surely compassion was key feature of Buddhism and therefore his teacher would not reject him. This indeed proved to be the case.

I also once worked with a woman once whose Christian faith was very important to her. It became clear to me that she could not forgive herself for what to me was not that big an issue. But to her it was and it had remained unresolved. I gently raised the question of forgiveness; was it not a crucial element in Christianity, featuring in the Lord's Prayer which is used regularly in Christian Church services and in private prayer? I suggested to her that if she had sought forgiveness then surely God would grant it to her. I also advised her that if this remained unresolved for her she could seek forgiveness via her minister.

Attitude of the individual therapist to religious faith

I have been surprised to find out that many therapists are interested in spirituality but less so than in religion. However, there is a significant group whose religious faith is important to them which is perhaps not surprising given that most faiths are committed to good works and that people of faith played a key role in the founding of modern counselling and psychotherapy, and continue to do so. Considering, then, the possible positions adopted by therapists in relation to religious faith:

1. **Religious**: although they may carry their religious faith and belonging lightly, it will nevertheless impact on the values that underpin their work with clients. I would argue that being a person of faith does at some subtle level impact on our clients. In Peter Gubi's (2002) research into the use of prayer in counselling, he found that many counsellors did pray for their clients but were often reluctant to talk about it in their supervision sessions, which I find disturbing as supervision should cover all the important interventions that are used; even those that may not be spoken out loud.

2. **Spiritual but not religious**: as stated earlier, this is quite a common position for people in the UK today – as reflected in the YouGov poll mentioned above. It also reflects my experience of discussing these issues with therapists and trainee therapists. This is what Grace Davie (1994) calls 'believing but not belonging'. Consider the wide popularity of religious practices such as mindfulness, yoga and meditation, which may or may not be taught within a spiritual or religious framework.

3. **Not spiritual**: some people do not get it and do not want it and wonder what the fuss is about! However, I have noticed that people can use non-spiritual language to discuss experiences, meanings and interactions that I and others would regard as 'spiritual'. Sometimes the word 'spiritual' just gets in the way!

4. **Anti religious**: a subset of 'not spiritual', this grouping has been strengthened by the polarisation of opinions for and against religion that has occurred this century, perhaps fed by social media. People in this group will sometimes carry hurt and anger in relation to their experiences of organised religion, which may or may not have been therapeutically processed.

It is worth thinking about which attitude(s) you the reader hold towards spirituality and/or religious faith and the challenges you might then face working with a client who has a differing attitude.

I remember working with a client many years ago who had recently left a rather closed Buddhist community. She was no longer able to be in contact with her fellow Buddhists in that community and was feeling very alone with no friends. It was as if she had fled a religious cult and was suffering the consequences of breaking away. It was clearly the right decision for her to leave that community but also some hard and painful therapeutic work was necessary.

Spirituality in psychotherapy

Table 12.1: Challenges of working with spirituality in therapy			
	Client's issues around spirituality	Spirituality in therapy sessions	Therapist's spirituality
Experience	Can I listen to my client's description of their spiritual experiences in an open, accepting and respectful manner?	Can I allow the apparent loss of boundaries that may be involved, and face the possible fears of both of us?	Can I allow myself to connect in this profoundly spiritual way and face my possible fears and vulnerabilities?
Meaning making	Can I suspend judgement of the meanings my client makes of their spiritual experience?	Can I make sense of such experiences within my therapeutic, or even spiritual frame of reference?	Am I willing to explore what this means to me, and to do the therapeutic work involved?
Values	Can I sit comfortably with the spiritual and religious values of the client, implicit and explicit? Even when they differ widely from my own?	How do such experiences sit within my value system?	Does this change how I approach the therapeutic encounter? And can I embrace this change?

(From West, 2012)

Drawing on this table we can consider spirituality within the therapeutic encounter:

1. **Experiences that people have they refer to as 'spiritual'.** This could well be clients talking about their own experiences of spirituality. This might even include spiritual moments within the therapeutic encounter which either therapist or client, or both, regards as spiritual. These may well be experienced as moments of deep encounter and connectedness in which the separation between client and therapist seems to disappear. (See my discussion below about working with a Sufi client.)

2. **The beliefs that people have in relation to their spirituality.** People who are alive to their spirituality will often have a belief system within which they make sense of these experiences. This is not always so and sometimes spiritual

experiences can shake up our belief systems. There is a history of misdiagnosis of spiritual or religious elements in mental health services. In contrast, there are a number of religious and spiritual understandings including 'dark night of the soul' and 'spiritual emergencies', which do not dismiss such experiences as merely 'psychotic' or 'crazy' (discussed in West, 2000). However, for many people, their mental and physical health is strengthened by their faith. "An increasingly substantial evidence-base that supports the hypothesis that religious belief can sustain health and promote recovery, in both physical and mental health, is emerging" (Gilbert & Parks, 2011, 19).

3. **The value system, explicit or implicit, people have in relation to their spirituality**. There is a value system, morality if you like, that usually underpins people's spirituality. People who are engaged with their spiritual side tend to be more altruistic and more ecologically minded(see Elkins *et al*, 1988; Hay, 1982; discussed in West, 2000). It can be challenging to work with a client who has a very different value system to one's own. I would personally struggle to work with someone who was homophobic or against gay marriage. The important thing is to consider why the client holds such a belief system and what is served by it.

Finally, we need to consider where this all fits in with organised religion or not. As previously stated, many people in the UK today actively explore spirituality and this is not contained within conventional religious groups. This can lead to difficulties, for example when people need support with what they are facing on their spiritual journey.

Once I worked with a man who was a Sufi. He did not initially disclose his faith but it was soon apparent that spirituality was important to him. There were times of extended silence within the therapy sessions that for me had a deep spiritual quality to them, akin to deep meditation, except I stayed alert to his presence in the room rather than going off into a deeper state of consciousness. I found out later that such group spiritual silences were often part of the Sufi experience. I did become worried that my role with this client was shifting away from therapist to spiritual counsellor. I shared my concern with him. He replied that I had not become his spiritual teacher but that he did want a therapist who was accepting of his spiritual side. We wrote together about some aspects of his therapy with me (see chapter 5 in West, 2004).

Access to therapy

Access to therapy is not a level playing field. Men access therapy less than women; working class people access/get referred to therapy less than middle class people; people from BAME communities are less likely to access or be referred for therapy.

I think it is important to state that no therapist has to work with any one client; indeed, there may be very good reasons why this is so. The client and their issues may be outside or beyond the therapist's competence. Or it may be clear from an initial meeting with a would-be client that they need to work with someone from their own faith tradition. In either circumstance, an appropriate referral would be recommended.

Therapists practising in Britain have their work supervised by experienced colleagues on a regular basis. It is important that any therapists working with client issues around spirituality and religion receive effective supervision. Not all supervisors are willing and able to do this.

Conclusion

What I have learnt as a therapist, colleague or friend, when meeting people from differing cultures, ethnicities or faiths, is that if I can approach this other person in a spirit of curiosity then the encounter is much more likely to go well and furnish me with some interesting experiences. I have enjoyed learning yoga within an Indian religion framework; food from differing cultures delight and surprise me; I am intrigued by how differently people live out their spiritual faith. Of course, it is not always pain free to have such encounters and I have had to be aware of my ignorance and lack of awareness in these issues, as well as what privileges are attached to me as a white, educated British man. But it has been worth it, and we live in a multi-cultural, multi-faith world so somehow we have to get our heads, bodies and souls around this reality.

References and further reading

De Botton A (2012) *Religion for Atheists: A non-believer's guide to the uses of religion.* London: Hamish Hamilton.

Davie G (1994) *Religion in Britain since 1945.* Oxford: Blackwell.

Dawkins R (2007) *The God Delusion.* London: Black Swan.

Elkins, D. N., Hedstorm, L. J., Hughes, L. L., Leaf, J. A. and Saunders, C. (1988) Towards a humanistic-phenomenological spirituality, *Journal of Humanistic Psychology*, **28**(4): 5-18.

Gubi P (2002) Practice behind closed doors: challenging the taboo of prayer in mainstream counselling culture. *Journal of Critical Psychology, Counselling and Psychotherapy* **2** (2) 97-104.

Gilbert P & Parkes M (2011) Faith in one city: exploring religion, spirituality and mental wellbeing in urban UK. *Ethnicity and Inequalities in Health and Social Care* **4** (1) 16-27.

Hay, D., (1982) *Exploring inner space: scientists and religious experience*. Harmondsworth: Penguin.

Harborne L (2008) *Working with issues of spirituality, faith or religion, BACP Information Sheet G13*. Lutterworth: British Association for Counselling and Psychotherapy.

Jenkins C (2011) When clients' spirituality is denied in therapy. In W West (Ed) *Exploring Therapy, Spirituality and Healing*. Basingstoke: Palgrave, pp. 28-47.

West W (2000) *Psychotherapy and Spirituality: Crossing the line between therapy and religion*. London: Sage.

West W (2004) *Spiritual Issues in Therapy: Relating experience to practice*. Basingstoke: Palgrave.

West W (2012) Addressing spiritual and religious issues in counselling and psychotherapy. *Thresholds*, Winter, 13-17.

Chapter 13:

Research and spirituality in mental health: generating, interpreting and disseminating evidence

By Wilfred McSherry, Adam Boughey & Alexis Carey

Summary

This chapter explores why research is important to the advancement and integration of spirituality within mental health. A description of the hierarchy of evidence is outlined discussing how quantitative, qualitative and mixed-methods may be used to enhance understanding of spirituality and how this may impact on mental health care. The chapter draws upon three studies undertaken as part of a programme of mixed-methods research evaluating the impact of a 'Chaplains for Wellbeing' (CfW) service. The different phases of this research illustrate how research may be conducted and used to appraise the effectiveness of a service and capture the voice of those accessing care. An overview of the research process is provided and some published examples of research into spirituality and mental health used to illustrate the different stages. The chapter demonstrates that research and spirituality in mental health is a dynamic and ever-evolving field with the unique goal of generating, interpreting and disseminating evidence to enhance care and services.

Broad aims

1. Explore why research is fundamental and essential to the ongoing advancement of spirituality in mental healthcare.

2. Investigate the different approaches that may be used when conducting research within mental health settings.

3. Offer an insight into the steps and stages involved in the research process, highlighting why knowledge of this is crucial to producing high-quality evidence.

Introduction

The field of mental health and spirituality was for several years poorly researched and underdeveloped. Spirituality within the context of mental health has been described as the forgotten and neglected dimension (Swinton, 2001). Perhaps one of the main reasons for this was the prevailing model of mental health services and treatments that existed. For several decades, mental health services had been driven by a greater understanding of pathology with the emphasis on a curative model that shaped the discipline of psychiatry. There is now more of a multidisciplinary approach to the delivery of mental health services. This has provided a space for the spiritual dimension to be explored. This dimension has been considered subjective and contentious but there is now a growing realisation of the potential benefits of engaging with this dimension and offering a more holistic, person-centred and recovery-oriented approach to care. In addition, aspects of this dimension such as religious belief and practice were often mistakenly categorised as contributory factors to some of the mental health classifications. Despite this very chequered and ambivalent history, there is no escaping the importance of research to the advancement of psychiatry and the wider field of mental health and wellbeing. Research, in all its forms and the wider context of evidence, have shaped and will continue to shape the landscape of mental health services internationally. The main outcome of all clinically focused research is to enhance the overall quality of care and ensure this care is informed by the voices of those providing, accessing and utilising mental health services.

Part 1: Generating research evidence

The hierarchy of evidence

■ **Before continuing with this chapter, you may want to pause and reflect upon the different types or approaches to research that you know. If you had to list them in order of importance, what might be first and last on your list?**

As part of your reflection, you may have identified that research can be conducted in many ways and the most important point to consider is whether the methodology and methods used answer the research question or the research helps us to better understand or develop a situation by providing appropriate evidence. The evidence generated as part of a research investigation could be statistical (numerical) or even written, taking the form of narratives perhaps obtained during an interview or capturing a patient story. If we consider this a little more closely, the term 'evidence' could be used to mean any sort of information that supports or does not support a belief, claim or position. In the delivery of mental health services and care, this evidence is often used to support the development of best practice or standards. By its very nature, evidence is not static but rather continually evolving as new insights emerge that inform the development of treatments, therapies and services for those using them.

The term 'hierarchy of evidence' has been used to diagrammatically represent the order of importance of specific designs of research (Burns *et al*, 2011). The diagram most used is that of a pyramid, which classifies at the base the least reliable form of evidence (such as anecdotal opinion-oriented), and at the pinnacle (apex) of the pyramid, the most reliable forms of evidence (Figure 13.1). While this hierarchy may be helpful to distinguish the least reliable from the most reliable designs, it can tell us very little about the quality of the research conducted and the significance of the findings. This hierarchical view of research is also not very representative at expressing the potential contribution that the different research paradigms are at generating evidence. For example, with reference to understanding spirituality, early studies exploring this dimension in healthcare used quantitative approaches such as surveys. While these might provide numerical and statistical data about what practitioners or patients understand by spirituality, such approaches may not be able to fully answer 'why' they hold these beliefs, or how these beliefs may impact upon their mental health and wellbeing.

So, a limitation of adopting a purely quantitative approach when conducting research is that it may not provide us with a rich insight and understanding of the totality of an individual's experience. One important observation about the use of the 'hierarchy of evidence' is that there is no real consistency in how the triangles or pyramids are presented, which can cause confusion and, more crucially, they do not address questions about the patient's experience (Ingham-Broomfield, 2016). Given all the drives to ensure the patient's voice is captured and used to inform the development of mental health service, this would appear to be a significant omission (Murad *et al*, 2016).

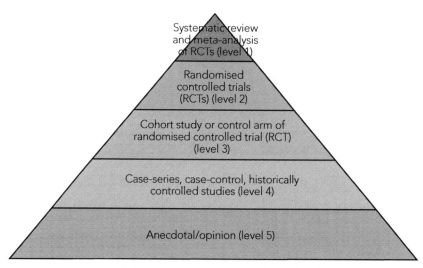

Figure 13.1: Pyramid heuristic of hierarchy of evidence

The authors would like to offer a different interpretation of the triangle used in Figure 13.1. This might be particularly helpful when conducting research into spirituality and mental health which does not really lend itself to a purely quantitative paradigm. The left side could be taken to represent a quantitative approach, while the right side represents a qualitative approach. The base side could represent mixed-methods research. This representation does away with evidence presented as a hierarchy and levels of reliability demonstrating that all research that is conducted ethically and rigorously has the potential to generate important evidence and insights.

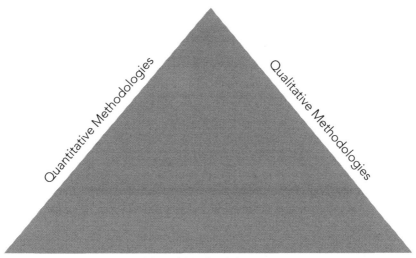

Mixed-Methodologies

Figure 13.2: Reinterpretation of the heuristic of hierarchy of evidence

The hierarchy of evidence may allude to the fact that quantitative approaches to research are more scientific, generalisable and reliable. However, this is an outdated approach to understanding the values and contribution that the different paradigms of research may bring to understanding and advancing spirituality research in mental health. Table 13.1 presents a brief overview of the three main paradigms of research (quantitative, qualitative and mixed-methods) as described in the section above. Having an understanding of these approaches is necessary when appraising or planning to conduct research into spirituality and mental health.

Table 13.1: Research paradigms	
Quantitative	Simply stated, this type of research involves the collecting and analysis of numerical data. This data may be to describe using frequency or percentages. It may be used to test causality, relationships, or associations between groups or treatments, or make predictions about treatment or therapy efficacy. This type of research is typically used when seeking to generalise findings to the wider population. The way to consider quantitative research is that the aim is to make deduction from the findings, thereby accepting or refuting the hypothesis. A vast number of research studies have been undertaken exploring spirituality within the context of mental health. One emerging area of interest in spirituality and mental health research is how we prepare practitioners to deal with this dimension of care.

Qualitative	This type of research may utilise a range of diverse methods to capture, the complex life experiences of participants in natural settings. This may include gathering data through interviews, focus groups, field observations or from documents, diaries, or other artefacts such as drawings, pictures and film. The data gathered is often not numerical in nature.
Mixed-methods	This approach may see the adoption of both quantitative and qualitative paradigms of research within a single study. There may be equal or greater emphasis on one or both paradigms depending upon the nature of the question to be answered. The key point to emphasise in this type of research is the notion of triangulation of data. For example, when exploring understandings of spirituality in mental health one part of the research may involve a survey while the other may utilise one-one interviews with participants to gain a more in-depth picture. The numerical and narrative data from both of these approaches will then be reviewed as a whole to identify commonality and difference.

The need for researching spirituality in mental health

■ **Considering the above section on the hierarchy of evidence, why might research be important to understanding spirituality in mental health? What type of research do you think is required to understand this area of practice?**

Spirituality in mental health is a very broad field of study and application. A look at the Royal College of Psychiatry 'Spirituality and Psychiatry Special Interest Group (SPSIG) (see www.rcpsych.ac.uk/members/special-interest-groups/spirituality) provides a robust justification and explanation for why this dimension is so fundamental to the delivery of high-quality services, treatments and care.

Your response to the question above may have indicated that researching spirituality in mental health is vital for several reasons, such as understanding experiences, testing the efficacy of treatments, developing services and ensuring practice is underpinned by sound evidence. 'Mental health' involves a diverse range of professions, disciplines and agencies providing services and care across many sectors and settings. Spirituality is relevant to all, but how spirituality and spiritual care may manifest or be applied in each context may require different sources of evidence to enhance understanding. Therefore, a one-size approach to research and spirituality in mental health does not fit. You may recall earlier, in the abstract, reference to the use of a mixed-methods approach to evaluating the impact of a 'Chaplains for Wellbeing' service. This will now be the focus of investigation in how research has been conducted that not only links strongly with spirituality and mental health, but also illustrates the importance of mixed-methodological approaches, which, as mentioned, is useful in understanding the richness of the human experience during times of immense challenges to maintaining mental health and wellbeing.

Part 2: Interpreting research evidence

Some examples of research that involve the area of spirituality and mental health

'Chaplains for Wellbeing' (CfW) represented one of several group and individual talking therapies provided in one region in the Midlands (UK) to improve mental health and wellbeing. Uniquely, CfW offered services to all users of the primary/community healthcare Trust and received referrals from general practitioners (GPs), other healthcare professionals, and self-referrals from service users. The evaluation of the CfW service took three phases each with different aims:

1. Phase 1 evaluated *quantitative* changes in patient wellbeing concurrent with chaplaincy interventions, along with the resource implications for the healthcare Trust.

2. Phase 2 *quantitatively and qualitatively* (mixed-methods) captured the experiences of a group of two experienced and three new CfW regarding chaplain training, pressures of their role, and development of resilience.

3. Phase 3 *qualitatively* explored what impact the introduction of the CfW had on the patient experience and perception of health and wellbeing along with identifying extrinsic or intrinsic factors influencing the long-term viability and sustainability of the CfW service.

These three phases can be mapped onto the pyramidal heuristic of the hierarchy of evidence (Figure 13.2). Phase 1 comprised the left side of the triangle (quantitative), whilst phase 2 comprised the left and right (qualitative) side of the triangle (mixed-methods), and phase 3 comprised the right side of the triangle (qualitative). All phases of the evaluation provide a comprehensive approach of mixed methodologies (base of the triangle) which help to address some of the complexities in researching spirituality in mental health.

However, there is some polarisation in how spirituality in mental health might be researched effectively. For instance, Koenig (2008) states that over the years quantitative measures have sought to reflect the trend of measuring spirituality not only in terms of religiosity, but also those considered on the margins of having a religion and those without any religion. Consequently, such measures have become 'contaminated' with questions assessing psychological personality traits and general wellbeing, and as a result Koenig (2008, p349) recommends that, "spirituality should be defined and measured in traditional terms as a unique, uncontaminated construct, or it should be eliminated from use in academic research". In contrast, the influential Mental Health Foundation states that the open nature of spirituality renders it difficult to quantify within the limitations of traditional scientific methods and that in-depth qualitative research can explore deeper meaning and relevance of spirituality for individuals that is not always accessible through questionnaires/surveys (Cornah, 2006). Fundamentally, "a balanced approach to reviewing the literature is required" (Cornah, 2006, p8). Carefully balancing how quantitative and qualitative methods were used to evaluate the CfW service was particularly important, especially because of the complex way that CfW were operating. Specifically, CfW were incorporated into a 'wellbeing hub' and collaborating inter-professionally with other healthcare services to offer a unique blend of whole-person care through employing counselling-type support but also religious and/or spiritual support. Key aspects of each of these phases for the CfW evaluation will be discussed consecutively to highlight the utility of mixed-methodology research into spirituality and mental health.

■ **You might want to make some notes or reflect on what 'mental health' and 'wellbeing' mean to you (and those who you may work with), and how it might be possible to assess mental health and wellbeing.**

Phase 1, including changes in patient wellbeing (Kevern *et al*, 2015a) and resource implications (Kevern *et al*, 2015b), required a quantitative methodology for two reasons. Firstly, given the larger sample size (n = 107), and secondly by ensuring statistical standardisation of measuring mental wellbeing (using the Warwick and Edinburgh Mental Wellbeing Scale [WEMWBS]) (Tennant *et al*, 2007) pre- and post-test to assess changes in health and wellbeing that might have been attributable to the support provided by CfW service.

Phase 2 also featured a quantitative element in the form of a questionnaire that was developed directly from CfW job description items. Three new CfWs completed this questionnaire at three-monthly intervals during their first year of work, and two experienced CfWs completed it once on the assumption that they had arrived at a settled view of the nature and role of CfW. This questionnaire was used to provide data on how CfWs understood their role and the challenges it presented. Although no sophisticated quantitative analysis was possible given the sample size of five CfWs, the Likert-scale responses helped to inform the development of an interview schedule for semi-structured interviews with each CfW. This qualitative element was the main aspect of phase 2 and ascertained aspects of CfW training and support by identifying sources of strength and stressors. Collectively, these qualitative findings provided insights into how CfWs addressed religious and/or spiritual needs in the care of their clients' mental health and wellbeing, which helped to inform considerations for future recruitment and longer-term viability of the service.

As with phase 2, phase 3 (McSherry *et al*, 2016) concentrated on qualitative methodology but with 16 patients. No quantitative elements featured in this phase. Semi-structured interviews used an interview schedule to ensure discussions focused on the impact of the CfW service rather than the interview being an extension of the patient's therapy. However, it was clear that issues of significant loss and destabilisation of the patient's existence had significant impacts on their mental health and wellbeing, and this became a focal point for interviews as the context in which the CfW service supported them through those challenging times.

In phases 2 and 3, smaller samples allowed for deeper investigation into participants' direct/lived experience (phenomenology) of either providing the CfW service, or in receiving support from the service respectively. Two qualitative analyses (thematic analysis [TA] and interpretative phenomenological analysis [IPA]) were used in phases 2 and 3 respectively. Although both analyses are quite similar in terms of process, TA focuses on the identification and analysis of patterns and themes within the data itself (Braun *et al*, 2006), whereas IPA uses a similar approach but also applies a hermeneutic (interpretative) element where lived experience is explored and uncovering intentions in the context of the language used (Smith *et al*, 2009").

The form of chaplaincy had evolved from that first implemented at a single primary care centre in 1997 (Bryson *et al*, 2012), but retaining key aspects in the way a community healthcare chaplain (CHC) worked. Specifically, CHCs (later as CfWs) focused on the importance of "listening, compassionate presence, facilitating the search for meaning, discerning the signs of life [sic], offering appropriate ritual, offering prayer, providing support in death and dying, and pastoral care of staff" (Bryson *et al*, 2012, p20). Prior to the CfW evaluation, the local team of CfWs and general practitioners (GPs) reported for the Professional Association of Community Healthcare Chaplaincy (PACHC, 2011) on the importance of providing whole-person spiritual care in primary care/general practice. It was noted that general practice was considered to be falling behind palliative care and mental healthcare in respect of effective spiritual care provision, which might have been due to significant barriers in general practice such as having insufficient time to address complexities of spiritual care and mental wellbeing, and a narrower focus on the biomedical model of health. From having implemented CHC since 1997, it was clear that this service positively impacted upon patients' physical health, coping, supporting frequent attenders of healthcare services, and those with medically undiagnosed symptoms (PACHC, 2011). Two key aspects of the successes with the CHC role included (1) the better inter-professional collaboration between primary care professionals in recognising the importance of spiritual care in mental health and wellbeing, and (2) having sufficient time to be with patients and their family and carers (of all or no faiths) to feel valued and safe to tell and reflect upon their stories.

- **Considering your own practice in healthcare, academia, or both, please identify any specific barriers and facilitators to implementing effective spiritual care to promote mental health and wellbeing.**

These more qualitatively focused aspects of the effectiveness of CfW providing spiritual care and supporting mental health and wellbeing are crucial, but so too is quantitative data which enables results and conclusions to be confidently extrapolated to the wider population. This is important to clinical commissioners who require assurance that their service provision positively impacts upon the health and wellbeing of the wider population in which the service operates (Robertson *et al*, 2016). Phase 1 reported non-significant differences between the characteristics of the sample and those of the population from which the data was drawn, and therefore results could be confidently extrapolated. The use of a statistically valid and reliable scale such as WEMWBS ensured that results accurately measured the mental wellbeing construct in question (construct validity) and that repeated administration of the scale resulted in stable and consistent results (test-retest reliability and internal consistency). WEMWBS itself was a useful scale as this measured mental wellbeing rather than mental illness, that might overlook changes in a 'healthy' population's mental wellbeing (Steward-Brown *et al*, 2008). Results indicated a statistically significant clinical improvement pre- post-test in patients accessing the CfW service, and that those patients who reported the lowest mental wellbeing pre-intervention also reported the most improvement in their mental wellbeing having received spiritual support from the CfW service.

Qualitative findings from phase 2 indicated the complex ways CfWs were working to provide spiritual support to patients with challenging life situations. CfWs reported on the intensity of the therapeutic work in consulting with "very poorly patients" and navigating the challenges in the "variety, vulnerability, and diversity" of patients' life situations. The intensity of therapy depended on CfWs needing to maintain their own spiritual care and resources by having "spiritual routines, bible study, reflection and prayer, and meditative techniques". As with other healthcare professionals, clinical supervision was "incredibly valuable and a good opportunity to offload". The intensity, maintenance of one's own personal spirituality and seeking supervision illustrated CfWs' personal wellbeing (theme 1). The extent to which CfWs were suitably qualified and experienced for their role linked to theme 2: training and development. Three chaplains were experienced healthcare professionals (e.g., registered nurses, health visitors, midwives, counsellors, or ordained ministers) and this experience was vital preparation for their role as CfWs. However, unlike the generally well-defined roles of their background as healthcare professionals, CfWs suggested that it was challenging to continue to develop the CfW service due to the complexity in quantifying its effectiveness on patients' spiritual wellbeing and mental health. Although the quantification of service effectiveness was challenging (and itself a case for support of the CfW evaluation), it was clear that in theme 3 (interaction with patients and staff), CfWs were using a complex range of therapeutic intervention skills and working in partnership with patients and colleagues to strive for the best possible spiritual care to support mental wellbeing. Being able to demonstrate compassionate presence by "imparting to any one given person that you are interested in who they are, what they are, and what they've brought to you" is crucial in building therapeutic alliances.

Qualitative findings from phase 3 detailed how CfWs developed therapeutic alliances with patients in creating suitable therapeutic environments in which they maintained a professional but also friendly and kind demeanour. It was clear that the theme of 'loss' was pertinent to most patients participating in the CfW evaluation, who had reported on relationship/family breakdown, bereavement, or loss of self-identity. If IPA were not used to interpret patients' narratives, there might have been an overly superficial analysis of the complexity of how 'loss' manifested. Through complex interpretation it became evident that patients experienced a significant spiritual or existential displacement following their loss. For CfWs to have been effective in helping patients to attend to these losses on a psychological, emotional, and spiritual level, required a depth of therapeutic alliance that went beyond counselling-type intervention alone. For example, the exploration of these losses through a spiritual lens assisted patients in readjusting and reengaging in their life situation with newfound meaning and purpose.

- **Consider whether the CfW evaluation might have been conducted differently given what might be important from a research methodological perspective and clinical commissioners.**

Part 3: Disseminating research evidence

From the above discussions you may have sensed that conducting any form of research requires careful preparation if the outcomes and data obtained are to be beneficial to the advancement of spirituality within mental health. Figure 13.3 presents an overview of what has become commonly known as the 'research process' (Lacey, 2013).

■ **In Figure 13.3, consider why each of the eight stages that make up the 'research process' are essential to conducting high quality research.**

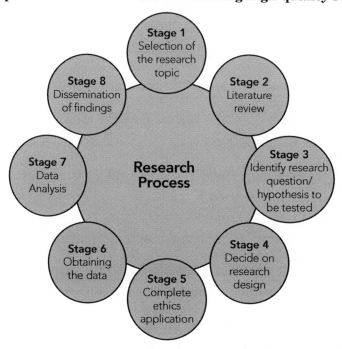

Figure 13.3: The research process

Preparing to undertake clinically focused research:

There are many aims of clinically focused research. For example, enhancing the quality of service provision; influencing changes in patient wellbeing and mental health outcomes; or to lead to practical improvements to policies, procedures and systems. When preparing clinically focused research, it is crucial to first develop an understanding of the topic area through thoughtful and honest dialogue between relevant healthcare professionals involved in the provision of mental healthcare and spiritual care, along with experts in the field and patients to identify how the research would be beneficial to the advancement of spirituality within mental health.

- **Take a moment to consider an area you would be inspired to research. What would be the impact of researching this topic? Could researching this topic area lead to conceptual and attitudinal outcomes by stimulating curiosity and learning or investigating meaning and values? Who would benefit because of this research and how?**

To develop a more detailed understanding of the research topic and develop an argument and justification for the proposed study, undertaking a literature review is imperative. It allows for the extraction and synthesis of key points and findings, and identifies discrepancies, inconsistences and knowledge gaps in the literature.

- **Pause for a moment to reflect on what type of questions a literature review should answer.**

As part of your reflection, you may have uncovered several questions that a literature review might address:

- What is known about the research area?
- What are the relationships between key ideas in the field?
- What are the current theories, empirical findings and/or best clinical practice guidelines?
- What are the significances, inconsistencies and limitations of previous studies?
- What warrants further inquiry because evidence is lacking, inconclusive, conflicting and/or limited?
- What methodological approaches have been utilised and why?
- Are the methodological approaches justified?
- Why does this area of research need to be studied?
- What contribution will your research make to the current knowledge base and impact on the generation of evidence-based practice?

An example of a literature review was carried out by Pesut *et al* (2011) who reviewed the literature on religion and spirituality in relation to bipolar disorder, a mental health condition that can cause episodes of low mood and episodes of over activity and mania. Findings indicated the relevance of religious and spiritual strategies in the management of bipolar disorder for some service users. These authors advocated for the need for longitudinal, prospective, mixed-methods research in order to inform evidence-based practice. This was due to the limited research and methodological shortcomings of some of the existing research, which made it difficult to draw conclusions.

A very rigorous and exhaustive literature review can be considered a *systematic review*. Rather than critically reviewing the literature on a topic area, a systematic review aims to identify all the research on a topic area to ensure no knowledge or understanding is missed. This can be particularly useful when comparing what types of interventions incorporating spirituality in the treatment of mental healthcare are effective. For example, Gonçalves *et al* (2015) undertook a systematic review to identify and assess the impact of religious/spiritual interventions on mental health outcomes through randomised clinical trials (RCTs). They found that religious/spiritual interventions decreased stress, alcoholism and depression. In this review, the diversity of protocols and outcomes associated with a lack of standardisation of interventions pointed to the need for further studies evaluating the use of religiosity/spirituality as a complementary treatment in mental healthcare.

Both reviews highlight the need for more research, particularly longitudinal and prospective studies, into the area of spirituality and mental health. This is due to confounding variables such as differences in samples and changes in mental health and spirituality over time, which make it challenging to understand specific effects of spirituality on mental health. Chatters (2000) highlights that these challenges can be further exacerbated by divergences in how religious/spiritual interventions are conceptualised and methodological aspects utilised by researchers, specifically different measurement tools. Although research on spiritually integrated interventions for mental health are increasing, the available research does not yet provide guidance about "what works best for whom" (Park *et al*, 2017, p231). This highlights the value of continual evolution of new insights or areas requiring further enquiry through review to inform the development of treatments, therapies and services for those utilising them.

Once a review of the literature has been completed and the rationale or reason for a study emerges, it is time to focus on the design of the research. Increasingly, studies in psychiatry, spirituality and religion deal with the necessity of mixing religious teachings, cultural beliefs and convictions related to health in psychotherapeutic strategies to develop wellness within a biopsychosocial model (Aten *et al*, 2009; Pesut *et al*, 2011).

Implementation of clinically focused research:

One of the most fundamental aspects of any type of research is ensuring it is conducted ethically. All research undertaken needs to abide by four key principles: respecting autonomy, maximising benefits, minimising risk, and upholding integrity. Any actual or potential conflicts of interest need to be considered and declared. Ideological and practical considerations can emerge when undertaking research regarding mental health and spirituality. For example, Park *et al* (2017) recommend caution as some researchers can be reluctant to interpret their findings with respect to the spiritual dimensions of meaning-making that capture the beliefs and values of participants being studied. They argue that, in some cases, researchers might be explicitly prejudiced against spiritual beliefs and values that cannot be easily integrated into secular meaning-making, or by a narrower focus on the biomedical model of health. This can lead to the reporting of the benefits of a spiritual dimension in clinical treatment and outcomes being omitted, which clearly has negative implications for evidence-based clinical practice.

Research should be worthwhile and have beneficial effects that outweigh the risks posed by the study. The recipient of the benefit will vary from project to project but may include service development (such as the CfW evaluation), health improvements, and/or the quality of life of participants themselves.

Summary

This chapter has outlined the importance of research to the advancement of spirituality within mental health. It has provided a brief overview of the 'hierarchy of evidence' offering a new way of interpreting that affords a greater degree of equality to all the primary research paradigms. Research has been described as a cyclical process emphasising how each stage requires careful planning and implementation. The CfW evaluation, as a working example of interpreting research evidence, affirms the importance of using both quantitative and qualitative methods. It also reveals the strengths and benefits of utilising mixed-methods research, especially when evaluating the different services offering spiritual and psychological support.

Although research on spiritually integrated interventions for mental health is increasing, the available research does not yet provide guidance about "what works best for whom" (Park *et al*, 2017, p231). Only by conducting rigorous and robust research that is based on sound ethical principles and practices will research evidence be generated to answer such questions. This evidence when disseminated may shed light on the nature of spirituality and the vital role it has in the lives of those receiving and providing care. All forms of research are necessary to ensure that an in-depth insight into how spirituality might impact on mental health is gained. Only then will we be able to ensure that every aspect of mental health services, treatment and care are truly 'holistic' and fundamentally evidence-based.

Suggested reading

Hierarchy of evidence-based practice

Burns PB, Rohrich RJ & Chung KC (2011) The levels of evidence and their role in evidence-based medicine. *Plastic and Reconstructive Surgery* **128** (1) 305-310. doi: 10.1097/PRS.0b013e318219c171

Although orientated to plastic and reconstructive surgery, this journal article provides a useful overview of the history of levels of evidence since the late 1970s, and how those hierarchies of evidence have been modified, evolved, and been interpreted in practice.

For undertaking quantitative research

Clark-Carter D (2004) *Quantitative Psychological Research: A student's handbook* (2nd ed.). Psychology Press.

This book teaches readers a comprehensive range of statistical tools in order to ensure that quantitative research and the analysis of its findings go beyond description towards sound hypothesis formulation and testing.

For undertaking mixed-methods research

Howitt D & Cramer D (2017) *Research methods in psychology* (5th ed). Pearson.

This book provides a comprehensive overview of the entire research process and helpfully starts from the fundamental principles in research before moving onto specifics of the quantitative and qualitative methods. There is an excellent section also on generating ideas for research.

References

Aten JD & Worthington EL (2009) Next steps for clinicians in religious and spiritual therapy: An endpiece. *Journal of Clinical Psychology* **65** (2) 224-229. doi: 10.1002/jclp.20562

Braun V & Clarke V (2006) Using thematic analysis in psychology. *Qualitative Research in Psychology* **3** 77-101. doi: 10.1191/1478088706qp063oa

Bryson PHR, Dawlatly S, Hughes A, Jones D, Sheldon M, Stobert M & Waterson J (2012) *Honouring personhood in patients: The added value of chaplaincy in general practice*. Whole Person Health Trust, England.

Burns PB, Rohrich RJ & Chung KC (2011) The levels of evidence and their role in evidence-based medicine. *Plastic and Reconstructive Surgery* **128** (1) 305-310. doi: 10.1097/PRS.0b013e318219c171

Chatters LM (2000) Religion and health: Public health research and practice. *Annual Review of Public Health* **21** (1) 335-367. doi: 10.1146/annurev.publhealth.21.1.335

Cornah D (2006) *The impact of spirituality on mental health: A review of the literature*. Mental Health Foundation. Retrieved February 25, 2021, from https://www.mentalhealth.org.uk/sites/default/files/impact-spirituality.pdfhttps://www.mentalhealth.org.uk/sites/default/files/impact-spirituality.pdf

Gonçalves JPB, Lucchetti G, Menezes PR & Vallada H (2015) Religious and spiritual interventions in mental health care: A systematic review and meta-analysis of randomized controlled clinical trials. *Psychological Medicine* **45** (14) 2937-2949. doi: 10.1017/S0033291715001166

Ingham-Broomfield R (2016) A nurses' guide to the hierarchy of research designs and evidence. *Australian Journal of Advanced Nursing* **33** (3) 38-43.

Kevern P & Hill L (2015a) 'Chaplains for well-being' in primary care: Analysis of the results of a retrospective study. *Primary Health Care Research Development* **16** (1) 87-99. doi: 10.1017/S1463423613000492

Kevern P & Ladbury I (2015b) Resource implications of a measured change in patient wellbeing: A retrospective cohort analysis study. *The Journal of New Writing in Health and Social Care* **2** (1) 47-54.

Koenig HG (2008) Concerns about measuring "spirituality" in research. *The Journal of Nervous and Mental Disease* **196** (5) 349-355. doi: 10.1097/NMD.0b013e31816ff796

Lacey A (2013) The research process. In: K. Gerrish (Ed.) *The research process in nursing* (pp. 13-26). Wiley-Blackwell.

McSherry W, Boughey A & Kevern P (2016) "Chaplains for Wellbeing" in primary care: A qualitative investigation of their perceived impact for patients' health and wellbeing. *Journal of Health Care Chaplaincy* **22** (4) 151-170. doi: 10.1080/08854726.2016.1184504

Murad HM, Asi N, Alsawas M & Alahdab F (2016) New evidence pyramid. *BMJ Evidence-Based Medicine* **21**, 125-127. doi: 10.1136/ebmed-2016-110401

Park CL, Currier JM, Harris JI & Slattery JM (2017b) *Trauma, Meaning, and Spirituality: Translating research into clinical practice*. American Psychological Association.

Chapter 14:

Spiritual competencies: key ways to address spirituality in mental health care

By Dr Cassandra Vieten

Spirituality and mental health

Hundreds of studies indicate that spiritual and religious backgrounds, beliefs and practices (SRBBPs) are relevant to most people's mental health (Kao *et al*, 2020). Spiritual beliefs influence how people make meaning of (and therefore respond to) everything from getting a flat tire on the freeway, to the unexpected death of a loved one.

Involvement in religious and spiritual (R/S) practices and communities are related to lower depression, anxiety, suicide ideation and attempts, post-traumatic stress disorder and substance abuse, and are also associated with higher purpose in life, hope, optimism and self-esteem (Sharma *et al* 2017; Oman, 2018). Over 60% of mental health clients agree or strongly agree to items such as "Engaging in my religious/spiritual practices [e.g., prayer, religious services, reading religious texts] improves my mental health"; "I consider my religion/spirituality to be relevant to my mental health"; "Relying on my religious/spiritual beliefs helps me to feel mentally healthy"; and "My religious/spiritual beliefs help me to reach my mental health potential" (Oxhandler *et al*, 2021). A survey of 406 mental health service recipients showed that more than 80% relied on spiritual and religious beliefs and behaviors to help them cope with frustrations and daily difficulties (Tepper *et al*, 2001). Another survey of 2,050 individuals receiving mental health services and their family members again found that more than 80% agreed or strongly agreed that spirituality was important to their mental health, with frequent practices including prayer (73%), meditation (47%), reading sacred texts or spiritual self-help books (36%), and attending religious services (40%) (Yamada *et al*, 2019).

People use their SRBBPs to cope with stress and difficult life events experiencing benefits such as self-regulation, positive attachment, emotional comfort and meaning (Pargament & Lomax, 2013). Evidence shows that spiritual and religious coping is prevalent and beneficial for combat veterans (Smith-MacDonald *et al*, 2017), disaster survivors (Aten *et al*, 2019), recovery from interpersonal trauma (Bryant-Davis & Wong, 2013), and multiple mental health and quality of life outcomes (Gall & Guirguis-Younger, 2013).

Spirituality and religion are important aspects of multicultural diversity (Richards & Bergin, 2014), overlapping with race, ethnicity and culture, and intersecting with other elements of diversity such as gender and sexual orientation. Similar to other areas of diversity, persecution and discrimination based on religious or spiritual beliefs are now and have historically been widespread (Hodge, 2019). Biases based on spiritual or religious orientation, or lack thereof, are built into the fabric of our society. Both holding and being the target of such biases, positive and negative, are intertwined with people's mental health.

Mental health professional training

With the prevalence of R/S in the general public, the frequency of use among mental health care patients, and the strength of evidence for the relevance of SRBBPs in mental health, it seems clear that professionals should receive training in how to address R/S ethically and effectively in clinical practice. But in a recent survey, about half of mental health care professionals report receiving little to no training in R/S competencies. Nearly 45% of the sample indicated they had received "none" or "not very much" training in R/S as a form of diversity they might encounter in their clients, and over 50% reported receiving no courses and no information on how to integrate clients' R/S into their clinical practice (Vieten *et al*, manuscript in preparation).

Indeed, professional and training guidelines in each of the mental health professions require that diversity, including religious diversity, must be taken into account when understanding and treating mental health issues. However, the majority of such training focuses on racial, cultural and gender diversity. Counseling and clinical training programs pay inadequate attention to religious and spiritual aspects of diversity in multicultural training (Magaldi-Dopman, 2014; Shafranske, 2016).

Over 70% of psychologists agree that they should receive training in, and be required to demonstrate, spiritual and religious competence (Vieten *et al*, 2016). Across mental health professions, 80% and 96% of clinicians "somewhat" or "very much" agree that professionals should receive training in the 15 competencies, with over 50% "very much" agreeing for all competencies (Vieten *et al*, manuscript in preparation). Another survey of 543 psychology doctoral students indicated that most received no formal training in SRBBPs, and almost universally endorsed the idea that mental health patients should be asked about R/S (Saunders *et al*, 2014). A nationwide survey of social workers likewise shows a strong majority (56% – 98%) hold positive attitudes toward integrating clients' R/S into treatment, but fewer than half actually do so (Oxhandler *et al*, 2015), in part due to lack of training.

Spiritual competencies

To address this gap, our team has developed a set of 15 competencies that we believe all mental health professionals would benefit from receiving training in and being required to demonstrate. In an initial study to develop and assess the feasibility of these competencies, mental health professionals rated a provisional set of competencies on clarity and relative importance, resulting in a proposed set of 16 competencies (three in the area of 'Attitudes', seven in the area of 'Knowledge', and six in the area of 'Skills' (Vieten *et al*, 2013). In a subsequent survey of psychologists, 73% and 94.1% (depending on which of the 16 areas of competency) of respondents agreed that psychologists should receive training and demonstrate competence in these areas and 52.2% - 80.7% of respondents reported receiving "little" or "no" training in these competencies, with 29.7% - 58.6% reporting "no" training at all (Vieten *et al*, 2016). One competency involving staying abreast of the scientific literature on R/S and psychology was removed due to repeated low endorsement suggesting this was too high a bar for basic competence.

Table 14.1 provides a list of these proposed spiritual and religious competencies in order of the strength of endorsement in our most recent survey of 1,269 mental health professionals (mean on a scale of 0-3, standard deviation, and percentage of professionals reporting that they "very much" believe that each competency should be included in training) (Vieten *et al*, manuscript submitted).

Table 14.1			
"Do you believe that mental health care providers should receive explicit training in this area?"	All Participants (n = 1,269)		
	mean	SD	% Very Much
Demonstrating empathy, respect and appreciation for clients from diverse spiritual, religious or secular backgrounds and affiliations.	2.78	0.50	82.10
Being able to conduct empathic and effective psychotherapy with clients from diverse spiritual and/or religious backgrounds, affiliations and levels of involvement.	2.75	0.58	81.40
Being aware of how as clinicians, their own spiritual and/or religious background and beliefs may influence their clinical practice, and their attitudes, perceptions and assumptions about the nature of psychological processes.	2.75	0.59	81.20
Viewing spirituality and religion as important aspects of human diversity, along with factors such as race, ethnicity, sexual orientation, socioeconomic status, disability, gender and age.	2.74	0.58	79.60
Knowing that there are many diverse forms of spirituality and/or religion, and being willing to learn about spiritual and/or religious beliefs, communities and practices that are important to their clients.	2.69	0.61	76.40
Recognising the limits of their qualifications and competence in the spiritual and/or religious domains, including their responses to clients spirituality and/or religion that may interfere with clinical practice, and being willing to 1) seek consultation from and collaborate with other qualified clinicians or spiritual/religious leaders (e.g. priests, pastors, rabbis, imam, spiritual teachers, etc.), 2) seek further training and education, and/or 3) refer appropriate clients to more qualified individuals and resources.	2.63	0.72	74.90
Being able to inquire about spiritual and/or religious background, experience, practices, attitudes and beliefs as a standard part of understanding a client's history.	2.62	0.68	71.70
Being aware of legal and ethical issues related to spirituality and/or religion that may surface when working with clients.	2.50	0.82	66.70

Knowing some ways that spiritual and/or religious beliefs, practices and experiences can develop and change over the lifespan.	2.50	0.77	63.70
Being able to identify spiritual and religious experiences, practices and beliefs that may have the potential to negatively impact mental health.	2.46	0.82	63.90
Being aware of spiritual and/or religious resources and practices that research indicates may support psychological wellbeing, and recovery from psychological disorders.	2.46	0.80	62.20
Being able to describe ways that clients may have experiences that are consistent with their spirituality or religion, yet may be difficult to differentiate from psychopathological symptoms.	2.43	0.80	59.40
Being able to describe how spirituality and religion can be viewed as overlapping, yet distinct, constructs.	2.42	0.82	59.40
Knowing how to help clients explore and access their spiritual and/or religious strengths and resources.	2.39	0.85	58.10
Being able to identify and address spiritual and/or religious problems in clinical practice.	2.35	0.86	55.50

Response Set: Not at All = 0, A little bit = 1, Somewhat = 2, Very Much = 3

Scammell and Vieten's book, *Spiritual and Religious Competencies in Clinical Practice: Guidelines for Psychotherapists and Mental Health Professionals* (2015) describes these competencies in detail, and provides preliminary training guidelines for teaching new mental health professionals.

Spiritual and religious competence, similar to other forms of multicultural competence, includes basic attitudes, knowledge and skills we propose all psychologists should possess, rather than advanced expertise. Spiritual and religious competencies do not require a mental health professional being religious or spiritual, any more than cultural competencies require them identifying with any one particular cultural group. An agnostic or atheist psychologist can recognise that SRBBPs shape multiple aspects of many of their clients' or participants' lives, can respect their SRBBPs as often helpful and sometimes disruptive influences in their lives, and learn to inquire about and address them at a general practice level. Competencies include a specific measurable set of knowledge base and skills, as opposed to a general familiarity with the topic. Personal involvement in religion or spirituality does not confer competence.

To summarise, it is clear from polls of the general public cited earlier that religion and spirituality are important in most people's lives. There is evidence that clients would prefer to have their spirituality and religion addressed rather than avoided in psychotherapy. Religion and spirituality have been empirically linked to a number of psychological health and wellbeing outcomes, as well as some psychological problems. Most mental health professions have already included religion and spirituality in their definitions of multiculturalism and already require training in multicultural competence. Yet most psychotherapists receive little or no training in religious and spiritual issues.

This proposed set of competencies are intended to be reasonable guidelines that mandate no particular worldview. They are equally applicable to religiously oriented and atheist/agnostic psychotherapists, and advocate a patient-centered approach emphasising appreciation, respect, knowledge and skills for appropriately inquiring into and, when appropriate, harnessing spirituality and religion to foster clients' psychological wellbeing. A recent online course on the EdX platform entitled Spiritual Competency Training in Mental Health (SCTMH), incorporating these and other spiritual and religious knowledge, attitudes and skills, has proven effective for increasing clinicians self-reported competency and decreasing perceived barriers to integrating spirituality and religion in clinical practice (Pearce *et al*, 2019a; 2019b). Currently, the author is chairing a task force that is developing practice guidelines which will be formally proposed for adoption by the American Psychological Association. We hope this will be adopted and will be helpful to other mental health fields.

It is important to note that psychologists should integrate R/S interventions into psychotherapy only when they have adequate training and clinical competence to do so. Even among highly competent psychologists, spiritual and religious issues may arise in clinical practice that require consultation, additional training, collaboration or referral. At times, coordination between psychologists and clergy can be useful to address the R/S needs of clients.

Competent mental health clinicians need not shy away from the religious and spiritual domains of people's lives. Asking about clients' spiritual and religious beliefs and practices, if any, can be integrated as a routine part of mental health care. Helping clients utilise their spiritual and religious beliefs and practices as resources for their mental and emotional wellbeing should reduce suffering and enhance wellbeing for the millions who seek help from mental health professionals each year.

References

Aten, J.D., Smith, W.R., Davis, E.B., Van Tongeren, D.R., Hook, J.N., Davis, D.E., Shannonhouse, L., DeBlaere, C., Ranter, J., O'Grady, K. and Hill, P.C.,. (2019). The psychological study of religion and spirituality in a disaster context: A systematic review. *Psychological Trauma: Theory, Research, Practice, and Policy,* **11**(6), 597.

Bryant-Davis, T., & Wong, E. C. (2013). Faith to move mountains: Religious coping, spirituality, and interpersonal trauma recovery. *American Psychologist,* **68**(8), 675.

Gall, T. L., & Guirguis-Younger, M. (2013). Religious and spiritual coping: Current theory and research. In K. I. Pargament, J. J. Exline, & J. W. Jones (Eds.), *APA handbook of psychology, religion, and spirituality* (Vol. 1): Context, theory, and research (pp. 349–364). American Psychological Association.

Hodge, D. R. (2019). Spiritual assessment with refugees and other migrant populations: A necessary foundation for successful clinical practice. *Journal of Religion & Spirituality in Social Work: Social Thought,* **38**(2), 121-139.

Kao, L.E., Peteet, J.R. & Cook, C. C. H. (2020) Spirituality and mental health, *Journal for the study of Spirituality* **10** (1): 42-54.

Magaldi-Dopman, D. (2014). An "afterthought": Counseling trainees' multicultural competence within the spiritual/religious domain. *Journal of Multicultural Counseling and Development,* **42**(4), 194-204.

Oman, D. (Ed.). (2018). *Why religion and spirituality matter for public health: Evidence, implications, and resources* (Vol. 2). Springer.

Oxhandler, H. K., Parrish, D. E., Torres, L. R., & Achenbaum, W. A. (2015). The integration of clients' religion and spirituality in social work practice: A national survey. *Social work,* **60**(3), 228-237.

Oxhandler, H. K., Pargament, K. I., Pearce, M. J., Vieten, C., & Moffatt, K. M. (2021). Current Mental Health Clients' Attitudes Regarding Religion and Spirituality in Treatment: A National Survey. *Religions,* **12**(6), 371.

Pargament, K. I., & Lomax, J. W. (2013). Understanding and addressing religion among people with mental illness. *World Psychiatry,* **12**(1), 26-32.

Pearce, M. J., Pargament, K. I., Oxhandler, H. K., Vieten, C., & Wong, S. (2019a). Novel online training program improves spiritual competencies in mental health care. *Spirituality in Clinical Practice,* **6**(2), 73–82.

Pearce, M. J., Pargament, K. I., Oxhandler, H. K., Vieten, C., & Wong, S. (2020). Novel online training program improves spiritual competencies in mental health care. *Spirituality in Clinical Practice,* **7**(3), 145.

Richards, P., & Bergin, A. E. (2014). Handbook of psychotherapy and religious diversity. American Psychological Association.

Saunders, S. M., Petrik, M. L., & Miller, M. L. (2014). Psychology doctoral students' perspectives on addressing spirituality and religion with clients: Associations with personal preferences and training. *Psychology of Religion and Spirituality,* **6**(1), 1.

Shafranske, E. P. (2016). Finding a place for spirituality in psychology training: Use of competency-based clinical supervision. *Spirituality in Clinical Practice,* **3**(1), 18.

Sharma, V., Marin, D. B., Koenig, H. K., Feder, A., Iacoviello, B. M., Southwick, S. M., & Pietrzak, R. H. (2017). Religion, spirituality, and mental health of US military veterans: Results from the National Health and Resilience in Veterans Study. *Journal of affective disorders,* **217**, 197-204.

Smith-MacDonald, L., Norris, J. M., Raffin-Bouchal, S., & Sinclair, S. (2017). Spirituality and mental wellbeing in combat veterans: A systematic review. *Military medicine,* **182**(11-12), e1920-e1940.

Tepper, L., Rogers, S. A., Coleman, E. M., & Malony, H. N. (2001). T*he prevalence of religious coping among persons with persistent mental illness.* Psychiatric Services, **52**(5), 660-665.

Vieten, C., Oxhandler H., Pearce, M. Fry, N., Pargament, K. (manuscript in preparation) Mental Health Professional Perspectives on Religion and Spirituality in Mental Health and Clinical Practice.

Vieten, C., & Scammell, S. (2015) *Spiritual and religious competencies in clinical practice: Guidelines for psychotherapists and mental health professionals*. New Harbinger Publications.

Vieten, C., Scammell, S., Pierce, A., Pilato, R., Ammondson, I., Pargament, K. I., & Lukoff, D. (2016). Competencies for psychologists in the domains of religion and spirituality. *Spirituality in Clinical Practice*, **3**(2), 92-114

Vieten, C., Scammell, S., Pilato, R., Ammondson, I., Pargament, K. I., & Lukoff, D. (2013). Spiritual and religious competencies for psychologists. *Psychology of Religion and Spirituality*, **5**(3), 129.

Yamada, A. M., Lukoff, D., Lim, C. S., & Mancuso, L. L. (2020). Integrating spirituality and mental health: Perspectives of adults receiving public mental health services in California. *Psychology of Religion and Spirituality*, **12**(3), 276.

Mental Health, Spirituality and Wellbeing

Themes & Journeys

Chapter 15:

Psychological and Christian perspectives on mental health

By Fraser Watts

Introduction

There are often both psychological and religious aspects of mental health problems, and it is fruitful to consider them together. People can be religious in a variety of different ways, for example in how central religion is to their lives, or how open-minded they are. Whether or not people are religious, there are almost always spiritual aspects of mental health problems, if that is broadly understood as what is sacred for them. It is often possible to discern the impact of underlying psychological problems in the form that a particular person's religious life takes. Similarly, the various different modes of psychological work with people with mental health problems, such as psychodynamic, person-centred and cognitive-behavioural, can all be mapped onto a Christian framework, though in somewhat different ways. Under some circumstances it can be helpful for psychological work to culminate in an explicitly religious practice such as prayer.

Christian psychologists who are offering pastoral care are always operating from two perspectives at the same time, looking at things as psychologists, but also as Christians. In this chapter, I want to explore the connection between these two approaches and how to integrate them in pastoral care (Webb, 2017). This is an example of the more general problem of how to relate scientific and religious perspectives. The psychology of religion and spirituality (Watts, 2017) is particularly relevant to the work of a Christian psychologist (Watts *et al*, 2002).

My first assumption is that is there is almost always both a psychological and a Christian perspective, rather than it being a matter of deciding whether a particular problem is a psychological or religious. It is almost always a mistake to think in those either/or terms. The challenge for the Christian psychologist is to be aware of both angles and to integrate them. There has been a tendency in the counselling and psychological work of Christians to go to extremes, and either to go over entirely to a psychological perspective, or to ignore it (Pattison, 1988). In this chapter I will take a balanced and integrative approach.

How this is done depends on the faith of the person seeking pastoral care, and the professional context in which care is being offered. These are complex matters. It is right to respect the faith position of a person seeking pastoral care, rather than using their need for pastoral care try to bring them to faith. Also, much pastoral care is provided in contexts in which the funding or employing authority would not consider it appropriate to exercise religious influence over the people to whom care is being provided.

Nevertheless, it may be permissible to offer a spiritually integrated approach to pastoral care. There is growing professional recognition there are 'spiritual' aspects of many presenting problems, and that it is helpful to take a whole-person approach to them that considers the spiritual aspects of a problem alongside the psychological ones (e.g. Pargament, 2007). Spiritual aspects of a person's life should normally be approached with the same matter-of-fact professional detachment as psychological ones.

A brief map of religion and spirituality

The domain of religion and spirituality is very broad and diverse, and it will be helpful to give a brief map of the terrain before considering the interface between psychological and religious issues. Religious people are also quite diverse. One classic distinction, going back to the research of Gordon Allport (1950), distinguishes between 'intrinsic' religious people, for whom religion is the dominant motivating force in their lives, and 'extrinsic' religious people, who may be involved in religion more for extraneous reasons, including social ones (see Watts, 2017). Extrinsic religion is probably declining more than intrinsic religion.

Some religions are more a matter of ethnic identity than others, and Christianity and Western Buddhism are less connected with ethnicity than most other religions. That leads to a question about whether or not particular people, for example in the Jewish tradition, 'practice' their religion. In a society where one religion is predominant, as in the UK, there is a danger of there being less recognition and understanding of minority religions.

There is an important distinction between open-mindedness and closed-mindedness in religion, which can be framed in terms of differences in integrative complexity about religion (Savage, 2013). Closed-minded (or dogmatic) religious people not only hold their views strongly, they also make a sharp distinction between those who agree with them and those who don't, and tend to see things from just one point of view, rather than being able to integrate multiple perspectives. Closed-minded religious people are inclined to be disparaging about open-minded religious people and think that their religion is simply weak. Closed-minded religion is very appealing and fulfilling, even though it can become problematic.

Atheists are also quite heterogeneous (Bullivant & Ruse, 2013). There is an important distinction between those who have strong views about religion, even if they are opposed to it, and those who are indifferent to religion and have no interest in it at all. There is a sense in which atheists can be quite religiously committed about their atheism. There is sometimes an element of anger in atheism, whether that is anger with God (Exline & Martin, 2005), or with religion and the church. Just as there are psychological reasons that explain why some people become religious, so there are psychological reasons that explain why some people become atheists. Atheism sometimes intertwines with psychological problems, just as religion does.

Whether or not people are religious, there are almost always spiritual aspects of mental health problems, if that is broadly conceptualised. It is helpful for psychologists and mental health professionals to be aware of what may broadly be called someone's 'spirituality', i.e. their values, ideals, ultimate concerns and the philosophy they live by, or what is 'sacred' for them. Defined in this way, almost everyone has something that is so important to them that it can be regarded as 'sacred'. There are many ways of steering a conversation towards a particular person's ultimate concerns, exploring what they value, what they aspire to, what they would miss most, what really matters to them etc.

There can be spiritual problems, just as there can be psychological problems. In some people, there is a problematic discrepancy between aspiration and reality in their ultimate concerns, in that people are looking for spiritual satisfaction in contexts that are not providing it. That can lead to considerable distress and dissatisfaction. Sometimes people may have a pattern of spiritual life which is failing to meet their spiritual needs, even if they are not themselves registering that there is any problem.

Sociologists are increasingly classifying some people as 'spiritual but not religious' (Watts, 2019). Many people now have an experiential religion, or a 'religion of the heart', even if they don't consider themselves religious. Such people usually have a spiritual worldview and assume that there is 'something more' than the material world they see around them (Hay, 2006). They also probably have spiritual practices, but are more likely to meditate them to pray. They might even believe in God, or at least would probably say that the spiritual side of life was important to them. However, they may not have any religious affiliation or pattern of attendance.

Religious aspects of psychological problems

Having mapped out the religious/spiritual landscape, let us examine the connections that can arise between people's religious or spiritual positions and their presenting psychological issues or problems. For example, there is often such a strong parallel between how people talk about their parents and how they conceptualise God, that it is hard to resist the conclusion that many people's understanding of God is shaped by their experiences with their parents (Rizutto, 1979). Also, how people understand the significance of the crucifixion of Jesus may be shaped by their emotional tone, whether that is guilt, shame or anxiety (Pruyser, 1991).

Sometimes psychological issues affect people's religious life, and religion then becomes simply another domain in which their pervasive psychological issues are manifest. For example, people who have a tendency to obsessionality may become highly obsessional about their religious practices as well as everything else. Equally, people who are depressive and have a strong sense of inadequacy may, in their religious life, have a sense of unworthiness (or shame or guilt) before God. Yet again, someone who is inclined to be angry will probably import their anger into their religious life and be angry with God, or with people whose religion is different from their own.

There are many ways in which psychological issues can be projected onto religion, and religion may then simply consolidate and entrench the person's psychological problems. Once a psychological problem moves into the religious domain, religion can give it a spurious authentication. Because people see religion as a matter of principle, they are often more closed-minded and dogmatic about it than about other things. So, when psychological issues enter the religious domain, people can become very dogmatic and defensive about them.

It is very difficult to guide someone out of this, although some of the methods that Sara Savage has developed for increasing integrative complexity are useful (Savage, 2013). It is always wise to avoid getting into disputes, but to look for ways in which it is possible, gradually and gently, to broaden the person's outlook, and to encourage them to entertain perspectives other than their own. As Iain McGilchrist

(2009) has pointed out, the analytical, cognition of the left brain is always inclined to be more arrogant and dogmatic, and it is a problem when religion becomes dominated by that kind of thinking. Right-brain thinking tends to be humbler and to have an instinct for reaching out to the other. It is also a more embodied mode of cognition, better connected with feeling, and it is more imaginative. So, if people can be nudged towards that mode of cognition, they become more open-minded and more open to change (Savage, 2013).

Religious resources for psychological problems

Though religion can all too often get sucked into psychological problems, there are also religious resources that can liberate people from their psychological problems, and I will now give some examples of that.

Worry is an interesting example. It is a very common mental health problem, and also one about which Jesus is recorded in the Gospels as saying something explicitly (Matthew 6; Luke 12), seeing worry as arising from lack of trust. It is likely to be a particular problem in those who have either never developed what Eriksen calls 'basic trust' (Erikson, 1950), or whose basic trust has been undermined by traumatic events. Trust can be rekindled by a person taking small safe steps outside their comfort zone, and finding that they do not lead to disaster (Vanzant, 2015). There is also an interesting connection between worry and prayer, which are closer psychologically than is often realised (Cook, 2021). Prayer can be a very effective way of rebuilding trust, and the inclination to worry can often be diverted into prayer.

There are also religious resources for the transformation of despair and hopelessness. It is helpful here to make a distinction between hope and optimism (Eagleton, 2015). Optimism is more about prediction, whereas hope is more a matter of attitude and commitment. It is possible to remain constructively hopeful in situations where there are no grounds for optimism. Indeed, it is in very difficult circumstances that hope comes into its own. The classic example is of Victor Frankl, who learned to cultivate hope in a Nazi concentration camp (Frankl, 2006). The psychology of hope has often linked it to a sense of self efficacy, and the belief that one can transform circumstances for the better (Snyder, 1994). For a religious person, hope will be grounded more in trust and a sense of providence, and in working with God to bring some kind of resurrection out of whatever crucifixion they are undergoing.

Religion has also taken a particular interest in the use of forgiveness to transform resentment and anger. Forgiveness is one of the most powerful tools in the Christian armoury, and it has recently been the subject of much psychological research. That has yielded specific guidance on how to go about forgiveness when it is proving difficult (e.g. Worthington, 2006). Recent psychological work on forgiveness has focused mainly on helping people to extend forgiveness to others, but there are also issues about receiving forgiveness oneself, which is often not straightforward. It is people who have a strong sense of guilt who most need to be reassured of the forgiveness of God. Christians have developed powerful ways of giving people that reassurance, though they are perhaps less good at giving a sense of being accepted by God to those who have a strong sense of shame. There can be a fruitful convergence between psychological and religious approaches to forgiveness (Watts & Gulliford, 2004).

There is also a particular religious perspective on psychosis, which can be interpreted as a spiritual struggle, as Clarke has argued (2008). That makes sense of the fact that there is often a particular religious focus in psychotic thinking, albeit one that can appear somewhat deranged. This is part of a wider debate about whether psychotic experiences and conversation should be taken seriously on their own terms, or whether they should be dismissed as mere symptoms of a psychiatric illness. My own view is that there is value in both approaches, and that they are complimentary (Watts, 2018). There is sometimes value in medication, which can make people more accessible to conversation. However, I also think that it can be very helpful to a person to take their apparently strange and psychotic religious experiences seriously, and to engage in conversation about them. I don't think there is any necessary opposition between these two approaches.

Case study

It is often quite difficult to disentangle organic and spiritual aspects of a presenting problem. That is illustrated by Rob, who felt that there was often an unseen person around him, out to get him, poking him in the ribs, interfering with his sleep etc. He was convinced that there really was someone there, a dark force of some kind. However, various factors suggest that what he was experiencing arose in part from brain damage. It started ten years ago when he had a serious accident on his motorbike; the symptoms he described correspond closely to the classical neurological symptom of "sense of presence"; the presence was often over his left shoulder, and the damage had been mainly on his left side. Nevertheless, his problem seemed to be affected by spiritual factors. When he attended a healing service at his local church he was free of the sense of presence throughout his time there, and said that 'it' knew it couldn't get at him in church. He also got similar help from prayers for protection from evil forces, such as St Patrick's Breastplate. The interaction between organic and spiritual factors seemed subtle and complex.

Maybe the brain damage made him more sensitive to spiritual influences, both good and bad. For more discussion of this case see Watts (2018).

> ### Question for reflection
>
> Consider how religious or spiritual factors influence the kind of psychological problems that you mainly work with, and how psychological and spiritual factors have interacted in one or two particular people.

Integrating psychological therapy with Christian pastoral care

Most forms of psychological therapy can be integrated with a Christian approach (Watts *et al*, 2002). However, it will depend on the clients and the healthcare setting whether that integration is just in the mind of the psychologist, or whether it is made explicit with the client.

Psychodynamic therapy is fundamentally concerned with building up an interpretive narrative that helps the person to understand how their problems have arisen and, through that, to be able to find liberation from long-standing, dysfunctional patterns of interaction and emotional responsiveness (Jacobs, 1985). Christianity has also developed a narrative about salvation, and it is possible in principle for the psychodynamic narrative to be nested within that broader Christian one.

Person-centred counselling emphasises the importance of therapeutic qualities of empathy, unconditional positive regard and congruence (or genuineness). Brian Thorne has argued that these are essentially the qualities of Christian love, and that a therapist who provides them is in effect providing people with the Christian love that can heal them (Thorne, 2012). That opens the way to an interpretation of the Christian gospel from the perspective of person-centred psychology.

The more practical advice found in cognitive behaviour therapy has much in common with the advice which has been developed over the centuries in Christian pastoral care and spiritual direction. For example, the approach of the 17th-century spiritual director Augustine Baker about intrusive and unsettling thoughts is entirely consistent with the methods that have been developed more explicitly within cognitive behaviour therapy (Watts & Williams, 1988).

The question remains whether there is a place for explicitly religious practices alongside psychological ones (Rose, 2013). My own view is that psychological methods are always important, and it is not helpful to rush into religious approaches before problems have been properly understood at a psychological level. However, where it is appropriate to the particular client and to the healthcare setting, it can be fruitful for psychological work to culminate in praying with the client in an explicitly religious way. The moment at which to do that needs to be carefully chosen but, at the right time, it seems able to crystallise an energy for change, and to invoke resources that are not available in ordinary psychological work.

Questions for reflection

Spend a moment considering how your own religious outlook and practices affect your work as a psychologist, and how you would place the therapeutic methods you use most within a Christian framework? What place is there for prayer in your work as a psychologist?

References

Allport GW (1950) *The Individual and His Religion: A psychological interpretation*. Oxford: Macmillan.

Bullivant S & Ruse M (2013) *The Oxford Handbook of Atheism*. Oxford: Oxford University Press.

Clarke I (2008) *Madness, Mystery and the Survival of God*. Winchester: 'O' Books.

Cook CCH (2021) Worry and Prayer: Some Reflections on the Psychology and Spirituality of Jesus's Teaching on Worry. In: R Re Manning (Ed) *Mutual Enrichment between Psychology and Theology* pp 163-175. Abingdon: Routledge.

Eagleton T (2015) *Hope Without Optimism*. New Haven CT: Yale University Press.

Erikson EH (1950) *Childhood and Society*. New York: WW Norton

Exline JJ & Martin A (2005) Anger toward God: a new frontier in forgiveness research. In E L Worthington (Ed) *Handbook of Forgiveness* pp 73-88. New York: Routledge.

Frankl V 2006) *Man's Search for Meaning*. New York: Beacon Press.

Hay D (2006) *Something There: The biology of the human spirit*. London: Darton, Longman & Todd.

Jacobs M (1985) *Presenting Past: Core of psychodynamic counselling and therapy*. London: Harper & Row.

McGilchrist I (2009) *The Master and His Emissary: The divided brain and the makings of the Western world*. New Haven: Yale University Press.

Pargament K I (2007) S*piritually Integrated Psychotherapy: Understanding and addressing the sacred*. New York: Guilford Press.

Pattison S (1988) *A Critique of Pastoral Care*. London: SCM Press.

Pruyser P (1991) *Religion in Psychodynamic Perspective: the contributions of Paul W. Pruyser* (Eds H N Maloney & B Spilka) New York: Oxford University Press.

Rizzuto A-M (1979) *The Birth of the Living God: A psychoanalytic study*. Chicago: The University of Chicago Press.

Rose J (2013) *Psychology for Pastoral Contexts: A handbook*. Norwich: Canterbury Press.

Savage SB (2013) Head and Heart in preventing religious radicalization. In: F Watts and G Dumbreck (Eds) *Head and Heart: Perspectives from Religion and Psychology* pp 157-94. Philadelphia: Templeton Press.

Snyder CR (1994) *The Psychology of Hope: You can get there from here*. New York: Free Press.

Thorne B (2012) *Counselling and Spiritual Accompaniment: Bridging faith and person-centred therapy*. New York: John Wiley.

Vanzant I (2015) *Trust: Mastering the Four Essential Trusts: Trust in Self, Trust in God, Trust in Others, Trust in Life*. New York: Smiley Books.

Watts F (2017) *Psychology, Religion and Spirituality: Concepts and applications*. Cambridge: Cambridge University Press.

Watts F (2018) Theology and science of mental Health and wellbeing. *Zygon* **53** (2) 336-355.

Watts F & Gulliford L (2004) *Forgiveness in Context: Theology and psychology in creative dialogue*. London: T & T. Clark.

Watts F, Nye R & Savage S B (2002) *Psychology for Christian Ministry*. London: Routledge.

Watts F & Williams M (1988) *The Psychology of Religious Knowing*. Cambridge: Cambridge University Press.

Watts G (2019) Religion, science and disenchantment in late modernity. *Zygon* **54** (4) 1022-35.

Webb M (2017) *Toward a Theology of Psychological Disorder*. Eugene OR: Cascade Books.

Worthington E L (2006) *Forgiveness and Reconciliation*. New York: Routledge.

Chapter 16:

Voices, visions and the spiritual journey

By Isabel Clarke, LH and Adam J Powell

What is the meaning of life? The question has almost become a joke, perhaps because our logical minds can get nowhere with it, but still it persists. Surely, the journey of life is about more than just 'getting by'? That experience of a deeper connection, of meaning behind the vagaries of everyday life, that sense of the spiritual, hard to pin down but fervently defended, must tell us something, surely?

The journey becomes spiritual when it spills out beyond the mundane confines of the everyday. Gateway events – the birth of a baby; falling in love; death – all these will reliably draw back the thin veil, to use a common metaphor, between the ordinary world and something other; something deeper, with the potential to be either more wonderful or more terrible. This is the place that is accessed when that everyday world hits an impasse and there is no good way forward. It is accessed when the props, the containment, that maintain our sense of self fall away; our roles and relationships that tell us who we are and where we fit in. This happens at times of transition and crisis.

At such times we can find ourselves reaching out beyond the confines of our individual self-perceptions. This experience can be creative, leading to growth and transformation; an opening to new horizons – provided we make it back to solid ground. For those who do not find their way back so easily, this journey can prove testing. For those who get lost, it signals breakdown; madness. Yet even here, the breakdown can be a prelude to break through, to fuller life. The secret is to be able to get back. The right support is helpful here, hence my commitment to the Spiritual Crisis Network – to be explained below.

To summarise: all human beings have the potential to engage with the world in two distinct ways. Normally, we weave in and out of the two without noticing it. We concentrate on a difficult text or some calculation, then let the mind drift as we turn to enjoying music or taking a walk in nature. Our logical faculty is engaged by the text or calculation. For the other, we switch to feeling and experience. At some point, it can become possible to cross a threshold between these two ways of knowing. We then find ourselves in the realm of extreme experience, whether mystical or mad, or both. These two ways of being and knowing arise from the way our brains function, see Box 16.1 for more detail here.

Box 16.1: How our brains give us two distinct ways of experiencing.

Cognitive research has tracked which pathways in our brains are connected and which are not. The Interacting Cognitive Subsystem model of cognitive architecture reveals two central meaning making systems. See Figure 16.1.

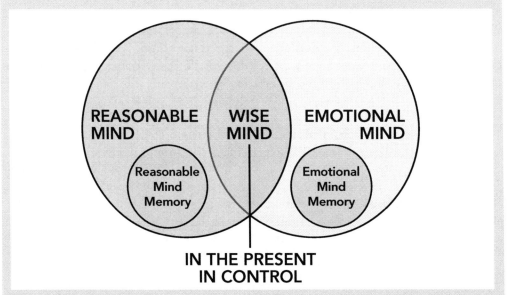

REASONABLE MIND

WISE MIND

EMOTIONAL MIND

Reasonable Mind Memory

Emotional Mind Memory

IN THE PRESENT IN CONTROL

The Emotion Mind, which connects our senses and bodies, looks out for the self. The other, Reasonable Mind, connects the more recently evolved verbal systems, and holds precise knowledge. Mostly they work together and give us ordinary consciousness. At high and low arousal they start to separate. When they become really disjointed, this gives us that other way of knowing. Their memories are similarly separate. Reasonable Mind memory knows about time and place, whereas Emotion Mind memory is interested in threat to and value of the self. When they separate, past bad memories get mixed up with current ones, as knowledge about time is lost.

Box 16.1 explains how time becomes collapsed when we leave our everyday functioning, hence the re-accessing of trauma memories, just when things are most challenging in the present; a process that can hasten breakdown.

This double nature means that, while we feel as if we are a coherent, self-conscious unity, we in fact exist within a web of relationship.

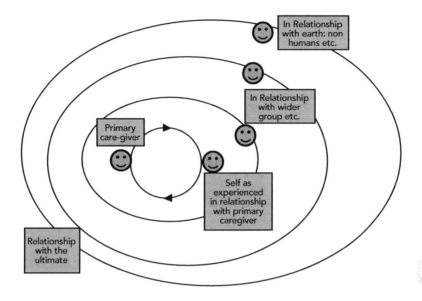

Figure 16.2: Web of relationships

For each one of us, there are important relationships, such as those with our early care-giver, that define us, but these are contained within others. The relationship that is furthest and deepest is a relationship honoured by peoples throughout the ages. In our precise, everyday way of being we want things pinned down, so assign names – God, Goddess, Spirit etc. – but in this relational mode of being, we know through experience, through feeling. We can feel more than we can precisely know. This chapter concerns what happens when life's journey strays far into that other way of being, perhaps too far. Once the individual has left behind the safety of their individuality, the familiar boundaries are lost; things merge; the interior world is experienced as if outside – in the form of voices, visions and other strange happenings. This is a place of extreme and of paradox. It might feel deeply meaningful and directed; abounding in synchronicities, or it might feel dead, meaningless and void.

LH's story

I am grateful to the assistance of LH in order to illustrate how the spiritual journey can take someone to strange, frankly psychotic, places, and still come through safely to new and broader perspectives. First, a word about the Spiritual Crisis Network

(SCN), where I am volunteer secretary and where I met LH. Having worked in acute mental health services, I am only too aware that the messages we give people about their experiences can make all the difference between the sort of despair that does not motivate people to undertake the work of re-joining consensus reality, and the type of positive outcome I have been suggesting is possible. There is a robust strand of research showing that people making sense of their experiences in ways that offer hope do much better. Seeing it as part of the spiritual journey is an example of this type of interpretation. The Spiritual Crisis Network spreads awareness of this perspective, provides peer support groups (now over Zoom) and responds to emails from those in crisis.

LH first contacted SCN in crisis after leaving psychiatric hospital. He received support and validation, joined a peer support group and later became a volunteer, responding to crisis emails and helping to train other volunteers. However, his journey to these roles involved an involuntary hospital admission, a locked ward and a long period when his life was in ruins.

The first question is, why did LH's life journey take him to such extreme places? There are two strands to this in LH's background. Psychic gifts ran in his family, with bards and freemasons among his ancestors, as did vulnerability. His brother had had a breakdown in early adulthood resulting in a life-long diagnosis of schizophrenia. Openness to this type of experience has physical foundations in levels of arousability, the action of neurotransmitters etc. However, that vulnerability does not need necessarily to lead to a life of disability, as we will see.

Another factor that often facilitates this openness is trauma, and I asked LH about this. He said that as a boy he was severely bullied; he was gay, and always felt an outsider. At home, too, his father could be aggressive, so that fear was a constant. Even when he came into his stride socially in his later teens, he felt an outsider. His interests were different; esoteric and philosophical. In his 20s and 30s, his job involved travel and he took the opportunity to explore sacred places and practices, being particularly drawn to ancient Egypt and the Valley of the Kings. Psychic experiences broke into his normal life every now and then. He says that, looking back, the way he viewed those things now seems limited and arrogant to him.

Transition: awakening and underworld

Times of transition have been identified as the occasion for opening to the other way of experiencing. At the age of 40, after various spiritual experiences, LH travelled to India to study Ayurvedic healing and massage and was embarking on Reiki training when the awakening happened. He was learning to work with energy, and suddenly energy took over his whole self, shaking his body, and connecting him with others in uncanny ways. He now views this as a shamanic awakening. His life became full of coincidences, and initially it felt liberating, and as though his eyes were opened and he could see through and beyond the conventional world. Straying beyond the ordinary, world view, which is limited and made predictable by the two parts of our processing working together, is often experienced like this – a spiritual revelation. The boundaries and divisions that delineate our normal thinking fall away. Everything can feel connected and meaningful in a cosmic sense. However, this is not a safe place to remain in. Without those boundaries, the sense of self becomes fluid and permeable, and we need to be able to get back and ground ourselves in the shared world if we are to safely explore the other. In LH's case, he plunged in too deeply and got seriously lost, beyond the bounds of consensus reality.

In the middle of his work as a massage therapist in London, shortly after his Reiki initiation, he experienced feelings of blissfulness, connectedness and love. This lasted for about three days, culminating in a profound experience when he found himself proclaiming: 'LH is dead! You must listen to me; this is the voice of God'. The following day he felt compelled to go to St. Paul's and proclaimed himself to be Christ, asking to preach on the Apocalypse. Everywhere, uncanny coincidences appeared to confirm this identification. Being apprehended by police with dogs and bundled off to hospital did nothing to resolve his internal turmoil. Still battling with supernatural powers and far from consensus reality, he accidentally injured a nurse, leading to forcible sedation and seclusion.

This ushered in LH's period in 'the underworld'. External and internal worlds merged and collapsed. He lost his job and was embroiled in a court case. Once out of hospital, he lived like a hermit, plagued by obsessions and synchronicities and strange experiences. It was a synchronous encounter with a chakra worker that LH feels helped him to turn the corner. After taking essences sent by this man, he started to evolve in a positive direction. The resolution of the court case, which reduced stress levels, will also have helped. It was at this juncture that he contacted SCN. Attending his first meeting of the London group, he was encouraged to hear the facilitator share that he had believed himself to be Jesus too at the height of his crisis, now some years distant.

Re-entry and new direction

During the dark period, LH had been exploring every avenue to make sense of the wealth of symbolic material bombarding him. Part of that exploration involved taking up photography, capturing the mythic and symbolic in the everyday; the shapes of the clouds and the architecture of the South Bank in London where he lived. At the same time, he was taking neuroleptic medication, and he tried to get himself re-admitted to hospital in desperation on a number of occasions. Once he had turned the corner, when taking the essences and the desperation had left him, he was able to gradually come off the medication that was dulling his faculties, and the researches he had been undertaking started to come together in a more coherent and communicable fashion.

The alchemical journey of transformation, or the Hero's Journey (see Joseph Cambell's 1993 book on the subject), of descent into the underworld and rebirth, leading to re-entry bearing gifts, can be seen as a framework. The revelation of rebirth came to LH when he recognised symbols from Egyptian and other ancient mysteries in the paintings of the Renaissance Gallery of the National Gallery and archetypal figures at the British Museum. The gifts bestowed were a new confidence and fearlessness, an ability to use imagination and discern symbolic meaning, which were to enable the new direction that his life took at this point.

Taking up acting was a central part of this new direction. He has portrayed the High Priest in Boris Godunov at the Royal Opera House and played Oedipus Rex in Sophocles' Greek tragedy, Oedipus Tyrannus, something he says his shyness would never have permitted him to accept previously. He was able to contribute his deeper knowledge of the mythic depths of the piece to the production. Also, his photographical representation of the unseen world led to three pieces of work being exhibited at the Tate Modern. When Covid caused that work to dry up, his fearlessness showed in his taking a job in a care home at the height of the pandemic.

Where previously, contact with the transliminal had thrown LH's life into turmoil, now that he was finding his ability to engage with this dimension of reality at the same time as keeping his feet on the ground and operating effectively in the shared world, he found that it was giving direction to his life in a sound way. Where he accessed that archetypal, mythic dimension, he reported that it was as if that direction came from outside of himself. It further helped him to use and redefine imagination to motivate himself to attempt things he would otherwise have avoided, and to communicate effectively with the people around him, who had previously rejected his new enthusiasms as craziness.

LH concluded by saying that the journey is ongoing, and he has no idea where it will lead, but with his newfound trust in direction from the level of symbols, coupled with the power of imagination to create reality, he has confidence in it.

To conclude, LH's inherited openness to crossing the threshold to the other way of experiencing launched him on this journey. It started slowly with his esoteric interests earlier in life; it took over and submerged him when he was undergoing a sensitive, transition period. With some external validation and support, and a lot of investigation on his own part, he has come through to fuller expression of the creativity and spirituality this openness brings with it, and his life in the shared world is on course. He now views these profound experiences as a gift.

Everyday voices and spiritual speech

We are now going to turn attention to the particular case of 'hearing voices'. Indeed, whether experienced as excessive self-scrutiny in which the 'I' turns an alienating gaze inward, or as a form of transcendence in which something perceptually 'other' interrupts (however briefly) the unity of self, extraordinary quasi-sensory events break many of our taken-for-granted experiential rules. Although striking, these episodes may be relatively common and, for some, rather mundane. For example, hearing voices in the absence of any physical speaker seems to occur on a sort of continuum, ranging from the mental conversations we have with ourselves on a daily basis to the emotionally distressing auditory voices accompanying various forms of psychosis.

Between those two poles exist a whole range of voice-hearing phenomena. It is estimated, for instance, that the majority of people will hear voices if deprived of sleep or sensory input for multiple days. Drugs – synthetic and organic – may induce voice-hearing, and nearly one third of people grieving the death of a loved one will hear the deceased's voice in the weeks and months after their death. Many children hear and converse with imaginary friends, while approximately 1% of the general public hears voices every month without requiring psychological or psychiatric care.

Voices may elicit positive, neutral or negative thoughts and feelings. They may seem to originate from within the mind or outside of the head. Some voices are perceived as thought-like, while others are reportedly heard aurally through the ears. The voices may be understood as belonging to an unknown agent or an easily recognisable intimate. The Hearing Voices Network, an international user-led linkage of voice-hearers, clinicians and advocates, has also raised awareness of how important it can be to acknowledge the words spoken by voices in addition to their perceived agency. The messages conveyed may reflect individual histories (including personal traumas) and cultural inheritances, even if they sometimes remain entirely ambiguous to the hearer. That said, in some instances initially meaningless voices acquire transformative meanings or interpretations over time – having first seemed benign or even ordinary.

One example might be a childhood imaginary companion whose voice and communications are later transformed by the voice-hearer's own encounter with new beliefs in the light of emerging psychological needs – the once blithe imagined playmate becoming a sage spiritual guide or relative visiting from beyond the grave. Indeed, evidence suggests that one of the most common forms of hallucinatory experiences, the voices and visions experienced during the transition between waking and sleeping (and vice versa), can sometimes receive profound spiritual attributions. In these transitional moments, waking life literally merges with dream consciousness, producing vivid quasi-perceptual experiences that may be difficult for the experiencer to categorise. Was that a dream, a hallucination, or something uniquely intended for me? Many turn to their social networks and cultural resources to answer that question. In doing so, some have concluded that the blurring of boundaries – between self and environment, waking and sleeping, etc. – indicates a spiritual or supernatural significance for the vision or voice.

Such spiritual voices, for example, are common among mediums and psychics, particularly those who report receiving clairaudient communications. While Spiritualists believe that spirits continue to live on beyond the death of the physical body and may attempt to communicate verbal messages to relatives or others via mediums during séances or other public events, not all reported clairaudient communications are experienced in this way. In fact, many clairaudient mediums join Spiritualist circles or churches only after having had unusual auditory experiences. For some, this may include early childhood experiences of seeing, hearing and/or speaking to a figure in their room, in the garden, or when walking along the beach. For others, the earliest relevant memory is of hearing their name called when falling asleep – one of the most common voice-hearing experiences among the general public. In all of these cases, however, the early experience is eventually interpreted within the paradigm of Spiritualism. The figure in the room or the voice calling the name is believed to be the spirit of a deceased loved one. In turn, the experiences subsequently lead to participation and to additional training in mediumship practices, transforming initially relatively mundane episodes into meaningful instances of spirit communication and proof of life after death.

Thus, the identification of voices heard with spiritual speech can bring comfort and clarity, a feature of many spiritual and religious voices that sets them apart from the distressing or aggressive voices most often reported by those with a mental health diagnosis. For instance, Protestant Christians who report experiences of hearing supernatural voices, typically the voice of God, also describe the experiences in overtly positive terms. Indeed, studies reveal that the vast majority of Christians who hear spiritual voices receive comfort or clarity concerning a dilemma or source of anxiety being faced in their lives. Just as striking are the number who cite hearing the voice of God as a moment of identity transformation. Usually described in terms of religious conversion, the individual first recalls being an atheist, sceptic, or stuck on a desultory path in life. However, as a result of hearing the divine voice, whether it spoke words of deep enlightenment or nearly meaningless banality, they claim to have emerged with fresh hope, faith and purpose. In this way, new directions are sometimes discovered by voice-hearers at the intersection of their interior lives (emotions, needs, perceptions and hauntings) and external possibilities (social contexts and spiritual/religious resources). One clinical/therapeutic aspiration is that those new transformative paths are just as much part of the journey for emotionally distressed psychosis patients as they are for non-clinical psychic mediums or Christian converts.

Conclusion

There are several messages that follow from this perspective on the spiritual journey.

First, that journey can take people to strange places, involving hard-to-fathom experiences, such as voices that are compelling for the individual but that others do not hear; a strong sense of meaning and direction that can make sense metaphorically, but be misleading when taken literally, and a loss of the grounded sense of self accompanied by an openness to the whole that can be both exhilarating and terrifying. Though such experiences might be labelled as an illness, it is argued here that they are part of the available spectrum of human experience. Properly supported, they can lead out of a stuck period of life into new horizons, as illustrated by LH's account. It is accessing the spiritual dimension of experience that clears the way to these possibilities.

References

Campbell J (1993) *The Hero with a Thousand Faces*, Fontana: London

Clarke I (2008) *Madness, Mystery and the Survival of God*. Winchester: 'O'Books.

Further Resources

Spiritual Crisis Network: https://www.spiritualcrisisnetwork.uk
Isabel Clarke's Website: https://www.isabelclarke.org
Hearing Voices Network: https://www.hearing-voices.org/
Understanding Voices: www.UnderstandingVoices.com

Chapter 17:
Return to Eden… Two journeys

By Jeremy Timm & Sally Coleman

Introduction

There is significant research to show that those identifying as LGBTQIA+ are more at risk of mental health issues due to factors such as discrimination, isolation and homophobia (Chakraborty *et al*, 2011). However, one study also found that people who were open about their sexuality with family and friends had lower stress hormone levels and fewer symptoms of anxiety, depression and burnout than those who were not open about their sexuality (Juster *et al*, 2013). Therefore helping those who identify as LGBTQIA+ to feel secure in who they are and confident to share that with those in their lives is an important factor in wellbeing.

This chapter explores the intersectionality of spiritual identity and sexual identity and its relationship to wellbeing. A further layer of identity to consider is racial identity, which can be particularly relevant for those from BAME communities. Those who are from a sexual minority as well as an ethnic minority may feel particularly vulnerable in 'coming out', for fear of losing the support of family and community that can be protective factors against racism (Carr, 2010).

The following accounts of our personal experiences of this journey reflect that process of both spiritual identity and sexual identity formation. As you read these personal experiences you may wish to reflect on how you may have supported us in our journeys if we had come to you for support during this process of self-awareness and self-acceptance.

Jeremy's journey

The place I am writing this from feels very safe and comfortable; a warm office in a country cottage in East Yorkshire, with an old dog in the chair snoring steadily. My now husband, with whom I have been in a relationship with for more than 20 years, has just waved as he sets off for his walk. Part of my comfort arises out of the fact that I no longer have any engagement with institutional religion, and its ongoing angst and often angry debate about the place of LGBTI+ folk in its life and ministry. I am, however, a member of a dispersed contemplative community which from its founding has been an inclusive community. As the founder once told me, inclusivity is in its very DNA. Thus now, stillness, meditation and nature are all an integral part of my spirituality and sense of wellbeing, which has allowed me to move on from the guilt and talk of 'sin' that was once a part of my journey. The story of the Garden of Eden in the Christian scriptures has always held a deep appeal for me. The strange paradox being that the very same story has been taken by some to diminish and exclude, and indeed still continues to be used in this way.

This is Eden for me... A place of flourishing and growth, where an individual's glorious gay potential can blossom, guilt free, owning and loving themselves, partners and lovers, completely comfortable in their own skin. In terms of spirituality, Eden provides a potent image, where Adam and his partner Eve are completely comfortable in their nakedness and their relationship in the presence of God. Guilt or shame have no place here; there is a healthy wholeness to their relationship together and with their God, which I know now is possible to enjoy as a gay man, but the journey has not been easy, nor without its challenges to my mental health. As I tell but a fraction of my story, I will point out some of the pressures I have experienced which have forced me to pretend to be someone who I was not, which clearly is far from flourishing or wholesome.

I have often been asked, "When did I first know I was gay?" which I have always found impossible to answer. I equate it with being asked, "When did I first know I had a pulse?" Of course, there is no one moment in time to identify who you simply are. However, I do remember one hot summer day when I was out in the garden with my parents, probably at the age of four or five, enjoying my paddling pool, which I can still strangely remember as being pale blue, when our neighbours invited us round to their garden for tea. So, we moved camp to the semi-detached next door, me still in my swimming trunks, or cossie as my mum called them. During tea, their adolescent son, in his swimming trunks too, lifted me up and sat me on his lap. I can remember vividly that it simply felt good, thrilling, an experience I enjoyed, sun-warmed flesh on flesh. This was an Eden experience for me... There was no guilt or shame, no word to describe my feeling of enjoyment, it simply felt good. Would that all life's experiences downstream were as innocent.

At the age of eight, I went to an all-boys boarding school in Wakefield as a boarding pupil. They were generally happy days for me, but they were days when that subtle pressure to be someone else began to exert itself. I became aware of a few boys who were different in that they were camp and effeminate, and I saw how they were the butt of jokes, verging on bullying, imitated and ridiculed. At the same time as I was aware of my own sexual awakening and attraction to certain other boys, invariably, way older than myself and usually in the First XV rugby team. Although I never had any sexual experiences with them, the truth was dawning that to avoid the same treatment I had to be "one of the boys". So from my early schooldays I began my training for an Oscar, which led me away from Eden, and owning who I was, which continued throughout my time at school. In the 1960s and 70s in public schools there was no such thing as sex education, as it may have squeezed Latin off the timetable, so I could not speak to anyone of my feelings, nor had I any idea that I was far from alone.

Perhaps one of the most pressured times to act out a role which I felt was expected of me was when I went to university in Leicester. Student days, which should have been a time of learning, growth and development, for me turned out to be three years of real inner struggle. Early on I made contact with The Christian Union, a very conservative evangelical group, who were for the first time in my experience all my own age and serious about their faith, and offered real friendship to a rather shy public school boy, which was deeply valued. The group had clear, prescriptive guidelines as to sexual intimacy, which was not permitted, as the place for sex was understood to be within a marital relationship. This actually provided a great cover for me as I had a girlfriend, and we could be seen walking hand in hand across campus, the ideal Christian couple, all the while I was able to hide the fact, thanks to these conservative teachings, that I was not sexually attracted to her.

The mantra of this group, oft repeated, when it came to homosexuality was, "Hate the sin, love the sinner", which is such a false dichotomy; being gay is deeply who I was and how I related to the world, a far deeper, richer thing than just a sex act. As I went to the big student church twice on a Sunday, there was a fellow student who was openly gay, handsome and apparently happy. How I secretly envied him, with his tight jeans, big smile and curly hair; my sense of almost suffocation increased, to near panic come the day when my girlfriend wanted me to meet her parents, one of the milestones along the road of conventional relationships in these Christian circles.

One small release I found in these difficult days was a strange anonymous correspondence with a fellow student via the student union pigeon holes, our letters being addressed to Mr Friendly. In these letters to someone I never met, many an erotic fantasy was shared on A4 notepaper and the equally sexual responses were eagerly awaited. Although exciting, this correspondence only served to make my respectable role as the now President of the Christian Union, with my smiling girlfriend, more painful and confusing.

Following university, I was selected for training for the ordained ministry in the Church of England, and organised a place at Durham University to start my training. Of course, during the whole selection procedure, there was no chink in my defences as to the real me, so with another Oscar-worthy performance behind me, I launched into the world of theological college. It was during my time at college that I met a man from the town who was openly gay, and we struck up a secret friendship. I had many difficulties about anything physical at this stage as I was carrying with me the internalised baggage of way too much guilt, but he was wonderfully warm and generous and did not make any demands on his strange theologian friend. One day he sprung on me that he would like to go with me to a gay club in Newcastle, which was a whole new experience for me. I can so clearly remember going to the now long-gone, exotically name Casablanca Club, and timidly walking through the doors into a world of high energy music, men dancing holding hands and kissing. Like the Pope visiting a new country, I wanted to drop to my knees and kiss the ground, as it felt then, and still does now, like a homecoming. Walking through those doors brought me to a crossroads, and I finally read the sign pointing back to Eden, and began the journey towards owning who I was and what it meant.

When I finished my theological training I was not ordained, and returned home to begin working in the family business of flour milling. For a while I was involved with the local church in lay ministry, before that eventually ceased and I had a long period with no church involvement at all, which allowed me to finally mature into a relational gay man. It does seem interesting that this finally took place once I had no involvement with the church, and being exposed to the heated debates which still continue today about the place of LGBTQIA+ people in the life and ministry of the church.

I briefly returned to lay ministry many years later within the church of England when they accepted civil partnerships, on the understanding that they were celibate! Yet more guilt-inducing teaching. This was a short-lived spell, as when I married my partner my Permission to Officiate was withdrawn which caused upset and tears, and I vowed never again to let teaching force me to act out a role that was expected of me, rather than experience the flourishing which I now enjoy.

Sally's story

As I sit in my office to write this, looking out at the city of Sheffield spread before me, I am conscious that I am not where I expected to be, my life journey has contained a number of twists and turns that have led me to discover my true self; some painful, some joyful. I also reflect that I have spent a lot of my life hiding, from others and from myself. I ask myself if I am happy, but that word seems too emotive. What I can say, however, is that I am content. I am content with my life even though living alone had never featured in my plans. That said, my two cats may dispute my aloneness, and so would numerous friends who, even in the midst of a global pandemic (this is 2021), ensure that I am not lonely.

Just under three years ago I was visiting one of these friends. We had come to know one another very well in a short space of time, sharing life stories in all of their joy and trauma. Our conversation had turned to sexuality, and I found myself saying for the first time, that despite all appearances (I had been married to a man for 32 years and that marriage had produced five children), I was not attracted to men at all. My friend, to his credit, didn't blink, and went on to support me as I came out to family, friends and colleagues over the course of the next year. Perhaps the best reaction to my news came from my youngest son, who simply said, "Really, mum, I am not surprised!"

As I look back over my life I can remember times of awakening, of being deeply attracted to the female form with the curves that I find beautiful. I can also remember an inner call, a sense that somehow, somewhere, all was right with the world, and I was right with the world; perhaps that was Eden awakening within. All could be perfect, all could be right!

I remember the amazing feeling of being in my body during swimming lessons, and the joy of moving in synchronization with the water and with others just felt joyful. Swimming was my solace, and I was fortunate enough as a child to be able to swim every day after school, one of the perks of an ex-pat childhood in Kuala Lumpur, Malaysia. There weren't many others, because keeping up appearances was all important, and being different was not seen as a good thing.

My parents had wanted a boy, and obviously I wasn't one. I was a tall and, pre-puberty, somewhat plump girl. I was awkward in my own skin and I didn't know why, I hid at the back of ballet classes feeling that I could never attain the perfection that I craved or read about in magazines. I can only say that I am glad that I wasn't exposed to social media as it would have probably bruised my fragile ego to the point of breaking.

In all of this I was a sensitive soul with a deep spiritual yearning. Every morning I awoke to the sound of the call to prayer from the mosque that was broadcast by loud hailers over the city. It stirred something in me. Years later, and on moving to England at the age of 11, I amazed my parents by wanting a Bible and being fascinated by the huge and inaccessible Priory Church at Deeping St James in Lincolnshire, which stood opposite our bungalow. I say inaccessible because it never occurred to me to try to go in!

Life twisted and turned. My parents divorced following a move to Nottinghamshire and my father's plunge into alcoholism. Another move, this time to Essex, where my mother married a childhood friend of hers who had been recently widowed. I don't remember any tender moments as a child, being held, caressed or even loved. Life was layered with expectations and these continued into my teenage years, so much so that I now wonder whose they were, and whether they were self-imposed. Enough to say I was hungry for touch and thoroughly mixed and muddled up. Love and sex became the same thing and I craved both. I also sought the divine, this time finding God in a small church on top of a hill overlooking the Blackwater Estuary in Essex. It was old with beautiful stained glass windows, and I found a sense of peace in the repetition of the liturgy even though I didn't really understand it. In this place I found a sense of acceptance and belonging, and yet I also didn't belong, something didn't quite fit, and in my hiddenness I couldn't work out what it was.

Interestingly, two things were never spoken about at home: one was sex, the other religion. Sex was a taboo subject (don't ask, don't tell) and religion was just weird, why a 16-year-old would want to go to church was beyond my agnostic family. As for the don't ask, don't tell, if there was one instruction it was don't come home pregnant, but of course that is what this mixed-up teenager did at the age of 19. My mum and step-father felt the best solution was abortion. My ex-husband's family had other plans, we were to do the right thing, which was of course to get married. I remember a deep intuition stirring within me in the months before the wedding that something was not right, this was not what I wanted, but I went ahead anyway. Over the next nine years, four more children came along; there was a joke that we may one day find out what was causing it! That stung.

Life continued: a busy home, a struggle to make ends meet, and a son with a complex congenital heart condition kept us busy and drove us to prayer. The support of the local community took us to church, not the peace-filled sanctuary of the building on the hill where the liturgy washed over me, but a more austere Congregational Church, with an emphasis on believing the right things. It was in this context that I sensed the call of God to ordination, and it was in this context that I was told that I had stolen my husband's ministry. I didn't fit.

As a family we moved to Texas and back within a four-year period, and on returning I began to study theology and found that I had an academic gift. Another move, this time to Norfolk, took us in a completely different direction: a job share in a Methodist Church that was to lead very quickly for me to ministerial training and ordination. I learned about the Methodist emphasis on prevenient grace, the God who goes before us and makes a way no matter what our path. I was also privileged to be offered the chance to complete an MA and to study Feminist and Liberation theology. I began to awaken to myself. This inevitably caused friction in my marriage, though in all honesty it had always been there. Nine years ago my marriage came to an end; divorce followed a year later. While I couldn't see it at the time, we had set one another free.

Free but in hiding, I began to catch glimpses of who I might be, I remember driving towards Blackpool sea front (I was serving there at the time) and catching a glimpse of the sunset that filled me with utter joy, and let me see that my queer way of looking at the world, one that hadn't ever quite sat with the heteronormative expectation that I had been surrounded by, was a reflection of the beauty and creative energy of the divine. It was okay for me to see things through a queer lens, because that is how I see them, and while it confuses others so often, it simply is authentically who I am.

Over the last few years I have begun to be at home within my own skin, from that first tentative owning that I am not straight, and not who people assumed me to be, I have told my story in many places, even on local radio when they wanted an interview following Philip Scofield's story hitting the press. Can you come out in your 50s? Yes you can, and perhaps it isn't so much of a coming out as it is a coming home, a return to Eden.

Eden for me is not external but internal. I am finally at home in and with myself, it has been a challenging journey, one that has led me into and out of religion, and then back into what I see as a kinder and deeper relationship with the creator who declares both male and female, and all of our myriad ways of being and wholesome relating, to be good. I still love swimming for that reason, but when I was young it was one of the times when I felt that I could be myself, at ease with who I was, both powerful and female.

Conclusion

If we had sought therapy from mental health services, we would have wanted to find a safe space to voice our experiences and to reflect on our identity as a whole person; integrating our sexuality and spirituality in order to find that sense of Eden. Therapy services need to offer an inclusive space for people to explore their sexual and gender identities and how this relates to their spiritual identities. This is particularly important when people are young and when there may be a sense of conflict during adolescence, of wanting to express themselves but also wishing to keep parts of their identity hidden (Rivers & Carragher, 2003). Various resources are available to support therapists to develop skills in this area and some are listed below. Mental health services have been improving over the years to become more inclusive and to raise awareness amongst staff with equality and diversity training, but there is still some way to go.

References

Carr S (2010) Seldom heard or frequently ignored? Lesbian, gay and bisexual (LGB) perspectives on mental health services. *Ethnicity and Inequalities in Health and Social Care.* **3** (3) 14-23.

Chakraborty A, McManus S, Brugha T, Bebbington P & King M (2011) Mental health of the non-heterosexual population of England. *Journal of Psychiatry* **198** 143–148.

Juster R-P, Smith N, Ouellet E, Sindi S & Lupien S (2013) Sexual orientation and disclosure in relation to psychiatric symptoms, diurnal cortisol, and allostatic load. *Psychosomatic Medicine* **75** (2) 103-116.

Rivers I & Carragher D (2003) Social-developmental factors affecting lesbian and gay youth: A review of cross-national research findings. *Children and Society* **17** 374-385.

Useful resources

www.pinktherapy.com

https://www.theproudtrust.org/for-young-people/faith-and-culture/groups-and-support/

https://imaanlondon.wordpress.com/

https://www.onebodyonefaith.org.uk/

Spirituality, Services, Leadership and Training

Chapter 18:
Love and leadership leads to conscious caring

Chrissie McGinn & Richard Hewitt

Summary

In this chapter we show how an environment of kindness and appreciation can be created to support staff wellbeing. By their example, leaders can set the tone for those around them, but everyone has a sphere of influence. Everyone can choose to consciously set the tone for a culture of care that benefits staff, as well as patients and clients. This then leads to individuals taking care of themselves, each other and patients, in a more conscious, compassionate way.

Staff benefit by feeling less stressed, more supported, and able to maintain their integrity. Staff can be proud of their work and of their organisation. The organisation becomes one that people want to work for, and staff recruitment and retention improves.

We also include some reflective exercises, and an example from the Irish Health Service (HSE), where a project focusing on staff wellbeing is developing a culture of restorative conscious caring.

Everyone is a leader

Most people in the workplace do not think they are leaders, but everyone has an influence on those around them. This affects the way people are cared for. It is possible for everyone to make a positive difference.

Some leaders have a vision and take a strategic view of an organisation. Managers lead their teams, and they can create an environment of care. Some have a gift for taking their teams with them during times of change and crisis. Others have a sense of goodness and compassion towards their colleagues and their patients or clients. So what can help everyone recognise themselves as leaders and make the most of their influence?

We would like to share a few principles that could help you create a caring, supportive environment. But before we do, we would like to ask you to take a couple of minutes' silence to contemplate what you have appreciated so far today. Cast your mind back and remember what you have liked about the day. Perhaps you enjoyed your first cup of coffee of the day, working with a colleague you like, doing something that you think made a difference to someone, or maybe you just appreciated the warmth of the sunshine on your face.

Having done that, how do you feel now? Usually, people realise that, in amongst the hustle and bustle of their day, there have been good moments, and thinking about the day like this lifts their spirits.

Generating positive feelings

If we are working with a group in an organisation, we might ask them what they have appreciated about their day and why. They then share their thoughts in pairs, for a few minutes. This usually creates a buzz in the room. It comes from people feeling good and expansive, as they share their energy of enjoyment. This is how we would like people to feel at work because when they feel good it changes the way they care for one another.

We have worked in some organisations where teams have chosen to start team meetings in this way to generate a positive, creative energy before starting to solve problems.

When a leader consciously creates an environment of kindness and appreciation it sets the tone for everyone around because kindness is infectious. Perhaps you can think of ways that you could encourage a few minutes of regular reflective silence and appreciative conversation in your workplace.

A patient's experience of a kind and appreciative environment: two operations – two different experiences

A couple of years ago, Chrissie had to have two operations. Both, we are pleased to say, were successful. Each one only needed local anaesthetic. One, on her eye, took 15 minutes and the only time she had to wait was for the anaesthetic to take effect. The other one, on her arm, took three quarters of an hour and she had to wait all day at the hospital for the operation to begin. She came home from both procedures with instructions about what to do to take care of herself at home.

On the day following the operation on her eye, the one that had only taken 15 minutes, she felt shaken and was literally shaking. She did not feel confident to manage. She was tearful and unsure of herself.

On the day following the operation on her arm, the one that had taken three quarters of an hour, she had some pain in her arm and had it in a sling, but she did not feel too bad, all things considered. She felt positive and hopeful.

So, what was the difference between Chrissie coming home and believing that she could manage, and coming home and believing that she could not cope? The difference was nothing to do with the surgeons. They were both extraordinarily skilful. The difference between the two experiences was in the way that the teams cared for her.

How not to do it

Chrissie was taken to the theatre for the procedure on her eye by someone who spoke to her but did not make any eye contact. While they were operating on her eye, Chrissie could not see anything except a bright light and so there could not be any eye contact. The protocol was read out at the beginning so that the team was sure it was the right patient, and then there was silence. There was no physical contact except for the surgeon carrying out the procedure.

When the surgeon had finished, Chrissie had difficulty getting up because of previous injuries. She had told three different people that this would be the case, but the person helping her seemed surprised and said, "Oh, well, take your time". Back on the ward, the conversations of the nurses talking in the next bay were negative and the instructions for going home were simply read out to her.

How to do it

During the procedure on her arm, although she had to wait all day for it and the theatre team then had to work past their shift time to do it, the theatre sister smiled and talked to her as she was taken to the theatre. The team talked to one another and included her. A nurse held her hand and told the surgeon if she thought Chrissie was in pain. Even though they were late finishing, the staff were cheerful and the Sister thanked them genuinely for still being there. They were fully present during the procedure, kind and caring to Chrissie, and kind to one another.

The contrast was quite extraordinary in the way that these two procedures were carried out, and the contrast on Chrissie's level of anxiety and healing were equally extraordinary. The difference it made – being treated kindly, and as one human being to another, rather than as one role to another – was significant.

The learning

There is so much we can learn from these two examples. They show how a kind and caring environment makes a difference to a patient's sense of being seen and heard, and to their belief that they will be able to cope with their situation when they go home. But not only do patients benefit from a caring environment, staff also feel less stressed and more appreciated. The first situation highlighted the effect of a disenchanted and undervalued team. The second showed what a kind and caring environment looks like, and how staff can consciously care for each other, even when they are under pressure and tired. It is worth the effort as it improves our relationships, our sense of self-worth and our wellbeing. It seems that kindness is good for us all.

Reflective exercise

You might like to take a moment to reflect on a time when you think that you connected with kindness with a patient, a client, or a colleague. A time when you really connected with the person as one human being to another, rather than seeing them from your role. Cast your mind back and remember that time in as much detail as you can – what was the situation where you were able to really connect with kindness and see beyond roles? Where were you? Who else was around? Was it a quiet time or a busy time? Was it at night or during the day? Just recall yourself being with that person. How did you feel? Remember the difference you made to that person.

Come back to the present and notice how you are feeling now, as you recall that kind connection.

Reflecting like this is an aspect of being conscious. Remembering what we did and how we felt about it is part of what we mean when we talk about conscious caring.

Kindness is natural

The act of reflecting and remembering something you have done well, or when you connected with kindness with someone, has probably raised your energy, so now you feel good, too. It will encourage you to be kind again.

As we said in our chapter entitled 'Creating an Environment of Kindness and Conscious Caring' in *Sharing Compassion – A Fortuitous Journey of Illumination* (2018), kindness not only makes the receiver feel good, accepted and appreciated, it also makes the giver feel good as oxytocin and serotonin are released. Oxytocin makes us want to be loving. It is released when a mother loves her baby. It is there when we are in love. It is there when we are kind to one another, and when we see others being kind. The release of oxytocin makes us want to be kind again.

One of the reasons our species has survived and thrived is because it is natural for us to be kind and compassionate. We would not have survived in more primitive times if we had not worked together. Our children would not have survived if they had not been nurtured.

During the COVID-19 pandemic, people had opportunities to work together and care for each other. It allowed us to release our natural compassion and it made a difference to people's lives. We saw many examples of communities working together and people showing kindness to one another. However, it also meant that some workers were under great pressure in extraordinarily stressful situations. A kind and appreciative environment is most needed in such situations, but it is also a time when kindness can easily be forgotten. We may have to make the effort to consciously choose to be kind.

Creating an environment of kindness and appreciation

We know that it is sometimes difficult to create an environment of kindness, an environment where oxytocin is being released. When we are caught up with thoughts and words about what we have done wrong or what we cannot do, it drags our mood down. We start withdrawing, rather than being expansive and outward looking. However, when we are pleased with what we have done, or appreciate what we have, we start to feel better. We are then more likely to be kind to someone. It helps to be:

- **Conscious of our feelings**: We all have times when we do not feel good. We may feel anxious, or angry, or just plain grumpy. And this is where consciousness comes in. If we do not want to react to those feelings, we need to recognise that we have them, and then make a choice. We need to acknowledge our feelings and then be compassionate to ourselves for having them. We can be kind to ourselves.

  Acknowledging our feelings helps us to step outside of them. Once I have stepped outside of my feelings, I can look at them and then choose to modify them, or begin to let them go, or deal with them later. I can be conscious of my feelings and thoughts, but I do not have to act from them.

- **Present**: The main lesson from the earlier examples of Chrissie's care was about being present. The one team was there with each other, conscious of each other and communicating with each other, and with the patient, Chrissie. We do not know where the other team was as they were wrapped up in themselves and not giving anything away.

- If I want to be present, I bring my whole self to the party. I am not thinking about what has passed, or worrying about the future, or even whether I am being professional or not. I am here with you; listening and wanting to understand you and wanting to be understood by you. I am picking up clues. Clues about what you have understood, what you have missed, what you disagree with and so on. I can do this because I am connecting with you.

- **Non-judgemental**: If I am judging or categorising you, I am thinking about you and not being with you. Judgement also means that I treat you as I have judged you, rather than as you really are. If I have judged that you are the one who is always whinging and whining, then I will probably have an attitude that is less than open hearted.

- Move beyond roles: Of course, we will all deliver a competent and professional service to everyone, no matter how we have judged them, or how grumpy we are feeling. However, I may not be able to connect with you unless I can step beyond my role and meet you, one human being to another.

   Moving beyond roles can sometimes make us feel vulnerable, and so disinclined to connect. We have the choice.

Connection, reflection and service

If we are able to make a connection with others while being ourselves, and being fully present we will also be connected to the Divine, God, the Universe (whatever you call the 'Something Greater than Ourselves'). We can feel supported and safe in this connection. When we feel safe, we are more able to be ourselves, to give of our best, and to be open to kindness from others. It becomes a continuous cycle as kindness generates kindness.

William Bloom (2011) speaks of Connection, Reflection and Service as the basis of contemporary spirituality. We all know the value of reflection. It is part of professional practice in most areas these days. In this context we are considering our thoughts, feelings and behaviour and checking their effect. For example, how am I feeling as I walk along the corridor to meet my boss? Perhaps a bit anxious. Perhaps I am thinking about how I am going to ask for something and I'm concerned that she will say no. If I carry these thoughts and feelings with me into the meeting, I am not fully present. I am not totally engaged. However, if I am conscious of my thoughts and feelings, I can step outside of them. I can choose to set them aside and be more present during the meeting.

Let us consider Service. We all want to provide a good professional service to patients or clients. However, we can also serve our colleagues as well as our patients. I can serve you more deeply if I am connected to you from my heart as well as my head.

You will see from Figure 18.1 that the heart is central. As a leader, when we are connecting as one human being to another, we support other people around us. We encourage them by loving and appreciating their humanity. We do this when we help someone understand what is happening to them and what they can do to help themselves and their colleagues.

In difficult situations, people can often feel stressed, and yet think that they should be stoical (and perhaps hide behind their roles). We can help people understand that it is natural to feel stressed at such times and help them to acknowledge their stress with compassion. This encourages them to have compassion for themselves as well as relieving their levels of stress.

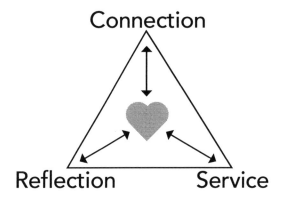

Figure 18.1: Contemporary Spirituality

Reflective exercise

■ How and when do you connect with something greater than you?
■ How and when do you reflect on each day?
■ How and when do you serve others?

Love

As leaders we need to be self-aware, able to look after ourselves and able to care for others. We then give others permission to do the same as we set the tone and expectation for "the way we do things around here". Many years ago we worked for a Sussex hospital group on a project called "The Worthing Way", which was created to establish a more caring environment. We trained many managers, and our philosophy of Conscious Caring underpinned all the management courses.

At that time, conscious caring was not overtly spoken about. We certainly would not have used the word 'love'. As it is now acceptable to use words like love and self-compassion, it shows how much staff development in healthcare has changed in the last 25 years.

Creating an environment of kindness and appreciation in the Irish Health Service

We have been working on a project in Ireland that is overtly founded on compassion and love. The project was initiated to promote self-care in the Irish health service (the Health Service Executive – HSE). It is based on the premise that self-care is not a selfish approach to life, but a way of enhancing life so that a person has more to give to others. Mary Prendergast, the Director of Nursing, Innovation & Research, has introduced a Restorative Conscious Caring Programme for staff.

Over the last ten years, Mary has organised an annual conference on compassion in healthcare. This has led to a raft of interventions in the form of training programmes, seminars and workshops. Healthcare providers can now apply for accreditation of their healthcare centres and hospitals if they can demonstrate a sustainable culture of self-care and conscious caring. A programme has been introduced for all levels of staff and from different disciplines. The programme consists of a one-day, 12 Steps of Restoration Programme, a three-day Conscious Caring Programme and the training and development of Self-Care Champions. As part of their training days, teams are also offered the opportunity for restorative practice, e.g. mindfulness training, retreats, meditation and wellbeing workshops

The Restorative and Conscious Caring Programme

As Mary's Restorative Practice Booklet (2018) explains, "the programme aims to facilitate staff to feel grounded in their own professional and personal wisdom, while exploring their innate capacity to feel deeply, and understand their values and beliefs. It aims to help staff think clearly and act with integrity, while demonstrating high standards of professional care and behaviour. It supports physical and emotional health to ensure restorative self-care needs are met."

The programme gives staff the understanding and skills to create a kind and appreciative environment. It includes recognising and managing emotional triggers, being conscious of thoughts, feelings, and behaviour, being present and non-judgemental, going beyond roles, spiritual connection, peaceful listening and reflection, and the power of silence. The focus is on understanding the nature of stress and increasing awareness of stress management, resilience and self-care.

Benefits for staff wellbeing

The project supports, motivates and sustains staff to initiate appropriate change by encouraging them to maintain and restore themselves using the techniques and tools offered in the programme.

Staff are introduced to concepts, models and techniques so that they can work together to implement their learning in their own work settings. This emphasis helps staff take responsibility for their own wellbeing with the support of the organisation.

The programme is seen as a valuable training resource which can be used to improve recruitment and retention of staff by using Self-Care Champions and initiatives to create and encourage a restorative working environment in the organisation. A service accreditation process has been introduced and the first awards were given in 2020. There is a bronze, silver and gold level of accreditation.

Completing the various stages of the accreditation journey enables a real recognition of services and their achievements in restorative practice as examples of best practice. The Restorative Practice Accreditation process has been shown to be relevant for good governance and management, as well as for staff wellbeing.

Accreditation provides a reward to the service area for their commitment to promoting and facilitating the practice of self-care management. Organisations and service areas provide evidence that the programme is established, ongoing and sustainable. They can also provide evidence of any other wellbeing and restorative programmes they would like the accreditation team to consider.

Some examples of the practical outcomes include the establishment of a quiet room for reflection and meditation, a reduction in staff turnover, less conflict, and fewer grievances. It has also led to a reduction in long-term sickness as people manage their stress levels better. Feedback from staff involved in the programme shows that they have enjoyed the process and feel more valued and empowered. They are pleased that self-care is recognised as important.

We have enjoyed working on this project and think that this approach to staff wellbeing is crucial during the difficult times and pressures that healthcare is currently facing. Mary Prendergast has had the vision and determination to establish a caring and sensitive approach to meet the wellbeing needs of healthcare staff in the present healthcare climate.

Setting our intent

So, what have we covered? We have explored what a kind and appreciative environment looks like. We have shown how a kind and conscious caring environment can be created, and we have highlighted the importance of connection, reflection and service. We have seen how a culture of kindness and appreciation can help people take responsibility for, and manage, their own health and wellbeing.

A culture like this can be created when people remember to be conscious as they connect, reflect and serve one another, and when they learn the skills that they need to develop support for each other and themselves. We have demonstrated how this approach has worked with the Restorative Practice and Conscious Caring Programme in Ireland.

One last thought. A conscious leader can set her intent to be the best that she can be each day. She can focus on a quality that she thinks will make a difference to her day, e.g. courage, kindness, calmness, peacefulness, patience. The intent becomes a touchstone to reflect on during the day. She can encourage others to do the same each day. The setting of an intent gives everyone a focus to remind them to appreciate who they truly are and to see that spark of goodness in everyone. What will your intent be today?

References

Bloom W (2011) *The Power of Modern Spirituality – How to Live a Life of Compassion and Personal Fulfilment* Piatkus.

McGinn & Hewitt R (2018) *Creating an Environment of Kindness and Conscious Caring* in ed. Prendergast & Brophy *Sharing Compassion – A Fortuitous Journey of Illumination* Rainsford Press pp 21–30.

*Mary Prendergast 2018 *Restorative Practice Booklet* accessed 07.11.20 www.restorativecaring.com

Chapter 19:

Coming at it obliquely: spiritual training for healthcare staff in an age of uncertainty

By Nirmala Ragbir-Day & Mike Gartland

Summary

The goal of developing a spiritually competent and skilled workforce has shaped the implementation of a staff training strategy within a large NHS provider of mental health services in West Yorkshire. At the heart of this approach has been the promotion of a largely experientially based model of training. This has included retreats and residential courses, fully funded by the NHS available to all staff groups.

Striving to engage creatively with an ethnically and religiously diverse workforce which includes a significant minority identifying as secular or non-religious, has been the catalyst for a process of experimentation, innovation and inclusivity in training design and delivery.

Recognition of the universality of spirituality in human experience alongside its ultimate transcendence of the spheres of logic and language have required trainers who are at ease with tentativeness, humility, adaptability and openness.

'Coming at it obliquely' encapsulates this understanding as it has sought to take root and bear fruit within a major healthcare provider.

Introduction

Tell all the Truth but tell it slant
Success in Circuit lies
Too bright for our infirm delight
The Truth's superb surprise

As Lightning to the Children eased
With explanation kind
The Truth must dazzle gradually
Or every man be blind

Emily Dickinson

How are moral or spiritual truths taught or communicated? This is a key question that has shaped the development of a staff training and support programme within a large NHS provider of mental health services in the North of England.

Emily Dickinson's poem reflects a wisdom that is universal within our great spiritual traditions, perhaps nowhere as beautifully or succinctly expressed as by the anonymous author of the 14th century English classic, *The Cloud of Unknowing*[15]. The author writes, 'By love may He be gotten and holden but by thinking never'. The parables of Jesus reflect a similar strategy of coming at things obliquely, telling it slant, using allegory, symbol and metaphor to encourage the listener into the liminal spaces where eyes may be opened and new understandings glimpsed.

How otherwise than by these or similar approaches are a set of estimable corporate values[16] (e.g. we put the person first and in the centre; we are respectful, open honest and transparent) actually moved from head to heart and individually and organisationally enculturated?

Disturbing recent examples of statutory health care providers found guilty of delivering care which is seriously lacking in compassion whilst claiming to adhere to admirable person-centred principles illustrate the challenge precisely.

---

15 An English classic, *The Cloud of Unknowing* is an anonymous work of Christian mysticism written in Middle English in the latter half of the 14th century. The text is a spiritual guide on contemplative prayer in the late Middle Ages.

16 SWYPT corporate values - https://www.southwestyorkshire.nhs.uk/about-us/why-were-here/vision-mission-and-values/

Bearing in mind the above caveats, what is it possible to say meaningfully about the domains of spirituality, spiritual truth and spiritual care? The monastery may be comfortable with imprecision with a recognition in this area, above most others, of the limitations of language. Healthcare funders, however, generally require the hard evidence of tangible even measurable characteristics and outcomes. So in developing a case for resourcing a spiritual care service, one of the initial tasks was to undertake a piece of research (Greasley *et al*, 2001) which used focus groups to obtain the views of mental health service users, carers and professionals about the concept of spirituality and the provision of spiritual care in mental health nursing.

Key themes which emerged in the group discussions related to spiritual care needing to acknowledge a person's sense of meaning and purpose to life (which may or may not find expression through formal religious beliefs and practices). Spiritual care was also associated with the quality of interpersonal care in terms of love and compassion. For the majority of service users who participated, the domain of spirituality was of vital concern and the researchers suggested that this was indicative of a recognition that it was the language of spirituality, more than any other discipline, which came closest to articulating 'deeply subjective, ultimately ineffable, yet crucially important dimensions of human experience – especially as these relate to the processes of illness and healing'.

On the basis of this research, the South West Yorkshire Partnership Trust (SWYPT) Board of Directors gave approval for the re-designation of the existing chaplaincy service as 'Pastoral and Spiritual Care' and provided resources for additional staffing.

This gave the service both a higher profile within the organisation and also permitted greater attention to be given to the development of a staff training and support programme which put spiritual care at the centre of a holistic understanding of personal and professional development.

As the then Chief Executive further commented at the time, it also demonstrated a growing corporate recognition of the importance and, indeed for many service users, the crucial significance of spiritual care to their self-maintenance and recovery processes.

Oblique: 'At an angle; slanting; not done in a direct way

SWYPT is a large NHS organisation employing over 4,000 staff in the provision of mental health, learning disability and community health services to a population of over a million people in South and West Yorkshire. It also draws upon the skills and commitment of volunteers many of whom contribute to the outreach of the Pastoral and Spiritual Care service in the roles of Befrienders and volunteer chaplains.

Shortly before the implementation of the service developments described above the lead chaplain had undertaken an NHS funded travel research project designed to investigate the potential for introducing meditation practice into staff training and patient support programmes. This had involved experience of Vipassana and Samatha meditation within UK Buddhist communities and also of the Hesychast contemplative practice of Orthodox monastic communities on Mount Athos in Greece[17]. An early outcome of this project was the funding by SWYPT of an inaugural residential retreat for 15 staff members in 2003. The venue was an Anglican retreat house in North Yorkshire. This first event was promoted as a personal development opportunity for staff seeking to understand and incorporate holistic approaches within their own clinical practice. Positive feedback and evaluations led to increased funding and within a couple of years the number of retreats offered increased to four. Shortly afterwards regular residential retreats for both service users and carers operating on a similar model were offered.

At the same time the remit for the staff retreats was widened to directly support a staff wellbeing strategy by emphasising the value of 'time out' for staff experiencing work related or domestic stress. The dual focus on wellbeing and personal development has continued to the present with innovations such as 'Returner' retreats for those wishing to deepen or refresh their practice and non-residential retreats - one day events promoted as 'Urban retreats' – for those unable or hesitant at making a commitment to a longer residential event.

The overall outcome of the retreat programme has been the opportunity for many hundreds of staff to have had direct experience of inner work on themselves and thereby come to a fuller appreciation of the value of attending to deeper, spiritual, areas of human need and functioning. At the same time the embedding of the retreats within the corporate consciousness of the organisation – bolstered by the consistently high levels of positive feedback - has undoubtedly opened the door and paved the way for further service development.

---

17 Hesychasm: a tradition of contemplative prayer and ascetical discipline in the Eastern Orthodox Church. Vipassana: a Buddhist meditation practice that seeks insight into the nature of reality. Samatha: one of the two qualities of mind developed in Buddhist meditation (Vipassana is the other). Trans. 'tranquillity of the mind'.

The mindfulness revolution

Among the first of the spin offs from the early retreat programme were requests from staff for further training in meditation and for ongoing opportunities for practice. This propitiously coincided with the beginnings of a more widespread curiosity within the organisation about 'Mindfulness'. Mindfulness, particularly in relation to stress reduction, had come to the attention of an increasing number of psychological practitioners. This resulted in Pastoral and Spiritual Care taking a lead within SWYPT organising Introduction to Mindfulness workshops. These sessions created the foundation for establishing a regular ongoing programme of Mindfulness themed events which more recently has been extended to include input on loving kindness, self-compassion and self-care.

Participation in Mindfulness, Compassion and Wellbeing themed regional conferences has formed part of the ongoing training of several members of the Pastoral and Spiritual care team. Skills and experience gained have consolidated the service's high profile in this area of staff and service user support.

A component of the early staff retreats had been the inclusion within each of an experiential complementary or alternative therapy workshop. These included crystal healing, the Enneagram, chanting, Myers-Briggs training, spiritual healing, Yogic breathwork and Chi Kung. This early experimentation led to regular spiritual healing sessions being made available to all trust staff at a central location. This remains a popular and valued wellbeing option with between 20 and 40 individual sessions available each month. Similarly, for many years, bodywork in the form of outdoor tai chi sessions has been a standard feature of the retreats. Also offered on each residential retreat is an individual complementary therapy session with a qualified practitioner. Options regularly include aromatherapy, Indian head massage, breathwork and reflexology.

Spiritual care training in the context of SWYPT values and ethos

In February 2011, *No Health without Mental Health: A Cross-government Mental Health Outcomes Strategy for People of All Ages* (Department of Health and Social Care, 2011) was published. This presented clear guidelines about the requirement to embed Pastoral and Spiritual care into service delivery.

At this point SWYPT had already made considerable strides in this direction. In particular the experience of several years of offering staff retreats and meditation workshops alongside a more traditional training programme, which included such modules as 'Recognising Spiritual Needs; Understanding the Processes of Loss and Bereavement and Holistic Approaches to Care', led in 2010 to the creation of a dedicated spiritual care trainer post.

Employed under a modified Chaplaincy role job description, this part-time post represented a very real commitment by the organisation to expand the reach of the existing service. Support for this development had followed the successful evaluation of the piloting within SWYPT of a modular staff training and development programme developed by The Janki Foundation for Spirituality in Healthcare[18].

Aimed at healthcare professionals, *Values in Healthcare: A spiritual approach*[19] (VIHASA) offers a values-based approach to learning and practice. Its seven modules encourage the development of values like peace, positivity, compassion co-operation and resilience through groupwork, personal reflection and discussion. As such, VIHASA offers an alternative to a more traditional training model based largely on the acquisition of knowledge and practical skills or spiritual tools. A model which tends to attach less significance to the development of communication and interpersonal skills, and even less, if any, to self-care.

A before and after study accompanying the pilot scheme showed a clear need for more training with an emphasis on self-care and support. This was regarded as vital to improving coping skills, raising morale and restoring a sense of purpose. As a consequence, it was also seen as instrumental to promoting staff retention, preventing burnout, and having a positive impact on staff absentee and sickness levels. This endorsed one of the conclusions of the 2009 report *Spiritual Care Matters* by NHS Scotland, which stated, 'It is now widely accepted that those organisations which have a 'spiritually-friendly' culture show universally lower than average rates of absenteeism, workplace stress and staff turnover'.

Central to the VIHASA strategy is the encouragement of self-enquiry, seen as a crucial component to the process of both individuals and teams coming to a deeper understanding of their core values and beliefs. Beyond this lies a recognition that, on an individual level, the achievement of clarity in this domain can lead to a process of profound personal re-vitalisation and renewal.

The implementation of a Pastoral and Spiritual Care strategic framework (South West Yorkshire Partnership, 2012) included a commitment to making experientially based training on spiritual values available to all staff disciplines. This was seen as providing strong support to the organisational aim of providing services that,

---

18 The Janki Foundation for Spirituality in Healthcare: www.jankifoundation.org/

19 The Values in Healthcare: A Spiritual Approach: www.jankifoundation.org/values-in-healthcare/

in reflecting the core corporate values, were sensitive to the needs of a diverse population and would therefore enable people to reach their potential and live well in their communities.

The Strategic framework stated: 'SWYFT recognises that a person-centred holistic approach to recovery and wellbeing must engage deeply with spiritual issues and so respond effectively to the spiritual needs of service users, carers and staff'. Recognising our oneness with others, with the cosmos, and with the Divine (however understood) brings about a deepening inner congruence. From this healing for ourselves and a deep compassion for others spontaneously arises expressed both in word and deed.

The still point in a changing world

The training strategy over the past decade has continued to build on the earlier foundations by providing a diverse range of opportunities for staff to deepen their understanding of what is involved in spirituality and spiritual care. The strategy draws on a participative and experientially focused model of personal and professional development designed to encourage self-awareness, self-confidence, develop relevant competencies and spiritual skills.

Regular residential staff retreats fully funded by SWYPT continue to be a mainstay of the training programme. Held in a peaceful and secure rural location, the retreats continue to evolve by offering a variety of approaches to personal and spiritual development. Interest in the potential of these events for staff support has also been expressed by a wide range of other healthcare providers following the publicity the retreats received as finalists in the 2012 *Nursing Times* annual awards.

Mindfulness and self-compassion training are integral components of both residential and **1-day 'Urban' retreats**. Shorter taster sessions as well as more extensive trainings are also incorporated into other experiential and educational events.

The service continues to take a lead in promoting the benefits of Mindfulness practice for staff through regular one-day workshops, with eligibility for study leave. Seen as a core skill for enhancing both personal and professional life, the workshop trainings have broadened to include targeted events for particular professional groups and for mixed groups of service users and staff. More recently, the growing recognition of the ethical dimension to mindfulness training has led to the routine incorporation of self-awareness, self-compassion and loving kindness practice into training schedules.

Meditation sessions, which have been held weekly for over a decade in one of the hospital chapels and since April 2020 have also been available on-line. Several 'quiet' rooms in clinical areas have also been developed to allow patients and staff 'time out' for quiet reflection, prayer and meditation. Typically, these are centred on a large natural stone or similar non-religious object of particular beauty and furnished to include meditation stools, prayer mats and a variety of spiritual and devotional texts.

Lifting Your Spirits[20] – A multi-sessional programme on how to respond positively to personal difficulties or illness is an offshoot of the VIHASA training (see above). Designed to enable participants to develop skills for confident self-expression, deeper empathy and greater emotional resilience, the sessions also use breathwork and bodywork to explore techniques for achieving states of deep relaxation and tranquillity. The core training is in learning to practice and incorporate in daily life seven simple tools which enhance physical, mental and spiritual wellbeing:

- Meditation
- Visualisation
- Appreciation
- Creativity
- Listening
- Play
- Reflection

Optional monthly support sessions are available to help strengthen reflective practices of these tools.

Annual Spirituality in Healthcare Conferences, often with a national speaker, have allowed the service to reach out to a wide cross section of interested colleagues and to showcase developments and achievements over the previous year. From 2011 conference themes have included:

- Enhancing Spiritual Values and Wellbeing at Work
- Science and Consciousness
- The Science of Spirituality
- Spiritual & Faith Communities and Mental Health

An annual spiritual skills competencies training programme, with a focus on mindfulness-based stress management and training in spiritual values, is available to staff who want to go further in incorporating holistic approaches into their clinical

---

20 Lifting Your Spirits: www.jankifoundation.org/lifting-your-spirits/

or professional practice. The programme, which includes ongoing mentorship, reflects the overarching service strategy of developing a spiritually skilled workforce to deliver care that is highly responsive to patients' religious and spiritual needs.

A 20-metre diameter outdoor labyrinth was created at the NHS Fieldhead site in Wakefield and opened in April 2013. It offers a beautiful and unique space to unwind and return to a centre point of peace and stillness. The outer spiral journey to the centre of the labyrinth can be seen as symbolic of the journey inwards – towards a reconnection with the deep self via the path of compassion and self-acceptance. Surrounding the labyrinth, flower beds in colours representing each of the four seasons with seating areas, including a forum for meetings, have been constructed. Located in the Caring Garden[21] away from the hospital buildings, this space provides a beautiful relaxing environment, one which naturally offers itself as a much-appreciated resource for retreat days and similar types of event.

Conclusion and way forward

The overarching strategy of enabling as many staff as possible to deepen their understanding of spiritual issues and to develop spiritual skills has engendered constantly evolving patterns of service engagement at both an individual and corporate level. As a consequence, increasing numbers of staff have been able to recognise and respond more effectively to patients' spiritual needs and to develop greater personal resilience and job satisfaction.

Organisationally, this has led to a growing recognition that the provision of spiritual care, led by a small dedicated team, is something in which the entire workforce has a part to play. Spiritual care, the core of a holistic approach to care, extends from how someone is greeted in the corridor to how the need for religious ritual is met at a time of profound personal crisis.

An outreach project launched in 2017 by the Pastoral Care service 'Spirit in Mind'[22] (SIM), seeks to respond more effectively to the mental health needs of people living in the community by working closely with local faith-based organisations. The SIM initiative follows encouragement at national level by government agencies and the NHS for greater cross-sector collaboration. Faith leaders and community activists engage in training to deepen their understanding of mental health issues and are supported in initiating local projects such as befriender services, bereavement support and drop-in groups.

---

21 Caring Garden: www.southwestyorkshire.nhs.uk/2012/03/02/tree-planting-at-fieldhead-to-mark-the-start-of-caring-garden-project/

22 Spirit in Mind: www.southwestyorkshire.nhs.uk/spirit-in-mind/home/

The continued evolution of the Pastoral and Spiritual Care staff development programme at SWYPT is based on research, innovation, adaptability and, above all, on a willing acceptance of the necessity of trial and error in moving from theory to practice.

Case Study 1: Mental Health Team Manager (since 2006)

It was a difficult period in my personal life that prompted me to access pastoral care about seven years ago. I have utilised the meditation and mindfulness techniques to help establish and maintain a regular practise which has been particularly invaluable during this Covid-19 situation. My regular practice helps me to manage a very demanding role. It also helps me support my team to develop and utilise such skills, and the team I manage actually runs daily meditation, health and wellbeing sessions for staff (these were set up at my request). Several of my team have also accessed the urban and residential retreats. I think by accessing the training I am open to encouraging my staff to seek creative ways of self-managing their health and wellbeing.

I have helped to co-facilitate sessions and have supported residential and urban retreats. Taking the opportunity to complete the spiritual skills training helped me to build my skills and confidence, both with co-facilitating sessions and delivering health and wellbeing sessions. This has allowed me the opportunity to meet different people with different life experiences and I have built relationships across the Trust. Assisting the pastoral and spiritual care dept enables me to develop a personal interest that I can utilise when supporting my large staff team.

Case Study 2: Community Support Worker (over 30 years)

Before I started practicing mindfulness and using spiritual tools, I felt lost through grief. There was no focus in my life and I lacked confidence. Mindfulness has allowed me to accept my past and enjoy being in the present. Knowing what I have control of and letting go of what I do not have control of enables me to overcome my anxiety.

At present, I am confident in life both personally and professionally. I feel alive, at peace, and I love myself. In meditation, I have re-found my faith. I practice gratitude and I know all will be ok, no matter what. I am more patient and in control of my thoughts and actions. I journal and do mindfulness colouring which relaxes me. All these things boost my mind, body and soul. I have learnt that I can't fix anyone but myself. My relationship with my mom has done a 360 degree turn for the best; it is fantastic! Friends and family have noticed my calmer demeaner especially whilst driving. I am also more able to have a voice and my listening skills have improved. Lifting Your Spirits sessions and being part of the support group form the bedrock in enabling my self-care! My work performance has improved and my clients are happy. One client commented: 'My support worker is amazing, passionate in what she does, caring, and is making a difference in our lives though supporting us in dealing with anxiety'.

Reflections on Retreat 2012
(Senior Manager)

3 Nights, 4 days away from home
How will I cope? No family all alone
So why are you here? You might ask
The answer is clear, To rid me of this mask
As the song goes ---
I can see clearly now!
The fog has lifted
No stiff joints, the pain has shifted
No heavy weight upon me
Only a lightness, I hope others can see
I arrived with some in trepidation
And leave here today with Elation!

References

Department of Health and Social Care (2011) *No Health without Mental Health: A Cross-government Mental Health Outcomes Strategy for People of All Ages.*

Greasley P, Chiu LF, Gartland M (2001) The concept of spiritual care in mental health nursing. *Journal of Advanced Nursing* **33** (5).

NHS Scotland (2009) Spiritual Care Matters [online]. Available at: https://www.nes.scot.nhs.uk/media/23nphas3/spiritualcaremattersfinal.pdf (accessed July 2021).

South West Yorkshire Partnership (2012) *Pastoral and Spiritual Care strategic framework* [online]. Available at: www.southwestyorkshire.nhs.uk/wp-content/uploads/2018/04/Pastoral-and-spiritual-care-strategic-framework.pdf

Chapter 20:

Compassionate leadership for an interconnected world

By Michael West

Summary

This chapter proposes that compassionate leadership is essential for nurturing cultures and communities of compassion and interconnection. Such communities enable us to experience our interconnectedness with other people, species and our ecosystems, and express the associated kindness which is at the heart of spirituality, whether from the perspective of established religions, main streams of philosophical thought or other belief systems. This chapter endeavours to answer the question 'How?'

Introduction

The pandemic has taught us that we must promote understanding of our interconnectedness with each other – across professional boundaries, across hierarchies, across sectors, across communities and across nations. And to develop our understanding of our connectedness with other species and the planet of which we are a part, not a separate and controlling entity. It is vital to grasp this moment and model and promote compassion within and across our communities in an enduring way, because connection and compassion are certain, unchanging, and provide a safe refuge in the face of major threats to our health, lives and communities.

Living in greater harmony as a result of the experience of compassionate interconnection, with each other, with other species and with our planet, will also enable us to respond to the greatest existential threats we face – such as pandemics and climate change. This chapter begins by suggesting that our need to belong, which is powerful and profound, also harbours within it the seeds of our destruction and destructiveness – intergroup discrimination and prejudice.

Belonging and intergroup hostility

What helps us also ails us. Meeting our need to belong is fundamental to our health and wellbeing. Loneliness and social isolation are profoundly damaging to our health and wellbeing, whereas connection, love and inclusion enable us to thrive (Baumeister & Leary, 1995). Evolution has equipped us with the means to get this core need met, such as the hard wiring of babies to make eye contact with their mother (or father and other caregivers) and thereby nurture connection. Evolution has also given us our impulse to help, the ubiquity of compassion and the value of altruism. Being kind to others, helping them and showing we care, enables bonding and connection, and builds trust in relationships – effectively reinforcing a sense of mutual belonging.

It is rewarded at a biochemical level through the release of oxytocin, and in life experience by feelings of happiness and safety. Empathy, forgiveness and caring have deeply beneficial effects upon wellbeing and resilience. Neglect, incivility, exclusion, bullying and harassment have quite opposite and profound effects. Throughout our evolutionary history, by bonding and creating supportive social groups we could survive far more effectively. We could share food, mate, safely raise our young and be protected from the predations of other animals (including some humans). Bonding and thereby building social groups are powerful and fundamental currents in the flow of human experience.

Yet, contained within the impulse to connect and bond is a key challenge for modern humanity. We come to identify with the groups of which we are part – where we feel that our needs to belong are met – such as male, young, White, British, football supporter, jazz lover, vegetarian etc. 'We come to identify' means we use these categories to construct an identity which we project out into the social world as a story of 'who'.

And preserving a positive sense of our constructed identity is important because it enables us to feel more secure with and happier about ourselves. By extension, those who belong to other categories I evaluate in slightly (or considerably) less positive terms because they are not members of the groups by which I define myself. This can apply to even the most arbitrary or superficial of category differences, such as accent, skin colour or eye colour. Thus I may come to dislike or denigrate those with different political views, coming from other countries, who eat meat, who are from a different religious tradition to my own, or even whose shade of skin colour is darker or somehow different from mine. Such social identity processes are underlying causes of discrimination, prejudice and cruelty in human society (Hewstone & Swart, 2011). Wars, racism, sexism, genocide, violence against women, ageism, populism and religious persecution are expressions of this underlying human tendency to create identities based on group and intergroup processes.

It is particularly salient now at a time in our history when we face threats to our existence that can only be neutralised by working together across all of humanity with a sense of shared identity. These threats are real. Pandemics are the most obvious, given our recent shared experience, but even greater are climate change and the destruction of other species threatening the biodiversity upon which the health of the ecosystem depends. Other threats we have created ourselves, such as weapons of mass destruction, which could eliminate human life as a result of accident or intent.

Our growing awareness of our interdependence and interconnectedness with each other, with other species and our fragile ecosystems, as well as the planet, demands we learn how to create a wider sense of identity. This will be based on our experienced sense of shared humanity and intergroup similarity. There is a powerful existential imperative that we act with compassion towards all we are connected with, if we are to ensure healthy evolution of the ecosystems and communities we are part of as well as our own species. Compassionate leadership within and across boundaries is essential for us to succeed in facing these challenges and overcoming them.

Compassion: a universal value

Compassion is a sensitivity to suffering in self and others with a commitment to try to alleviate and prevent it (Gilbert, 2013). We are motivated to notice and become aware of the distress of the other and pay attention to this distress, while having an empathic insight into the needs of others.

Compassion is a universal value because it is care that flows naturally from a deep part of ourselves. Across cultures it is celebrated as a positive value and behaviour – there are paragons across cultures; communities everywhere celebrate compassion. Compassion binds us together, creates a sense of safety and interconnectedness and is a manifestation of love in an encompassing rather than exclusive sense. It nurtures a feeling of belonging to others beyond our immediate circles.

It also implies having the motivation to help. The 'commitment to alleviate/prevent suffering' requires courage and wisdom – taking 'wise' action. Compassion includes the motivation to relieve the suffering of others as well as cognitive empathy – stepping into the other's shoes, which helps to guide an appropriate response. These are basic human reactions for which most of us are pre-programmed.

Four elements of compassion

The increase in thinking and research on compassion in the last decade is perhaps because of the global movements to nurture a greater sense of connection across our communities and in relation to our planet more widely. Compassion can be understood simply as having four components[23]: *attending*, *understanding*, *empathising* and *helping* (Atkins & Parker, 2012).

Compassion is a means of connecting with all others – those we love, those to whom we are neutral or indifferent and those who we find difficult – and establishing trust and warmth. It is a way of transcending boundaries and establishing our shared humanity with a commitment to help, support and nourish. When we become more aware, open and curious about the world and those around us through attending (being present), seeking to understand, empathising and with a commitment to helping, life has greater meaning and richness. It enables us also to respond more wisely to personal challenges and to manage our anxieties, anger and pains with greater confidence and ease. In short, it transforms our mental and physical health.

Compassion and health

Below we describe the importance of compassion as protective of health, drawn largely from a powerful recent research review (Trzeciak & Mazzarelli, 2019). There is a strong link between human connection (closeness rather than number of connections) and risk of death from all causes. Having good relationships is associated with 50% higher odds of survival over time, revealing how fundamental belonging and connection are to us humans. Loneliness is deeply damaging to human wellbeing and is associated with higher mortality than obesity and high blood pressure, and comparable in terms of mortality to smoking and alcohol abuse. Being lonely is associated with between 26% and 50% higher odds of early death.

For those who are already ill, connection and a sense of belonging are protective. Heart attack patients who reported lacking emotional support had three times higher odds of death. The corollary is also true. A study with 406 volunteers monitored their stress, conflict and social support over a two-week period. They

---

23 A more sophisticated breakdown, based on extensive theorising and research, is offered in Gilbert (2013).

were then exposed to the cold virus, following which they were quarantined to determine who succumbed and what factors appeared to protect those who didn't. The study showed that those with high stress and conflict in the previous two weeks were more likely to develop the infection. Social support in contrast protected against infection. Thirty-two per cent of the protective effect of social support was attributable to the number of hugs the volunteers had had in the previous 14 days!

RCTs were also used by researchers from Harvard Medical School and Massachusetts General Hospital in Boston to determine whether additional compassion ('special care') shown by anaesthetists prior to surgery had an impact on patient care and outcomes. Half of the patients were assigned an extra visit from the anaesthetist prior to surgery, with the explicit purpose of building rapport through showing compassion to patients. 'Special care' was associated with a 50% lower requirement for opiates post-surgery and patients had a significantly lower length of stay following surgery. The compassion intervention had more than double the effects of pentobarbitone in achieving adequate sedation.

What about chronic conditions? A study of 49 physicians in consultations with nearly 900 people with diabetes categorised the physicians into those with low, medium and high emphasis on compassion. Those treated by the physicians with a high compassion emphasis had (on average) 80% higher optimal blood sugar control.

Research reveals how compassion is a powerful intervention in the treatment of HIV. In a sample of 1,700 HIV patients, where the clinician treating the patient showed high compassion, there was 33% higher adherence by patients to their chemotherapy and 20% higher odds of no detectable virus in the blood.

The effects extend also to survival rates following an early diagnosis of terminal lung cancer. An RCT compared normal early cancer diagnosis treatment of 97 patients with this treatment plus early compassionate palliative care. The study was designed to examine the impact on quality of life but revealed the surprising finding that those randomly assigned to receive early palliative care versus standard care survived 30% longer.

Powerful effects have been demonstrated in primary care also. A UK study of GPs showed that GP compassion during a patient visit, on average, was associated with improved patient wellbeing at one month following the surgery visit. Compassion is of course powerful in the treatment of mental health difficulties. A meta-analysis of the psychology literature on 21 RCTs involving 1,285 participants showed significant impacts of compassion in reducing patients' depression, anxiety, distress and improving their wellbeing.

A systematic review shows that most studies find an inverse relationship between compassion and burnout – the more clinicians and carers are compassionate the less likely they are to subsequently experience burnout. Moreover, being compassionate appears to make us happier. Neuroscience studies suggest that the most potent activator of brain circuits associated with happiness is compassion or helping others.

How then can we apply this knowledge about compassion in the context of the challenges we face as a species at this stage in our evolution and our location on one tiny planet amidst the (in effect) infinite vastness of the cosmos?

Compassionate leadership for compassionate cultures

Given the profound importance of compassion in human health and wellbeing and, as this chapter has proposed, for interconnection, how do we create the conditions for compassion to be nurtured and expressed in our communities? The answer to this is *culture* – culture is the manifestation of our values in norms, rituals, behaviour, symbols and implicit and explicit rules and expectations.

How then do we shape culture? Every interaction by every one of us every day is an opportunity to shape the culture of our communities, work organisations and even families. But the role of leaders (both formal and informal) is particularly powerful. We focus on leaders – we are vigilant around them, what they pay attention to, talk about, monitor, approve and disapprove of, and (particularly) model in their behaviour – and this tells us what it is they value.

To nurture and sustain compassionate cultures, leaders at every level of our society must therefore embody the value of compassion in their leadership (West & Chowla, 2017). What does this mean in practice?

Compassionate leadership involves the same four compassion behaviours described above but understood and applied in the context of leading others.

Attending: The first element of compassionate leadership is being present with and attending to those we lead. Leaders who attend will model being present with those they lead and 'listening with fascination'. Listening is probably the most important skill of leadership and involves taking the time to listen to the challenges, obstacles, frustrations and hurts people experience as well as the successes and pleasures.

Understanding: The second component involves leaders appraising the situations with which those they lead are struggling, to arrive at a measured understanding. Ideally, leaders arrive at their understanding through dialogue with those they lead.

Empathising: The third component of compassionate leadership is empathising. Compassionate leadership requires being able to feel the distress or frustration of those we lead without being overwhelmed by the emotion and therefore unable to help.

Helping: The fourth and final component is taking thoughtful and intelligent action to help the other. Leadership, according to all definitions, includes helping and supporting others.

Self-compassion

Compassion is rooted in the relationships shared between people. But it is also about the relationship we have with ourselves. This is particularly important in the context of spirituality and mental health. Developing and sustaining our leadership compassion is dependent on our ability to develop and sustain compassion towards ourselves.

Our relationship with ourselves is the basis for our relationships with others. It is at the core of our being. We spend our lives with ourselves, in an inner world made of thoughts that can sometimes feel like an 'inner voice', and feelings and emotions that can well up in response to our own thoughts, or what we perceive to be happening in our 'outer world'.

Self-compassion means being warm and understanding toward ourselves in situations where we suffer, behave badly or 'fail', rather than denying our pain or punishing ourselves. Self-compassion involves a recognition that being imperfect, failing and experiencing life difficulties is inevitable.

Self-compassion also involves recognising that suffering and personal inadequacy are what it is to be human – it is part of the shared human experience.

Self-compassion helps us take a balanced approach to negative emotions so that feelings are both accepted and regulated. This requires that we observe our feelings and thoughts openly and clearly and (ideally) in a non-judgmental way, perhaps through mindfulness or meditation (West, 2016). We don't ignore pain but neither do we over-identify with associated thoughts and feelings, so that we are caught up and swept away in a negative spiral. When we create a sense of safety, acceptance and love in our experience of self, we are less likely to bring our fear, anger, guilt, resentment and shame into our interactions with others. The relationship with self can be anxious because we feel shame, blame ourselves, feel inadequate or inconsistent and that makes us anxious in our relationships with others. This can manifest as needing to please others and always seeking their approval.

At another extreme, an authentic relationship with ourselves can be avoided and suppressed and we simply create a superficial, artificial and narcissistic self-concept. We fashion a well-defended sense of self as being always right, powerful, immune to criticism or challenge, and this enables us to avoid an authentic and loving relationship with ourselves or anyone else. It often manifests as a bullying and overbearing leadership. It is notable that these behaviours are many times more likely amongst senior organisational and political leaders than in the general population because they are often mistaken for signs of strong and effective leadership.

Self-compassion then helps us create a sense of deep connection with our sense of being in a secure, grateful and wonder-full way. And this in turn helps us connect with others authentically, honestly, with humility, with a sense of ease, optimistically, appreciatively and compassionately. It also makes it more likely that we will care for ourselves in fundamentally important ways. Self-compassion makes us more likely to be open to our core instinct of altruism – to help others. When we help ourselves and have a warm, accepting sense of ourselves we are better able to have a warm and accepting sense of others, thereby enabling us more easily to show them compassion.

Conclusion

Interconnectedness is our reality. To meet the challenges we face, we must increasingly understand how to develop belonging and trust and create cultures of compassion in our communities and societies. Humans make up these communities. Leaders must come to see those they lead and work with across boundaries as more collaborative, compassionate and caring than is typically portrayed. We need to repeat the stories and models that emphasise the success of compassion and collaboration, as we saw throughout the pandemic. As individuals, we can learn the skills of compassion in the way we work with others in order to create the collaborative and supportive institutions of the future – at every level of society. Where our interactions are underpinned by cultures of compassion, they foster individual, group, inter-organisational and community interconnection characterised by justice, trust, thriving and wellbeing. That is the challenge and the imperative for leaders at every level for the benefit of the communities we serve.

References

Atkins PWB & Parker SK (2012) Understanding individual compassion in organizations: The role of appraisals and psychological flexibility. *Academy of Management Review* **37** (4), 524–46.

Baumeister RF & Leary MR (1995) 'The need to belong: desire for interpersonal attachments as a fundamental human motivation'. *Psychological Bulletin* **117** (3) p497-529.

Collins B (2015) *Intentional whole health system redesign: Southcentral Foundation's 'Nuka' system of care*. London: The King's Fund.

Gilbert P (2009) *The Compassionate Mind*. London: Constable.

Hewstone M & Swart H (2011) 'Fifty-odd years of inter-group contact: from hypothesis to integrated theory'. *British Journal of Social Psychology* **50** (3) 374–86.

Trzeciak S & Mazzarelli A (2019) *Compassionomics: The revolutionary scientific evidence that caring makes a difference*. Pensacola, FL: Studer Group.

West MA & Chowla R (2017) Compassionate leadership for compassionate health care. In: Gilbert P (ed.) *Compassion: Concepts, research and applications*. (pp237-257). London: Routledge.

West MA (2016) *The Psychology of Meditation: Research and practice*. Oxford: Oxford University Press.

Chapter 21:

Burnout: a spiritual crisis, from trauma to transformation

By Rev. Prof. Stephen G Wright

"Between the probable and the proved there yawns
A gap. Afraid to jump, we stand absurd,
Then see behind us sink the ground and, worse,
Our very standpoint crumbling. Desperate dawns
Our only hope: to leap into the Word
That opens up the shuttered universe."
Sheldon Vanauken (2009)

Introduction

As I write, in the midst of a pandemic, there has been a steady stream of reports in the media (for example, Quinn, 2020; Moss, 2021; Weaver, 2021; Saner, 2021) telling of health care staff burning out under the pressure of caring. There is no doubt that healthcare practitioners (HCPs) have endured exceptional pressures as the effects of Covid-19 have spread worldwide. The pandemic has both exacerbated and thrown into sharp focus a long-standing predicament of caring work – the stress that it causes, the causes and effects of that stress, and the connection with burnout.

The causes are invariably seen as circumstances beyond the control of carers – the patients' demands, the limitations of resources and inhospitable organisational cultures. This tends to reinforce the sense of victimhood – heroic carers giving their all in the face of impossible odds. This paradigm is too simplistic, ignoring the complexities of the joy-suffering predicament of caring and locking burnout into a model where it is but an extension of stress. It also ignores spiritual dimension of burnout (Lanara, 1981; Snow & Willard, 1989; Grof & Grof, 1989; Vaughan, 1996; Glouberman, 2007; Borysenko, 2012: Wright, 2021). In a world where being human is reduced to the merely psychobiological, notions of the non-material, enchanted and spiritual are often dismissed. Yet it is precisely the disenchantment and dispiriting of our experience of reality that causes burnout, and lies at the root of the crisis of modern Western civilisation (Guenon, 2004; Cheetham, 2005; Diamond, 2011; Wright, 2017)

The exploration of burnout in this chapter lies not only in theories and evidence of burnout as a spiritual crisis, but also almost 40 years' experience of the Sacred Space Foundation (www.sacredspace.org.uk). This is a charitable trust in the UK created to help those suffering from the extremes of stress and burnout. Likewise, the Sheldon Community (www.sheldon.uk.com) and the work of Dina Glouberman (www.dinaglouberman.com) have sought to offer wider responses to burnout than the stress models. Recent studies on the effects on HCPs when spiritual approaches are integrated into staff support programmes (Cheshire and Wirral NHS Trust 2015; Hall & Nelligan, 2015; Donald *et al*, 2019) show how the spiritual and the practical need not be separated.

Although burnout is often portrayed as a consequence of extreme and sustained stress (Maslach, 1982), the two are quite different. Stress is the 'flight or fight' response when the mind and body prepare to deal with threat and challenge. The accompanying excitement and fear normally pass away when the cause of the stress does. We can feel physically and mentally exhausted as a result, but these diminish as we recover and continue with life. The stress that tips over into burnout carries with it more serious and long-term consequences, for we do not recover from it, even when the stressor has gone. The symptoms, physical and psychological, persist with an added dimension – the spiritual – whereby we lose a sense of meaning, identity, connectedness and purpose.

Who burns out?

A great many evidence-based studies are available on stress, burnout and HCPs, as well as others involved in caring work such as fire and police officers, teachers, social workers and clergy. It also affects lay people involved in caring situations, such as those supporting a disabled person at home, volunteers working for charities and international aid workers (Wright, 2021).

Caring work tends, internationally, to be downgraded in value and rewards, hence struggling to claim its fair share of resources. This sets up a dynamic between external pressures and the inner motivations of the carer that can lead to the unique experience that is burnout.

If our daily activities are heart-centred, involving giving of care to others or even caring attention to organisations and tasks, where we are invariably required to put other people first and give of our all, then there are higher risks of stress and burnout. Thus, while the focus of burnout has often been on those in caring professions, those with caring qualities in industrial and commercial settings can find themselves equally at risk. While studies into stress and burnout and suggestions for a 'cure' are many and have been reported and acted upon to varying degrees, the scale of the problem has not diminished (Wright, 2021). This suggests that even if the circumstances that produce stress-burnout are righted, for example through improvements in workloads and other stress relief methods, then there may be factors other than work-related stress producing burnout.

An internet search for the word 'burnout', at the time of writing (June 2021), revealed over 140 million hits. Alongside the tragedy of the pandemic is the widespread acknowledgement of the stress leading to burnout among 'key workers' – health care staff, police, transport workers and many other front line workers who have kept essential services running (Johnson, 2020; Kale, 2020). One survey (Quilter-Pinner *et al*, 2020) found that half of all UK health workers are suffering from debilitating stress alongside deteriorating mental health during the pandemic. The figure rose to nearly three quarters among less experienced staff and with women being more severely affected than men. Another report (Glover, 2021) suggested that critical care staff were showing high levels of stress, depression and self-harming and suicidal thoughts. Similar evidence has been found among health care staff in the city of Wuhan, currently deemed the source of the outbreak (Jianbo *et al*, 2020).

Even before the pandemic, the evidence for high levels of stress in the caring workplace was strong, along with the enormous financial costs to organisations. A report from the UK Health and Safety Executive (2019) suggests that work-related stress, depression or anxiety accounted for 44% of work-related ill health and 54% of working days lost in 2018/19, and the health and public sectors of the economy are consistently the worst affected. One account (Kay, 2017) of the personal effects of stress and burnout cites the impact upon medical staff in which it is noted that 85% of junior doctors experience mental health issues and 13% admit suicidal feelings, while young female doctors in the UK are two-and-a-half times more likely than other women to kill themselves.

However, such reports tend not to differentiate stress and burnout, conflating the primary causes in excessive workloads, lack of resources and managerial and structural support, and organisational change. What is going on inside the carer (other than judgements about personal weakness in the face of stress or being seen as the victim of impossible forces) is rarely explored. If burnout is only a product of stress, then logically the problem is solvable by getting out of the situation or removing the causes of that stress e.g. impossible workloads or hostile managers. However, the evidence cited above of the continued and escalating levels of stress and burnout suggests that existing psychological and organisational measures are not fully addressing the problem.

At a conference organised by Sacred Space in 1996, on the theme of spirituality and health, one participant commented (Wright & Sayre-Adams, 2012) how she had come to see the causes of suffering at work for herself and her team differently: "How can I go back there," she cried, close to tears, "when my heart and soul are not welcome there?" Notice how she was not complaining about the lack of staff, material resources or effective HR policies. Her heartfelt cry came from a longing for some other need to be met.

Spirituality?

Burnout is indeed related to stress in the workplace, but it is contended here that there are invariably deeper issues at work. Thus, if burnout was only a stress product because life is tough at work, we can feel much restored after a holiday or when the bullying boss is dismissed or when staffing levels improve.

However, when the stress is alleviated and the signs and symptoms of burnout remain, then it may be deduced that something else is afoot. Work and caring pressures are factors in burnout it is true, but these are often the *agents provocateurs* rather than the root causes. Burnout in this context is the desperate cry of the very essence of who we are/the highest self/the soul to break free. It is symptomatic of a longing to be liberated, no longer defined by roles and identities or who or what others say we are. It is the struggle to be in the world in which we find and give love and compassion, and have work and relationships that have heart and meaning for us. It is the longing to be free of old wounds and other unconscious processes that limit our definitions and understanding of ourselves and our freedom to be who we truly are in the world, fully and authentically (Wright, 2017).

This struggle for truth and authenticity, when we are trapped in work and relationships that inhibit or edit us and which no longer nurture us, can lead to an experience of profound exhaustion. It is an exhaustion made worse by confusion if we can see no way out, or understand why we feel so bad, or try to help ourselves by injecting even more effort into getting things back to 'normal'. It is an exhaustion that is fed and festered in contexts of inhospitable working environments that provide the petri dish for the deeper crisis to grow and be made visible.

"How can I go back there when my *heart and soul* [my emphasis] are not welcome there?" Such words illuminate the dilemma of burnout, that it is more than a stress/job related phenomenon and, at least for some individuals, a deep personal crisis when what has heart and meaning for us no longer fits with the work and other circumstances in which we find ourselves.

Spirituality and its impact upon health has only relatively recently been given more attention. It inevitably gets caught up in reservations associated either with fluffy, touchy-feely therapy or hard-boiled religiosity. Such hesitation is borne out in studies among HCPs, yet awareness is expanding and demands are growing for increased education and research (Kirwan & Armstrong, 1995; Vaughan, 1996; Salvage, 1997; Nursing Times, 1997; Williams *et al*, 1998; McManus *et al*, 2004; Mateen & Dorji, 2009; Dean, 2010; McSherry & Jamieson, 2011; Neuberger & Wright, 2012; 2013; Maslach & Leiter, 2016).

Spirituality is all about the way each person finds meaning, purpose and connection in the world – how we relate to ourselves, to each other, and perhaps (for many people) to the Transcendent, the wholly Other, an Absolute, God, Ultimate Reality. It has countless names and forms. In the post-war, working-class Manchester of my youth it had largely only one name and form: Christianity. The modern spiritual supermarket nowadays provides a smorgasbord of spiritual options to explore, from the deep to the shallow, from weekend workshops or online courses of inner exploration, to retreats and in-depth study nurturing profound transformation.

Spirituality helps us to find our grounding in the world, our purpose for living, to seek and find the answers to questions such as who am I? Why am I here? Where am I going? And how do I get there? (Wright, 2017). Some people find the answers to these questions in religion, others do not, although everyone seems to ask them at some point in life, if not always; that is part of the nature of what it is to be human. Thus on this basis, everyone is spiritual but not everyone is religious. Spirituality as meaning, purpose and connection is given attention in authors who move away from the causes of burnout as purely psychological (Snow & Willard, 1989; Vaughan, 1996; Wright, 2005; Glouberman, 2007; Borysenko, 2012; Patton, 2014; Murray, 2018; Wright 2021).

The spiritual crisis of burnout occurs when everything that we once thought of as normal or valuable or certain in our lives is thrown into turmoil. Vaughan (1996) writes:

"Anyone who has experienced burnout, a common occupational hazard among helping professionals, has probably had the feeling of being trapped in a web of necessity and impossible demands. Most recommended treatments for burnout

consist of stress reduction or setting boundaries. They overlook the fact that burnout usually indicates a state of spiritual aridity, and the effective treatment may call for spiritual renewal or awakening the soul.”

Borysenko (2012) further comments:

“It is a spiritual crisis. The way I see it, when we're burned out, we've lost our way. Our sense of meaning and purpose has disappeared from view and we don't know which way to turn. One definition of the soul is 'a quintessential human organ whose purpose is to create meaning.' In burnout, our meaning-making apparatus goes awry”. Patton (2014) takes a similar perspective noting, *“Burnout is a tell-tale malady of our times. It's a state of physical, emotional, and spiritual depletion. It manifests in depression-like symptoms such as lost motivation, decreased productivity, and feelings of cynicism and hopelessness. It shows up in physical symptoms of extreme stress, including digestive shut-down, inflammation, adrenal fatigue, and a compromised immune system.”*

This 'spiritual aridity', 'tell-tale malady' and 'meaning gone awry' is burnout. It is what happens when the energy we are investing in trying to keep things 'normal', to keep control of our lives, to keep things the same becomes more and more demanding. As the effort increases, we become increasingly depleted, exhausted and heartsick. This comment from Michael, a retreatant at the Foundation, summarises the experience:

“Last year my body, mind and soul started playing up. I was slow to ask for help; those around me tried to help, and for a while things seemed all right. However life was not normal. Bit by bit everything was falling apart. I was slow starting in the morning. I had no concentration, and the slightest pressure tipped the balance. Emotional breakdown, “burnout”, followed. At one point I described it as the worst thing I had ever experienced, although I wasn't to know it would get worse still. I appealed to my Maker, but there was silence. Silence, I guess, because I was unable to listen.”

Another wrote:
“Everything and I mean everything, came unstuck. Nothing seemed to mean anything anymore. One morning I tried to force myself to go to work as usual. Two hours later I was still sitting in the car in the drive. I was immobile. I couldn't even turn the engine on. My partner got me back in the house. I sobbed for the best part of two days and my GP wanted me to take sedatives or go into the psychiatric hospital. I couldn't get them to understand what I felt like, how everything that I'd assumed was fixed about me, my life, my work, who I am, no longer felt solid. One thing was sure, I didn't want to be a doctor anymore, but that was terrifying to admit and too terrifying to consider that if not that, then what?”

The greater the exhaustion, the closer we get to an almost complete state of mental, physical, social and spiritual collapse. At some level, one or more relationships is changing, or change is being demanded, perhaps with work, a primary personal relationship or with our deepest truth about ourselves and our beliefs. Often the process is an unconscious one as we call to ourselves challenge after challenge that brings us closer to the edge, even though consciously we may think we do not want these things to be happening. Things seem to fall apart despite our best efforts – one thing after another goes wrong. We may feel that the cause lies in something outside ourselves – a bullying boss, new demands on us at work but without the resources to meet them, a relationship at home that has grown cold, the demands of a loved one for care, or a sudden trauma in life that throws all our cherished values into question. While these external factors are indeed happening, what is going on in the person, often unconsciously, is a deep unrequited desire to transform and live more authentically and meaningfully.

Responding to burnout

From the experiences of organisations such as the Sacred Space Foundation and individuals such as Dina Glouberman (2007) working in this field, some approaches have been found to be effective which have yet to find their way into mainstream staff support. Assessing whether what we are experiencing is an extreme of stress, or whether it is stress plus a 'heart and soul' cry for personal change is part of the process. Various questionnaires have been devised to help those in stress and burnout to discern what is going on (Wright, 2021; Glouberman, 2007) and map a way out of it – from stress relief measures, to better self care, to deep personal inquiry.

On balance, being in burnout is not a time for action or trying to make solutions happen – the effort to do so can make things worse; this is a time to come to stillness, to wait and see, to get out of the situation and find the space to allow the solutions that are waiting within to emerge. This is a time to:

Retreat: When burnout arises, an immediate requirement is to step back from ordinary life and the unhealthy circumstances and take stock. Finding the space, the sacred space, is a priority – time for ourselves to permit new insights and healings to emerge, to be receptive to our inner promptings, to renew or forge a relationship with the Divine however this is experienced by us, and to seek supportive guidance to help us discern what is true. It might be necessary to take 'sick leave' or move to the home of a friend or place of retreat where we feel safe and taken care of. A GP aware of burnout will be able to offer suggestions. He or she can help with authorising sickness leave to cover time off work if necessary, and medication as a temporary aide (if, for example, depression is part of the struggle), so that we become more grounded and able to see more clearly what is going on and ways out of it.

Rest, Re-energise, Recuperate: looking after our physical wellbeing by eating, exercising and sleeping better are part of the process, coupled with time to look deep within at what is going on in ourselves.

Reconnection: this problem cannot be solved alone, despite often very strong feelings otherwise. Disconnection in retreat is not the answer, reconnection is what is called for, and so the support of a wise counsellor who can guide us through the reflective process is essential. Birthing within us what needs to come forth is unsafe alone – we need a 'spiritual midwife', one or more helpers skilled in the art of spiritual direction, to accompany us through this phase.

Recollection, Reflection, Re-visioning: as we recollect what has gone on, we can start a process of re-visioning our lives. Using all kinds of reflective, insight and awareness building processes, such as guided meditation, the Enneagram, inspiring literature, prayer, spiritual direction and so on. Thus we can begin to return to that place in ourselves where we feel at home.

In essence the application of a spiritual perspective and practices are necessary if the unique spiritual crisis that is burnout is to be resolved. The Sacred Space Foundation is but one example of organisations that have collaborated to apply and research these methods, and to develop programmes of awareness raising so that burnout is prevented.

For example, studies have found that setting up teaching programmes where staff can explore issues of identification with roles, develop self-care and minimise work-based stress, found that as a result staff were less stressed, had a greater sense of wellbeing, more positive team relationships, more able to be compassionate with patients and each other, less likely to go off sick and less likely to leave (Cheshire & Wirral, 2015; Hall & Nelligan, 2015: Donald *et al*, 2019). Setting up 'time out' and retreat days for NHS staff have been shown to help (Cheshire & Wirral, 2015; Wright, 2018), in which they can learn some stress management and self care skills, and gain deeper insight into their stresses at work and how to find healthier responses, and use assessment tools to measure the risk of burnout.

In exploring the significance of the spiritual dimension to burnout, it must be emphasised that this does not preclude discerning where proper support in the caring workplace is needed and for right action by organisations to be instituted so that staff suffer minimal stress. Where stress does arise at work, it may be seen as acceptable only insofar that it is a short term and positive source of creativity, achievement and innovation. Healthy workplaces always have systems in place to monitor stress levels to ensure that they are temporary when they arise and do not tip over into harmful effects upon those who work there.

Conclusion

Burnout is more than an extreme version of stress. Stress goes away when the source is removed or we remove ourselves from it. Burnout persists. As a defence, burnout disconnects us from unhealthy situations or deep unconscious drives (to succeed, fix others, be worthy or to control, for example) that no longer serve us. It is a response from the depths of who we are that refuses to continue with the status quo. It's as if our heart, our soul, our highest self, is saying to our everyday, functional personality, the I-who-I-think-I-am, "Right, I've had enough of this and you're not paying attention to me so I will stop you in your tracks until you listen to me and follow a completely different way of being in life".

In this sense, burnout is also full of potential for personal transformation, for living life anew and connecting more deeply to the very source of life itself.

A spiritual crisis demands spiritual solutions. Seeing burnout as simply a psychosocial or psychiatric problem may lead us into closing the gates of opportunity for transformation that burnout may offer us.

Burnout is a summons to take stock of our lives, why we cling to things where our heart and soul are not welcome. That summons is a painful, frightening, chaotic, lonely place, but if nurtured through it healthily, it is pregnant with potential to initiate us into new depth and authenticity in life; less about doing, more about being.

On balance, burnout is not a time for action or trying to make solutions happen – the effort to do these can make it worse; this is a time to come to stillness, to wait and see, to get out of the situation and find the space and support to allow the solutions that are waiting within to emerge. It is a time to retreat, rest, re-energise, refocus, reconnect, renew, reflect.

Some of the changes we need to make can take a lot of time to integrate, but starting small, first by tackling one or two achievable issues than can make a difference is a more realistic and healthy approach. The workplace culture that may have been one of the catalysts for burnout may need radical reappraisal as well, but that is often beyond the remit of the burned-out person... More enlightened employers avail themselves of the widely available guidance on building healthy workplaces. However, the dynamic between the burned-out person, workplaces and inner-outer-relationships is a complex one. Stress models, organisational change and fix-it approaches alone are inadequate responses to what is a demand for a new way of being.

That way of being may require a complete reappraisal of work and relationships in our lives where we either change them or change the way we are in them. Burnout is not an endpoint. It is always temporary; we can reignite. It does not necessarily mean we have to leave our jobs or relationships, but it does require us to be different in them if we are to remain in them. The suffering that is burnout always contains the seeds of a way out of it. Indeed we may come to a point of resolution and forgiveness where we no longer see ourselves as victims of circumstances or our own weakness. Instead we may come to see that burnout was a blessing, a catalyst for change that was needed to shift us into a more meaningful, authentic and joyful life.

References

Borysenko J (2012) *Fried: Why You Burn Out and How to Revive*. New York. Hay House.

Cheshire and Wirral Partnership NHS Foundation Trust (2015) Heart of leadership project part 1; Inspiring cultural change through leadership and training [online]. https://youtu.be/YUMBKXjgEN0 (accessed July 2021).

Cheetham T (2005) *Green man, earth angel*. New York. SUNYP.

Dean E (2010) Survey reveals spirituality to be a 'forgotten dimension of care'. *Nursing Standard* **24** (35) 9.

Diamond J (2011) *Collapse*. London. Penguin.

Donald G, Wilson I, McCarthy J, Hall I, Crossley B, Adshead P, Shaw V, Dunne R & Dwyer T (2019) Experience of nurses and healthcare staff participating in a reflective course on compassion-based care. *British Journal of Nursing* 28 (15) 1020-25.

Glouberman D (2007) *The Joy of Burnout; how the end of the world can be a new beginning*. London. Hodder Mobius.

Grof S & Grof C (1989) *Spiritual emergency: when personal transformation becomes a crisis*. New York. Tarcher.

Grover N (2021) Nearly half of NHS critical care staff report PTSD, depression or anxiety [online]. Available at: www.theguardian.com/society/2021/jan/13/nhs-icu-staff-ptsd-severe-depression-anxiety?CMP=Share_iOSApp_Other (accessed July 2021).

Guenon R (trans. Pallis M, Osborne A & Nicholson R 2004) Hillsdale. Sophia.

Hall I & Nelligan M (2015) Helping nurses reconnect with their compassion. *Nursing Times* **111** (41) 21-23.

Health and Safety Executive (2019) *Work-related stress, anxiety and depression statistics in Great Britain 2019*. London. Health and Safety Executive.

Jianbo L, Simeng M, Ying W, Zhongxiang C, Jianbo H, Ning W, Jiang W, Hui D, Tingting C, Ruiting L, Huwei T, Kang L, Lihua Y, Manli H, Huafen W, Goahua W, Zhonqchun L & Shaohua H (2020) Factors Associated With Mental Health Outcomes Among Health Care Workers Exposed to Coronavirus Disease. *Journal of the American Medical Association* **3** (3) :e203976 doi:10.1001/jamanetworkopen.2020.3976.

Johnson S (2020) 'We're all approaching burnout': paramedics on the toll of tackling coronavirus [online]. Available at: www.theguardian.com/society/2020/apr/23/approaching-burnout-paramedics-tackling-coronavirus (accessed July 2021).

Kale S (2020) 'People were like animals'. How supermarket staff watched the coronavirus crisis unfold [online]. Available at: www.theguardian.com/lifeandstyle/2020/may/26/people-were-like-animals-how-supermarket-staff-watched-coronavirus-crisis-unfold (accessed July 2021).

Kay A (2017) *This is going to hurt*. London. Picador.

Kirwan M & Armstrong D (1995) Investigation of burnout in a sample of British general practitioners. *British Journal of General Practice* **45** (394) 259-60.

Lanara V (1981) *Heroism as a nursing value*. Athens. Sisterhood Evniki.

McManus I, Keeling A & Paice E (2004) *Stress, burnout and doctors' attitudes to work are determined by personality and learning style: a twelve year longitudinal study of UK medical graduates*. London. Department of Psychology, University College.

McSherry W & Jamieson S (2011) An online survey of nurses' perceptions of spirituality and spiritual care. *Journal of Clinical Nursing* 20 (11-12) 1757-1767.

Maslach C (1982) *Burnout: the cost of caring*. New York. Prentice-Hall.

Maslach C & Leiter M (2016) Understanding the burnout experience: recent research and its implications for psychiatry. *World Psychiatry* **15** (2) 103-111

Mateen F & Dorji C (2009) Health-care worker burnout and the mental health imperative. *Lancet* **22:374** (9690) 595-7.

Moss J 2021 Beyond burned out [online]. Available at: https://hbr.org/2021/02/beyond-burned-out Harvard Business Review (accessed July 2021).

Murray S (2018) *The burnout solution*. Dublin. Gill.

Neuberger J & Wright S (2012) Why spirituality is essential for nurses. *Nursing Standard* **26** (40) 19-21.

Neuberger J & Wright S (2013) Spiritual expression. *Nursing Standard* **27** (41) 16-18.

Nursing Times (1997) The spiritual dimension. *Nursing Times* **93** (30) 22-23.

Patton J (2014) Back from Burnout [online]. Available at: https://experiencelife.com/article/back-from-burn-out/ (accessed July 2021).

Quilter-Pinner H, Thomas C, Harvey R & Wastell D (2020) *Covid-19: One in five healthcare workers could quit after pandemic unless urgent government action is taken*. London. Institute of Public Policy Research.

Quinn B (2020) Survey of female NHS staff raises concerns over burnout in pandemic [online]. Available at: www.theguardian.com/society/2020/aug/25/survey-of-female-nhs-staff-raises-concerns-over-burnout-in-covid-pandemic (accessed July 2021).

Salvage J (1997) Journey to the centre. *Nursing Times* **93** (17) 28-32.

Snow C & Willard P (1989) *I'm dying to take care of you*. Redmond. Professional counsellor books.

Vanauken S (2009) *A severe mercy: a story of faith, tragedy and triumph*. London. HarperOne.

Vaughan F (1996) *Shadows of the Sacred*. Wheaton. Quest.

Weaver M (2021) NHS staff face burnout as covid hospital admissions rise [online]. Available at: www.theguardian.com/world/2021/jan/01/nhs-staff-face-burnout-covid-hospital-admissions-rise?CMP=Share_iOSApp_Other (accessed January 2021).

Williams S, Mitchie S & Pattani S (1998) *Improving the health of the NHS workforce*. London. Nuffield.

Wright S (2021) *Burnout: a spiritual crisis*. Penrith. SSP.

Wright S (2018) Making (sacred) space for staff renewal and transformation. *Journal of Holistic Healthcare* **15** (1) 38-40.

Wright S & Sayre-Adams J (2012) *Sacred space: right relationship and spirituality in healthcare*. Penrith. SSP.

Chapter 22:
Spiritual care in general practice

By Ross Bryson and Liz Bryson

Summary

This chapter begins with a description of general practice in the UK, focusing on its aspirations to be holistic in the assessment and treatment of patients. Following this is a discussion of the difficulties in defining spiritual factors and spiritual care which could be part of this holistic approach. This is illustrated by reflecting on a case study. The chapter concludes by describing advances in holistic care where expertise in spiritual care has been added to primary healthcare and considers how these services may develop within an integrated model of holistic care.

A perspective on general practice in the UK today

General practice has been described as 'the jewel in the crown of the NHS' (Marshall, 2015) and much is expected of this precious commodity. Almost unique amongst world healthcare systems, it is led by doctors who are highly trained generalists and who work in teams of increasing diversity. The Royal College of General Practitioners (RCGP) published a report on the contribution made by General Practitioners (GPs), who are described as 'medical generalists' and 'experts in whole person medicine' (RCGP, 2012). Medical generalism is here defined as 'an approach to the delivery of health care that routinely applies a broad and holistic perspective to the patient's problems' (RCGP, 2012). The RCGP Core Curriculum Statement *Being a General Practitioner*, describes a core capability of 'practising holistically and promoting health' which requires the consideration of the 'physical, psychological, socioeconomic and cultural dimensions of health'. This involves 'caring for the whole person in the context of the person's values, their family beliefs, their family system, and their culture in the larger community'. It acknowledges that 'holistic care can only be interpreted in relation to an individual's perception of holism', and 'that people have inner experiences that are subjective, mystical and, for some, religious, which may affect their health and wellbeing' (RCGP, 2016). Advice from the General Medical Council for all doctors, regardless of speciality, compliments this approach. It is stated that in good medical practice, doctors must 'adequately assess the patient's conditions, taking account of their history (including the symptoms and psychological, spiritual, social and cultural factors), and their views and values' (GMC, 2019).

General practice resides within the complex and ever-changing NHS healthcare system, and at its heart is the doctor-patient relationship. This has always had both 'transactional and relational' elements (Heath, 2020). In recent decades, the transactional aspect of general practice care has become more prominent. Its effects are more easily measured and the targets required to achieve funding are more easily attained. Increasing public demands for healthcare in an economic climate of austerity are also factors which have combined to challenge the relational element of general practice. General practice has a long-held value of continuity of personal care which is known to result in more effective healthcare (Freeman & Hughes, 2010) and is more satisfying for patient and doctor alike.

Conversations with those who are training to be doctors often reveal a desire to bring the possibilities of modern science to bear in the care of patients. Students are taught to be both compassionate and curious in their clinical work. What is really going on in this patient? Who are they and what makes them tick? How can this be understood so that they are given the healthcare that is most appropriate to them? This is described by one of the General Medical Council standards that future doctors should achieve in their training:

'Newly qualified doctors must be able to work collaboratively with patients, their relatives, carers or other advocates to make clinical judgements and decisions based on a holistic assessment of the patient and their needs, priorities and concerns, and appreciating the importance of the links between pathophysiological, psychological, spiritual, religious, social and cultural factors for each individual.' (GMC, 2018)

This approach by the UK regulatory body for all doctors is in line with the World Health Organisation's (WHO) understanding of health. In 1997, the WHO added spiritual wellbeing to the previous definition (WHO, 1997). It was also stated that 'addressing the scientific link between religion, spirituality and health has too often been a forgotten subject or avoided for irrational, emotional or political reasons. It is time for the scientific community to integrate religious and spiritual factors, which have guided human behaviour over centuries, into health and human sciences' (Richardson, 2002). This appeal has not gone unheeded. The search to understand more fully the complexity of the human being has led to new disciplines such as neuropsychology, neuroendocrinology and psychoneuroimmunology, which are exploding the myths about human beings having separate functions regarding mind/body/spirit. Concepts are now being discussed within and beyond the scientific community such as 'the science of good and evil' (Zak, 2012), with publications appearing such as *Wired for God: The Biology of Spiritual Experience* (Foster, 2010), *The Neuroscience of Spirituality* (Fenwick, 2011) and *The Moral Molecule* (Zak, 2012).

Pause for reflection

What might all this mean for general practice in the UK?

At times we are all 'patients'.

■ What are your experiences and aspirations regarding the healthcare you receive?

■ Has it been the 'whole person medicine' which general practice leaders describe?

■ How could it have been different?

What is meant by 'spiritual factors' in primary healthcare'?

General practitioners are pragmatists. They have learned to distil the complexity of conditions as described by specialist colleagues and apply it to the patient they care for, who often has more than one co-existing condition. This same process can apply to spirituality, spiritual factors and spiritual care. To understand these terms and how they might relate to a patient in general practice, it is imperative not to create firm boundaries between spiritual factors, social factors, cultural factors and religious factors. Boundaries that do not exist outside the world of academia.

Whole-person care encompasses the interconnections between the physical, psychological, emotional, social and spiritual dimensions of health (Freeman, 2005). It recognises that the individual's story is at the centre of the personal healthcare process (Tarrant *et al*, 2003) and encourages patients to understand the impact of their story on their health. Whole person care prioritises the patient in decisions about appropriate courses of action (Sheldon, 2004). Many people have some form of long-term illness. They cannot be cured, but are recognised to have 'needs for personal, social, psychological and spiritual support' (DOH, 2005), which the NHS should seek to meet. This is to be done, according to NHS policy, by 'services which promote physical, psychosocial and spiritual wellbeing and emphasise quality of life' (DOH, 2005). NHS policy also recognises that people who have some form of mental illness should be regarded as 'whole people with interrelated psychological, social, physical and spiritual needs' (DOH, 2006).

It has been stated by the National Institute of Clinical Excellence (NICE) that:

'...spirituality usually includes reference to a power other than self, often described as God, a higher power, or forces of nature. This power is generally seen to help a person to transcend immediate experience and to re-establish hope. Formal religion is a means of expressing an underlying spirituality, but spiritual belief, concerned with the search for the existential or ultimate meaning in life, is a broader concept and may not always be expressed in a religious way.' (NICE, 2004)

This aligns with the concepts of 'deepest human needs' (Bryson, 2010) or spiritual needs which can be understood as being 'the universal needs of the human spirit to have a sense of meaning and purpose in life; a sense of being loved and valued, of belonging to some community and being part of something bigger than oneself' (Bryson, 2020).

The potential has long been acknowledged in general practice (Brown *et al*, 1989) and demonstrated by research that UK GPs are often aware of the spiritual needs of their patients but are frequently unable to meet such needs because of a lack of training or resources (Murray *et al*, 2003). A review of the literature has suggested that, 'most GPs see it as their role to identify and assess patients' spiritual needs, despite perceived barriers such as lack of time and specific training. However, they struggle to find appropriate language to discuss spiritual factors and experience feelings of discomfort and fear that patients will refuse to engage in the discussion' (Vermandere *et al*, 2011). It has also been shown that GPs have varying views on what spirituality is, and that these relate partly to individual beliefs and experiences. These differences 'create considerable variation in the delivery of spiritual care' (Appleby *et al*, 2018).

Pause for reflection

Have you ever discussed spiritual factors with your GP or a member of the primary healthcare team?

If so, in what way was this helpful?

If not, would you like that opportunity and why?

What is meant by 'spiritual care'?

'Spiritual care can be defined as care that recognises and responds to the needs of the human spirit when faced with trauma, ill health, or sadness. It includes the need for meaning and self-worth, to express oneself, for faith support or simply for a sensitive listener. It is usually given in a one-to-one relationship, is person centred, and makes no assumptions about personal conviction or life orientation' (Hamilton *et al*, 2017).

Spiritual care intervention can be associated with health gain (Post *et al*, 2000; Walsh *et al*, 2002; Speck, 2004; Sveidqvist, 2003; Kliewer & Saultz, 2005). In the *Handbook of Religion and Health*, a critical and comprehensive analysis of over 1,200 studies and 400 reviews of empirical research found statistically significant benefits of spiritual care in terms of prevention of ill-health, aiding recovery and encouraging equanimity (Koenig *et al*, 2001). While its role in promoting wellbeing is developing (Merchant, 2006), the relationship between religion and spirituality in a multicultural society is complex (King *et al*, 2006). Spiritual care services are well established in hospice and hospital settings (Wright, 2001; Sheikh *et al*, 2004), especially within oncology and palliative care (NICE, 2004), and have been increasingly developed in mental health services (Royal College of Psychiatrists, 2006; Merchant *et al*, 2008; Gilbert, 2008). Much has been written about the components of spiritual care, including listening to patients' experience and questions, affirming patients, and protecting their dignity, self-worth and identity, all from within the framework of the patient's belief system or philosophical framework (Marie Curie Cancer Care, 2003; Health Care Chaplains Code of Conduct, 2005; NHS Scotland, 2008). Nevertheless, the question of whether or not GPs should offer spiritual care is far from agreed; how GPs should be trained in spiritual care (Appleby *et al*, 2019) and how to measure the effectiveness of spiritual interventions is still in its infancy (Hamilton *et al*, 2017).

It is into this vortex of conflicting opinions that some general practices have in recent decades been offering specialists in spiritual care as part of the primary healthcare team. These health professionals have been called Chaplains for Wellbeing, or Primary Care Chaplains, and their service described as Listening and Guidance or Primary Care Chaplaincy. The research to date suggests that they can make a significant difference to some patients' wellbeing (Kevern & Hill, 2013; Kevern & Hill, 2015; McSherry *et al*, 2016), that they may be as effective as anti-depressant medication (MacDonald, 2017), and that they can be a useful additional resource for patients with complex problems (MacDonald, 2018). Which patients are likely to be most helped by this service and how they interface with the relatively new social prescribing link workers in England is the subject of healthy debate.

The delivery of healthcare is not only changed by the results of quantitative research published in scientific journals. Sometimes, people's stories are a more effective means of communicating concepts which actually lead to a change in practice. Such use of story was illustrated by the inaugural speech of the then new Royal College of General Practitioner's chairperson in 2017, 'Enid's story' (Stokes-Lampard 2017). Here we have an elderly lady who has been widowed, who is lonely, lacking in purpose, and seeking human contact by attending general practice. Her GP did not medicalise her condition. Instead, she honoured her bereavement and the importance of the grief process, but also helped her to find a role in the community that addressed her real needs, while noting that 'human beings are spiritual creatures' and that 'to deny our spirituality diminishes us'.

> **Pause for reflection**
>
> How would you describe your own spiritual needs and the care that they require?

Learning from a case study

Case study

Ed (pseudonym) is a White British man who lives alone. He did not do well at school due to dyslexia. He remained living at home with his parents after his siblings left home and he worked as a glazier until his early 40s, when he stopped work to care for his aging father who died when Ed was 44. He then remained living at home to care for his mother who became gradually more frail over many years. In her later years she was physically immobile with dementia but, because of Ed's care, she was able to remain at home until her death. Ed began to see the family doctor more often, not only about his raised blood pressure. He was aged 59, he had lost both parents, lost his role in life and his 'family' home was in fact not in his name and the council wanted him to leave. His low mood was made worse by the anxiety arising from the threat of being made homeless and the seeming impossibility of finding paid work with his lack of suitable skills. Temporary work as a driver caused an increase in anxiety as he felt trapped in a strange context so he could not continue. The Covid-19 pandemic made him more isolated and worsened his chances of finding employment.

> **Pause for reflection**
>
> If, in line with the General Medical Council's advice, you considered the pathophysiological, psychological, spiritual, religious, social and cultural factors, what would your holistic assessment of Ed's situation lead you to conclude?
>
> What would a whole person medicine approach to treatment look like?

If you were an expert in whole-person medicine, how would your assessment and treatment plan unfold? Might you conclude that his pervasive anxiety, which is worsened when alongside other people, is indicative of pathophysiological dysfunction and would benefit from medication? Perhaps there is an underlying low self-esteem which needs psychological approaches such as Cognitive Behavioural Therapy with stress management techniques?

However, could it be that his dyslexia and years of not being part of a workplace could be helped by volunteering in a context in which he could safely build his social skills and gain confidence? Perhaps this could align with acquiring new skills which would make him more employable. Understanding that his cultural background is that of a working class, White British nuclear family with no wider community might increase your conviction that addressing social factors was critical.

Allowing him to tell his story more fully reveals that in his childhood he was part of a church and a youth group. In later years he did not attend church, but his parents maintained their religious faith. He tells of an experience of a 'presence' giving him an uncharacteristic sense of calm which stayed with him after being prayed for by a chaplain, and he describes a 'presence' that was almost tangible in the room just after the death of his parents at home. These may lead you to conclude that religious factors are significant for him. Perhaps he would be helped by being able to talk about these experiences? Perhaps he thinks that they indicate a dimension of existence which transcends death and which might give him strength to face the remaining years of his life? But where could you suggest he found a safe place to have such conversations?

What, in addition to these factors, could be made of 'spiritual factors' in your holistic assessment of Ed's situation? If spiritual factors were understood as the universal human need for a sense of belonging, meaning, purpose and hope, would that enable you to usefully frame his needs?

His limited human contact with his small family; his ambivalence about connecting with new people; his memories of being part of a youth and church community in days of old; his questions about whether his parents 'live on' in some other dimension; are these not declaring that he longs to belong, to know that his life is not an isolated island but is securely intertwined with others?

In the hours he spends alone, contemplating the fact that he has neither the skills, experience, or the benefit of youth which could lead him into a fulfilling job; reflecting on the fact that he gave the most productive years of his life to being a carer for his parents; that he has had no life partner and the years ahead contain no guarantee of a secure home and worthwhile activity; that his days and weeks are punctuated mainly by futile job applications online and interviews which are required to ensure an extension of his benefits; are these not unmistakable signs that he is looking for meaning and purpose in life?

As he talks to you about all those things which suggest he has only a partial sense of belonging and a limited sense of meaning and purpose; as he talks about his tentative faith in a larger dimension of life, is he not also wanting you to recognise that, like all human beings, he is searching for hope?

Ed's treatment plan contained several facets. He was offered regular appointments with a GP he knew and trusted; he was considered as suffering from an anxiety disorder and unable to apply for work. He was given 'sick notes' and anxiety-reducing medication and was reviewed regularly. He was referred to two members of the extended primary care team: the social prescriber, with a view to exploring options for activities in his community, and the Chaplain for Wellbeing, who was able to offer appointments with enough time to explore spiritual factors.

Ed's care is ongoing and he has given permission for his story to be told.

Perhaps this case study will lead you to consider that spiritual factors – the universal human need for a sense of belonging, meaning, purpose and hope – are factors which should be considered as fundamental to all clients and patients. It may be that facilitating conversations about them early in the holistic assessment and formulation of a treatment plan, would result in much more effective care. It is conceivable that all practitioners would find themselves offering 'spiritual care' without labelling it as such. It may also lead to the widespread recognition that there is great value in having 'spiritual care practitioners' who have additional expertise in this area, readily accessible in all areas of healthcare. Would that not be the logical conclusion of the General Medical Council's directive 'to make clinical judgements and decisions based on a holistic assessment of the patient and their needs' (General Medical Council, 2018)?

The challenge of enabling spiritual care in general practice

It is a profound challenge for general practice to rise to its noble aspiration to be expert in whole-person medicine and for spiritual factors to be understood as integral to this holistic, not reductionist, care. If this is accepted then all practitioners will find that, in part, they are offering aspects of spiritual care. However, they will be reluctant to embark upon unpacking these deeply personal and significant issues with patients unless there is the specialist resource within primary care to support this aspect of care. Some of the pioneering work in this field, which started in the late 1990s, is told in *Honouring Personhood: The added value of Chaplaincy in General Practice* (Bryson *et al*, 2012).

Subsequent discussion and publications related to spiritual care in general practice are collected by the Association of Chaplaincy in General Practice (ACGP, 2021), which is also the body that sets the professional standards for these primary care spiritual care practitioners. The Association of Chaplaincy in General Practice has also produced a GP Chaplaincy handbook which is a practical guide to service provision. This consists of guidelines and recommendations covering the role of the chaplain working in general practice; management and supervision; training and continuing personal development; and the importance of measurement, evaluation and research. Prompted – in part by this guide – the specialist service is appearing in more general practices across the UK. These are sometimes entirely local arrangements where the appointee may or may or not be paid. More recently, with the advent of social prescribing in England, some Primary Care Networks are using NHS funding to enable this service in various ways. In England, the NHS Long Term plan includes not only a commitment to social prescribing but also opportunities for new primary mental health services within primary care networks (Naylor *et al*, 2020). These are opportunities to make whole person medicine more of a reality for all.

The impact of the Covid-19 pandemic is incalculable. One of its long-term consequences is its 'legacy of grief' (Heath, 2020) and a 'tsunami of mental illness' (RCPsych, 2020). Covid-19 has also confronted society with how fundamental to our humanity is our need for a sense of belonging, meaning, purpose and the hope for a better future. These are the spiritual factors we need to include in healthcare if we are truly to enable people to heal.

> **For more information about how the Association of Chaplaincy in General Practice is supporting spiritual care in General Practice see the website** www.acgp.co.uk

References

Books

Bryson P, Dawatly S, Hughes A, Bryson E & Petra H (2012) *Honouring Personhood in Patients; the added value of Chaplaincy in General Practice*. UK: Whole Person Health Trust

Foster C (2010) *Wired for God: the biology of spiritual experience*. London: Hodder and Stoughton.

Kliewer SP & Saultz J (2005) *Healthcare and Spirituality*. Oxford: Radcliffe.

Koenig HK, McCullough ME & Larson DB (2001) *Handbook of Religion and Health*. Oxford: Oxford University Press.

Richardson P (2002) *Spirituality: The New Frontier", Psychological Testing at work*. p138. New York: MC Graw Hill.

Zak PJ (2012) *The Moral Molecule: The source of love and prosperity*. London: Bantam Books.

Journal articles

Appleby A, Swinton J & Wilson P (2019) Spiritual care training and the GP curriculum: where to now? *Education for Primary Care* **30** (4) 194-197.

Brown C & Sheldon M (1989) Spiritual healing in general practice. *Journal of Royal College of General Practitioners* **39** (328) 476-477.

Freeman J (2005) Towards a definition of holism. *British Journal of General Practice* **55** 154-55.

Hamilton IJ, Morrison J & MacDonald S (2017) Should GPs provide spiritual care? *British Journal of General Practice* **67** (665) 573-584

Heath I (2020) COVID-19 and the legacy of grief. *British Journal of General Practice* **70** (698): 428.

Kevern P & Hill L (2013) Chaplains for wellbeing in primary care: analysis of the results of a retrospective study. Peter Kevern and Lisa Hill. *Primary Health Care Research and Development* 00: 1–13.

Kevern P & Hill L (2015) Chaplains for wellbeing in primary care: analysis of the results of a retrospective study. *Primary Health Care Research & Development Journal* 16:87-99.

King M, Weich S, Nazroo J & Blizaard B (2006) Religion, mental health and ethnicity. EMPRIRIC – a national study of England. *Journal of Mental Health* **15** (2) 153-162.

Marshall M (2015) A precious jewel — the role of general practice in the English NHS. *New England Journal of Medicine* **372** (10):893–897.

MacDonald G (2017) The efficacy of primary care chaplaincy compared with antidepressants: a retrospective study comparing chaplaincy with antidepressants. *Primary Health Care Research & Development Journal* **18** (4):354-365.

Macdonald G (2018) Primary Care Chaplaincy: an intervention for complex presentation. *Primary Health Care Research & Development Journal* **20** (69) 1-12.

McSherry W, Boughey A & Kevern P (2016) Chaplains for wellbeing in primary care: a qualitative investigation of their perceived impact for patients' health and wellbeing. *Journal of Health Care Chaplaincy* **22** (4): 51-170.

Merchant R (2006) Promoting health and wellbeing: the role of spirituality. *Journal of the Royal Society for the Promotion of Health* **126** (5) 408-9.

Murray SA, Kendall M, Boty K, Worth A & Benton TF (2003) General practitioners and their possible role in providing spiritual care: a qualitative study. *British Journal of General Practice* **83** 957-959.

Post SG, Puchalski CM & Larson DB (2000) Physicians and patient spirituality: professional boundaries, competency and ethics. *Annals of Internal Medicine* **132** (7) 578-583.

Sheikh A, Gatrad AR, Sheikh U, Panesar SS & Shafi S (2004) Hospital chaplaincy units show bias towards Christianity. *British Medical Journal Letters* **329** 626.

Sheldon M (2004) Whole person medicine. *Nucleus* July 18-25.

Speck PW (2004) Spiritual care in health care. *Scottish Journal of Healthcare Chaplaincy* **7** (1) 21-25.

Sveidqvist V (2003) Who am I, and why am I here? Young people's perspectives on the role of spirituality in the promotion of their mental health. *International Journal of Mental Health Promotion* **5** (3) 36-44.

Tarrant C, Windridge K, Boulton M & Freeman G (2003) Qualitative study of the meaning of personal care in general practice. *British Medical Journal* **326** 1310.

Vermandere M *et al* (2011) Spirituality in general practice: a qualitative evidence synthesis *British Journal of General Practice* **61** (592) 749.

Walsh K, King, M, Jones L, Tookman A & Blizard R (2002) Spiritual beliefs may affect outcome of bereavement: prospective study. *British Medical Journal* **324** 1551-1556.

Wright MC (2001) Chaplaincy in hospice and hospital: findings from a survey in England and Wales. *Palliative Medicine* **15** 229-242.

Online articles

Appleby A *et al* (2018) *What GPs mean by spirituality and how they apply this concept with patients: a qualitative study*. BJGP Open; 2 (2). https://bjgpopen.org/content/2/2/bjgpopen18X101469.abstract (accessed July 2021)

Association of Chaplains in General Practice, ACGP (2021) Evidence Base -articles http://acgp.co.uk/resources/ (accessed July 2021).

Merchant R, Gilbert P & Moss B (2008) *Spirituality, religion and mental Health: a brief evidence resource*. https://www.rcpsych.ac.uk/docs/default-source/members/sigs/spirituality-spsig/spirituality-special-interest-group-publications-gilbert-evidence-resource.pdf?sfvrsn=c0a26fd8_2 (accessed July 2021).

Royal College of Psychiatrists (2006) *Spirituality and Mental Health*. https://www.rcpsych.ac.uk/mental-health/treatments-and-wellbeing/spirituality-and-mental-health (accessed July 2021).

Royal College of Psychiatrists - RCPsych (2020) *Psychiatrists see alarming rise in patients needing urgent and emergency care and forecast a 'tsunami' of mental illness*. https://www.rcpsych.ac.uk/ (accessed July 2021).

Stokes-Lampard H (2017) RCGP Conference Speech https://www.gponline.com/read-professor-helen-stokes-lampards-rcgp-conference-2017-speech-full/article/1447175 (accessed July 2021).

WHO Report (1997) https://apps.who.int/gb/archive/pdf_files/EB101/pdfangl/eb1017.pdf. (accessed July 2021).

Presentations

Bryson PHR (2010) *Spiritual Needs in Holistic Care – a Human Given. Deepest Human Needs* Consultation Tool. Queen Elizabeth Post-graduate Centre Birmingham

Fenwick P (2011) *The Neuroscience of Spirituality*. Royal College of Psychiatrists.

Guidelines

Department of Health DOH (2005) *The National Service Framework for Long Term Conditions*.

Department of Health DOH (2006) *From Values to Action: the chief nursing officer's review of mental health nursing*.

Freeman G & Hughes J (2010) The King's Fund: *Continuity of care and the patient experience*.

General Medical Council (2018) *Outcomes for Graduates* Section 14.

General Medical Council (2019) *Good Medical Practice*, Section 15a.

Gilbert P (2008) *Guidelines on spirituality for staff in acute care services*. Staffordshire University.

Health Care Chaplains Code of Conduct (2005) Association of Hospice and Palliative Care Chaplains, The College of Health Care Chaplains and the Scottish Association of Chaplains in Healthcare. *Health Care Chaplains Code of Conduct, (2nd edition)*.

Marie Curie Cancer Care (2003) *Spiritual and Religious Care: competencies for specialist palliative care.*

National Institute for Clinical Excellence NICE (2004) *Improving Supportive and Palliative Care for Adults with Cancer.*

National Institute for Clinical Excellence NICE (2004) Spiritual Support Services *Guidance on Cancer Services Improving Supportive and Palliative Care for Adults with Cancer* Section 7 p95.

Naylor C, Baird B, Gilburt H, Bell A & Heller A (2020) The King's Fund: *Mental health and primary care networks: understanding the opportunities.*

NHS Scotland (2008) *Spiritual Care and Chaplaincy in Scotland, Revised Guidance: report and recommendations.*

Royal College of General Practitioners (2012) *Medical Generalism: Why expertise in whole person medicine matters.*

Royal College of General Practitioners, RCGP (2016) *The RCGP Curriculum: Core Curriculum Statement.*

Unpublished

Bryson ER (2020) M.A. Dissertation: *A Critical Analysis of How Children and Young People with Cancer Explore Spirituality.*

Chapter 23:

Beyond the here and now: the challenges for the formal mental health system of embracing spiritually informed models of care

By Paul Jenkins

Over the decades there has been a battle for the soul of mental health services based on very differing understandings of the nature and causes of mental illnesses. Most prominent in this battle has been a clash between the proponents of physical and biological perspectives and those who have advocated for an approach grounded in the understanding of life experiences and social systems.

No one perspective has held the ascendancy, in part because the complexity of the human mind and emotions have, so far, defeated any attempt to establish a single unifying theory of mental illness or a single dominant approach to relieving the distress it causes.

In this chapter, I would like to offer some reflections on the role of spirituality in mental health services, the challenges it raises for the formal mental health system and some suggestions on how these might be overcome.

Spirituality in services: a definition

First of all, it will be important to define what I mean by 'spirituality'. For me, it reflects a willingness to acknowledge a dimension to services beyond the narrow business of clinical assessment and treatment and a recognition of the importance of belief systems and a wider sense of connectedness as crucial ingredients of promoting recovery. It also describes elements of the values and behaviours of mental health professionals which should be fundamental to the holistic delivery of care.

As a student I spent a lot of time on archaeological excavations. One of the most fascinating aspects of archaeology, and in particular prehistoric archaeology, is the identification and interpretation of 'ritual' features. At one level the term was used to explain a whole series of phenomena for which we have no practical explanation. At another level it reflects the recognition of fundamental and longstanding human desire for a sphere of meaning beyond the strictly utilitarian and material. There are, similarly, aspects of mental distress which go beyond a purely practical or scientific explanation.

This recognition of an aspect of human experience beyond the everyday should also be an important element of how we approach the delivery of mental health services. Spirituality is not the same as formal religion, important though that is for many people who use services. It plays out in a number of dimensions, all of which are eloquently spoken to in different chapters of this book. The key elements are:

- First, encouraging a discourse in society about mental health and mental illness which recognises the significance for our sense of wellbeing and resilience of conscious and unconscious beliefs.

- Second, ensuring we include these issues, including an individual's expressed beliefs around spirituality and religion in our understanding of their mental distress and how best to work with them.

- Third, helping us design services that are culturally sensitive for the communities we are serving, and which respect different perspectives in those communities on the meaning and significance of mental distress.

- Fourth, supporting approaches such as mindfulness which encourage individuals to manage distress by tapping into a deeper awareness of themselves and the world around them.

- Fifth, building services that are based on an empathetic and non-judgmental approach to understanding the experience and feelings of people using services.

In line with the last point, it is my firm belief that any attempt to develop spiritually informed models or approaches to care must be sensitive to the beliefs and preferences of individual services and practitioners. Indeed, their value is set within a pluralistic framework of services where there is no dominant orthodoxy of what works and what can be provided. That very plurality of approach and the empowerment of patient choice and sense of agency in an individual's recovery is some of what gives most meaning to spiritually based approaches.

The barriers to developing spiritually informed and holistic models of care

These perspectives and values, however, can be difficult to translate into the formal structures of care. There are a number of barriers which stand in the way which I would like to consider at greater length together with some of the actions we could take to overcome them.

The first reflects the perceived reduction in the importance of religion in society and an increasing emphasis on secular values.

There are a number of aspects to this. At one level there is a clear decline in formal adherence to religion and religious institutions. Church attendance has declined by a half in the last 40 years and the prominence of religion and religious leaders in public discourse has declined. However, religion and spirituality are far from dead. In a 2016 poll, 28% of the population were reported as believing in God or a higher spiritual power, and 20% believing in some kind of higher spiritual power.

Furthermore, there is ongoing evidence, as Richard Layard highlights in his writing on the science of happiness (2005), that there is an established correlation between a belief in God and greater reported levels of happiness. For many, religion and religious beliefs have served to provide the sense of meaning in life which is a central part of a sense of individual and collective wellbeing.

The second relates to a growth in a dominant narrative that is antagonistic to religion and where 'science' is held up as the singular principle on which social interventions, including mental health, should be based.

This is unhelpful. Not because there is not an enormous value in good quality objective evidence in the development of thinking about mental health. But rather because any oversimplification of our understanding of the causes of mental distress and its alleviation is unnecessarily restrictive and reduces meaningful options for those experiencing that distress and those trying to help them.

In particular, an over-emphasis on the 'positivist' model of science, first promoted by Hume, with its emphasis that science must be grounded in objects that are directly observable, is dangerous in a field where so much depends on the interpretation of the unconscious processes of the mind.

Throughout history mental health practitioners have tried to compensate for the relative lack of status accorded to their work by attempts to overly imitate the scientific norms of physical health care. In doing so, the risk is that mental health loses the diversity of approaches it has to offer. Rather than doing so, it should be bolder in offering to physical health care the richness of psychological, emotional and spiritual understandings of distress which might also have benefit in those settings, especially in areas such as medically unexplained symptoms which go beyond the traditional paradigm of medical thinking.

In particular, spiritual perspectives can be of great significance in confronting mortality. As is so powerfully described in Atul Gawande's work *Being Mortal* (2014), modern medicine, for all its potency, can struggle greatly in helping people at the end of their lives, when medical intervention can often do more harm than good. There has always been a big role for religious practitioners in this space and I remember with great respect what my late father-in-law, an Anglican clergyman, had to say about the importance of his work with the dying and the bereaved.

The third barrier is a related one and concerns the availability of evidence of impact. Despite what I have just said about the dangers of a narrow adherence to science as the guiding principle of care, it is not unreasonable to place an emphasis on evidence in making important decisions about the allocation of resources.

The availability of evidence of impact has, over the years, been a wider challenge for mental health services. It is, however, a particular challenge for interventions such as art and music therapy, which are often greatly valued by patients but operate outside the usual parameters of clinical care. Even within the fields of psychology and psychotherapy, and with the exception of CBT, the empirical evidence base can be limited.

Spirituality and spiritual-based interventions are not totally without an evidence base. A 2006 review of the literature by the Mental Health Foundation (2006) listed good examples of the positive relationship between spirituality and better mental health in relation to a number of mental health problems. There are problems, however, with the extent of the evidence and the over reliance of quantitative studies in an area where the relationship between cause and effect may, inevitably, be more complex.

Those who wish to argue for broader approaches to provision cannot afford to ignore this deficit. There is a need to argue for greater investment in research in non-traditional forms of care. There is also a methodological challenge here. The paradigms of scientific research, such as Random Controlled Trials, so beloved of physical health care, do not always lend themselves to concepts such as spirituality. As well as arguing for more research, the case needs to be made for a wide range of methodologies. There is a particular case, in this instance, for user-led research.

The fourth issue standing in the way of incorporating spiritual approaches to care relates to scale. Given the enormous levels of unmet need in mental health, improving access has understandably become the most important driver of policy. This is clearly visible in the priorities and targets set out in the NHS Long Term Plan.

In response to this challenge, there has been an emerging focus on how we can best 'industrialise' the delivery of care, combining, at the same time, organisational efficiency and adherence to evidence based best practice. The IAPT (Improving Access to Psychological Therapies) programme has been the most obvious example. While IAPT has had its critics, there is no doubting its achievements in offering talking therapies to very large numbers of people who would have previously been able to access only medication, or in many cases, nothing at all.

Traditionally, mental health services have been something of a cottage industry which have struggled to respond to the challenge of scale, and which have tended to be inconsistent in their approaches and their quality and outcomes. Given our success as mental health campaigners in arguing for the unacceptability of excluding great swathes of those in need for accessing care, there is a need to ensure that the system can respond to the ensuing demand as those who, due to stigma which surrounded mental illness, would have previously suffered in silence start to come forward to seek help.

There is a danger, however, that industrial models of care fail to have the space to accommodate more nuanced approaches such as those embraced by those advocating a spiritually informed model of care. In embracing more efficient models of evidence-based care we must not throw away other ways of engaging with people who use services, including the ability to engage with the spiritual aspects of their distress and beliefs and the potential wellbeing it may bring.

Strategies for developing and promoting spiritually based approaches

So, what would I say, as a long-standing chief executive in both the NHS and the voluntary sector, in support of a broader vision of mental health services which includes the space for spiritually informed approaches, including the many examples of inspiring thinking which are set out in this volume?

The first is to continue to have the conversation. To talk about ideas and identities which go beyond the scientific and purely material is a natural response to the complexity of human psychology and distress. We must not reduce mental health to a narrow debate about chemical imbalances. While science has it is place, it is not the only key to healing in a field where personal identity and agency has such an important role to play. This must be part of a movement within mental health to improve outcomes and reach, and not just headline, measures of access. It will be crucial that the stories of individual service users and practitioners are heard in this debate.

This is particularly important when we look at the question of inequities of access and the cultural acceptability of service models. It is to the great shame of all of us in the sector that we have tolerated for so long the gross inequalities experienced by patients from BAME, and in particular the overrepresentation of Black men in the most restrictive parts of the mental health system.

Amongst the many things we need to do to address this is to embrace, again, a community-focused approach to the development of services. Part of this will be the recognition of the importance of religious and spiritual beliefs in certain communities and the role of faith leaders and faith institutions as important players in supporting the mental health and building bridges with statutory services.

It is interesting and to some extent shaming to see the focus being put on community engagement as part of the vaccine programme. Mental health urgently needs to regain a sense of momentum in this respect if it is to make any serious response to the glaring inequalities in access and outcomes experienced by some minority groups.

This may also require statutory services to recognise the limitations of their own models and interventions. More local and community-based organisations may be better placed both to improve access and engagement but also in providing services which are more culturally specific.

Faith organisations of all kinds already have a major formal and informal role in supporting people in mental distress, including many of those at the most marginalised edges of society. In a US study quoted in *Shunned*, Graham Thornicroft's landmark book on mental health stigma (2006), 25% of people with a mental illness first seeking help went to a member of the clergy, compared to 17% going to a psychiatrist and 17% going to a general practitioner. While a US paradigm may not be totally applicable to this country, it would be foolish to ignore the ongoing importance of faith institutions as sources of help.

Faith organisations need to recognise their own role, as indeed many have. One of the most inspiring events I attended while being involved in the Time to Change anti-stigma programme was a summit for faith leaders organised by the then Archbishop of Canterbury, Rowan Williams. Across different faiths there were common messages about the role that faith communities played in supporting people with mental health problems. There was a healthy recognition, too, of the situations in which religion can, itself, be a source of distress, in particular when it is judgmental of the actions of individuals.

Such an approach fits well with the principles of population health and integrated care which sits at the heart of the latest reforms proposed for the health and care system. This should privilege efforts to invest in prevention and community resilience, building on and strengthening individual and community resources which promote and protect physical and mental health. Spirituality and faith communities are one such crucial asset.

Conclusion

We have been here before. During the early 2000s, a number of mental health trusts developed work on spirituality in mental health services encouraged by a programme established by the National Institute for Mental Health in England (NIMHE) in the wake of 9/11. The late Peter Gilbert, editor of the first edition of this handbook, was instrumental in leading something of a social movement for raising the profile of spirituality within the mental health community.

The flames of interest in that work have not subsided. As I have set out in this chapter there are plenty of reasons, in the current circumstances, to seek to revive them. Whether it's through the construction of formal strategies and policies or by a broader encouragement of spiritually informed and compassionate models of care and practice, a renewed interest in spirituality will be valuable at all levels of the system. At a time when mental health has rightly risen to a place of greater prominence in public policy and discourse, it is a healthy reminder that some of the less tangible ways of how we relate to individuals in mental distress as people are just as important as access to formal treatments and therapies.

References

Layard R (2005) *Happiness: Lessons from a New Science*.

Gawande A (2014) *Being Mortal: Medicine and What Matters in the End*.

The Mental Health Foundation (2006) *The impact of spirituality on mental health*.

Thornicroft G (2006) *Shunned: Discrimination against People with Mental Illness*.

New Landscapes

Chapter 24:
Reflections on race, religion and wellbeing

By Yvette Arthur, Prabhleen Sandhu, Nancy Nsiah & Haben Ghezai

The year 2020 was filled with a series of generation-defining moments, particularly for the ethnic minority population. Across the UK, evidence has shown that the Covid-19 pandemic, which has gripped the world, has disproportionately affected BAME[24] communities (Public Health England, 2020). Through social media, the world shared stories that were historically denied or buried from society's conscience. Hashtags and trending stories highlighted the murder of George Floyd and Kisaan (Indian farmers) demonstrations, which catalysed global protests against racial injustice that have long been experienced by BAME communities worldwide. These incidents also saw the emergence and popularisation of a language for these racial experiences (e.g. racial trauma, anti-racism, micro-aggressions), which provided a voice for invisible narratives and acted as a vehicle to move society towards liberation.

These moments resulted in a palpable sense of collective grief, with a domino effect of secondary losses; including the burden of social isolation, worries about our health, loss of financial security and much more. Consequently, these experiences have offered fresh focus on the importance of mental health and wellbeing as growing evidence points to ever-widening mental health inequalities (Institute for Fiscal Studies, 2020). Alongside social, emotional, and cognitive coping strategies, religious and spiritual practices have also served as a comforting balm amidst periods of trauma (Park *et al*, 2017). Nguyen (2020) describes that since religions have a narrative of determination and hope in the face of adversity and discrimination, it is an important source of strength for BAME communities. Spirituality in Black communities may further have socio-political roots, tied to liberation and survival (Beagan *et al*, 2012). Mattis (2002) argued that religion/

---

24 We recognize that the use of this term is problematic as it homogenises all non-white ethnic groups, making invisible the various differences between cultures, ethnicities and lived experiences. For the purpose of this chapter, the term BAME has been used to represent solely Black and Asian communities.

spirituality have historically served as transgressive and transformative spaces, in which Black women have been able to use religion/spirituality for meaning-making and to confront and go beyond limitations.

Religion offers a rich source of meaning which can provide a comprehensive framework that influences our ability to cope with periods of suffering and uncertainty (Park, 2013). Various studies attest to how religious beliefs offer both an understanding and a way to respond to mental health difficulties amongst BAME communities (e.g. Taylor *et al*, 2000; Krause, 2003; Haque, 2004). Religious practices can also provide a rich tapestry of connections, with God/a higher power, our sense of self and our communities, the latter having been further disrupted through the implementation of social distancing guidelines that have prevented religious communities from meeting in their traditional formats.

As authors of this chapter, we identify as clinical psychologists of Black and Asian heritage who also hold religious beliefs. Crenshaw (1989) describes the combination of identities such as these as intersectionality, highlighting the importance of understanding how one's identity characteristics interact to contribute to heterogeneous experiences.

We have noted the renewed interest in mental health support specifically targeting the needs of BAME communities, namely through addressing racial trauma and supporting mental health in the context of Covid-19. This need is evidenced in the launch of popular third-sector initiatives such as Black Minds Matter UK, who raised funds to provide therapy by Black therapists. Similarly, the South Asian Therapists directory was created to offer culturally sensitive therapy.

Mirroring the collective drive for anti-racism work, we have personally been encouraged and sustained by our religion, which has pushed us to continue anti-racism work. Whilst there is no agreed definition of the term 'anti-racism', it's generally been viewed as acts of resistance, any opposition to racism, and refusal to adopt White supremacist assumptions (Gilborn & Ladson-Billings, 2004). Our faith, as illustrated in the scriptures below, has given us permission to rest knowing that the task is not ours alone, but bigger than us, contributing to our sense of connectedness to others in our drives for social justice.

> *"Learn to do right; seek justice. Defend the oppressed"*
> **Isaiah 1:17, Bible**

> *"Why do you waver, O mortal being? The creator Lord Himself shall protect you. He who created you, will also give you nourishment"*
> **Sri Guru Granth Sahib Ji**

Our collective experiences as trainees and qualified psychologists have highlighted the missed opportunities to meaningfully attend to both ethnicity and spirituality/religion in the therapeutic and professional space. Challenging the myth of the monolithic minority, we take the position that the role of religion/spirituality in how an individual navigates mental health challenges needs to be considered in the context of ethnicity. This is part of our calling to anti-racist practice.

We acknowledge the complexities of multi-layered experiences of religion, mental health, and ethnicity. We hope to share our insights through reflections and illustrations of cases from clients and our personal experiences. We aim to encourage readers to thoughtfully consider how they can shape meaningful collaboration towards healing.

The relationship between religion/spirituality and ethnicity

Our ethnicity means that we are usually the only, or one of a few ethnic minorities within the psychology field, which has sometimes led to an unconscious tendency to 'monitor' our comments. For example, in group supervision, we have individually noticed that reflections around the impact of a client's racial background were omitted and we felt apprehensive about encouraging further exploration. Such challenges leave us worrying about appearing 'too outspoken or too strong', reflecting the legacy of negative stereotypes against Black individuals. This echoes the narratives of other BAME clinical psychology trainees, who engage in multifaceted and effortful emotional work to manage similar experiences (Shah, 2010). Such internalised stereotypes about BAME communities lead us occasionally to feel as though we cannot be our true selves. This leaves us and many others feeling powerless in speaking about our experiences and culture (Paulraj, 2016).

Whilst ethnicity is an important aspect of our identity, our religious beliefs are also important. These two components have sometimes resulted in us feeling as though we do not 'fit' the traditional image of a clinical psychologist, which is usually White and non-religious (Leeds Clearing house, CHPCCP, 2020). Moreover, the minimal inclusion of topics about race and religion on the clinical psychology doctoral programme and in standardised clinical assessment tools implies that these areas are incongruous with the discipline of psychology. An impact of this is the 'double silencing' because of being a minority in both religion and ethnicity within the profession, and uncertainty of how we use our unique position. Arthur (2018) highlighted that Christian and Muslim psychologists from BAME backgrounds often felt silenced by the perceived need to protect themselves to avoid judgement and negative comments from colleagues. Cole (2009) highlights the importance of considering the hierarchies of power, privilege or oppression within identities, such as the different experiences of a White male compared to a Black female who are both Christian.

The previous book chapters detail the positive impact of religious commitment upon one's mental health. Rajaei (2010) argues that moral discipline derived from religion has important effects on the feelings, behaviour and experiences of individuals. Although religious experiences and psychological wellbeing were studied by early psychologists (e.g. James, 1917; Jung, 1969), we argue that the relationship between religion and ethnicity continues to be neglected in therapy, unless being considered in the context of managing risk such as in the anti-terrorism 'Prevent' programme or increased religiosity associated with psychosis within BAME communities (Loewenthal, 2006).

In contrast to this, a study found that individuals from BAME communities regard their religious beliefs to be a central part of their identity, as compared to White Christians (O'Beirne, 2004). Also, involvement in religious activity enables people from BAME groups to hold onto their cultural traditions in a society in which the dominant culture holds different values (King *et al*, 2006). In terms of addressing mental health difficulties amongst BAME communities across Hinduism, Christianity, Islam and Judaism, there was a preference to respond to distress with private prayer. This was due to the communities' perceptions of mental health difficulties being a weakness and placing the family's reputation at stake, as compared to White Catholics (Cinnirella & Loewenthal, 1999). By not facilitating open dialogue around issues that are profoundly important to our clients, we inadvertently send a message that talking about religion/spirituality and/or race is unwelcome and separate from presenting concerns.

Unconscious bias

To integrate religion/spirituality and race into therapeutic practices, the therapist must be aware of their own unconscious biases and assumptions, which are influenced by the environment they grew up in and how they are socialised to race within the community. These biases and assumptions are often made on an implicit level, without realising we are doing it. For example, if a therapist does not consider religion or race important, they might refrain from talking about it in the therapy space or hold off from exploring it further if a client does not bring it up (Crossley & Salter, 2005). Research has shown that these biases can be experienced by Black clients in the form of microaggressions including minimising the impact of cultural experiences and pathologising cultural values (Constantine, 2007).

So how do we deal with these unconscious biases? The first step is to develop our self-awareness, by reflecting on our beliefs, values, attitudes, behaviours and social contexts. Freire (2006) developed the idea of critical consciousness, which refers to an awareness of the socio-political context of daily life. This involves illuminating the often taken for granted assumptions and realities about the way the world operates (Afuape, 2011). For example, noticing our reactions to things clients say, especially those that may evoke strong or negative feelings. Burnham (1993; 2012) developed a useful way of exploring differences in the therapy room and supervision by using the mnemonic 'Social GGRRAAACCEEESS', which encompasses aspects of identity (See Table 24.1).These can be voiced/unvoiced and visible/invisible. The focus on each part of one's identity permits for the exploration of aspects that are dominant or marginalised. Such a tool enhances the exploration of religion/ spirituality in the therapy room, as a client's religious beliefs may be invisible, or clients may intentionally avoid voicing it due to perceptions that it is not relevant to the therapy domain. For example, not acknowledging an individual wearing a pagh/ dastar (a Sikh turban).

Table 24.1: Social GGRRAAACCEEESS mnemonic
Gender
Geography
Race
Religion
Age
Ability
Appearance
Class
Culture
Ethnicity
Education
Employment
Sexuality
Sexual orientation
Spirituality

(Burnham (1993; 2012)

Shellenberger et al (2007) argue that when an individual and therapist do not share a common culture, misunderstandings can occur. This can leave the individual feeling disrespected, uncomfortable, or receiving care that is inconsistent with important cultural practices. Smedley (2003) argues the importance of cultural competence education in shifting ethnic and racial inequalities in health care. A cultural genogram (Shellenberger et al, 2007; Hardy & Laszloffy, 1995) is a tool to support healthcare professionals to integrate and address people's cultural beliefs and practices in their work. It moves beyond a traditional genogram and explores an individual's family and cultural beliefs, such as country of origin, ethnic identification, religious practices, family definitions of health and wellbeing, use of alternative health practices, how emotional illness is viewed, and more. By using the cultural genogram tool, we can begin to offer interventions that are more in line with an individual's worldview.

When our personal beliefs and values are so strong that we struggle to remain self-reflective on our biases/judgements, it may impact the therapeutic relationship. Supervision can be a useful space to provide alternative perspectives to the therapist-client dyad. Through supervision, we can continuously reflect on these challenges and find ways to build healthier and more transparent relationships. We often reflect on our own biases and wonder why we hold off from exploring religion/spirituality and race in the therapy space. Perhaps it is because we are part of a BAME community and we are aware of the negative stereotypes this brings, such as being viewed as 'pushing religion onto others'. Or perhaps it is because we never spoke about the intersection of religion/spirituality, race, and mental wellbeing during training. Maybe this set a precedent?

As psychologists, we believe that it is our role to commit to anti-racist practice. This includes challenging Eurocentric psychological theories and practices, which make it difficult to bring religion/spirituality and race into the therapy room, by asking questions and being curious. As well as those in Table 24.2, Patel & Keval (2018) also have a useful list of questions to reflect on race and social injustice.

Table 24.2: Reflective exercise

- What connects you and keeps you going in social justice work?
- How can you nourish and sustain your motivation to engage in anti-discriminatory practices?
- As therapists, how would your assessments, formulations and interventions change if we were to centre the narratives of faith and race within the therapy room?
- What aspects of your practice needs to be de-centered to make space for this?
- How can you centre the client and their experiences, without placing the burden of educating the professional upon them?
- How can we seek to understand the needs of those closest to the pain of injustices?

Call to action

Belonging to a BAME and religious community in a non-religious, White profession, we have felt it essential to develop our critical consciousness, allowing us to take 'action' against the oppressive elements of our reality. We also recognise particular privileges such as the level of education, socio-economic class and professional title we hold. We recognise that these privileges enable us to support change when addressing issues of mental health and inequalities related to race. In raising our critical consciousness by placing our previous experiences in political and historic contexts, we are better able to challenge the difficulties we have reflected on in this chapter and move towards anti-racist practices. For example, considering the prevalence of Covid-19 vaccine hesitancy amongst the Black population within the wider socio-historical and political context of relationships to vaccinations. Including distrust towards Western pharmaceutical companies facilitating mass immunisation campaigns for Polio across Nigeria (Jegede, 2007), admissions of the intention to 'test' Covid-19 vaccines across Africa by European scientists (Busari & Wojazer, 2020), and a history of long-standing health inequalities within the UK (Geddes, 2021), further fuelling hesitancy around biomedical research.

Further, there is a higher prevalence of schizophrenia among Black males in the UK (Fearon *et al*, 2006), despite this increased prevalence not seen within Black populations outside of the UK (Mahy *et al*, 1999). The historical context of schizophrenia details how the diagnosis became associated with Black males during the late 1960s, coinciding with the Civil Rights movements (Metzl, 2014). This is evidenced in an advertisement describing Haloperidol as the 'drug of choice' to medicate "assaultive and belligerent" Black males (Archives of General Psychiatry, 1974). The effects of this are still seen today as Black people are more likely to be prescribed Haloperidol rather than newer antipsychotics which have better outcomes and fewer side effects (Opolka *et al*, 2004). Furthermore, concerns about risk and violence among Black service users has led to an over-reliance on medication and restrictive methods (Keating & McCulloch, 2002). This has led us to advocate for alternative forms of support for mental health difficulties.

Throughout history 'anti-racism' has consisted of ordinary people, outside the control of the state, agencies, or political parties, taking continued action against racism and oppression (Bonnett, 2000). In the context of 2020 and the various protests, activism and political stances adopted, it is important that these strides must not be carried out in the 'hype' of defining moments in history. We should remain active in creatively resisting and responding to injustices within society and the various spaces we occupy, including the therapeutic/professional space.

One way in which we have chosen to resist oppression and take an anti-racist stance is by taking a non-neutral position in our therapeutic work. For example, Haben has chosen to name experiences of racism and injustice when working with torture survivors; Nancy has chosen to promote critical engagement in issues concerning ethnic minority populations within physical health sectors; Yvette has chosen to name experiences of racism as a contributory factor to the development of psychosis and religion as a protective factor of mental health and Prabhleen has chosen to explore the impact of intergenerational racial trauma when supporting children, young people, and their families. Thus, moving away from the medicalisation and individualisation of racism and oppression and reframing it as a systemic disease, infiltrating all aspects of society.

Through these anti-discriminatory practices, we hope to stay connected to our preferred ways of engaging with and supporting those who come to consult us for support. It is important, however, to not limit acts of resistance and anti-racist thinking to the therapy room. We have often found it important to think about how we can impact the organisations and systems that we work within, as not doing so may leave us complicit in perpetuating oppressive systems and at risk of re-enacting harm. For example, supporting staff and senior management to reflect on and address organisational practices which have allowed for a lack of BAME representation in senior or paid roles and an over-representation of BAME workers in key non-paid service user roles.

While it is important to seek opportunities for resistance and anti-racist work within the psychology profession, we have often felt 'unsafe' to do so in environments where we and our experiences are the minority. As psychologists, we hold degrees of power, similarly in these spaces we may be left feeling disempowered.

Psychology and educators have often spoken about the need for 'safe spaces' to create environments where individuals can authentically engage in dialogue. Where the spaces we inhabit may not always feel safe to hold a dialogue about diversity, power, privilege, and religion, the idea that we need a 'safe space' before we can engage in conversation on such topics becomes increasingly problematic. Such notions may lead some to conflate 'safety' with 'comfort' and towards ideas that certain dialogues are risk-free (Arao & Clements, 2013). Arao & Clements (2013) go on to argue that authentic learning about social justice often requires qualities of risk and discomfort which are incompatible with the notion of 'safety'. The conversation around racism, race and religion may often feel risky in certain environments. It is important for us to consider whose comfort or safety is being centred when we choose not to engage in these discussions. We argue that notions of safety may hinder the therapeutic relationships and cause systemic harm if it comes at the cost of further silencing the silenced and the ability to challenge social injustices.

Moving away from a 'safe space' paradigm towards notions of 'brave spaces' may help us to pursue courageous conversations when addressing issues of race, religion/spirituality and mental health (Arao & Clements, 2013). We have noted that these principles better fit spiritual teachings regarding the importance of being brave in the face of things that bring anxiety and discomfort. Spirituality/religion can guide and sustain individuals in anti-racism work and to actively move towards meaningful change.

We would like to leave you with extracts from religious texts that we have often used to encourage us in anti-racist work and persevering in our profession.

> *"Have I not commanded you? Be strong and courageous, do not be afraid;*
> *do not be discouraged..."*
> **Joshua 1:9, Bible**

> *"Recognise the entire human race as one"*
> **Sri Guru Gobind Singh Ji**

References

Afuape T (2011) *Power, resistance and liberation in counselling and psychotherapy: To have our hearts broken*. Routledge.

Arao B & Clemens K (2013) From safe spaces to brave spaces. *The art of effective facilitation: Reflections from social justice educators* 135-150.

Archives of General Psychiatry (1974) *Archives of General Psychiatry* **31**(5) 732-733.

Arthur Y (2018) Narratives of Christian and Muslim qualified and trainee clinical psychologists working in the NHS. Professional doctoral thesis: University of East London.

Beagan B L, Etowa J & Bernard W T (2012) "With God in our lives he gives us the strength to carry on": African Nova Scotian women, spirituality, and racism-related stress. *Mental Health, Religion & Culture* **15** (2) 103-120.

Bonnett A (2000) *Anti-racism*. Psychology Press, pp 88.

Burnham J (1993) Systemic supervision the evolution of reflexivity in the context of the supervisory relationship. *Human Systems* **4** 349-381.

Burnham J (2012) Developments in Social GGRRAAACCEEESS: visible-invisible and voiced-unvoiced. In I-B Krause (Eds) *Culture and reflexivity: Mutual perspectives (systemic thinking and practice)* pp 139-160 London: Karnac.

Busari S & Wojazer J (2020) French doctors' proposal to test Covid-19 treatment in Africa slammed as 'colonial mentality. *CNN* 21 January.

Cinnirella M & Loewenthal K M (1999) Religious and ethnic group influences on beliefs about mental illness: A qualitative interview study. *British Journal of Medical Psychology* **72** 505-524.

Cole E R (2009) Intersectionality and research in psychology. *American Psychologist* **64** (3) 170–180.

Constantine M G (2007) Racial microaggressions against African American clients in cross-racial counseling relationships. *Journal of Counseling Psychology* **54** 1–16.

Crenshaw K (1989) Demarginalizing the Intersection of Race and Sex: A Black Feminist Critique of Antidiscrimination Doctrine, Feminist Theory and Antiracist Politics. *The University of Chicago Legal Forum* **1** (8) 139-167.

Crossley J P & Salter D P (2005) A question of finding harmony: A grounded theory study of clinical psychologists' experience of addressing spiritual beliefs in therapy. *Psychology and Psychotherapy: Therapy, Research and Practice* **78** 295-313.

Freire P (2006) *Education for Critical Consciousness*. London UK: Continuum

Geddes L (2021) Health inequalities in UK are major factor in high BAME Covid cases. *The Guardian* 28 January.

Gillborn D & Ladson-Billings G (Eds.) (2004) *The RoutledgeFalmer reader in multicultural education*. Psychology Press.

Haque A (2004) Religion and Mental Health: The Case of American Muslims. *Journal of Religion and Health* 43 45–58.

Hardy K V & Laszloffy T A (1995) The cultural genogram: Key to training culturally competent family therapists. *Journal of Marital and Family Therapy* **21** 227–237.

James W (1917) *The Varieties of Religious Experience, A Study in Human Nature Being the Gifford Lectures on Natural Religion Delivered at Edinburgh in 1901-1902*. Longmans, Green, And Co.

Jung CG (1969). *Psychology and Religion: The Terry Lectures. In: Jung CG, Adler G, Fordham M, eds. The Collected works of C.G. Jung*. Routledge and Kegan Paul.

Jegede A S (2007) What led to the Nigerian boycott of the polio vaccination campaign?. *PLoS Med* **4** (3) e73.

Keating F & McCulloch A W (2002). *Breaking the circles of fear*. United Kingdom: The Sainsbury Centre for Mental Health.

King M, Weich S, Nazroo J & Blizard B (2006) Religion, mental health and ethnicity. EMPIRIC – A national survey of England. *Journal of Mental Health* **15** (2) 153-162.

Krause N (2003) A preliminary assessment of race differences in the relationship between religious doubt and depressive symptoms. *Review of Religious Research* **45** 93–115.

Leeds Clearing House CHPCCP (2020) Equal opportunities [online]. Leeds: Leeds Clearing House. Available at: https://www.leeds.ac.uk/chpccp/equalopps.html (accessed January 2021).

Loewenthal K (2006) *Religion, culture and mental health*. USA: Cambridge university press.

Mahy G E, Mallett R & Bhugra D (1999). First-contact incidence rate of schizophrenia in Barbados. *The British Journal of Psychiatry* **175** 28-33.

Mattis J S (2002) Religion and spirituality in the meaning–making and coping experiences of African American women: A qualitative analysis. *Psychology of Women Quarterly* **26** (4) 309-321.

Metzl J (2014) *The protest psychosis*. Boston: Beacon Press.

Nguyen A W (2020) Religion and mental health in racial and ethnic minority populations: A review of the literature. *Innovations in Aging* **4** (5) 1-13.

O'Beirne M (2004) *Home office research study 274: Religion in England and Wales: findings from the 2001 home office citizenship survey*. London: Home Office.

Opolka J L, Rascati K L, Brown C M & Gibson P J (2004) Ethnicity and prescription patterns for haloperidol, risperidone, and olanzapine. *Psychiatric Services* **55** (2) 151-156.

Patel, N & Keval, H (2018). Fifty ways to leave……your racism. *Journal of Critical Psychology, Counselling and Psychotherapy* **18** (2) 61-79.

Park C L (2013) The meaning making model: A framework for understanding meaning, spirituality, and stress-related growth in health psychology. *European Health Psychologist* **15** (2) 40-47.

Park C L, Currier J M, Harris J I & Slattery J M (2017) *Trauma, meaning, and spirituality: Translating research into clinical practice*. American Psychological Association.

Paulraj P S (2016) *How do Black trainees make sense of their 'identities' in the context of clinical psychology training?* Professional doctoral thesis: University of East London.

Public Health England (2020) COVID-19: review of disparities in risks and outcomes [online]. United Kingdom: Gov.uk. Available at: https://www.gov.uk/government/publications/covid-19-review-of-disparities-in-risks-and-outcomes (accessed January 2021).

Rajaei A R (2010) Religious cognitive–emotional therapy: A new form of psychotherapy. *Iranian journal of psychiatry* **5** (3) 81.

Shah S (2010) *The experience of being a trainee clinical psychologist from a Black and Minority Ethnic group: A qualitative study*. Professional doctoral thesis: University of Hertfordshire.

Smedley B (Ed.) (2003) *Unequal treatment: Confronting racial and ethnic disparities in health care*. Washington, DC: Institute of Medicine.

Shellenberger S, Dent M M, Davis-Smith M, Seale J P, Weintraut R, & Wright T (2007) Cultural genogram: A tool for teaching and practice. *Families, Systems, & Health* **25** (4) 367.

Taylor R J, Ellison C G, Chatters L M, Levin J S & Lincoln K D (2000) Mental health services in faith communities: The role of clergy in black churches. *Social Work* **45** (1) 73–87.

The Institute of Fiscal Studies (2020) The mental health effects of the first two months of lockdown and social distancing during the Covid-19 pandemic in the UK [online]. The IFS. Available at: https://www.ifs.org.uk/publications/14874 (accessed January 2021).

Chapter 25:
Ecology, mental health and eco-spirituality

By Peter Hawkins

Will you teach your children what we have taught our children?
That the earth is our mother?
What befalls the earth befalls all sons of the earth.
This we know: the earth does not belong to man, man belongs to the earth.
All things are connected like the blood that unites us all.
Man did not weave the web of life, he is merely a strand in it.
Whatever he does to the web, he does to himself?
(Chief Seattle First Nations Elder, Leader and Teacher in North America, 1855)

"No doubt about it, ecology drives people crazy, this has to be our point of departure – not with goal of finding a cure, just so we can learn to survive without … denial, or hubris, or depression, or hope for a reasonable solution, or retreat into the desert."
(Professor Bruno Latour, 2017:13)

"To heal the soul without reference to the ecological system of which we are an integral part is a form of self-destructive blindness". (James Hillman (p xvi))

Introduction

We need to recognise that we are the youngest children of creation, even if we are the loudest, most unruly and destructive. We need to develop the humility to learn from those who have been here much longer than we have and will survive long after our species is extinct.

We can no longer afford to treat mental illness as personal, as something that belongs to an individual, for our mental disturbances are species wide, and its consequences are affecting every aspect of our beautiful planet.

In 2019, I set out to discover why, in a world, particularly the 'Western' world, of growing human prosperity and education, increase in medical knowledge and services and global connectivity, there was such an exponential increase in mental illness, depression, anxiety and suicides. After a great deal of reading and talking to experts and colleagues around the world, I realised we had a collective human sickness. In the first part of this chapter, I will outline the five underlying causes that I perceive to be at the root of this human malady, and then in the second part I will outline what I believe will provide the healing needed, not only for us as a species, but for the split between the human and the more-than-human world, which is not only disturbing the human species, but taking our whole shared earth to the precipice of an ecological collapse. The ecological crisis and the climate emergency cannot be healed or resolved through a human-centric focus, as human-centricity is one of the fundamental causes of what has taken us to the state of a disturbed and diseased Anthropocene world. Rather, we must find healing for humanity, through focusing on healing the split between ourselves and the more-than-human world and discover a new participatory consciousness through an eco-spirituality.

The human illness

A 2016 index of 301 diseases found mental health problems to be one of the main causes of the overall disease burden worldwide, with 800,000 suicides, accounting for 1.4% of all deaths worldwide, making it the 18th leading cause of death. Globally, an estimated 300 million people are affected by depression (WHO/GHO 2017), and nearly half of adults (43.4%) think that they have had a diagnosable mental health condition at some point in their life.

So why, when the human species is getting richer, healthier and more resourced, is mental illness becoming more prevalent and happiness not increasing? I suggested in Hawkins and Ryde (2020), and much of the next section draws heavily from this book (with kind permission of the publishers, Jessica Kingsley, and my co-author Judy Ryde), that there are four main factors that go some way to explaining this:

- psychological overload
- the conscious or unconscious registering of ecological devastation leading to 'eco-anxiety' and species 'loneliness'
- the fragmentation of the psychological containers in and through which we psychologically process our experience and form our sense of meaning and our individuality
- human-centrism and living in what we have termed 'The Age of More'; an addicted society that is searching for happiness in ways that can never be satiated.

We will take these four and explore them in more detail.

Psychological overload

We now connect with more people than ever before, play a greater variety of roles, and are exposed to more sources of data and information than ever, and yet have less space alone or time to digest what we daily absorb. Today more information is instantaneously available to us at the click of the cell-phone or computer, than our grandparents would have accessed in their lifetime. We no longer need to wonder or argue about who wrote a book, or appeared in a film, for Google can tell us! But our information arrives in bite-sized fragments – by Twitter, YouTube, Facebook, television headlines and e-mail. We lack the time to engage in the process of turning data into information, information into knowledge and knowledge into wisdom, before the next flood of data arrives.

Us 'privileged' members of the world wide web are inundated every day with the equivalent amount of 34 Gb (gigabytes) of information, a sufficient quantity to overload the average laptop within a week (Bohn 2012). In addition, screen experience is very addictive in nature. The average British person checks their mobile phone once an hour, or 10,000 times a year, and many people check it much more often than that – in the middle of meals, meetings or even in bed (Independent, 1st December 2017).

In Hawkins and Ryde (2020) I wrote:

"Not only do we take in more, but we move through a greater variety of roles in each day, from parents negotiating our children's education with a teacher, to care-giver for our own parents; from our partner's lover to co-parent, to joint manager of the family house and finances; from work roles where we now may belong to multiple teams, or have a portfolio career involving many different ways of being; and from being a passionate sports fan to volunteering on the local soup run to the homeless. Yet psychotherapy encourages us to be authentic and autonomous and discover our integration in this one-man or one-woman, ever changing repertory show."

"Additionally many have written about how life is becoming increasingly VUCA, which stands for Volatile, Uncertain, Complex and Ambiguous (Stiehm, & Townsend, 2002). Psychological overload is not just about the amount of information we take in; the range of experience and virtual experience we absorb; and the multifarious roles we are required to play; but also that we know more, but can predict less in our lives. The contexts we inhabit are changing faster and with more interconnected complexity than ever."

Human beings have been incredibly successful at adapting to multiple environmental niches, from the tropical jungle to the artic tundra, and from the desert to urban living, but now, for better or worse, we have created one interconnected, fast changing, global niche, and as a species we have no idea how to thrive within this context.

The pain of ecological devastation

For many years human beings have been wilfully blind to the ecological destruction that has resulted from their so called 'success'. The massive pollution of the atmosphere from the carbon-driven economies originated in the industrial revolution and the effects of this will last for hundreds of years. The climate changes that emerge from the effect of greenhouse gasses are already driving more extreme weather patterns in many parts of the world and sea level rises from melting polar icecaps and glaciers. The devastation of many ecological niches of the world through exploitation of nature's resources include: deforestation of many of the worlds jungles and forests, what some term 'the earth lungs'; the hunting of many animals that has caused unprecedented loss of species diversity; the mining of carbon sources (coal, gas, oil) and of minerals to fuel and adorn and enable human lifestyles; and the conversion of diverse wild natural areas into human controlled mono-cultures.

The devastation of our shared planetary home has enormous and increasing impact on the mental and emotional lives of each and every one of us, for some consciously and for all unconsciously. This gives rise to direct or indirect feelings of: grief and loss; guilt for one's part in the destruction; fear for oneself, one's community and/ or for future generations; or anger at others who the individual sees as more responsible for the devastation than themselves. It can emerge through the dreams, reactions to current events, or even through nameless and unlocatable emotions. Whatever way, the wider ecology and what is happening to it, arrives, bidden or unbidden, recognised or unrecognised.

Nature has traditionally been a significant source of physical and mental healing. Yet with the unprecedented migration of human beings to urban environments and the parallel destruction and humanisation of many natural ecologies, this resource is less and less available to larger percentages of the human population. Many have lost their living connection to other mammals and to plants, or ease of access to places of unspoilt beauty away from human noise and interference. Many of us have lost our healthy living connection to our source, and life has become plastically packaged, humanised, noisy and crowded.

Fragmentation

The materials from which we build our identity and meaning have become much more fractured and fragmented in recent years:

- **Families** are more transitory, with parents changing partners, and many children having life split between separated parents, engaging with different half and step brothers and sisters.

- **Community**, which was our holding container in previous generations, was not just our immediate nuclear family, for this was often contained within a wider extended family of grandparents, aunts, uncles and cousins who lived locally. The local village or urban estate would be a known community with and through whom you created an identity. Our communities are now often spread round the world and consist of people we connect with digitally via Facebook, Snapchat, Instagram, etc.

- **Place**. In the past children would grow up in a rooted location. Even 50 years ago, two-thirds of the world's population were rural, intimately connected with growing their food and looking after their animals within an ecological locale with which they felt deeply connected. Now nearly all of us have become indigenous orphans, migrants who have left the soil of our childhood, and have lost the sense of creating our meaning in relation to a given ecological context (Hawkins 2018a; 2018b).

- **A collective rhythm and shared belief**. Traditionally, cultures would have collective rhythms that gave shape and meaning to the day, week, seasons and year. As a child, I went to church on Sundays, experiencing a clearer distinction between the working week and the weekends. The school day began with an assembly of prayers and hymns. We experienced the fasting of Lent, harvest festivals, May Day dancing around the maypole and Christmas that was not just a consumerist indulgence. Our family, community, town or village and festivities were an interconnected web which expressed and communicated shared beliefs. In the last 100 years, not only have we become more migratory and less rooted, but much more secular and individualistic in our beliefs. This is particularly true in the Western world. We need to find new non-sectarian rituals that reconnect us to our shared earth.

- **Digitalisation of human interactions**. A 75-year-old friend of ours told us that in the past he would, whilst collecting his pension, have a conversation with the local post office counter-clerk; buy his train ticket in conversation at the ticket office; and discuss his finances with the bank manager. All of these conversational interactions have now been replaced with digital online transactions with faceless processes on his computer. Even playing with his grandchildren happens over Zoom.

There is increasing global evidence that many individuals and social communities and groups are struggling to create a positive sense of identity in the midst of the exponential changes of our time. Some argue that the political move back to nationalism and more right-wing agendas is fuelled by people's reaction to this fragmentation and loss of social identity.

The coming of human-centrism and the 'Age of More'

Central to human mental health and wellbeing is a sense of purpose which gives meaning to one's life (Frankl, 2013). Today we are the daughters and sons of the Age of Enlightenment and the birth of 'Liberal Humanism', which Harari (2016) argues is the dominant religion of our time in the West. Whereas the Copernican revolution put the Sun at the centre of our solar system and relegated the Earth to an orbiting planet, the Protestant revolution put the individual mind and conscience at the centre of the universe and relegated the priest to an orbiting organism that would sometimes come for tea. Secular liberal humanism has put individual feelings and happiness at the centre of the universe and the environment as something to fulfil our individual human needs. Liberal Humanism brings with it its own shadow. For capital markets rely on growth, and growth relies on constantly increasing consumerism.

Alan During (1992) wrote:
"Our enormously productive economy… demands that we make consumption our way of life, that we convert the buying and use of goods into rituals, that we seek our spiritual satisfaction, our ego satisfaction, in consumption… We need things consumed, burned up, worn out, replaced, and discarded at an ever-increasing rate." (p 69)

Armies of advertisers, marketing experts and 'spin doctors' have to convince human beings that to be happy, to be healthy, to be successful, they need to acquire 'more': more food, drink, clothes, cars, travel, holidays, books, films, electronic gadgets, computers, belongings of every kind. More recently in the rich cultures, 'more' has begun to move away from acquisition of material things, to acquisition of experiences, which you can tell your friends about via social media; a move, from: 'you are what you own', to 'you are what you have experienced'.

'The Age of More' is also the age of the sore neck, for everyone is looking upwards, to those that have more than they do. Consumerism requires conspicuous inequality and rich and attractive celebrities to increase the mass aspiration for more. Some of us may be in the wealthiest 1% of the world's population, but if the people they see on our televisions and YouTube, the celebrities in our sports events and popular entertainment, the top executives in our organisations, are much wealthier than they are, they feel hard-up and under-privileged. Durning quotes Lewis Lapham the ex-editor of Harpers as saying:

"… a depressing number of Americans believe that if only they had twice as much, they would inherit the estate of happiness promised them in the Declaration of Independence. The man who receives $15,000 a year is sure that he could relieve his sorrow if he had $30,000 a year; the man with $1 million a year knows that all would be well if he had $2 million a year … Nobody ever has enough." (Durning, 1992, p70)

Harari (2016) writes about how: "modernity … inspired people to want more, and dismantled the age old disciplines that curbed greed". Furthermore, globalisation and the internet has meant that "the rest know what the best are having" (Hawkins, 2021), and, in 'The Age of More', this has led to massive increase in migration.

As experiences have become more valued than material possessions for those who live in the materially more affluent societies, many have become consumers of experiences, many are centring their sense of purpose on a 'healthy body', 'great relationships', 'more mindfulness', 'an expanded and enlightened consciousness'. These too have their armies of marketing advertisers and seductive sales forces.

The nature of addiction is that, whatever you become addicted to, you need increasing amounts of it to meet your habituated need. 'More' no longer brings you the pleasure it once did. 'More' no longer brings you happiness, but instead brings you the longing for 'even more'. The Age of More, with its aspiration, acquisition and addiction, supports gross inequality and the exponential growth of consuming the earth's resources beyond sustainable levels. With over three times more people in the world than when I was born, all being globally connected, all being encouraged to want more, our human species urgently needs to find a new sense of personal and collective meaning. I believe that 'Liberal Humanism' has reached its apotheosis and humans have already played at being God far too long for the good of the planet's eco-system. What is needed is a major paradigm shift in human consciousness, from human centricity to humility; and from seeing the environment as being there to serve human want, to seeing the environment as being part of us, without which we have no healthy or sustainable life.

Healing the split

"Unless we see the Earth as a planet that behaves as if it were alive, at least the extent of regulating its climate and chemistry, we will lack the will to change our way of life and to understand that we have made it our greatest enemy." (James Lovelock, 2007)

There are thousands of challenges facing human beings, but at heart there is only one: the need for us to evolve human consciousness fast enough for homo sapiens to be fit to remain as part of the biosphere by the late 21st century". In response to the great challenges facing our globe, most human beings respond either through denial or through the forlorn hubristic attempts to develop science and technology fast enough for the human species to stay one step ahead of the challenges. The need is for us, the human species, to evolve its consciousness to be able to respond fully to the complexity of the world we have been responsible for co-evolving.

I see eco-spirituality as a path that leads individuals, communities and our one global human family, back from species separation and alienation, to experiencing ourselves once again as nested within the wider complex and endlessly creative ecological life of our living planet. It recognises the flow of what the poet Coleridge called "the one life in us and abroad". The holy book of eco-spirituality is the shared nature that surrounds us and flows through us and is our wisest teacher.

Satish Kumar, a great eco-spiritual teacher, builds his eco-spirituality on a new inter-connected trinity, of Soul, Soil and Society (Kumar, 2002). James Hillman, the late great Imaginal Psychologist, wrote:

"At the heart of the coming environmental revolution is a change in values, one that derives from a growing appreciation of our dependence on nature. Without it there is no hope. In simple terms, we cannot restore our own health, our sense of wellbeing, unless we restore the health of the planet. .....airs, waters and places play as large a role in the problems psychology faces as do moods, relationships, and memories. (Hillman 1995 p xvi- xxii)

Eco-spiritual practices

"To the eye of the seer, every leaf of the tree is a page of the holy book that contains divine revelation." Hazrat Inayat Khan

Eco-spirituality is not a theory, or a set of intellectual spiritual beliefs. It is a practical and embodied way of being. It is a path along which we are constantly stumbling, learning and discovering new ways of returning to a participatory consciousness with the wider world. It takes daily practices and disciplines, and here I offer just five of the simple practices I have found helpful.

1. **Find you unique purpose**: Victor Frankl (2013), based on his experience in the Nazi concentration camps, wrote: "He who has a why can bear almost any how". Life becomes meaningful when we discover our unique purpose – "what we can uniquely do, that the world of tomorrow needs" (Hawkins, 2021). No one occupies the same place in the ecology as we do, and all other places are taken!

2. **Service and compassion**: opening to another's need, seeing the world from their eyes, and walking a mile in their shoes, or lack of them. Moinuddin Chisti, who brought Sufism from Persia to India, interpreted religion in terms of human service and exhorted his disciples "to develop river-like generosity, sun-like affection and earth-like hospitality". The highest form of devotion, according to him, was "to redress the misery of those in distress – to fulfil the needs of the helpless and to feed the hungry".

   Elias Amidon, a contemporary Sufi teacher, in his notes from the Open Path, puts it beautifully:

   "The cry of the world is still there – it's everywhere – and you are seamless with it. There is an old person living alone just a few houses from yours who hasn't smiled in weeks; there is your own son or daughter or father or mother with whom you haven't been fully present; there are refugees from Syria in your city who need to learn your language and be welcomed, there are people on the other side of the world who have no idea of the freedom you enjoy and the creativity they are capable of. Of course, you can't respond to all of it. You can only respond to what is yours to do – what comes to you to do."

   How do we know what is ours to do? Notice what arises in you as a need and turn it into an offering to others. Elias Amidon goes on to say that kindness is "a gesture, pure in itself because it is not burdened with any notions of self-importance or pre-conceived ideas about fixing anything... it arises from your natural seamlessness with the world – either the world far away or the world close at hand". So let me pause and ask each of you, "What is knocking on your door, asking you to respond with the natural gesture of kindness?"

3. **Gardening**: *"Plant a garden. It's good for the health of the earth and its good for the health of people. A garden is a nursery for nurturing connection, the soil for cultivation of practical reverence.... Once you develop a relationship with a little patch of earth, it becomes a seed itself.... Medicine for broken land and empty hearts."* (Robin Wall Kimmerer, 2020, p126). One of the things that happy centenarians around the world seem to share is that they continue to garden (Garcia & Miralles, 2017).

4. **Gratitude back to source**: Before you eat a meal, look at the plate of food and say 'thank-you'. First for the people who did the cooking, then for those who did the shopping, then for those in the shops and those who transported the food there. Then for those who harvested the food and grew it; then for soil in which it grew and the millions of micro-organisms that created the soil; then for the rain and wind and sun – the primary elements that created the life – and finally for the stars that died, that created the carbon on this beautiful planet and made life here possible. Much has died and lived to make possible each plate of food we eat.

5. **Let nature be your teacher**: I invite you to give yourself some time to take a discovery walk into nature, be it your garden, a local park, a woodland, coastal path or other part of nature that is important to you. Travel with open-hearted, wide-eyed and wide-eared curiosity. Try and be as unencumbered as possible – taking very little with you, either in what you carry physically or in the clutter of your mind. Be open to what comes. Lightly hold the question, "what can the wider ecology teach me about how to heal myself and others?" and allow yourself to wander and wait for whatever surprising answers may unfold. After a while the question may change to: "how can I help you, the wider ecology, heal humanity?"

6. **Opening the seven levels**: For a number of years, I have had the privilege of being an inter-faith spiritual celebrant, facilitating weddings, child blessings, funerals and other rites of passage. In more recent years I have trained other spiritual celebrants in this important work. One of the core practices happens before the ceremony and is for the celebrant to prepare themselves through the practice of opening to seven levels of awareness.

   1. The first level is to open to the individual or individuals, and to picture them with love and compassion.

   2. Then to refocus on the relational connections. In the case of a wedding, the relationship between those marrying; for a child blessing, the relationship between the parents, siblings and new arrival; and for a funeral, between the relatives and the deceased.

   3. Thirdly, to open to the wider community of family, friends and neighbours that will shortly gather.

   4. We then move our focus to those who will not be present, because they are ill or have died, or have not been invited – the previous wife or husband, the estranged sibling, the parent suffering from dementia.

   5. The attention then moves to the whole interconnected human family, all 7.7 billion of us that share this planet.

6. And then to the more-than-human world of all the sentient beings that surround us, and the elements that support and flow through us.

7. Finally, we open the door to the mystery of oneness – that which connects everything, beyond time and space, beyond words, and certainly beyond our own limited comprehension.

Every counselling or therapy session is in some way a *rite of passage*, so this is a practice we can do as mental health workers before every meeting. Picture the individual, their important relationships, the community they talk about in their sessions, and the community they leave out and ignore. Then the one human family, the more-than-human-ecology and the mystery of oneness. What we know from the experience of many practitioners is that when you open to some new awareness within you, even though you never mention it, the client starts talking to that same level, as though they had only been awaiting your readiness.

An ending and a beginning

Pope Francis, in his encyclical 'Laudato Si' (section 11), showed how:

"…if we approach nature and the environment without this openness to awe and wonder, if we no longer speak the language of fraternity and beauty in our relationship with the world, our attitude will be that of masters, consumers, ruthless exploiters, unable to set limits on their immediate needs. By contrast, if we feel intimately united with all that exists, then sobriety and care will well up spontaneously."

Eco-spirituality along with 'Deep Ecology' show how eco-literacy cannot just be conceptual, but must be emotional and embodied, where we overcome the dangerous splits of self and other; my tribe and the enemy; my species and others I can exploit; humans and so-called 'lesser beings'; humankind and nature. 'Them' are all 'us', and self-care and mental health now need to embrace the whole world, and in humility ask the more-than-human world to help us heal.

References

Amidon E (2020) Notes from the Open Path [online]. Available at: www.sufiway.org/teaching/notes-from-the-open-path/ (accessed July 2021).

Bohn R & Short J (2012) Measuring consumer information. *International Journal of Communication* **6** pp980-1000.

Durning AT (1992) *How Much is Enough?: The Consumer Society and the Future of the Earth*. New York: Norton.

Frankl V (2013) *Man's Search for Meaning*. London: Penguin Random House.

Garcia H & Miralles F (2017) *Ikigai: The Japanese Secret to a long and Happy life*. London: Hutchinson.

Harari NY (2016) *Homo Deus: A Brief History of Tomorrow*. London: Harvill Secker.

Hawkins P (2018a) *Leadership Team Coaching in Practice*. 2nd edition. London: Kogan Page.

Hawkins P (2018b) *Systemic Primer*. Renewal Associates.

Hawkins P (2021) *Leadership Team Coaching: Developing Collective Transformational Leadership*. London: Kogan page.

Hawkins P & Ryde J (2019) *Integrative Psychotherapy: A relational, systemic and ecological approach*. London: Jessica Kingsley.

Hillman J (1995) A Psyche the Size of the World: A Psychological. Foreword. In: T Roszak, ME Gomes & AD Kammer (Eds.), *Ecopsychology: Restoring the Earth Healing the Mind*. Berkley, CA: Counterpoint.

Kimmerer RW (2020) *Braiding Sweetgrass: Indigenous Wisdom, Scientific Knowledge and the Teachings of Plants*. London: Penguin Random House

Kumar S (2012) *Soil, Soul and Society: A New Trinity for our Time*. Brighton, UK: Leaping Hare Press.

Latour B (2017) *Facing Gaia: Eight Lectures on the New Climatic Regime*. Cambridge, UK: Polity Press.

Lovelock J (2007) *The Revenge of Gaia*. London: Penguin

Stiehm, JH & Townsend NW (2002) *The U.S. Army War College: Military Education in a Democracy*. Philadelphia: Temple University Press.

WHO/GHO (2017) *Mental Disorders* [online]. Available at: www.who.int/news-room/fact-sheets/detail/mental-disorders (accessed July 2021).

Wilber K (2000a) *Integral Psychology: Consciousness, Spirit, Psychology and Therapy*. Boulder, Colorado: Shambala.

Wilber K (2000b) *A theory of everything: An integral vision for business, politics, science, and spirituality*. Boston: Shambala.

Chapter 26:

The call of the new spiritualities: the unfolding mysteries of the universe and consciousness

By Paul Gilbert & Hannah Gilbert

The emergence of the new spiritualities

Nobody really knows when, but probably around a million years ago humans began to evolve a new type of brain (Baron-Cohen, 2020); a brain that had at least three types of new competencies (Gilbert, 2019; 2020). One is the ability to reason in new ways, which enabled us to see patterns in things and develop a systematic understanding of the world in which we live (Baron-Cohen, 2020). It is the 'reasoning brain' that works out 'not to eat seeds but plant them', and how to make tools, from spears to wheels to vaccines. A second type of competency is insight into the nature of mind itself, and that gives rise to empathy (Decety *et al*, 2012) and mentalisation (Luyten *et al*, 2020). We can recognise that people do and say things because of what is motivating them, which gives rise to new potential areas and depths of social interactions. A third competency is to have consciousness of consciousness. This gives rise to a competency for mindfulness. We are aware of existing (unlike other species), and that in the not-too-distant future, we won't exist; everything is impermanent. The Vietnamese Buddhist monk Thích Nhất Hạnh (1975) called it the *Miracle of Mindfulness*, to indicate how special and unique a competency this is. Mindfulness gives us a *knowing awareness*. As noted below, for thousands of years the cultivation of mindfulness has been used to try to connect with deeper levels of consciousness.

With the evolution of homo sapiens, all three competencies have played a role in the emergence of religion and spiritualties; sometimes for good and sometimes for very bad. Our reasoning brain gave rise to multiple theories about the nature of the universe, our place in it, and the role of deities that could control powerful forces in our lives. Some of these creations have been ones of terror, others more benevolent, and the competency of empathic insight has also fuelled religious and spiritual pursuits (Bering, 2002). Our problem, however, is that it may not be accurate. Although we think we might be intuiting the motives and intentions of another, it may be simple projection. This is a problem in religion, and quite a major one (Bering, 2002). For example, imagining and then trying to understand 'the mind of a God' requires us to use empathic competencies. But limited to using our evolved motivations and emotions as a basis means we can project all too human motives and emotions to God. That is why just about any type of God can be created. Hence, we have vengeful Gods, Gods that like sacrifice, Gods that drown the whole world, Gods that endorse everlasting pain in hell, Gods that require violence and wars in their name, and for their glory, Gods whose laws mean that certain groups or 'types' of people (e.g. lifestyle choices, etc.) are deemed abominable or heretical, and so must be 'dealt with'. Gods are related to the function for their group, as they need them. So, for example, people that live by the sea and have to risk its unpredictable patterns in order to feed their community, have Gods of the seas that they will pray to, and may sacrifice to... but you will not find Gods of the sea in the Himalayas. When groups and tribes went to war with each other they invented Gods around tribal identities with punishment for defectors, with each group believing their God will favour them and that they are somehow superior in the eyes of their God, or God gives them licence over land.

Clearly when it comes to mental health, the kind of God(s) people believe they are relating to can either be a source of comfort or a source of terror, and fear of punishment. In addition, as has been the case for centuries when pandemics strike populations, the first thing they ask themselves is 'is this punishment from God'? And, as history shows, some religious figures have seemed keen to suggest this, and so drive people back to their places of worship. Although we can change the archetypal form of God, from tyrant to benefactor or a loving presence (Armstrong, 1999), this does not remove the problem of projection of our own minds into the void.

Facing the suffering of life

There are many theories about why we use our new intelligence to imprison ourselves in these hierarchical, mostly patriarchal, projections that are potentially punitive, or that are loving attachment relationships but commonly divisive (Hinde, 2009). One reason is that the invention of agriculture, which enabled resource storage and individual wealth accumulation (unlike the immediate use and egalitarian lifestyle of hunter gathers), changed the nature of our minds from caring and sharing, into ones of control and hold. This reactivated more typical primate, dominant aggressive male control of groups, and we have suffered from this ever since (Gilbert, 2018, 2021; Ryan, 2019). Another more existential reason is that at a deep level, we are all traumatised by biological life itself. All living things just found themselves here. No living thing consciously asked to exist for a short while in the manner that it does, dependant on a genetic lottery. No living thing chose to be easy to injure and vulnerable to bacteria and viruses, which can decimate a species at a stroke, as one is right now. And the 'predator/prey' relationship is a part of life, because no animal can exist without eating other living things. No human asked to be built with a body and a brain that has such potential for mental suffering, depressions, and can also be a source of immense cruelty. Evolution built all that exists through a simple process of DNA replication. Probably the most accurate of all the religions is Buddhism, which highlights the fact that the whole nature of life is about suffering (Wright, 2017). For many, though, we try to dissociate from these realities, and hope that if we can create deities who will protect and look after us, we can escape somehow, or at least have the potential means to find protection. So we are faced with the reality that if a God made this world, as the creationists would have us believe, then apart from sunsets, red wine and the joys of affection, it is an often pretty dire place, full of suffering. The idea that we are souls to be tested, can also be seen as another cruel dissociative idea. Crucially, the seas of these beliefs that we all swim in can have major impacts on mental health.

Seeing through the veil

It is clear that, as education and our understanding of the nature of the universe, biology, physics, evolution, not to mention the fact that this world has seen five major mass extinctions (without which we certainly would not be here), our standard religions are on the wane. This calls us to use our third evolved competency, which is *consciousness of consciousness*. While the nature of consciousness itself is an interesting question, and some increasingly believe it to be a property of the universe rather than biological minds (Harris, 2020), what is even more startling is being conscious of being conscious (Gilbert, 2020). However, since consciousness along with consciousness of being conscious, aware of being aware, came into existence, this competency is a game changer. It allows us to begin to become mindful of the minds that we have (Thích Nhât Hạnh, 1975). We can begin to recognise the complexities of our evolved tricky brain. Our 'science brain' allows us to understand history, and in doing so, recognise that the last 10,000 years have not gone all that well for humans in many ways. In fact, as amazing as the human brain is, it is full of problems that that can make us one of the nastiest, most vicious species that have ever existed. We can use our science brain to invent weapons of war, frightful tortures and forms of execution and we can, and have, turned other human beings into objects of slavery and abuse, while our treatment of animals for food today remains deeply immoral.

The new spiritualities

The new spiritualities are on a path towards enlightenment, which means that we are beginning to open our eyes to the realities of the biological life we are all caught up in. Unlike many of the religions born out of fear of disease, drought and famine or tribal conflict, religions like Jainism and Buddhism had different origins. Indeed Siddhartha (or Buddha, meaning 'Enlightened one') was a prince and had everything he wanted, because his father kept him in a golden palace to shield him from the realities of life outside. But in escaping his golden palace one evening, he became aware of the realities of sickness, decay and death. As rich as he was, it was with shock that he realised he could not escape that destiny, and it was that awareness that broke him out of his bubble of pleasure and set him on the search for how to cope with such a dreadful reality. Today, neoliberalism and the sparkles of wealth blind us to these realities, and keep our eyes firmly on the carrots placed in front of our nose, looking neither left nor right at the suffering all around us.

Nonetheless, like Siddhartha, all of us can be open to awaken from our delusions and projections, our hiding in the pursuit of personal wealth or tribal superiority. We are invited to use our new *mind aware competency* that sets us apart from all other animal species, and to enter into and practise experiencing present-moment conscious awareness. When we do this and 'settle the mind', we begin to experience different textures to consciousness, and rather than separation, we experience a sense of interdependence. There is a lovely contemplative story that demonstrates this: There were two waves, a big wave and a little wave, rushing across the ocean. Suddenly the big wave said to the little wave, "Oh no! There are cliffs and rocks ahead, we are finished!" The little wave responds, "Do not worry, all is well." The big wave sighs and says, "You're not frightened because you can't see what I can see; but I'm telling you, there's foam everywhere, we are finished." And the little wave says, "There is no need to fear, because you are not a wave, you are water".

Delving into the mysteries

If we accept that the little wave is correct, that somehow consciousness is flowing through our biological forms, and our biological forms are patterning consciousness, but that this is itself not the ultimate reality, we can recognise a wisdom that has been at the heart of a specific tradition of spiritual pursuits. One example sometimes given is that our minds are like water, which can contain a poison or a medicine, but water itself is neither. But because water is crystal clear, it can mistake itself from its contents. The new spiritualities pose exactly that proposition: that our biological brains pattern consciousness, but do not create it. For example, the human eye and brain creates an experience of redness or greenness, but do not create the energy frequencies on which those experiences depend. If you somehow lose the receptors for energy frequency, then you can no longer experience red or green. We are beginning to understand that that the brain actually creates reality out of energy fields (Campero, 2019). In 2007, neurosurgeon Jill Bolte Taylor (see also Taylor, 2009) gave a TED talk about her experience of a major stroke. It knocked out her left hemisphere and made her incapable of speaking, but at the same time she became aware of a complex array of energy fields around her. Her biological brain was patterning these energy fields.

Before the advent of agriculture, there is evidence that humans were very aware of the possibility that our biological existence was only one type of existence. They used a whole range of plants, rituals, starvation and exhaustion to stimulate different experiences in the domain of consciousness (Rossano, 2006). Indeed, the use of psychedelics was probably one of the first efforts at really exploring the nature of mind. Despite thousands of years, and much wisdom in these traditions, we are at the point where Western societies, particularly the younger members, are becoming increasingly disillusioned with materialism, and increasingly interested in these domains.

Governments of the 1960s took it upon themselves to introduce prohibitions because of fears over their recreational use, but this is gradually softening to allow research into how these substances influence the relationship between the biological, the spiritual and mental heath (Nutt & Carhart-Harris, 2020). The ancient traditions understood very well (if in a slightly different way) that the chemistry of the brain is essentially the creator of the content of consciousness. Today psychedelics are being used to give people very different experiences of the nature of consciousness, and the nature of connectedness. This does not mean that they reflect any ultimate reality, only that they offer windows on different versions of what our minds can create. Giving people new experiences of interdependency and connectedness, can have very important effects on people with mental health difficulties. It's not the change in the physiology that is the key, but the experience they are left with. Indeed, these substances are not only being explored in relationship to mental health, but also in areas such as fear of dying (Anderson *et al*, 2018; Forstmann *et al*, 2017).

Observing the mind

You can produce brain changes in another way, which is through dedicated practises, particularly (but not only) mindfulness (Goleman & Davidson, 2017). The essence of mindfulness is learning how to use our consciousness of consciousness, to be aware of our mind as it exists in any one moment, and to settle the mind from the usual chatter of the 'reasoning mind' with its planning, ruminations, fixations, intrusions and so on. There is a saying that if you sit still in a muddy pool, the mud will settle, and the water will clear. The key, however, is that we need to do this with knowing intentionality. We need to have a conscious awareness in order to know that we can do this. No other animal species can have this insight, as far as we know; it is very unlikely that when chimpanzees are sitting under their trees, they are meditating and observing the nature of their minds. In this process, new experiences of interconnectedness can arise. However, many of the secular eight-week courses in mindfulness are very different trainings to the mindfulness practice that was originally intended (Coseru, 2012), and have been influenced by capitalist culture (Purser, 2019). So mindfulness is not intended as a spiritual journey, or to give insights into the nature of the mind itself, but as relatively straight forward way of helping people stabilise their mind and deal with mental health difficulties (Davis & Hayes, 2011).

The Compassion Motive

A third avenue of the new spiritualities is to really understand that we are capable of great cruelty and callousness. These spiritualities require the courage to speak against callousness and cruelty, including the hidden cruelties in religious beliefs. For example, those who believe in a loving God need to account for the absolute terrors and horrors of this biological life and existence. Why would a loving God create anything remotely like this? So, we have to come to compassion from a different way: that there are in fact two types of compassion, and two different paths to them. One is a form of compassion which exists because we have evolved motivational systems for caring. These originally evolved as a solution for infant survival (Carter *et al*, 2017). In the infant-parent bond, the parent is attuned to the needs and suffering of their infant, and seeks to alleviate it. This is the essence of compassion, which can be defined as *a sensitivity to suffering in self and others with the commitment to try to relieve it* (Gilbert, 2020). *At the root of compassion is not kindness, but courage and wisdom* (Gilbert *et al*, 2019). We need courage, because we often have to engage with suffering that is painful, and also the dark side of the mind. Compassion often requires us to sacrifice, or give up things for the benefit of others, and even risk ourselves. If we think about the sacrifice of Christ, we talk about the compassion of Christ, not the kindness of Christ, in recognition that compassion is very different to kindness. Secondly, we need a dedication to acquire wisdom, because it is not always clear what the best actions are. For example, today there are thousands of individuals risking their lives to help fight Covid-19, and so they need to be courageous and they need to be knowledgeable of their medical science. These are archetypal examples of compassion. Compassionate intention without compassionate wisdom is often unhelpful.

Note, too, that compassion differs from caring (which many other species do) precisely on the basis of a consciousness of suffering. While we can care for our gardens, cars and houses, if they are damaged, we would not have compassion for them, because they do not have sentience, or consciousness, so they cannot suffer. We are conscious that it is the *conscious suffering of others* that we target with compassion, which can be extended to animals as well. This brings us to the intimate connection between consciousness, suffering and spirituality.

In essence, therefore, we have the biological basis for compassion from hundreds of millions of years of evolution – it is a very old algorithm. The problem is that our biological capacity for caring and compassion can often be confined to those closest to us. We are far more likely to be compassionate to those we love and care about, and not to those we dislike or see as our enemies. Although many spiritualities put compassion at their heart, it is very clear that the tribal manifestation of those spiritualities have not. Once we introduce hierarchy and deities that have their own preferences we are supposed to pick up on, we are going to struggle. To create universal compassion requires us to break out of our biological biases, and extend an empathic awareness to all suffering beings. This is where we need wisdom, which is not reliant on emotion, and to bring our reasoning minds to the problem (Lowenstein & Small, 2007).

We can identify the physiology of these caring and compassion systems. There is increasing evidence that when we practise certain types of compassionate meditation we can change, at times quite profoundly, a range a physiological and neurophysiological circuits (e.g, Singer, & Engert, 2019; Weng *et al*, 2018). While we can see these approaches as conducive to spiritual values in terms of moral philosophy, there is another dimension to compassion that is quite different.

This is the dimension of the 'big wave and little wave'; it is seeking insights into the essential nature of consciousness itself, and its interdependency that creates a sense of connectedness and desire for compassion (Siegel, 2016). This is a very different path to compassion via sensing the subtleties of consciousness itself. For example, we know that the vagus nerve, as part of the parasympathetic nervous system, plays an important role in caring and compassion behaviour (Porges & Furman, 2011; Porges, 2017). We also know that this is linked to a sense of social safeness and calming (Gilbert, 2020). There is evidence that meditative practises stimulate the vagus nerve and facilitate this capacity for safeness and calming (Krygier *et al*, 2013). Meditative practise can therefore create states of body and brain that may well open the caring motive systems, as well as opportunities to experience domains of consciousness as interconnectedness. The degree to which that experience of interconnectedness via meditation is dependent upon these physiological systems is unknown. This does not mean that the experience of interconnectedness gained through years of meditation is a chemical trick, but it does mean that we might have to create certain states within the brain in order for us to have access to these experiences. If our brains are not in the 'right states' these insights might not be possible.

A fascinating question is that if some of the mass extinctions in our past had not happened, if a different intelligence had arisen, for example from solitary beings (like tigers or polar bears), or beings that reproduced by simply dividing themselves into clones, would they have had these experiences of spirituality? To what extent are these experiences and searching for interconnectedness a hallmark of the species we are, and the brain we have? The new spiritualities are on the search.

Conclusion

As a biological creation we are confronted with a life that is full of suffering. While some admire the miracle of biological life, others are rather more sanguine about it. Indeed, the inherent process of life and the evolutionary struggles that are really a game of the genes, are not on the face of it great creations. Humans therefore have constantly tried to understand why the world can be both extraordinarily wonderful, but also extraordinarily harsh, heartless and terrifying. Some people blame Adam and Eve, others the whole issue of sin. The Gnostics believed the creation of the biological world was either by an evil deity, or a mistake. Today, we are beginning to understand that life was not a *purposeful creation*, but that there is something in the nature of the physical universe that makes organic life possible and the rest, as they say, is history. There is no division between creator and created. How consciousness fits into this, and how that in turn helps us to understand our role in all this, is unfolding. The degree to which it addresses our existential questions is unfolding, and to which it opens the door on the spiritual seeking for something more than just a biological existence, is still unfolding. Is this biological life something of a dream? Is consciousness but a biochemical trick, or are we are trapped in these biological forms, and yearning for release? Is the existence of material universes part of how consciousness creates form; how it comes to experience itself; how the clarity of water understands itself as water? The new spiritualities do not turn to higher authorities for answers, rather they use our 'reasoning mind', with its consciousness of consciousness, as a spotlight of exploration, and with compassion as our motivation, we strive to liberate all beings from suffering

References

Anderson, T., Petranker, R., Rosenbaum, D., Weissman, C. R., Dinh-Williams, L. A., Hui, K., ... & Farb, N. A. (2019). Microdosing psychedelics: personality, mental health, and creativity differences in microdosers. *Psychopharmacology*, **236**(2), 731-740.

Armstrong, K. (1999). *A history of God: From Abraham to the present: The 4000-year quest for God*. Random House.

Baron-Cohen, S. (2020). *The Pattern Seekers: A New Theory of Human Invention*. London Allen

Bering, J. M. (2002). The existential theory of mind. *Review of general psychology*, **6**(1), 3-24.

Campero, A. (2019) *Genes vs Culture vs Consciousness: A brief history of our computational mind* ASIN B07TCD4JH7

Carhart-Harris, R. L., Erritzoe, D., Haijen, E., Kaelen, M., & Watts, R. (2018). Psychedelics and connectedness. *Psychopharmacology*, **235**(2), 547-550.

Carter, S., Bartal, I.,B & Porges, E. (2017). The roots of compassion: an evolutionary and neurobiological perspective. In, Seppälä, E.M., Simon-Thomas, E., Brown, S.L., Worline, M.C., *The Oxford handbook of compassion science* (p. 178-188). New York: Oxford.

Coseru, C. (2012). Mind in Indian Buddhist Philosophy. *Stanford Encyclopaedia of philosophy* October.

Davis, D. M., & Hayes, J. A. (2011). What are the benefits of mindfulness? A practice review of psychotherapy-related research. *Psychotherapy*, **48**(2), 198.

Decety, J., Norman, G. J., Berntson, G. G., & Cacioppo, J. T. (2012). A neurobehavioral evolutionary perspective on the mechanisms underlying empathy. *Progress in neurobiology*, **98**(1), 38-48.

Forstmann, M., Yudkin, D. A., Prosser, A. M., Heller, S. M., & Crockett, M. J. (2020). Transformative experience and social connectedness mediate the mood-enhancing effects of psychedelic use in naturalistic settings. *Proceedings of the National Academy of Sciences*, **117**(5), 2338-2346.

Gilbert, P. (2019b). Psychotherapy for the 21st century: An integrative, evolutionary, contextual, biopsychosocial approach. *Psychology and Psychotherapy: Theory, Research and Practice*. **92**, 164-189. DOI: 10.1111/papt.12226

Gilbert, P. (2020). Compassion: From its Evolution to Psychotherapy. *Frontiers in Psychology*. 11:586161.

Gilbert, P. (2021). Creating a compassionate world: Addressing the conflicts between sharing and caring versus controlling and holding evolved strategies. *Frontiers: Psychology*

Gilbert, P., Basran, J., MacArthur, M., & Kirby, J. N. (2019). Differences in the semantics of prosocial words: an exploration of compassion and kindness. *Mindfulness*, **10**(11), 2259-2271

Gilbert, P & Choden. (2013). *Mindful Compassion*. London: Constable Robinson.

Goleman, D., & Davidson, R. J. (2017). Altered traits: Science reveals how meditation changes your mind, brain, and body. Penguin.

Hinde, R. A., & Hinde, R. (2009). *Why Gods persist: A scientific approach to religion*. Routledge.

Krygier, J. R., Heathers, J. A., Shahrestani, S., Abbott, M., Gross, J. J., & Kemp, A. H. (2013). Mindfulness meditation, well-being, and heart rate variability: a preliminary investigation into the impact of intensive Vipassana meditation. *International Journal of Psychophysiology*, **89**(3), 305-313.

Luyten, P., Campbell, C., Allison, E., & Fonagy, P. (2020). The mentalizing approach to psychopathology: State of the art and future directions. *Annual Review of Clinical Psychology*, **16**, 297-325.

Nutt, D., & Carhart-Harris, R. (2020). The current status of psychedelics in psychiatry. *JAMA psychiatry*.

Porges, S. W., & Furman, S. A. (2011). The early development of the autonomic nervous system provides a neural platform for social behaviour: A polyvagal perspective. *Infant and child development*, **20**(1), 106-118.

Purser, R.E. (2019) *McMindfulness: How Mindfulness Became the New Capitalist Spirituality*. London: Repeater

Rossano, M. J. (2006). The religious mind and the evolution of religion. *Review of general psychology*, **10**(4), 346-364.

Siegel, D. J. (2016). *Mind: A journey into the heart of being human*. New York: Norton.

Singer, T., & Engert, V. (2019). It matters what you practice: Differential training effects on subjective experience, behavior, brain and body in the ReSource Project. *Current opinion in psychology*, **28**, 151-158.

Taylor, J.B (2009). My stroke of insight. New York Plume

Thích Nhất Hạnh (1975). The miracle of mindfulness: An introduction to the practice of meditation Beacon

Weng, H. Y., Lapate, R. C., Stodola, D. E., Rogers, G. M., & Davidson, R. J. (2018). Visual attention to suffering after compassion training is associated with decreased amygdala responses. Frontiers in psychology, 9, 771.

Wright, R. (2017). *Why Buddhism is true: The science and philosophy of meditation and enlightenment.* London: Simon and Schuster.

Chapter 27:

Beyond separation: Transpersonal and spiritual approaches to wellbeing

By Steve Taylor

Summary

From the perspective of transpersonal psychology – and many spiritual traditions which inform the field – the main source of human suffering (including mental health issues and general psychological discord) is a sense of psychological separation, or disconnection. A sense of separation leads to a sense of 'ego-isolation', with traits of anxiety and insecurity. Conversely, many spiritual traditions concur that wellbeing arises when separation is transcended and replaced by a sense of connection or union, both with the world and other human beings. I support this with evidence from my own research into temporary 'awakening experiences' and into the ongoing state of 'wakefulness', both of which are associated with a general sense of wellbeing and a sense of connection. Without a transcendence of separation, it is impossible to attain a stable, long-term state of wellbeing. At the same time, it is an error (made by some 'non-duality' teachers) to believe that transcending separation is the only factor in wellbeing.

The field of transpersonal psychology originated in the late 1960s, strongly influenced by the 'human potential' and counterculture movements of that decade. Through exposure to psychedelic substances, meditation and other practices, large numbers of people experienced unusual states of consciousness, and alternate perspectives on reality. To some extent, transpersonal psychology was – and remains – an attempt to understand the different perspectives that are revealed through such psycho-spiritual experimentation.

Another aim of transpersonal psychology has been to integrate mainstream psychology with the insights of spiritual traditions such as Buddhism, Hindu Vedanta and Taoism (as well as Western mystical traditions), with their emphasis on higher states of consciousness and higher stages of human development. One of the most prominent early transpersonal psychologists, Ken Wilber (2000), described this in terms of combining the enlightenment of the West (with its emphasis on reason and intellectual development) with the enlightenment of the East (with its investigation of higher reaches of human experience). Or as Caplan (2009) has put it, transpersonal psychology attempts 'to integrate timeless wisdom with modern Western psychology and translate spiritual principles into scientifically grounded, contemporary language' (p231). In this sense, the field is an attempt to develop a more integrated and holistic form of psychology which, in Caplan's words, 'addresses the full spectrum of human psychospiritual development' (ibid).

One of the essential insights of transpersonal psychology is that what we think of as a 'normal' state of being is in some ways limited. There are more expansive and more intense states of awareness which we can experience in certain circumstances. (I call these 'awakening experiences'.) What some psychologists might view as 'optimum' human psychological functioning – e.g. freedom from anxiety, irrational negative thought-patterns, an optimistic outlook, a strong sense of identity – is by no means the endpoint of our development.

Transpersonal psychology and wellbeing

Unlike positive psychology, the topic of wellbeing is not a central focus of transpersonal psychology. Positive psychology examines the sources of human wellbeing and develops strategies of cultivating and enhancing it (Seligman, 2012). Transpersonal psychology examines expansive ranges of human experience partly so that such states can be consciously cultivated. However, wellbeing is a prominent theme that emerges from the investigation of expansive ranges of human experiences, since they are often associated with wellbeing. In this way, transpersonal psychology has an important contribution to make to any discussion of wellbeing. In fact, transpersonal psychology – and the field of spirituality in general – offers a more complete and holistic understanding of wellbeing than mainstream psychology.

The first issue to bear in mind is that, from a transpersonal or spiritual perspective, human beings' *normal* state is one of psychological discord and mental suffering. Essentially, suffering is caused by an illusory state of separateness – the delusion that we are autonomous entities, living within our own mental space and our bodies, in a state of 'otherness' towards the world and other people. From this perspective, to become free of suffering and attain wellbeing means to transcend separateness, and to experience a state of connection with the world, and with other human beings.

On a simple physical level, separateness seems inevitable. All entities are physically limited and distinct and move through space with distance between them. We can touch each other's bodies, and can communicate through speech and gestures, but there is always space between us. From the perspective of standard scientific materialism (which is the primary worldview of modern secular cultures), the human mind is a product of brain activity, so we are separate on a mental level too, trapped inside our bodies like a genie in a bottle (Dawkins, 1998).

However, there are other perspectives that argue against a fundamental separateness and allow for connection and oneness. From a 'post-materialist' perspective, consciousness is not a by-product of brains – or simply equivalent to neurological activity – but is a fundamental universal principle (Beauregard *et al*, 2014). According to the philosopher David Chalmers (1995), for instance, since consciousness 'does not seem to be derivable from physical laws' it should be 'considered a fundamental feature, irreducible to anything more basic' (p83). There are various philosophical approaches based on this principle, including panentheism, dual-aspect monism and various forms of idealism (Marshall, 2019). In my own philosophical approach of 'panspiritism' (Taylor, 2018; 2020), the ground reality of the universe is a 'fundamental consciousness' that pervades all space and all material entities, and also constitutes the being of all living things. In my view, the primary function of the brain – and of all cellular structures – is to receive and transmit fundamental consciousness. Fundamental consciousness becomes 'canalised' into individual beings, so that they become individually sentient.

From the point of view of these approaches, all things are fundamentally one, since they are pervaded with – and emanate from – the same fundamental consciousness. It is therefore possible to transcend separateness by experiencing this shared consciousness. By doing so, we become aware of our connection to all our living beings, all physical entities, and the whole universe itself.

Perspectives from spiritual traditions

Similar perspectives are expressed by spiritual traditions. Many of them suggest that the root of human suffering and unhappiness is an illusory state of separateness that can be transcended.

According to the Buddha, suffering (or *dukkha*) is an inevitable part of human life, partly because of the physical suffering of disease, old age and death, but also because of the mental suffering that arises when human beings perceive themselves as separate, autonomous egos, who attempt to impose control and stability on an impermanent world. The Hindu philosophical traditions of Vedanta and Yoga also suggest that suffering arises from an illusory sense of separation. At their deepest essence, human beings are one with the universe itself, and with all of the phenomena that constitute the world. The inner spirit (*atman*) is one with the spirit of the universe itself (*brahman*). The Chandogya Upanishad describes *brahman* as 'an invisible and subtle essence' that fills the universe and goes on to say, 'That is Reality. That is Atman. Thou art that' (*The Upanishads*, 1990, p117). However, we human beings lose our sense of oneness with the universe because we identify with our minds and bodies. Under the influence of *maya* – or illusion – we come to believe that we are separate and limited entities. *Maya* covers up *brahman* like a veil, hiding the reality of essential oneness. While this state of separation and delusion exists, suffering is inevitable (Feuerstein, 1990). Similarly, the Chinese philosophy of Taoism suggests that suffering and discord arise when we lose connection to the 'Tao' (the universal principle of harmony that maintains the balance and order of the world) and experience ourselves as separate and autonomous beings.

From these perspectives, suffering ceases when the illusion of separateness is transcended. *The Upanishads* state that, 'when a man knows the infinite, he is free; his sorrows have an end' (1990, p86). In Buddhism, *bodhi* (enlightenment or wakefulness) entails a cessation of both separateness and suffering. In Taoism, wellbeing arises when we transcend the illusion of autonomy and experience ourselves as part of the flowing harmony of the world. In this state, we experience wu-wei – literally, actionless activity – when our actions are not dictated by individual will but arise naturally and spontaneously from the Tao flowing through us (Spencer, 1963). In line with this, all spiritual traditions suggest guidelines and strategies to help adepts overcome the illusion of separation and attain a state of connection or oneness, and at the same time a state of wellbeing. Examples of these are the Buddhist eightfold path, and Patanjali's eight-limbed path of Yoga.

In Vedanta, bliss is one of the qualities of consciousness itself, as in the term *satcitananda* (being-consciousness-bliss), which describes the nature of reality. The essence of Brahman itself is joy, in the same way that wetness is the nature of water. As the Taittiriya Upanishad (1990) puts it, 'Brahman is joy: for from joy all beings have come, by joy they all live, and unto joy they all return' (p111). To transcend separation is therefore to enter into a state of bliss, as the term *samadhi* (literally, ecstasy) describes. In Taoism, the term *ming* was used by the sage Chuang-tzu to describe a state in which the individual no longer experiences duality and separation, and realises their true nature as Dao, and so becomes one with it. This is also depicted as a state in which individual suffering ceases (Spencer, 1963).

In terms of Christian mysticism, Underhill (1960) noted that ecstasy is a characteristic of the stage of mystical illumination, while Happold (1986) stated that during the phase of recollection (one of the stages of contemplation) the soul is filled with a deep inner peace. Similarly, in Jewish spirituality, *devekut* – literally, cleaving to the divine – is described as a state of joy and exaltation (Hoffman, 2007; Lancaster, 2005), as is the Sufi state of *baqa* (abiding in God) (Azeemi, 2005).

From a spiritual perspective, therefore, the question of wellbeing is quite simple. Suffering and psychological discord arise from a sense of separation, and authentic wellbeing arises from transcending separation and experiencing a sense of connection or union with other beings and the world itself. The traditions also agree that wellbeing is a *natural* state. It is not a state that human beings need to strive for, because it is a quality that we already possess. We do not need to cultivate wellbeing so much as *allow* it to manifest itself, which means removing the obstacles that prevent it from doing so.

Psychological perspectives

In line with the principles of transpersonal psychology, we can view the above insights outside the perspective of individual spiritual traditions, from a more neutral psychological perspective.

From a psychological perspective, separation creates suffering because it brings a sense of 'ego-isolation' (Taylor, 2005; 2012c). There is a duality between the individual and the world, which creates a sense of apartness and aloneness. Separateness also brings a sense of *fragmented-ness*, as if we are fragments broken off the whole, with a feeling of loss and incompleteness. There is also a sense of vulnerability and fragility, with a feeling of being potentially overwhelmed by the vast reality outside. The world may seem overpowering in its otherness.

I have elsewhere suggested (Taylor, 2005; 2012c) that ego-isolation is at the root of a variety of negative traits, such as the desires to accumulate wealth, possessions, achievements power and status and the need for psychological attachments (such as ambitions, hopes, beliefs, roles and group identities). Collectively, there is a strong connection between ego-isolation and pathological group behaviour such as warfare and patriarchy (Taylor, 2005). All of these traits are rooted in a desire to strengthen the fragile ego, or to add attachments to it, to compensate for a sense of incompleteness and vulnerability.

Separation and ego-isolation are also associated with the constant stream of 'thought-chatter' (including images, memories, anticipations, reflections, and snippets of information) that runs through the human mind when a person's attention is not externally occupied. In fact, this thought-chatter helps to maintain the sense of separation, since thoughts are inextricably linked with identity, and continually strengthen it. Thought-chatter is a source of suffering because it generates a sense of inner disturbance and restlessness. In addition, because the general atmosphere of the mind is negative (due to ego-isolation), thought-chatter often assumes a negative tone, in the form of worry, rumination and other types of negative thinking. These negative thoughts often generate negative emotions and an overall negative mood.

In my view, the link the between the above factors and mental health issues has been underestimated. Under normal circumstances, these factors create a background sense of psychological unease, which makes it difficult for human beings to live 'inside' themselves. This unease generates a drive to immerse our attention outside ourselves, in tasks, activities and entertainments. However, when the sense of separation and isolation becomes stronger, it may manifest itself in the form of intense anxiety, as an existential *angst* that may be diagnosed as depression. When thought-chatter becomes chaotic and confused, it may be diagnosed as psychosis, especially if a person loses the ability to detach themselves from their thought-chatter, becoming completely immersed in it, and unable to distinguish it from reality. In a more general sense, the rumination and negative tone of thought-chatter is strongly associated with depression (Lyubomirsky & Nolen-Hoeksema, 1995).

My research on spiritual awakening

My own research confirms that spiritual awakening entails a transcendence of a sense of separation, enabling a transcendence of psychological suffering and the attainment of a state of intense wellbeing. In fact, the transcendence of separateness – and a corresponding sense of connection or union – is one of the primary characteristics of spiritual awakening, both in a temporary and ongoing form. I will summarise the main themes of this research below.

Awakening experiences

In my terminology, an awakening experience is a temporary expansion and intensification of awareness that brings significant perceptual, affective and conceptual changes. In awakening experiences, there is a sense that our consciousness opens up, as if limitations or filters fall away, allowing a fuller and more intense awareness of reality. There is a sense of revelation, including the insight that life is more meaningful and positive than previously suspected. There is a feeling that, in comparison to this fuller awareness, normal awareness is limited and even delusory. Such experiences (which can also be described as spiritual experiences) can last anywhere from a few seconds to a few days, before normal awareness returns. It is almost as if awakening experiences occur when normal psychological structures recede or dissolve away. At a certain point these structures re-establish themselves, with a loss of heightened awareness (Taylor, 2010; 2012b; Taylor & Egato-Szabo, 2017).

Awakening experiences may occur spontaneously, but in most cases they are linked to specific activities and situations. In particular, there is a strong link to psychological turmoil. For example, in a study of 90 awakening experiences (Taylor & Egato-Szabo, 2017), different types of psychological turmoil – including stress, depression, loss, bereavement, combat – were found to be the most frequent trigger, being linked to 37 of the experiences. The other significant triggers were contact with nature (23), spiritual practice (21) and reading spiritual literature (15).

The above research found that the three most common characteristics of awakening experiences are: positive affective states (including a sense of elation or serenity, a lack of fear and anxiety); a sense of connection (towards other human beings, nature, or the whole universe in general) and intensified perception. Other, less prevalent characteristics are a sense of love and compassion; altered time perception (which often includes a sense of being intensely present); and a sense of inner quietness (as if the normal associational chatter of the mind has slowed down or become quiet) (Taylor, 2010; 2012b; Taylor & Egato-Szabo, 2017).

Overall, there are different intensities of awakening (both in a temporary and ongoing form), at which the above characteristics manifest themselves at corresponding levels of intensity. For example, in terms of the characteristic of connection, a 'low-intensity' awakening experience may feature a sense of participation and harmony, as in the following example:

'I swam out as far as I could, to the middle of the lake and just looked around, treading water. I could see no houses, no people, no cars or roads. I could hear no noise, just my arms splashing. I felt completely alone, but part of everything… I felt in harmony with nature. It only lasted a few minutes but I remember a sense of calm ness and stillness and it soothes me now.' (Taylor, 2010, p0)

A correspondingly intense form of connection may manifest itself as a state of complete union and identification, as described here:

'I was vast and merged with the universe. No longer could I perceive myself as separate, I was in and of the universe, with time and space altered. I knew I could be everywhere all at once. There was no concept of distance or past and present… The sense of peace, blissful and oneness is hard to put into words.' (Taylor & Egato-Szabo, 2017, p54)

Wakefulness

Wakefulness is an ongoing and stable form of awakening, in which the characteristics of awakening experiences are established on a long-term basis. It is similar to Abraham Maslow's (1970) concept of the 'plateau experience' in relation to what he called the 'peak experience', which was temporary. Wakefulness can occur gradually, as a result of following spiritual practices and paths, or it can occur suddenly and dramatically, where it is usually linked to intense psychological turmoil such a long period of depression or addiction, bereavement or a diagnosis of serious illness (Miller & C'de Baca, 2001; Taylor, 2012a; 2020; 2021). In such awakenings, a person feels that they have suddenly taken on a different identity, with a wholly new set of attitudes, perspectives and values. They report a higher-functioning state with the ability to live more authentically, with new sense of meaning, appreciation and connection.

In wakefulness, an expansion and intensification of awareness occurs across four main areas. Awareness intensifies in a *perceptual* sense, as the phenomenal world becomes more vivid and alive. Awareness also intensifies in a *subjective* sense, as we become aware of increased depth and richness in our own subjective experience. In addition, awareness intensifies in an *intersubjective* sense, as we become increasingly empathic and compassionate towards other human beings, other living beings, and the whole of the natural world. And finally, awareness expands or intensifies in a *conceptual* sense, as we develop a more global or universal perspective. Table 1 shows a complete list of the main characteristics of wakefulness (Taylor, 2017).

Table 27.1: The main characteristics of wakefulness	
Category or aspect of wakefulness	Characteristics
Perceptual	Intensified Perception/Increased Present-ness/Timelessness
	Awareness of 'Presence' or All-Pervading Spiritual Energy
	Aliveness, Harmony and Connectedness
Affective	Inner Quietness//Less Identification with Thoughts
	Transcendence of Separation/Sense of Connection
	Empathy and Compassion
	Wellbeing
	Absence of (or Decreased) Fear of Death
Conceptual/Cognitive	Lack of Group Identity
	Wide Perspective - 'Universal' Outlook
	Heightened Sense of Morality
	Freedom from the 'Taking for Granted' Syndrome - Appreciation and Curiosity
Behavioural	Altruism and Engagement
	Enjoyment of Inactivity/Ability to 'Be'
	Beyond Accumulation and Attachment/ Non-Materialism
	Autonomy/Living more authentically
	Enhanced (more authentic) relationships

It is possible to interpret all four of these aspects of wakefulness (and the characteristics associated with them) in terms of connection. There is an increased sense of connection to the phenomenal world, through intensified perception. There is an increased connection to one's own self, as we uncover deeper aspects of our own being. There is an increased connection to other human beings (and other living beings) which manifests itself as empathy and compassion. Finally, there is an increased sense of connection to the human race a whole, and to the world as a whole, which manifests itself as a transcendence of group identity and a universal conceptual outlook.

Certainly, a deep sense of wellbeing and a sense of connection are two of the main themes of the phenomenology of the wakeful state. At the most basic level, a person may feel a strong sense of connection to other human beings, other living beings in generally, or to the whole of the natural world. For example, a man called Eric told me that, 'I feel a part of nature... I feel a connection with people, but I also feel connected with tree and birds and grass and hills' (Taylor, 2017a, p192). At a higher intensity of wakefulness, a participant called Kelly described how, 'The deep aliveness of space is so amazing it takes your words away. I do not feel connected to it. I feel like I am it.' (ibid.)

Mental health and wakefulness

Therapeutic approaches such as CBT aim to deal with mental issues by changing a person's mode of thinking. The field of positive psychology in general takes a similar approach, aiming to change a person's 'explanatory style' to a more positive form, and to encourage positive modes of thinking such as gratitude and forgiveness (Seligman, 2012). There is no doubt that such strategies are effective. However, from the point of view of transpersonal psychology (and spirituality in general), a different, perhaps even more effective approach, is recommended: transcending thought altogether. In other words, spiritual approaches do not teach the power of positive thinking, but the power of *not* thinking. They suggest that there is a natural sense of wellbeing and psychological harmony that emerges when the human mind becomes quiet, or even when our normal thought-chatter simply slows down to some degree. One of the aims of meditation is cultivate this state of no-thought, and this is one of the reasons why meditation is so strongly associated with wellbeing (Szekeres & Wertheim, 2015).

At the same time, there is a wellbeing that emerges when we *dis-identify* with our thought-chatter, developing the ability to watch thoughts and emotions flow by without attaching ourselves to them. This is the central principle of Buddhist *vipassana*-type meditation practices, which do not aim to suppress thought, but simply to create space between awareness and thought (Szekeres & Wertheim, 2015). In a wider sense, this may lead to a complete dis-identification with the entire construct of self, with the realisation that the separate self is not one's true identity. In my research, a man called Parker experienced this revelation after a long period of intense depression, which led to constant suicidal ideation. This led to a sudden spiritual awakening, which he experienced as an identity shift. As he described his present awareness of himself:

'I've spent my entire life creating an identity based on the thoughts that come to me, but that identity has now suddenly and spontaneously revealed itself to be a complete fiction… It's as if my entire identity just vanished and the realization came to me that my core, the true 'me' is just awareness itself.' (Taylor, 2021, p142)

The above example also reflects the role of mental health issues as a cause of awakening. As I have summarised, various forms of psychological turmoil – including depression, addiction, intense stress and bereavement – are the most frequent trigger of temporary awakening experiences and are also often a trigger of ongoing wakefulness (as in Parker's case above). Certainly, it appears that intense psychological turmoil holds a great deal of potential for spiritual awakening, and it may be that when challenges and crises arise in our lives, they can be approached in such a way that increases their transformational potential. This may include an attitude of acknowledgement, exploration and acceptance (Taylor, 2021).

Conclusion

All of the above suggests an expanded perspective on wellbeing which accords with transpersonal psychology's goal of creating a more holistic and integrated form of psychology. Positive psychology – and mainstream psychology generally – tends to conceive of wellbeing in terms of behaviour and cognition, as exemplified by cognitive-behavioural therapy. From a conventional psychological perspective, we can cultivate wellbeing by making changes to the way we live – for example, by socialising, being altruistic, practicing activities that generate 'flow', spending time in nature, exercising etc. We can also cultivate wellbeing by changing the way we think – for example, by developing a more positive explanatory style, developing a sense of gratitude, or following a cognitive-behavioural approach of identifying irrational negative thought patterns. In shorthand, this means conceiving of wellbeing in terms of *doing* and *thinking*. However, transpersonal psychology and spirituality add a third dimension of *being*. They suggest that wellbeing is strongly related to the nature of our inner being. We can attain wellbeing by changing the way we are as well as how we live and how we think. As described above, this may mean move beyond thought, experiencing periods of no-thought, and perhaps slowing and quietening thought-chatter on an ongoing basis.

Ultimately, this perspective suggests that wellbeing is a matter of connection. Without a sense of connection it is impossible to attain a stable, long-term state of wellbeing. This does not mean that wellbeing is *only* about connection. This is an error that some spiritual teachers and authors have made, particularly some associated with the contemporary 'non-duality' or Neo-Advaita movement (for example, Parsons, 1995; Foster, 2021). There is a tendency to believe that a state of non-duality makes all problems magically disappear, bringing a state of permanent ease and bliss. Foster (2021) has suggested that non-duality is the only real and valid form of therapy, since all other forms sustain the illusion of the separate self, under the misapprehension that it can be 'fixed.' This is simplistic and naïve and encourages a form of 'spiritual bypassing' (Welwood, 2002) in which psychological issues are avoided and repressed. Clearly, psychological issues (such as low self-esteem, negative explanatory styles, traumatic memories etc.) need to be addressed at the same time as cultivating a sense of connection. In other words, focusing on *being* as a means of cultivating wellbeing should not mean neglecting the elements of doing and thinking.

Another aspect to bear in mind is that there is no clear distinction between separation and connection, or between non-duality and duality. There is a continuum of connection, from a state of extreme separation to one of intense connection or union, with many gradations between. Spiritual development can be seen as movement along the continuum, towards greater connection. And as we move towards greater connection, we also move towards greater wellbeing.

Any wellbeing that arises from changing the way we live or the way we think will not be enduring unless there is also a change to our state of being. Authentic wellbeing can only arise when we transcend the state of separation that is the essential source of human suffering, when our self-boundary becomes soft and fluid, enabling us to sense that the essence of our own being is also the essence of every other being, and of the whole universe itself.

References

Azeemi, K.S (2005). *Muraqaba: The art and science of Sufi meditation*. Houston, TX: Plato.

Beauregard, M., Schwartz, G. E., Miller, L., Dossey, L., Moreira-Almeida, A., Schlitz, M. & Tart C. (2014). Manifesto for a post-materialist science. *Explore*, 10(5), 272-274. https://doi.org/10.1016/j.explore.2014.06.008

Caplan, M. (2009). *Eyes wide open: Cultivating discernment on the spiritual path*. Boulder, CO: Sounds True..

Chalmers, D. (1995.) The puzzle of conscious experience. *Scientific American* **273**(6), pp. 80-86.

Dawkins, R. (1998). *Unweaving the rainbow*. Boston, MA: Houghton Mifflin Harcourt.

Feuerstein, G. (1990). *Yoga: The technology of ecstasy*. Wellingborough, UK: Thorsons.

Foster, J. (2021). Therapy without a therapist: Nonduality, healing and the search for Wholeness. Available at https://www.lifewithoutacentre.com/writings/therapy-without-a-therapist

Happold, F. C. (1986) *Mysticism*. London, UK: Pelican.

Hoffman, E. (2007). *The way of splendour: Jewish mysticism and modern psychology*. New York, NY: Rowman & Littlefield.

Lyubomirsky, S. & Nolen-Hoeksema, S. (1995). Effects of self-focused rumination on negative thinking and interpersonal problem-solving. *Journal of Personality and Social Psychology*, **69**, 176–190.

Marshall, P. (2019). *The shape of the soul: What mystical experience tells us about ourselves and reality*. Lanham, MD: Rowman & Littlefield

Lancaster, L. (2005). *The essence of Kabbalah*. London, UK: Arcturus.

Maslow, A. (1970). *Motivation and personality* (2nd Edition). New York, NY: Harper and Row.

Miller, W., & C'de Baca., J. (2001). *Quantum change*. New York, NY: Guilford

Parsons, T. (1995). *The Open secret*. Shaftesbury: Open Secret Publishing.

Seligman, M. *Flourish: A visionary new understanding of happiness and wellbeing*. Miami, FL: Atria

Szekeres, R. A., and Wertheim, E. H. (2015) Evaluation of *Vipassana* Meditation Course Effects on Subjective Stress, Wellbeing, Self-kindness and Mindfulness in a Community Sample: Post-course and 6-month Outcomes. *Stress Health*, **31**: 373– 381. doi: 10.1002/smi.2562.

Spencer, S. (1963). *Mysticism in world religion*. London, UK: Pelican Books.

Taylor, S. (2005). *The fall: The insanity of the ego in human history*. Ropley, UK: Zero Books.

Taylor, S. (2010). *Waking from sleep: Why awakening experiences occur and how to make them permanent*. London, UK: Hay House.

Taylor, S. (2011). *Out of the darkness: From turmoil to transformation*. London, UK: Hay House.

Taylor, S. (2012a). Transformation through suffering: A study of individuals who have experienced positive psychological transformation following periods of intense turmoil and trauma. *Journal of Humanistic Psychology*, **52**, 30–52.

Taylor, S. (2012b). Spontaneous awakening experiences: Exploring the phenomenon beyond religion and spirituality. *Journal of Transpersonal Psychology*, **44**(1), 73–91.

Taylor. S. (2012c). *Back to sanity: Healing the madness of our minds*. London: Hay House.

Taylor, S. (2017). *The leap: The psychology of spiritual awakening*. Navato, CA: New World Library.

Taylor, S. (2018). *Spiritual science: why science needs spirituality to make sense of the world*. London: Watkins.

Taylor, S. (2020a). An Introduction to Panspiritism. *Zygon* **55** (4):898-923 (2020)

Taylor, S. (2020b). Transformation through Loss and Grief: A Study of Personal Transformation Following Bereavement. *The Humanistic Psychologist* (March 2020 doi:https://doi.org/10.1037/hum0000172.

Taylor, S. (2021). *Extraordinary awakenings: When trauma leads to transformation*. Navato, CA: New World Library.

Taylor, S. & Egeto-Szabo, K. (2017). Exploring Awakening Experiences. A study of awakening experiences in terms of their triggers, characteristics, duration and aftereffects. *The Journal of Transpersonal Psychology*, **49** (1), 45-65.

The Upanishads (1990). (J. Mascaro, Ed. and Trans.). London: Penguin

Underhill, E. (1911/1960). *Mysticism*. London, UK: Methuen.

Welwood, J. (2002). *Toward a psychology of wwakening: Buddhism, psychotherapy, and the path of personal and spiritual transformation*. Boston, MA: Shambhala.

Wilber, K. (2000). *One taste*. Boston, MA: Shambhala.

Chapter 28:
Epilogue and ending reflections: listening from the heart

By Sarajane Aris, Hilary Garraway, Hannah Gilbert

'In the end is my beginning', a line from TS Elliot's 'Little Giddings', the last poem in his Four Quartets, points towards the eternal nature of our journey.

We have travelled a broad territory and landscape in our journey through this handbook. We hope that you have found it both a rich resource and tapestry upon which to draw from the many perspectives shared here. It will be hard to do justice to the richness of these in this concluding chapter.

In this chapter, we will highlight some of the key themes and threads that we see as weaving throughout the handbook. However, there may be many more themes that hold significance for you personally. We will also highlight some of the 'gaps', areas or perspectives we have not covered, and touch on possible future directions, and landscapes moving forwards in the field of spirituality, mental health and wellbeing.

Summary of key themes and threads

As editors, we have chosen eight key themes and will refer to certain chapters that illustrate these themes, some in more nuanced ways than others. We also consider some further thematic areas hinted at or which emerge through our journey in crafting this collection. However, these themes weave their way through many more of the chapters than we can refer to here.

1. The current context and challenges society faces

Themes such as climate change, Black Lives Matter and similar movements striving to encourage authentic equality, the impact and long-term trauma arising from the Covid-19 pandemic, its mutations, is a common theme throughout the handbook. These are just some of the major issues society is facing. We are also living with and through the challenges of terrorism, human trafficking, knife crime, and many social injustices. These can lead to people raising existential questions of meaning and purpose, and issues around death and dying. There is a call to come together as a human race within this global context and to consider spirituality in a range of ways, but particularly as a source of hope, meaning, purpose and sustenance in these challenging times.

These themes run through many chapters, but are particularly salient in the following chapters:

■ Chapter 4: Finding meaning and purpose in a Covid world

■ Chapter 7: The need for spirituality in the dying process

■ Chapter 24: Reflections on race, religion and wellbeing

■ Chapter 25: Ecology, mental health and spirituality

■ Chapter 26: The call of the New Spiritualities

Many authors see this as heralding a time for meaningful change in our relationships with each other, in combatting racism and the climate crisis, though not all are optimistic that the societies in which they live will grasp the opportunity and enable substantive change. The path of spirituality and compassion is a significant and crucial way forward, as a source of and resource for our sustenance, resilience, wellbeing, courage and hope for change.

2. Compassion

This is essential to us all, everywhere, at all levels, and particularly within mental health services, and leadership at all levels. It is key in all relationships, related to spirituality, and our shared humanity. Whilst an implicit thread throughout most of the book, compassion is particularly reflected in Chapter 18: Love and leadership leads to conscious caring, Chapter 20: Compassionate leadership for an interconnected world, and Chapter 26: The Call of the New Spiritualities. Some of these chapters outline how and what compassion brings to care, developing a consciously caring environment, and the need to develop compassionate and conscious leadership. Self-compassion is a related theme and crucial when working within stretched services. It is related to staff, and staff's wellbeing, as is compassion for the Earth.

3. Connectedness and 'the collective'

Many chapters recognise the essential nature of our interconnectedness at the heart of, and at all levels of, our being and relationships. Connection with the Earth and its nature, especially with respect to climate change and the way this changes habits, working together collaboratively and collectively, are themes that run through many chapters. This is illustrated particularly in Chapter 2: Integrating spirituality into mental health services through the Essex case study, Chapter 3: African Psychology and spiritness in twin pandemics, and Chapter 20: Compassionate leadership for an interconnected world. These chapters emphasise community approaches and the significance of deep and meaningful relationships.

This theme is also picked up in Chapter 6: Spirituality and the older generation, which speaks of the scaffolding of our lives depending on a sense of community with others, in order to thrive and flourish in old age. This is also seen in Chapter 23: Beyond the here and now: The challenges for the formal healthcare system. It highlights the challenges for the healthcare system, and suggests ways of embracing spiritually informed models of care through community-focused approaches.

Our connectedness to each other and the Earth, 'the mystery of the oneness' connecting everything in the universe, is particularly highlighted in Chapter 25: Ecology, mental health and eco-spirituality', Chapter 26: The call of the new spiritualities and also in Chapter 27: Beyond separation, to name but a few.

4. The language of spirituality

How we define spirituality can be problematic – some see it as a nebulous term that can be surrounded in mystery. There are diverse views reflected in the handbook. How do we talk about spirituality and the challenges of building bridges to a shared understanding? What are the questions to ask and how do we start those conversations with each other to give voice to the personal or hard to define experiences? The value of ritual, myth and symbol as a way of expressing spirituality is explored in some chapters. It is particularly illustrated in Chapter 5: Children and young people's mental health and spirituality, which addresses the taboo of talking about spirituality, and also in Chapter 3 about African Psychology.

5. Diversity and inclusion

Valuing all voices and personal stories, spiritual and religious traditions, looking at the breadth of issues related to diversity and inclusivity across the lifespan has emerged as one of the compelling issues of our time. There is also the value of recognising the importance of unconscious bias and also of 'voices less heard', particularly raised and represented in Chapter 17: Return to Eden, Chapter 3: African Psychology, Chapter 24: Reflections on race, spirituality and wellbeing,

Chapter 16: Voices, visions and spiritual journey and Chapter 9: Spiritual crisis. The spiritual understanding of psychosis is explored in a number of chapters.

In Chapter 11: Faith and mental health, we hear an expert by experience's voice and journey, which also threads through a number of the chapters with examples of various experiences and stories. The 'Children and Young People's Mental Health and Spirituality (Chapter 5) and Spirituality and the Older Generation'(Chapter 6) also reflect similar themes related to diversity and inclusion.

6. Application and practice

Integrating spirituality into all aspects of service delivery is another theme. Various contributions explore spirituality within assessment, therapy, service development, leadership, research, chaplaincy, training, competencies, and the role of faith groups. This theme is evident in chapters such as Chapter 8: Assessing spirituality (Chapter 8), Chapter 10: Therapy for the whole person (Chapter 10) and most of the chapters in sections two and three of the handbook.

7. Wellbeing

This is an implicit thread running throughout many of the chapters, which is not surprising given the book's title. Staff and organisational wellbeing, as well as that of clients, is a key theme in the chapters related to burnout and compassion. What spirituality offers for individuals and organisations in sustaining wellbeing is particularly captured in Chapter 15: Psychology and religious perspectives on mental health, Chapter 11: Faith and mental health – the intersection, Chapter 23: Beyond the Here and Now – the challenges for the formal health care system in embracing spiritually informed models of care and Chapter 27: Beyond separation; transpersonal and spiritual approaches to wellbeing. A number of these offer a view on the sources of wellbeing and the significant place of forgiveness, love, faith and trust in sustaining it.

Staff wellbeing, created through developing kind, nourishing and sustaining environments is particularly highlighted in Chapter 18: Love and leadership leads to conscious caring and Chapter 4: Finding meaning and purpose in a Covid world. The theme of wellbeing is also salient in Chapter 6: Spirituality and older generation, which speaks of 'spiritual flourishing', and also Chapter 27: Beyond separation.

8. The whole person

This is a theme considering 'holistic wellbeing'. Spirituality can address what may be missing in mental health services – deeper life questions of meaning, purpose, values, identity and compassion within a holistic approach. This can bring a balance to and complement a purely scientific, measurable, outcome-driven style that is the current NHS approach. Chapter 7: The need for spirituality in the dying process illustrates this, by sharing examples of not just medicalising death, but honouring the process and celebrating life, of which death is an inevitable part.

Authenticity and bringing our whole self to relationships is particularly reflected in Chapter 22: Spiritual care in GP practice, focusing on our deepest human needs and also in Chapter 4: Finding meaning and purpose in a Covid world. The need for embodiment is also expressed in a number of chapters, which can be seen as another aspect of the whole person.

There are a number of other significant threads and themes that weave throughout many of the chapters in the handbook. We will therefore highlight a few of these that we think may be worthy of further exploration and research:

- The importance of creating space and 'safe' space.
- The importance of breath.
- Small gestures.
- Remembering.
- Journeying alongside.
- Integration of approaches and perspectives.
- The sacred and divine.
- The mystery of the oneness.
- The significance of prayer.
- Something deep inside me.
- Presence.
- Connections to a love and power both within and beyond us.
- A sense of being and 'compassionate interconnectedness'.
- Creating a compassionate culture.
- Illuminating the spirit of wellness.
- Reclaiming our knowing, our essence.
- Transformation and transmutation.
- Awakening and wakefulness.
- Integration and union.
- Transcending separateness.
- Our shared humanity and shared consciousness.

> ### Exploratory exercise
>
> As Editors, we have picked out eight key themes and 20 other threads here. We invite you to reflect on the eight most significant themes for you personally. What makes them the most significant for you?
>
> You may want to make a note of these as part of a 'learning journal' for yourself.

Gaps and perspectives not covered

The handbook, while attempting to be inclusive, cannot cover the entire landscape of each of the areas of spirituality, mental health and wellbeing for all people across the life cycle, in depth.

We are mindful of the absence of substantial writing here focused on those who suffer from neuropsychological problems or those experiencing mental health challenges, particularly those associated with health-related problems such as cancer, pain or dementia, and developmental issues such as those diagnosed along the autistic spectrum and those with learning difficulties.

The handbook also does not cover working with our bodies and the role of bodywork in both sustaining and maintaining our mental health and wellbeing and its significance within our spiritual development.

Also missing are materials and explorations related to paranormal experiences, such as 'near death' experiences and their links to wellbeing and spirituality. No single volume can cover all aspects of such a vast topic as spirituality. Despite this, we hope that some of the themes that the handbook covers will have some relevance for these areas.

We are also aware that we cannot fully represent every spiritual and holistic therapeutic perspective here. While we have a chapter on 'Spirituality and Psychotherapy', this reflects just one perspective. There are many more approaches and perspectives, such as various transpersonal and spiritually focused psychotherapies, that are beyond the scope of this handbook.

In terms of spirituality and research, the chapter that explores this offers an important perspective, but there is not adequate space to give justice to the wealth of research in this field. For example, there is the spiritually related research carried out at Liverpool's John Moores University in the 1980s-2000 as part of an MSc. This has now been transferred and is currently run through the Alef Trust.

The Alistair Hardy Trust has a Religious Experience Research Unit based at the University of Wales, Trinity St David. One of the main parapsychological research centres, which involves a number of studies interested in transpersonal and religious experience is now the University of Northampton, led by Professor Chris Roe.

The US has a number of research centres such as the Windbridge Research Centre based in Arizona, where spiritually related research is being conducted, run by Julie Beischel and Mark Boccuzzi. Jim Tucker, Bruce Greyson and Ed Kelly at the University of Virginia's Division of Perceptual Studies are also exploring similar areas. We have provided links below to their work, as this is beyond the scope of the current handbook.

We are also aware we have not covered some faith perspectives directly or in depth, such as Judaism, Buddhism, Hinduism, Vedanta, Jainism, Taoism, Native American, Canadian, Australian and other Indigenous Peoples, and Islamic perspectives. We also haven't included a Humanist perspective. Humanist ethics and principles are rooted in science rather than faith, are open to seeing meaning in life beyond the individual self, and are inspired by the mysteries of the universe that are beyond current scientific understanding. While each faith and culture has its own unique way of being, we hope what we have covered is inclusive and relevant for all the perspectives.

While this handbook has particular relevance for the current dilemmas and issues we are facing across the whole of society and the world, some of what we have covered may have timeless relevance, others may specifically relate to the current landscape, and therefore change in the next few years. You, as a reader, will need to decide this for yourself, and what resonates for you at this time. These changes and developments may warrant another update of this handbook, which will tackle some of the areas left unexplored, in more detail.

The potential landscape moving forwards/ future possibilities

'Let the waters settle and you will see the moon and stars mirrored in your own being' Rumi

'The journey of transformation lies deeply in our hearts, inner knowing and being. Just listen gently, graciously and spaciously with your inner ear, eyes and loving heart.' Sarajane Aris

The landscape of our potential future, our mental health, spirituality and wellbeing is painted in each of the chapters in this handbook, and shaped by the themes outlined in the previous section. We can choose to be influencers, or warriors of the heart, with wisdom and knowing. We can influence and shape our mental health, spirituality and wellbeing in our places of work and our communities, in some of the ways described in the handbook chapters. We can influence and transform circumstances, if we chose to do so.

We can never know for sure in our everyday lives, what lies ahead of us, other than uncertainty and impermanence. Things never stay the same, they continue to evolve, if we let them. It's what we choose to do with this, both individually and collectively, as humanity and as a society that matters, and will impact on each of us, the world and our universe. We need continuous open-hearted, honest and courageous dialogue together on these themes to move forwards.

Some questions and reflections to explore

As we end this journey, here are a number of questions and reflections for you to consider and explore:

- How can we remain with 'not knowing' and at the same time reach into and cultivate our 'inner knowing', holding both ends of the thread?

- How and what can we learn from the current disasters in society, such as Covid-19, climate change and the ensuing trauma, glaring inequalities and conflicts across the world, to work together, grow closer and in strength together, meaningfully and deeply, to transform our way of being?

- What needs to change for us all to work with what both unites and divides us in a true spirit of love, wisdom and truth, from the depth of our hearts, so that we go beyond our ordinary awareness and touch into an eternal dimension, where we can feel our true inter-connectedness? Can we sow these seeds individually and collectively?

- In all this, are we being called to attend to our spiritual dimension in order to truly and deeply connect, enable and sustain our individual and collective wellbeing?

- Could the current crises in society also be calling us to move beyond separation, as outlined particularly in Chapter 27: Beyond separation and Chapter 25: Ecology mental health and eco-spirituality, to become aware of and collectively attend to our mystical nature, the unseen threads, resonances and dimensions that deeply connect us, and to the more subtle energetic nature of our being, in moving forwards? By becoming more spiritually aware beings, could this not only help us in developing our individual and collective wellbeing but also enable us to evolve collectively, as indicated by the work of David Sloan Wilson?

- When the world is seemingly engaged in its own destruction, and at such risk, could attending and attuning to these subtle energetic realms therefore be a key to moving humanity forwards in creating new ways of being, and also part of our transformation? If so, can we learn to develop an awareness of this consciousness, touched on in the 'Call of the New Spiritualities' chapter? And by doing this, could we then individually and collectively create a subtle pattern of coherence that enables the manifestation of a new dimension of consciousness, thereby also enabling planetary evolution?

- What does each one of us therefore need to be doing differently to create these changes, to live more compassionately and with more conscious awareness? How can we enable this personally and collectively across the world, so that we can all be part of a transformation in consciousness?

We can all have a part to play in transformation, by engaging in our own inner work, being present to the moment, remaining curious, listening from our hearts, planting seeds of love, humour and understanding, questioning and challenging lovingly, looking for ways to open doors to create new understanding, bringing light into darkness, as torch bearers, so to speak, working with and healing the rifts and conflicts. Where this is not possible, learning to live with difference respectfully, honourably and peaceably, and as is mentioned in Chapter 6: Spirituality in an older generation, develop the ability to embrace and live with ambiguity, paradox and uncertainty.

It is our contention that if we can use some seeds of the wisdom shared in this handbook in our daily lives, moment by moment, consciously, with awareness and mindfulness, in whatever we do, then transformation is possible, and miracles surely do happen. This is both the work of integration and evolution, and can be our reality, path and continuing journey.

"Your task is not to seek for love, but merely to seek and find all the barriers within yourself that you have built up against it." Rumi

Our acknowledgement and thanks

It has been an honour and privilege putting this together – thank you to every author who has shared the wisdom of their special perspective. We all share a piece of the truth, together, that collectively shared offers a powerful and timeless gift.

We hope this handbook will offer each of our readers something to go away with, however small, on their journey.

A closing activity

As you finish reading this handbook, just close your eyes, take a few breaths, ask yourself the following questions:

1. What sense am I left with reading this handbook? What images, feelings, words and thoughts come to mind? You may want to capture these in a drawing or picture for yourself.

2. What do I want to take away to use in my own practice as a person and in my work/what I do?

3. What are 2 things I can take from this handbook to use personally and in my work?

You may want to record this in a 'learning journal' for yourself.

Resources to explore

The Alef Trust: https://www.aleftrust.org

The work of Prof Chris Roe:

https://www.northampton.ac.uk/directories/people/chris-roe/

Windbridge Research Center (USA): https://www.windbridge.org/

Perceptual Studies (USA): https://med.virginia.edu/perceptual-studies/

The Ethical Movement (Humanist Heritage): https://heritage.humanists.uk/the-ethical-movement/

Humanists UK: https://humanism.org.uk/

HeartMath: https://www.heartmath.com

David Sloan Wilson: https://www.this view of life.com

Prosocial World: https://www.prosocial.world

Mind and Life Institute: https://www.mindandlife.org/insight/evolution-of-the-heart/.

References

Levine T (2010) *In an Unspoken Voice: How the body releases trauma and restores goodness*. North Atlantic Books.

Solms M (2021) *The Hidden Spring: A journey to the source of consciousness*. Profile Books.

Van Lente E & Hogan MJ (2020) Understanding the nature of oneness experienced in meditators using collective intelligence methods. *Frontiers in Psychology* **11** 2092.

White F (2021) *The Overview Effect: Space exploration & human evolution*. Multiverse Publishing.